Embedded Linux Primer

Prentice Hall
Open Source Software Development Series

Arnold Robbins, Series Editor

"Real world code from real world applications"

Open Source technology has revolutionized the computing world. Many large-scale projects are in production use worldwide, such as Apache, MySQL, and Postgres, with programmers writing applications in a variety of languages including Perl, Python, and PHP. These technologies are in use on many different systems, ranging from proprietary systems, to Linux systems, to traditional UNIX systems, to mainframes.

The **Prentice Hall Open Source Software Development Series** is designed to bring you the best of these Open Source technologies. Not only will you learn how to use them for your projects, but you will learn *from* them. By seeing real code from real applications, you will learn the best practices of Open Source developers the world over.

Titles currently in the series include:

Linux® Debugging and Performance Tuning
Steve Best
0131492470, Paper, ©2006

The Definitive Guide to the Xen Hypervisor
David Chisnall
013234971X, Hard, ©2008

Understanding AJAX
Joshua Eichorn
0132216353, Paper, ©2007

The Linux Programmer's Toolbox
John Fusco
0132198576, Paper, ©2007

Embedded Linux Primer
Christopher Hallinan
0131679848, Paper, ©2007

The Apache Modules Book
Nick Kew
0132409674, Paper, © 2007

SELinux by Example
Frank Mayer, David Caplan, Karl MacMillan
0131963694, Paper, ©2007

UNIX to Linux® Porting
Alfredo Mendoza, Chakarat Skawratananond, Artis Walker
0131871099, Paper, ©2006

Rapid Web Applications with TurboGears
Mark Ramm, Kevin Dangoor, Gigi Sayfan
0132433885, Paper, © 2007

Linux Programming by Example
Arnold Robbins
0131429647, Paper, ©2004

The Linux® Kernel Primer
Claudia Salzberg, Gordon Fischer, Steven Smolski
0131181637, Paper, ©2006

Rapid GUI Programming with Python and Qt
Mark Summerfield
0132354187, Hard, © 2008

New to the series: Digital Short Cuts

Short Cuts are short, concise, PDF documents designed specifically for busy technical professionals like you. Each Short Cut is tightly focused on a specific technology or technical problem. Written by industry experts and best selling authors, Short Cuts are published with you in mind — getting you the technical information that you need — now.

Understanding AJAX:
Consuming the Sent Data with XML and JSON
Joshua Eichorn
0132337932, Adobe Acrobat PDF, © 2007

Debugging Embedded Linux
Christopher Hallinan
0131580132, Adobe Acrobat PDF, © 2007

Using BusyBox
Christopher Hallinan
0132335921, Adobe Acrobat PDF, © 2007

Embedded Linux Primer

A Practical, Real-World Approach

Christopher Hallinan

Prentice Hall Professional Technical Reference

Upper Saddle River, NJ • Boston • Indianapolis • San Francisco
New York • Toronto • Montreal • London • Munich • Paris
Madrid • Cape Town • Sydney • Tokyo • Singapore • Mexico City

PRENTICE
HALL

The publisher offers excellent discounts on this book when ordered in quantity for bulk purchases or special sales, which may include electronic versions and/or custom covers and content particular to your business, training goals, marketing focus, and branding interests. For more information, please contact:

U.S. Corporate and Government Sales
(800) 382-3419
corpsales@pearsontechgroup.com

For sales outside the United States, please contact:

International Sales
international@pearson.com

Visit us on the Web: informit.com/ph

Library of Congress Cataloging-in-Publication Data:

Hallinan, Christopher.

  Embedded Linux primer : a practical, real-world approach / Christopher Hallinan.

    p. cm.

  Includes bibliographical references.

  ISBN 0-13-167984-8 (pbk. : alk. paper) 1. Linux. 2. Operating systems (Computers) 3. Embedded computer systems—Programming. I. Title.

  QA76.76.O63H34462 2006

  005.4'32—dc22

                    2006012886

ISBN-13: 978-0-13-167984-9
ISBN-10: 0-13-167984-8
Text printed in the United States on recycled paper at R.R. Donnelley in Crawfordsville, Indiana.
Fourth printing, February 2008

This Book Is Safari Enabled

The Safari® Enabled icon on the cover of your favorite technology book means the book is available through Safari Bookshelf. When you buy this book, you get free access to the online edition for 45 days.

Safari Bookshelf is an electronic reference library that lets you easily search thousands of technical books, find code samples, download chapters, and access technical information whenever and wherever you need it.

To gain 45-day Safari Enabled access to this book:

• Go to http://www.prenhallprofessional.com/safarienabled

• Complete the brief registration form

• Enter the coupon code 2VEQ-8TDF-KJZM-VSG3-AC5I

If you have difficulty registering on Safari Bookshelf or accessing the online edition, please e-mail customer-service@safaribooksonline.com.

To my mother Edythe, whose courage, confidence, and grace
have been an inspiration to us all.

Contents

Foreword

Computers are everywhere.

This fact, of course, is not a surprise to anyone who hasn't been living in a cave during the past 25 years or so. And you probably know that computers aren't just on our desktops, in our kitchens, and, increasingly, in our living rooms holding our music collections. They're also in our microwave ovens, our regular ovens, our cellphones, and our portable digital music players.

And if you're holding this book, you probably know a lot, or are interested in learning more about, these embedded computer systems.

Until not too long ago, embedded systems were not very powerful, and they ran special-purpose, proprietary operating systems that were very different from industry-standard ones. (Plus, they were much harder to develop for.) Today, embedded computers are as powerful as, if not more than, a modern home computer. (Consider the high-end gaming consoles, for example.)

Along with this power comes the capability to run a full-fledged operating system such as Linux. Using a system such as Linux for an embedded product makes a lot of sense. A large community of developers are making it possible. The development environment and the deployment environment can be surprisingly similar, which makes your life as a developer much easier. And you have both the security of a protected address space that a virtual memory–based system gives you, and the power and flexibility of a multiuser, multiprocess system. That's a good deal all around.

For this reason, companies all over the world are using Linux on many devices such as PDAs, home entertainment systems, and even, believe it or not, cellphones!

I'm excited about this book. It provides an excellent "guide up the learning curve" for the developer who wants to use Linux for his or her embedded system. It's clear, well-written, and well-organized; Chris's knowledge and understanding show through at every turn. It's not only informative and helpful—it's also enjoyable to read.

I hope you both learn something and have fun at the same time. I know I did.

Arnold Robbins

Series Editor

Preface

Although many good books cover Linux, none brings together so many dimensions of information and advice specifically targeted to the embedded Linux developer. Indeed, there are some very good books written about the Linux kernel, Linux system administration, and so on. You will find references right here in this book to many of the ones that I consider to be at the top of their categories.

Much of the material presented in this book is motivated by questions I've received over the years from development engineers, in my capacity as an embedded Linux consultant and my present role as a Field Application Engineer for Monta Vista Software, the leading vendor of embedded Linux distributions.

Embedded Linux presents the experienced software engineer with several unique challenges. First, those with many years of experience with legacy real-time operating systems (RTOSes) find it difficult to transition their thinking from those environments to Linux. Second, experienced application developers often have difficulty understanding the relative complexities of a cross-development environment.

Although this is a primer, intended for developers new to embedded Linux, I am confident that even developers who are experienced in embedded Linux will find some useful tips and techniques that I have learned over the years.

Practical Advice for the Practicing Embedded Developer

This book contains my view of what an embedded engineer needs to know to get up to speed fast in an embedded Linux environment. Instead of focusing on Linux kernel internals, the kernel chapter in this book focuses on the project nature of the kernel and leaves the internals to the other excellent texts on the subject. You will learn the organization and layout of the kernel source tree. You will discover the binary components that make up a kernel image, and how they are loaded and what purpose they serve on an embedded system. One of my favorite figures in the book is Figure 5-1, which schematically illustrates the build process of a composite kernel image.

In the pages of this book, you will learn how the build system works and how to incorporate into the Linux kernel your own custom changes that are required for your own projects. You will discover the mechanism used to drive the configuration of different architectures and features within the Linux kernel source tree and, more important, how to modify this system to customize it to your own requirements. We also cover in detail the kernel command-line mechanism. You will learn how it works, how to configure the kernel's runtime behavior for your requirements, and how to extend this functionality to your own project. You will learn how to navigate the kernel source code and how to configure the kernel for specific tasks related to an embedded system. You will learn many useful tips and tricks for your embedded project, from bootloaders, system initialization, file systems, and Flash memory to advanced kernel- and application-debugging techniques.

Intended Audience

This book is intended for programmers with a working knowledge of programming in C. I assume that you have a rudimentary understanding of local area networks and the Internet. You should understand and recognize an IP address and how it is used on a simple local area network. I also assume that you have an understanding of hexadecimal and octal numbering systems, and their common usage in a text such as this.

Several advanced concepts related to C compiling and linking are explored, so you will benefit from having at least a cursory understanding of the role of the linker in ordinary C programming. Knowledge of the GNU make operation and semantics will also prove beneficial.

What This Book Is Not

This book is not a detailed hardware tutorial. One of the difficulties the embedded developer faces is the huge variety of hardware devices in use today. The user manual for a modern 32-bit processor with some integrated peripherals can easily exceed 1,000 pages. There are no shortcuts. If you need to understand a hardware device from a programmer's point of view, you will need to spend plenty of hours in your favorite reading chair with hardware data sheets and reference guides, and many more hours writing and testing code for these hardware devices!

This is also not a book about the Linux kernel or kernel internals. In this book, you won't learn about the intricacies of the Memory Management Unit (MMU) used to implement Linux's virtual memory-management policies and procedures; there are already several good books on this subject. You are encouraged to take advantage of the "Suggestions for Additional Reading" section found at the end of every chapter.

Conventions Used

Filenames and code statements are presented in `Courier`. Commands issued by the reader are indicated in **`bold Courier`**. New terms or important concepts are presented in *italics*.

When you see a pathname preceded with three dots, this references a well-known but unspecified top-level directory. The top-level directory is context dependent but almost universally refers to a top-level Linux source directory. For example, `.../arch/ppc/kernel/setup.c` refers to the `setup.c` file located in the architecture branch of a Linux source tree. The actual path might be something like `~/sandbox/linux.2.6.14/arch/ppc/kernel/setup.c`.

Organization of the Book

Chapter 1, "Introduction," provides a brief look at the factors driving the rapid adoption of Linux in the embedded environment. Several important standards and organizations relevant to embedded Linux are introduced.

Chapter 2, "Your First Embedded Experience," introduces the reader to many concepts related to embedded Linux upon which we build in later chapters.

In Chapter 3, "Processor Basics," we present a high-level look at the more popular processors and platforms that are being used to build embedded Linux systems. We examine selected products from many of the major processor manufacturers. All of the major architecture families are represented.

Chapter 4, "The Linux Kernel—A Different Perspective," examines the Linux kernel from a slightly different perspective. Instead of kernel theory or internals, we look at its structure, layout, and build construction so you can begin to learn your way around this large software project and, more important, learn where your own customization efforts must be focused. This includes detailed coverage of the kernel build system.

Chapter 5, "Kernel Initialization," details the Linux kernel's initialization process. You will learn how the architecture- and bootloader-specific image components are concatenated to the image of the kernel proper for downloading to Flash and booting by an embedded bootloader. The knowledge gained here will help you customize the Linux kernel to your own embedded application requirements.

Chapter 6, "System Initialization," continues the detailed examination of the initialization process. When the Linux kernel has completed its own initialization, application programs continue the initialization process in a predetermined manner. Upon completing Chapter 6, you will have the necessary knowledge to customize your own userland application startup sequence.

Chapter 7, "Bootloaders," is dedicated to the booloader and its role in an embedded Linux system. We examine the popular open-source bootloader U-Boot and present a porting example. We briefly introduce additional bootloaders in use today so you can make an informed choice about your particular requirements.

Chapter 8, "Device Driver Basics," introduces the Linux device driver model and provides enough background to launch into one of the great texts on device drivers, listed as "Suggestions for Additional Reading" at the end of the chapter.

Chapter 9, "File Systems," presents the more popular file systems being used in embedded systems today. We include coverage of the JFFS2, an important embedded file system used on Flash memory devices. This chapter includes a brief introduction on building your own file system image, one of the more difficult tasks the embedded Linux developer faces.

Chapter 10, "MTD Subsystem," explores the Memory Technology Devices (MTD) subsystem. MTD is an extremely useful abstraction layer between the Linux file system and hardware memory devices, primarily Flash memory.

Chapter 11, "BusyBox," introduces BusyBox, one of the most useful utilities for building small embedded systems. We describe how to configure and build BusyBox for your particular requirements, along with detailed coverage of system initialization unique to a BusyBox environment. Appendix C, "BusyBox Commands," lists the available BusyBox commands from a recent BusyBox release.

Chapter 12, "Embedded Development Environment," takes a detailed look at the unique requirements of a typical cross-development environment. Several techniques are presented to enhance your productivity as an embedded developer, including the powerful NFS root mount development configuration.

Chapter 13, "Development Tools," examines many useful development tools. Debugging with `gdb` is introduced, including coverage of core dump analysis. Many more tools are presented and explained, with examples including `strace`, `ltrace`, `top`, and `ps`, and the memory profilers `mtrace` and `dmalloc`. The chapter concludes with an introduction to the more important binary utilities, including the powerful `readelf` utility.

Chapter 14, "Kernel Debugging Techniques," provides a detailed examination of many debugging techniques useful for debugging inside the Linux kernel. We introduce the use of the kernel debugger KGDB, and present many useful debugging techniques using the combination of `gdb` and KGDB as debugging tools. Included is an introduction to using hardware JTAG debuggers and some tips for analyzing failures when the kernel won't boot.

Chapter 15, "Debugging Embedded Linux Applications," moves the debugging context from the kernel to your application programs. We continue to build on the `gdb` examples from the previous two chapters, and we present techniques for multithreaded and multiprocess debugging.

Chapter 16, "Porting Linux," introduces the issues related to porting Linux to your custom board. We walk through a simple example and highlight the steps taken to produce a working Linux kernel on a custom PowerPC board. Several important concepts are presented that have trapped many newcomers to Linux kernel porting. Together with the techniques presented in Chapters 13 and 14, you should be ready to tackle your own custom board port after reading this chapter.

Chapter 17, "Linux and Real Time," provides an introduction to one of the more exciting developments in embedded Linux: configuring for real time via the `CONFIG_RT` option. We cover the features available with RT and how they can be used in a design. We also present techniques for measuring latency in your application configuration.

The appendixes cover the GNU Public License, U-Boot Configurable Commands, BusyBox Commands, SDRAM Interface Considerations, resources for

the open source developer, and a sample configuration file for one of the more popular hardware JTAG debuggers, the BDI-2000.

Follow Along

You will benefit most from this book if you can divide your time between the pages
of this book and your favorite Linux workstation. Grab an old x86 computer to
experiment on an embedded system. Even better, if you have access to a single-
board computer based on another architecture, use that. You will benefit from
learning the layout and organization of a very large code base (the Linux kernel),
and you will gain significant knowledge and experience as you poke around the kernel and learn by doing.

Look at the code and try to understand the examples produced in this book.
Experiment with different settings, configuration options, and hardware devices.
Much can be gained in terms of knowledge, and besides, it's loads of fun!

If you are so inclined, please log on and contribute to a web site dedicated to this
book which can be found at www.embeddedlinuxprimer.com. Feel free to create an
account, add content and comments to other contributions, and share your own
successes and solutions as you gain experience in this growing segment of the Linux
community. Your input will help others as they learn. It is a work in progress, and
your contributions will help it become a valuable community resource.

GPL Copyright Notice

Portions of open-source code reproduced in this book are copyrighted by a large
number of individual and corporate contributors. The code reproduced here has
been licensed under the terms of the GNU Public License or GPL.

Appendix A contains the text of the GNU General Public License.

Acknowledgments

I am constantly amazed by the graciousness of open source developers. I am humbled by the talent in our community that often far exceeds my own. During the course of this project, I reached out to many people in the Linux and open source community with questions. Most often my questions were quickly answered and with encouragement. In no particular order, I'd like to express my gratitude to the following members of the Linux and open source community who have contributed answers to my questions:

Dan Malek provided inspiration for some of the contents of Chapter 2, "Your First Embedded Experience."

Dan Kegel and Daniel Jacobowitz patiently answered my toolchain questions.

Scott Anderson provided the original ideas for the gdb macros presented in Chapter 14, "Kernel Debugging Techniques."

Brad Dixon continues to challenge and expand my technical vision through his own.

George Davis answered my ARM questions.

Jim Lewis provided comments and suggestions on the MTD coverage.

Cal Erickson answered my gdb use questions.

John Twomey advised on Chapter 3, "Processor Basics."

Lee Revell, Sven-Thorsten Dietrich, and Daniel Walker advised on real time Linux content. Klaas van Gend provided excellent feedback and ideas for my development tools and debugging content.

Many thanks to AMCC, Embedded Planet, Ultimate Solutions, and United Electronic Industries for providing hardware for the examples. Many thanks to my employer, Monta Vista Software, for tolerating the occasional distraction and for providing software for some of the examples. Many others contributed ideas, encouragement, and support over the course of the project. To them I am also grateful.

I wish to acknowledge my sincere appreciation to my primary review team, who promptly read each chapter and provided excellent feedback, comments, and ideas. Thank you Arnold Robbins, Sandy Terrace, Kurt Lloyd, and Rob Farber. Thanks also to David Brief who reviewed the proposal and provided valuable input on the book's organization. Many thanks to Arnold for helping this newbie learn the ropes of writing a technical book. While every attempt has been made to eliminate mistakes, those that remain are solely my own.

I want to thank Mark L. Taub for bringing this project to fruition and for his encouragement and infinite patience! I wish to thank the production team including Kristy Hart, Jennifer Cramer, Krista Hansing, and Cheryl Lenser.

And finally, a very special and heartfelt thank you to Cary Dillman who read each chapter as it was written, and for her constant encouragement and her occasional sacrifice throughout the project.

—Chris Hallinan

About the Author

Christopher Hallinan is currently field applications engineer for Monta Vista Software, living and working in Massachusetts. Chris has spent more than 25 years in the networking and communications marketplace mostly in various product development roles, where he developed a strong background in the space where hardware meets software. Prior to joining Monta Vista, Chris spent four years as an independent Linux consultant providing custom Linux board ports, device drivers, and bootloaders. Chris's introduction to the open source community was through contributions to the popular U-Boot bootloader. When not messing about with Linux, he is often found singing and playing a Taylor or Martin.

Chapter 1

Introduction

In this chapter

- The license grants the user the right to study and modify the source code.

- The license grants the user permission to distribute the original code or his modifications.

- The license grants these same rights to anyone to whom you distribute GPL software.

When a software work is released under the terms of the GPL, it must forever carry that license.[3] Even if the code is highly modified, which is allowed and even encouraged by the license, the GPL mandates that it must be released under the same license. The intent of this feature is to guarantee access to everyone, even of modified versions of the software (or derived works, as they are commonly called).

No matter how the software was obtained, the GPL grants the licensee unlimited distribution rights, without the obligation to pay royalties or per-unit fees. This does not mean that a vendor can't charge for the GPL software—this is a very reasonable common business practice. It means that once in possession of GPL software, it is permissible to modify and redistribute it, whether it is a derived (modified) work or not. However, as defined by the GPL license, the author(s) of the modified work are obligated to release the work under the terms of the GPL if they decide to do so. Any distribution of a derived work, such as shipment to a customer, triggers this obligation.

For a fascinating and insightful look at the history and culture of the open source movement, read Eric S. Raymond's book referenced at the end of this chapter.

1.3.1 Free Versus Freedom

Two popular phrases are often repeated in the discussion about the free nature of open source: "free as in freedom" and "free as in beer." (The author is particularly fond of the latter.) The GPL license exists to guarantee "free as in freedom" of a particular body of software. It guarantees your freedom to use it, study it, and change it. It also guarantees these freedoms for anyone to whom you distribute your modified code. This concept has become fairly widely understood.

One of the misconceptions frequently heard is that Linux is "free as in beer." Sure, you can obtain Linux free of cost. You can download a Linux kernel in a few minutes. However, as any professional development manager understands, certain

---

[3] If all the copyright holders agreed, the software could, in theory, be released under a new license, a very unlikely scenario indeed!

costs are associated with any software to be incorporated into a design. These include the costs of acquisition, integration, modification, maintenance, and support. Add to that the cost of obtaining and maintaining a properly configured toolchain, libraries, application programs, and specialized cross-development tools compatible with your chosen architecture, and you can quickly see that it is a nontrivial exercise to develop the needed software components to deploy your embedded Linux-based system.

1.4 Standards and Relevant Bodies

As Linux continues to gain market share in the desktop, enterprise, and embedded market segments, new standards and organizations are emerging to help influence the use and acceptance of Linux. This section serves as a resource to introduce the standards that you might want to familiarize yourself with.

1.4.1 Linux Standard Base

Probably the single most relevant standard is the Linux Standard Base (LSB). The goal of the LSB is to establish a set of standards designed to enhance the interoperability of applications among different Linux distributions. Currently, the LSB spans several architectures, including IA32/64, PowerPC 32- and 64-bit, AMD64, and others. The standard is broken down into a core component and the individual architecture components.

The LSB specifies common attributes of a Linux distribution, including object format, standard library interfaces, minimum set of commands and utilities and their behavior, file system layout, system initialization, and so on.

You can learn more about the LSB at the link given in Section 1.5.1, "Suggestions for Additional Reading," section at the end of this chapter.

1.4.2 Open Source Development Labs

Open Source Development Labs (OSDL) was formed to help accelerate the acceptance of Linux in the general marketplace. According to its mission statement, OSDL currently provides enterprise-class testing facilities and other technical support to the Linux community. Of significance, OSDL has sponsored several working groups to define standards and participate in the development of features targeting three important market segments. The next three sections introduce these initiatives.

1.4.2.1 OSDL: Carrier Grade Linux

A significant number of the world's largest networking and telecommunications equipment manufacturers are either developing or shipping carrier-class equipment running Linux as the operating system. Significant features of carrier-class equipment include high reliability, high availability, and rapid serviceability. These vendors design products using redundant, hot-swap architectures, fault-tolerant features, clustering, and often real-time performance.

The OSDL Carrier Grade Linux working group has produced a specification defining a set of requirements for carrier-class equipment. The current version of the specification covers seven functional areas:

- **Availability**—Requirements that provide enhanced availability, including online maintenance operations, redundancy, and status monitoring

- **Clusters**—Requirements that facilitate redundant services, such as cluster membership management and data checkpointing

- **Serviceability**—Requirements for remote servicing and maintenance, such as SNMP and diagnostic monitoring of fans and power supplies

- **Performance**—Requirements to define performance and scalability, symmetric multiprocessing, latencies, and more

- **Standards**—Requirements that define standards to which CGL-compliant equipment shall conform

- **Hardware**—Requirements related to high-availability hardware, such as blade servers and hardware-management interfaces

- **Security**—Requirements to improve overall system security from various threats

1.4.2.2 OSDL: Mobile Linux Initiative

As this book is written, several mobile handsets (cellular phones) are available on the worldwide market that have been built around embedded Linux. It has been widely reported that millions of handsets have been shipped based on Linux. The only certainty is that more are coming. This promises to be one of the most explosive market segments for what was formerly the role of a proprietary real-time operating system. This speaks volumes about the readiness of Linux for commercial embedded applications.

The OSDL sponsors a working group called Mobile Linux Initiative. Its purpose is to accelerate the adoption of Linux on next-generation mobile handsets and other converged voice/data portable devices, according to the OSDL website. The areas of focus for this working group include development tools, I/O and networking, memory management, multimedia, performance, power management, security, and storage.

1.4.2.3 Service Availability Forum

If you are engaged in building products for environments in which high reliability, availability, and serviceability (RAS) are important, you should be aware of the Service Availability Forum (SA Forum). This organization is playing a leading role in defining a common set of interfaces for use in carrier-grade and other commercial equipment for system management. The SA Forum website is www.saforum.org.

1.5 Chapter Summary

- Adoption of Linux among developers and manufacturers of embedded products continues to accelerate.

- Use of Linux in embedded devices continues to grow at an exciting pace.

- In this chapter, we present many of the factors driving the growth of Linux in the embedded market.

- Several standards and relevant organizations influencing embedded Linux were presented in this chapter.

1.5.1 Suggestions for Additional Reading

The Cathedral and the Bazaar
Eric S. Raymond
O'Reilly Media, Inc., 2001

Linux Standard Base Project
www.linuxbase.org

Open Source Development Labs, Inc.
www.osdl.org

Chapter 2

Your First Embedded Experience

In this chapter

Often the best path to understanding a given task is to have a good grasp of the big picture. Many fundamental concepts can present challenges to the newcomer to embedded systems development. This chapter takes you on a tour of a typical embedded system and the development environment, with specific emphasis on the concepts and components that make developing these systems unique and often challenging.

2.1 Embedded or Not?

Several key attributes are usually associated with embedded systems. We wouldn't necessarily call our desktop PC an embedded system. But consider a desktop PC hardware platform in a remote data center that is performing a critical monitoring and alarm task. Assume that this data center is normally not staffed. This imposes a different set of requirements on this hardware platform. For example, if power is lost and then restored, we would expect this platform to resume its duties without operator intervention.

Embedded systems come in a variety of shapes and sizes, from the largest multiple-rack data storage or networking powerhouses to tiny modules such as your personal MP3 player or your cellular handset. Some of the usual characteristics of embedded systems include these:

- Contain a processing engine, such as a general-purpose microprocessor

- Typically designed for a specific application or purpose

- Includes a simple (or no) user interface—an automotive engine ignition controller, for example

- Often is resource limited—for example, has a small memory footprint and no hard drive

- Might have power limitations, such as a requirement to operate from batteries

- Usually is not used as a general-purpose computing platform

- Generally has application software built in, not user selected

- Ships with all intended application hardware and software preintegrated

- Often is intended for applications without human intervention

Most commonly, embedded systems are resource constrained compared to the typical desktop PC. Embedded systems often have limited memory, small or no hard drives, and sometimes no external network connectivity. Frequently, the only user interface is a serial port and some LEDs. These and other issues can present challenges to the embedded system developer.

2.1.1 BIOS Versus Bootloader

When power is first applied to the desktop computer, a software program called the BIOS immediately takes control of the processor. (Historically, BIOS was an acronym meaning Basic Input/Output Software, but the acronym has taken on a meaning of its own because the functions it performs have become much more complex than the original implementations.) The BIOS might actually be stored in Flash memory (described shortly), to facilitate field upgrade of the BIOS program itself.

The BIOS is a complex set of system-configuration software routines that have knowledge of the low-level details of the hardware architecture. Most of us are unaware of the extent of the BIOS and its functionality, but it is a critical piece of the desktop computer. The BIOS first gains control of the processor when power is applied. Its primary responsibility is to initialize the hardware, especially the memory subsystem, and load an operating system from the PC's hard drive.

In a typical embedded system (assuming that it is not based on an industry-standard x86 PC hardware platform) a *bootloader* is the software program that performs these same functions. In your own custom embedded system, part of your development plan must include the development of a bootloader specific to your board. Luckily, several good open source bootloaders are available that you can customize for your project. These are introduced in Chapter 7, "Bootloaders."

Some of the more important tasks that your bootloader performs on power-up are as follows:

- Initializes critical hardware components, such as the SDRAM controller, I/O controllers, and graphics controllers

- Initializes system memory in preparation for passing control to the operating system

- Allocates system resources such as memory and interrupt circuits to peripheral controllers, as necessary

- Provides a mechanism for locating and loading your operating system image

- Loads and passes control to the operating system, passing any required startup information that might be required, such as total memory size clock rates, serial port speeds and other low-level hardware specific configuration data

This is a very simplified summary of the tasks that a typical embedded-system bootloader performs. The important point to remember is this: If your embedded system will be based on a custom-designed platform, these bootloader functions must be supplied by you, the system designer. If your embedded system is based on a commercial off-the-shelf (COTS) platform such as an ATCA chassis,[1] typically the bootloader (and often the Linux kernel) is included on the board. Chapter 7 discusses bootloaders in detail.

2.2 Anatomy of an Embedded System

Figure 2-1 shows a block diagram of a typical embedded system. This is a very simple example of a high-level hardware architecture that might be found in a wireless access point. The system is centered on a 32-bit RISC processor. Flash memory is used for nonvolatile program and data storage. Main memory is synchronous dynamic random-access memory (SDRAM) and might contain anywhere from a few megabytes to hundreds of megabytes, depending on the application. A real-time clock module, often backed up by battery, keeps the time of day (calendar/wall clock, including date). This example includes an Ethernet and USB interface, as well as a serial port for console access via RS-232. The 802.11 chipset implements the wireless modem function.

---

[1] ATCA platforms are introduced in Chapter 3, "Processor Basics."

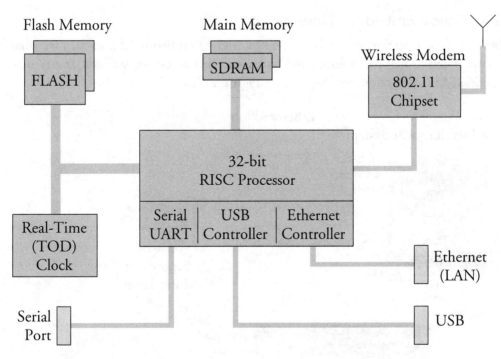

FIGURE 2-1
Example embedded system

Often the processor in an embedded system performs many functions beyond the traditional CPU. The hypothetical processor in Figure 2-1 contains an integrated UART for a serial interface, and integrated USB and Ethernet controllers. Many processors contain integrated peripherals. We look at several examples of integrated processors in Chapter 3, "Processor Basics."

2.2.1 Typical Embedded Linux Setup

Often the first question posed by the newcomer to embedded Linux is, just what does one need to begin development? To answer that question, we look at a typical embedded Linux development setup (see Figure 2-2).

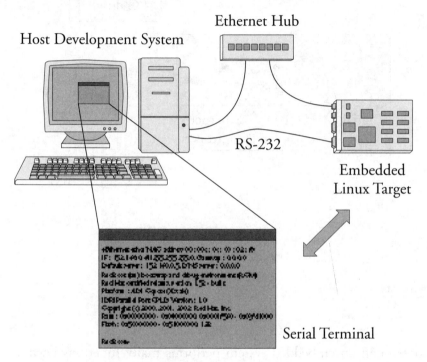

FIGURE 2-2
Embedded Linux development setup

Here we show a very common arrangement. We have a host development system, running your favorite desktop Linux distribution, such as Red Hat or SuSE or Debian Linux. Our embedded Linux target board is connected to the development host via an RS-232 serial cable. We plug the target board's Ethernet interface into a local Ethernet hub or switch, to which our development host is also attached via Ethernet. The development host contains your development tools and utilities along with target files—normally obtained from an embedded Linux distribution.

For this example, our primary connection to the embedded Linux target is via the RS-232 connection. A serial terminal program is used to communicate with the target board. Minicom is one of the most commonly used serial terminal applications and is available on virtually all desktop Linux distributions.

2.2.2 Starting the Target Board

When power is first applied, a bootloader supplied with your target board takes immediate control of the processor. It performs some very low-level hardware initialization, including processor and memory setup, initialization of the UART controlling the serial port, and initialization of the Ethernet controller. Listing 2-1 displays the characters received from the serial port, resulting from power being applied to the target. For this example, we have chosen a target board from AMCC, the PowerPC 440EP Evaluation board nicknamed Yosemite. This is basically a reference design containing the AMCC 440EP embedded processor. It ships from AMCC with the U-Boot bootloader preinstalled.

Listing 2-1

Initial Bootloader Serial Output

```
U-Boot 1.1.4 (Mar 18 2006 - 20:36:11)

AMCC PowerPC 440EP Rev. B
Board: Yosemite - AMCC PPC440EP Evaluation Board
        VCO: 1066 MHz
        CPU: 533 MHz
        PLB: 133 MHz
        OPB: 66 MHz
        EPB: 66 MHz
        PCI: 66 MHz
I2C:    ready
DRAM:   256 MB
FLASH:  64 MB
PCI:    Bus Dev VenId DevId Class Int
In:     serial
Out:    serial
Err:    serial
Net:    ppc_4xx_eth0, ppc_4xx_eth1

=>
```

When power is applied to the Yosemite board, U-Boot performs some low-level hardware initialization, which includes configuring a serial port. It then prints a banner line, as shown in the first line of Listing 2-1. Next the processor name and revision are displayed, followed by a text string identifying the board type. This is a literal string entered by the developer in the U-Boot source code.

U-Boot then displays the internal clock configuration (which was configured before any serial output was displayed). When this is complete, U-Boot configures any hardware subsystems as directed by its static configuration. Here we see I2C, DRAM,

FLASH, PCI, and Network subsystems being configured by U-Boot. Finally, U-Boot waits for input from the console over the serial port, as indicated by the => prompt.

2.2.3 Booting the Kernel

Now that U-Boot has initialized the hardware, serial port, and Ethernet network interface, it has only one job left in its short but useful lifespan: to load and boot the Linux kernel. All bootloaders have a command to load and execute an operating system image. Listing 2-2 presents one of the more common ways U-Boot is used to manually load and boot a Linux kernel.

Listing 2-2

Loading the Linux Kernel

```
=> tftpboot 200000 uImage-440ep
ENET Speed is 100 Mbps - FULL duplex connection
Using ppc_4xx_eth0 device
TFTP from server 192.168.1.10; our IP address is 192.168.1.139
Filename 'uImage-amcc'.
Load address: 0x200000
Loading: #################################################
         #####################################
done
Bytes transferred = 962773 (eb0d5 hex)

=> bootm 200000
## Booting image at 00200000 ...
   Image Name:    Linux-2.6.13
   Image Type:    PowerPC Linux Kernel Image (gzip compressed)
   Data Size:     962709 Bytes = 940.1 kB
   Load Address: 00000000
   Entry Point:  00000000
   Verifying Checksum ... OK
   Uncompressing Kernel Image ... OK
Linux version 2.6.13 (chris@junior) (gcc version 4.0.0 (DENX ELDK 4.0 4.0.0))
⌐ #2 Thu Feb 16 19:30:13 EST 2006
AMCC PowerPC 440EP Yosemite Platform
...
< Lots of Linux kernel boot messages, removed for clarity >
...
amcc login:    <<< This is a Linux kernel console command prompt
```

The `tftpboot` command instructs U-Boot to load the kernel image `uImage-440ep` into memory over the network using the TFTP[2] protocol. The kernel image, in this case, is located on the development workstation (usually the same machine that has the serial port connected to the target board). The `tftpboot` command is passed an address that is the physical address in the target board's memory where the kernel image will be loaded. Don't worry about the details now; we cover U-Boot in much greater detail in Chapter 7.

Next, the `bootm` (boot from memory image) command is issued, to instruct U-Boot to boot the kernel we just loaded from the address specified by the `bootm` command. This command transfers control to the Linux kernel. Assuming that your kernel is properly configured, this results in booting the Linux kernel to a console command prompt on your target board, as shown by the login prompt.

Note that the `bootm` command is the death knell for U-Boot. This is an important concept. Unlike the BIOS in a desktop PC, most embedded systems are architected in such a way that when the Linux kernel takes control, the bootloader ceases to exist. The kernel claims any memory and system resources that the bootloader previously used. The only way to pass control back to the bootloader is to reboot the board.

One final observation is worth noting. All the serial output in Listing 2-2 up to and including this line is produced by the U-Boot bootloader:

```
Uncompressing Kernel Image ... OK
```

The rest of the boot messages are produced by the Linux kernel. We'll have much more to say about this later, but it is worth noting where U-Boot leaves off and where the Linux kernel image takes over.

2.2.4 Kernel Initialization: Overview

When the Linux kernel begins execution, it spews out numerous status messages during its rather comprehensive boot process. In the example being discussed here, the Linux kernel spit out more than 100 lines before it issued the login prompt. (We omitted them from the listing, for clarity of the point being discussed.) Listing 2-3

---

[2] This and other servers you will be using are covered in detail in Chapter 12, "Embedded Development Environment."

reproduces the last several lines of output before the login prompt. The goal of this exercise is not to delve into the details of the kernel initialization (this is covered in Chapter 5, "Kernel Initialization"), but to gain a high-level understanding of what is happening and what components are required to boot a Linux kernel on an embedded system.

Listing 2-3

Linux Final Boot Messages

```
...
Looking up port of RPC 100003/2 on 192.168.0.9
Looking up port of RPC 100005/1 on 192.168.0.9
VFS: Mounted root (nfs filesystem).
Freeing init memory: 232K
INIT: version 2.78 booting
...

coyote login:
```

Shortly before issuing a login prompt on our serial terminal, Linux *mounts* a *root file system.* In Listing 2-3, Linux goes through the steps required to mount its root file system remotely (via Ethernet) from an NFS[3] server on a machine with the IP address 192.168.0.9. Usually, this is your development workstation. The root file system contains the application programs, system libraries, and utilities that make up a GNU/Linux system.

The important point in this discussion should not be understated: *Linux requires a file system.* Many legacy embedded operating systems did not require a file system, and this is a frequent surprise to engineers making the transition from legacy embedded OSs to embedded Linux. A file system consists of a predefined set of system directories and files in a specific layout on a hard drive or other medium that the Linux kernel *mounts* as its root file system.

Note that there are other devices from which Linux can mount a root file system. The most common, of course, is to mount a partition from a hard drive as the root file system, as is done on your Linux workstation. Indeed, NFS is pretty useless when you ship your embedded Linux widget out the door and away from your development environment. However, as you progress through this book, you will come to appreciate the power and flexibility of NFS root mounting as a development environment.

---

[3] We cover NFS and other required servers in Chapter 12.

2.2.5 First User Space Process: init

One more important point should be made before moving on. Notice in Listing 2-3 this line:

```
INIT: version 2.78 booting.
```

Until this point, the kernel itself was executing code, performing the numerous initialization steps in a context known as *kernel context*. In this operational state, the kernel owns all system memory and operates with full authority over all system resources. The kernel has access to all physical memory and to all I/O subsystems.

When the Linux kernel has completed its internal initialization and mounted its root file system, the default behavior is to spawn an application program called init. When the kernel starts init, it is said to be running in *user space* or user space context. In this operational mode, the user space process has restricted access to the system and must use kernel system calls to request kernel services such as device and file I/O. These user space processes, or programs, operate in a virtual memory space picked at random[4] and managed by the kernel. The kernel, in coop-eration with specialized memory-management hardware in the processor, performs virtual-to-physical address translation for the user space process. The single biggest benefit of this architecture is that an error in one process can't trash the memory space of another, which is a common pitfall in legacy embedded OSs and can lead to bugs that are difficult to track down.

Don't be alarmed if these concepts seem foreign. The objective of this section is to paint a broad picture from which you will develop more detailed knowledge as you progress through the book. These and other concepts are covered in great detail in later chapters.

2.3 Storage Considerations

One of the most challenging aspects of embedded systems is that most embedded systems have limited physical resources. Although the Pentium 4 machine on your desktop might have 180GB of hard drive space, it is not uncommon to find embedded systems with a fraction of that amount. In many cases, the hard drive is typically replaced by smaller and less expensive nonvolatile storage devices. Hard drives are bulky, have rotating parts, are sensitive to physical shock, and require

---

[4] It's not actually random, but for purposes of this discussion, it might as well be. This topic will be covered in more detail later.

multiple power supply voltages, which makes them unsuitable for many embedded systems.

2.3.1 Flash Memory

Nearly everyone is familiar with CompactFlash modules[5] used in a wide variety of consumer devices, such as digital cameras and PDAs (both great examples of embedded systems). These modules can be thought of as solid-state hard drives, capable of storing many megabytes—and even gigabytes—of data in a tiny footprint. They contain no moving parts, are relatively rugged, and operate on a single common power supply voltage.

Several manufacturers of Flash memory exist. Flash memory comes in a variety of physical packages and capacities. It is not uncommon to see embedded systems with as little as 1MB or 2MB of nonvolatile storage. More typical storage requirements for embedded Linux systems range from 4MB to 256MB or more. An increasing number of embedded Linux systems have nonvolatile storage into the gigabyte range.

Flash memory can be written to and erased under software control. Although hard drive technology remains the fastest writable media, Flash writing and erasing speeds have improved considerably over the course of time, though flash write and erase time is still considerably slower. Some fundamental differences exist between hard drive and Flash memory technology that you must understand to properly use the technology.

Flash memory is divided into relatively large erasable units, referred to as erase blocks. One of the defining characteristics of Flash memory is the way in which data in Flash is written and erased. In a typical Flash memory chip, data can be changed from a binary 1 to a binary 0 under software control, 1 bit/word at a time, but to change a bit from a zero back to a one, an entire block must be erased. Blocks are often called erase blocks for this reason.

A typical Flash memory device contains many erase blocks. For example, a 4MB Flash chip might contain 64 erase blocks of 64KB each. Flash memory is also available with nonuniform erase block sizes, to facilitate flexible data-storage layout. These are commonly referred to as boot block or boot sector Flash chips. Often the bootloader is stored in the smaller blocks, and the kernel and other required data

---

[5] See www.compactflash.org.

are stored in the larger blocks. Figure 2-3 illustrates the block size layout for a typical *top boot* Flash.

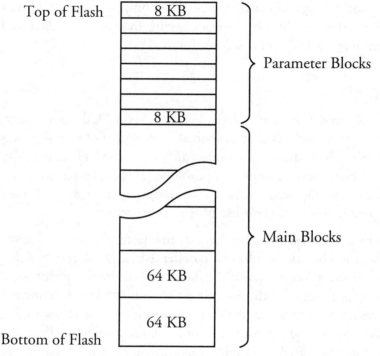

FIGURE 2-3
Boot block flash architecture

To modify data stored in a Flash memory array, the block in which the modified data resides must be completely erased. Even if only 1 byte in a block needs to be changed, the entire block must be erased and rewritten.[6] Flash block sizes are relatively large, compared to traditional hard-drive sector sizes. In comparison, a typical high-performance hard drive has writable sectors of 512 or 1024 bytes. The ramifications of this might be obvious: Write times for updating data in Flash memory can be many times that of a hard drive, due in part to the relatively large quantity of data that must be written back to the Flash for each update. These write cycles can take several seconds, in the worst case.

---

[6] Remember, you can change a 1 to a 0 a byte at a time, but you must erase the entire block to change any bit from a 0 back to a 1.

Another limitation of Flash memory that must be considered is Flash memory cell write lifetime. A Flash memory cell has a limited number of write cycles before failure. Although the number of cycles is fairly large (100K cycles typical per block), it is easy to imagine a poorly designed Flash storage algorithm (or even a bug) that can quickly destroy Flash devices. It goes without saying that you should avoid configuring your system loggers to output to a Flash-based device.

2.3.2 NAND Flash

NAND Flash is a relatively new Flash technology. When NAND Flash hit the market, traditional Flash memory such as that described in the previous section was referred to as NOR Flash. These distinctions relate to the internal Flash memory cell architecture. NAND Flash devices improve upon some of the limitations of traditional (NOR) Flash by offering smaller block sizes, resulting in faster and more efficient writes and generally more efficient use of the Flash array.

NOR Flash devices interface to the microprocessor in a fashion similar to many microprocessor peripherals. That is, they have a parallel data and address bus that are connected directly[7] to the microprocessor data/address bus. Each byte or word in the Flash array can be individually addressed in a random fashion. In contrast, NAND devices are accessed serially through a complex interface that varies among vendors. NAND devices present an operational model more similar to that of a traditional hard drive and associated controller. Data is accessed in serial bursts, which are far smaller than NOR Flash block size. Write cycle lifetime for NAND Flash is an order of magnitude greater than for NOR Flash, although erase times are significantly smaller.

In summary, NOR Flash can be directly accessed by the microprocessor, and code can even be executed directly out of NOR Flash (though, for performance reasons, this is rarely done, and then only on systems in which resources are extremely scarce). In fact, many processors cannot cache instruction accesses to Flash like they can with DRAM. This further impacts execution speed. In contrast, NAND Flash is more suitable for bulk storage in file system format than raw binary executable code and data storage.

---

[7] Directly in the logical sense. The actual circuitry may contain bus buffers or bridge devices, etc.

2.3.3 Flash Usage

An embedded system designer has many options in the layout and use of Flash memory. In the simplest of systems, in which resources are not overly constrained, raw binary data (perhaps compressed) can be stored on the Flash device. When booted, a file system image stored in Flash is read into a Linux ramdisk block device, mounted as a file system and accessed only from RAM. This is often a good design choice when the data in Flash rarely needs to be updated, and any data that does need to be updated is relatively small compared to the size of the ramdisk. It is important to realize that any changes to files in the ramdisk are lost upon reboot or power cycle.

Figure 2-4 illustrates a common Flash memory organization that is typical of a simple embedded system in which nonvolatile storage requirements of dynamic data are small and infrequent.

Top of Flash

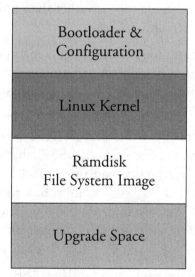

FIGURE 2-4
Example Flash memory layout

The bootloader is often placed in the top or bottom of the Flash memory array. Following the bootloader, space is allocated for the Linux kernel image and the ramdisk file system image,[8] which holds the root file system. Typically, the Linux kernel and ramdisk file system images are compressed, and the bootloader handles the decompression task during the boot cycle.

---

[8] We discuss ramdisk file systems in much detail in Chapter 9, "File Systems."

For dynamic data that needs to be saved between reboots and power cycles, another small area of Flash can be dedicated, or another type of nonvolatile storage[9] can be used. This is a typical configuration for embedded systems with requirements to store configuration data, as might be found in a wireless access point aimed at the consumer market, for example.

2.3.4 Flash File Systems

The limitations of the simple Flash layout scheme described in the previous paragraphs can be overcome by using a Flash file system to manage data on the Flash device in a manner similar to how data is organized on a hard drive. Early implementations of file systems for Flash devices consisted of a simple block device layer that emulated the 512-byte sector layout of a common hard drive. These simple emulation layers allowed access to data in file format rather than unformatted bulk storage, but they had some performance limitations.

One of the first enhancements to Flash file systems was the incorporation of wear leveling. As discussed earlier, Flash blocks are subject to a finite write lifetime. Wear-leveling algorithms are used to distribute writes evenly over the physical erase blocks of the Flash memory.

Another limitation that arises from the Flash architecture is the risk of data loss during a power failure or premature shutdown. Consider that the Flash block sizes are relatively large and that average file sizes being written are often much smaller relative to the block size. You learned previously that Flash blocks must be written one block at a time. Therefore, to write a small 8KB file, you must erase and rewrite an entire Flash block, perhaps 64KB or 128KB in size; in the worst case, this can take tens of seconds to complete. This opens a significant window of risk of data loss due to power failure.

One of the more popular Flash file systems in use today is JFFS2, or Journaling Flash File System 2. It has several important features aimed at improving overall performance, increasing Flash lifetime, and reducing the risk of data loss in case of power failure. The more significant improvements in the latest JFFS2 file system include improved wear leveling, compression and decompression to squeeze more data into a given Flash size, and support for Linux hard links. We cover this in detail in Chapter 9, "File Systems," and again in Chapter 10, "MTD Subsystem," when we discuss the Memory Technology Device (MTD) subsystem.

---

[9] Real-time clock modules often contain small amounts of nonvolatile storage, and Serial EEPROMs are another common choice for nonvolatile storage of small amounts of data.

2.3.5 Memory Space

Virtually all legacy embedded operating systems view and manage system memory as a single large, flat address space. That is, a microprocessor's address space exists from 0 to the top of its physical address range. For example, if a microprocessor had 24 physical address lines, its top of memory would be 16MB. Therefore, its hexadecimal address would range from `0x00000000` to `0x00ffffff`. Hardware designs commonly place DRAM starting at the bottom of the range, and Flash memory from the top down. Unused address ranges between the top of DRAM and bottom of FLASH would be allocated for addressing of various peripheral chips on the board. This design approach is often dictated by the choice of microprocessor. Figure 2-5 is an example of a typical memory layout for a simple embedded system.

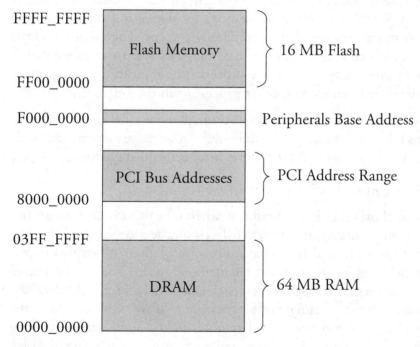

FIGURE 2-5
Typical embedded system memory map

In traditional embedded systems based on legacy operating systems, the OS and all the tasks[10] had equal access rights to all resources in the system. A bug in one process could wipe out memory contents anywhere in the system, whether it belonged to itself, the OS, another task, or even a hardware register somewhere in

---

[10] In this discussion, the word *task* is used to denote any thread of execution, regardless of the mechanism used to spawn, manage, or schedule it.

the address space. Although this approach had simplicity as its most valuable characteristic, it led to bugs that could be difficult to diagnose.

High-performance microprocessors contain complex hardware engines called Memory Management Units (MMUs) whose purpose is to enable an operating system to exercise a high degree of management and control over its address space and the address space it allocates to processes. This control comes in two primary forms: access rights and memory translation. Access rights allow an operating system to assign specific memory-access privileges to specific tasks. Memory translation allows an operating system to virtualize its address space, which has many benefits.

The Linux kernel takes advantage of these hardware MMUs to create a *virtual memory* operating system. One of the biggest benefits of virtual memory is that it can make more efficient use of physical memory by presenting the appearance that the system has more memory than is physically present. The other benefit is that the kernel can enforce access rights to each range of system memory that it allocates to a task or process, to prevent one process from errantly accessing memory or other resources that belong to another process or to the kernel itself.

Let's look at some details of how this works. A tutorial on the complexities of virtual memory systems is beyond the scope of this book.[11] Instead, we examine the ramifications of a virtual memory system as it appears to an embedded systems developer.

2.3.6 Execution Contexts

One of the very first chores that Linux performs when it begins to run is to configure the hardware memory management unit (MMU) on the processor and the data structures used to support it, and to enable address translation. When this step is complete, the kernel runs in its own virtual memory space. The virtual kernel address selected by the kernel developers in recent versions defaults to 0xC0000000. In most architectures, this is a configurable parameter.[12] If we were to look at the kernel's symbol table, we would find kernel symbols linked at an address starting with 0xC0xxxxxx. As a result, any time the kernel is executing code in kernel space, the instruction pointer of the processor will contain values in this range.

In Linux, we refer to two distinctly separate operational contexts, based on the environment in which a given thread[13] is executing. Threads executing entirely

---

[11] Many good books cover the details of virtual memory systems. See Section 2.5.1, "Suggestions for Additional Reading," at the end of this chapter, for recommendations.

[12] However, there is seldom a good reason to change it.

[13] The term *thread* here is used in the generic sense to indicate any sequential flow of instructions.

within the kernel are said to be operating in *kernel context,* while application programs are said to operate in *user space context.* A user space process can access only memory it owns, and uses kernel system calls to access privileged resources such as file and device I/O. An example might make this more clear.

Consider an application that opens a file and issues a read request (see Figure 2-6). The read function call begins in user space, in the C library read() function. The C library then issues a read request to the kernel. The read request results in a context switch from the user's program to the kernel, to service the request for the file's data. Inside the kernel, the read request results in a hard-drive access requesting the sectors containing the file's data.

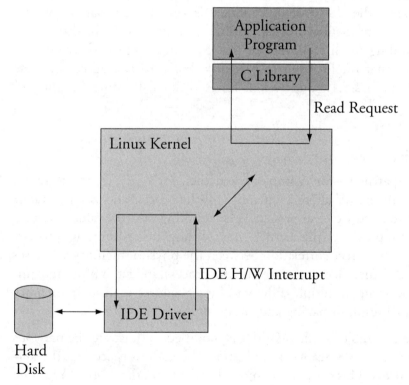

FIGURE 2-6
Simple file read request

Usually the hard-drive read is issued asynchronously to the hardware itself. That is, the request is posted to the hardware, and when the data is ready, the hardware interrupts the processor. The application program waiting for the data is *blocked* on a wait queue until the data is available. Later, when the hard disk has the data ready, it posts a hardware interrupt. (This description is intentionally simplified for the purposes of this illustration.) When the kernel receives the hardware interrupt, it suspends whatever process was executing and proceeds to read the waiting data from the drive. This is an example of a thread of execution operating in kernel context.

To summarize this discussion, we have identified two general execution contexts, user space and kernel space. When an application program executes a system call that results in a context switch and enters the kernel, it is executing kernel code on behalf of a process. You will often hear this referred to as *process context* within the kernel. In contrast, the interrupt service routine (ISR) handling the IDE drive (or any other ISR, for that matter) is kernel code that is not executing on behalf of any particular process. Several limitations exist in this operational context, including the limitation that the ISR cannot block (sleep) or call any kernel functions that might result in blocking. For further reading on these concepts, consult Section 2.5.1, "Suggestions for Additional Reading," at the end of this chapter.

2.3.7 Process Virtual Memory

When a process is spawned—for example, when the user types `ls` at the Linux command prompt—the kernel allocates memory for the process and assigns a range of virtual-memory addresses to the process. The resulting address values bear no fixed relationship to those in the kernel, nor to any other running process. Furthermore, there is no direct correlation between the physical memory addresses on the board and the virtual memory as seen by the process. In fact, it is not uncommon for a process to occupy multiple different physical addresses in main memory during its lifetime as a result of paging and swapping.

Listing 2-4 is the venerable "Hello World," as modified to illustrate the previous concepts. The goal with this example is to illustrate the address space that the kernel assigns to the process. This code was compiled and run on the AMCC Yosemite board, described earlier in this chapter. The board contains 256MB of DRAM memory.

Listing 2-4

Hello World, Embedded Style

```
#include <stdio.h>

int bss_var;         /* Uninitialized global variable */

int data_var = 1;    /* Initialized global variable */

int main(int argc, char **argv)
{
  void *stack_var;               /* Local variable on the stack */

  stack_var = (void *)main;    /* Don't let the compiler */
                               /* optimize it out */

  printf("Hello, World! Main is executing at %p\n", stack_var);
  printf("This address (%p) is in our stack frame\n", &stack_var);

  /* bss section contains uninitialized data */
  printf("This address (%p) is in our bss section\n", &bss_var);

  /* data section contains initializated data */
  printf("This address (%p) is in our data section\n", &data_var);

  return 0;
}
```

Listing 2-5 shows the console output that this program produces. Notice that the process called `hello` thinks it is executing somewhere in high RAM just *above* the 256MB boundary (0x10000418). Notice also that the stack address is roughly halfway into a 32-bit address space, well beyond our 256MB of RAM (0x7ff8ebb0). How can this be? DRAM is usually contiguous in systems like these. To the casual observer, it appears that we have nearly 2GB of DRAM available for our use. These *virtual addresses* were assigned by the kernel and are backed by physical RAM somewhere within the 256MB range of available memory on the Yosemite board.

Listing 2-5

Hello Output

```
root@amcc:~# ./hello
Hello, World! Main is executing at 0x10000418
This address (0x7ff8ebb0) is in our stack frame
This address (0x10010a1c) is in our bss section
This address (0x10010a18) is in our data section
root@amcc:~#
```

One of the characteristics of a virtual memory system is that when available physical RAM goes below a designated threshold, the kernel can swap memory pages out to a bulk storage medium, usually a hard disk drive. The kernel examines its active memory regions, determines which areas in memory have been least recently used, and swaps these memory regions out to disk, to free them up for the current process. Developers of embedded systems often disable swapping on embedded systems because of performance or resource constraints. For example, it would be ridiculous in most cases to use a relatively slow Flash memory device with limited write life cycles as a swap device. Without a swap device, you must carefully design your applications to exist within the limitations of your available physical memory.

2.3.8 Cross-Development Environment

Before we can develop applications and device drivers for an embedded system, we need a set of tools (compiler, utilities, and so on) that will generate binary executables in the proper format for the target system. Consider a simple application written on your desktop PC, such as the traditional "Hello World" example. After you have created the source code on your desktop, you invoke the compiler that came with your desktop system (or that you purchased and installed) to generate a binary executable image. That image file is properly formatted to execute on the machine on which it was compiled. This is referred to as *native* compilation. That is, using compilers on your desktop system, you generate code that will execute on that desktop system.

Note that *native* does not imply an architecture. Indeed, if you have a toolchain that runs on your target board, you can natively compile applications for your target's architecture. In fact, one great way to test a new kernel and custom board is to repeatedly compile the Linux kernel on it.

Developing software in a cross-development environment requires that the compiler running on your development host output a binary executable that is incompatible with the desktop development workstation on which it was compiled. The primary reason these tools exist is that it is often impractical or impossible to develop and compile software natively on the embedded system because of resource (typically memory and CPU horsepower) constraints.

Numerous hidden traps to this approach often catch the unwary newcomer to embedded development. When a given program is compiled, the compiler often knows how to find include files, and where to find libraries that might be required for the compilation to succeed. To illustrate these concepts, let's look again at the "Hello World" program. The example reproduced in Listing 2-4 above was compiled with the following command line:

```
gcc -Wall -o hello hello.c
```

From Listing 2-4, we see an include the file `stdio.h`. This file does not reside in the same directory as the `hello.c` file specified on the `gcc` command line. So how does the compiler find them? Also, the `printf()` function is not defined in the file `hello.c`. Therefore, when `hello.c` is compiled, it will contain an unresolved reference for this symbol. How does the linker resolve this reference at link time?

Compilers have built-in defaults for locating include files. When the reference to the include file is encountered, the compiler searches its default list of locations to locate the file. A similar process exists for the linker to resolve the reference to the external symbol `printf()`. The linker knows by default to search the C library (`libc-*`) for unresolved references. Again, this default behavior is built into the toolchain.

Now consider that you are building an application targeting a PowerPC embedded system. Obviously, you will need a cross-compiler to generate binary executables compatible with the PowerPC processor architecture. If you issue a similar compilation command using your cross-compiler to compile the `hello.c` example above, it is possible that your binary executable could end up being accidentally linked with an x86 version of the C library on your development system, attempting to resolve the reference to `printf()`. Of course, the results of running this bogus hybrid executable, containing a mix of PowerPC and x86 binary instructions[14] are predictable: crash!

The solution to this predicament is to instruct the cross-compiler to look in nonstandard locations to pick up the header files and target specific libraries. We cover this topic in much more detail in Chapter 12, "Embedded Development Environment." The intent of this example was to illustrate the differences between a native development environment, and a development environment targeted at cross-compilation for embedded systems. This is but one of the complexities of a cross-development environment. The same issue and solutions apply to cross-debugging, as you will see starting in Chapter 14, "Kernel Debugging Techniques." A proper cross-development environment is crucial to

---

[14] In fact, it wouldn't even compile or link, much less run.

your success and involves much more than just compilers, as we shall soon see in Chapter 12, "Embedded Development Environment."

2.4 Embedded Linux Distributions

What exactly is a distribution anyway? After the Linux kernel boots, it expects to find and mount a root file system. When a suitable root file system has been mounted, startup scripts launch a number of programs and utilities that the system requires. These programs often invoke other programs to do specific tasks, such as spawn a login shell, initialize network interfaces, and launch a user's applications. Each of these programs has specific requirements of the system. Most Linux application programs depend on one or more system libraries. Other programs require configuration and log files, and so on. In summary, even a small embedded Linux system needs many dozens of files populated in an appropriate directory structure on a *root file system*.

Full-blown desktop systems have many thousands of files on the root file system. These files come from *packages* that are usually grouped by functionality. The packages are typically installed and managed using a package manager. Red Hat's Package Manager (rpm) is a popular example and is widely used for installing, removing, and updating packages on a Linux system. If your Linux workstation is based on Red Hat, including the Fedora Core series, typing rpm -qa at a command prompt lists all the packages installed on your system.

A package can consist of many files; indeed, some packages contain hundreds of files. A complete Linux distribution can contain hundreds or even thousands of packages. These are some examples of packages that you might find on an embedded Linux distribution, and their purpose:

- initscripts—Contains basic system startup and shutdown scripts.
- apache—Implements the popular Apache web server.
- telnet-server—Contains files necessary to implement telnet server functionality, which allows you to establish Telnet sessions to your embedded target.
- glibc—Standard C library
- busybox—Compact versions of dozens of popular command line utilities commonly found on UNIX/Linux systems.[15]

---

[15] This package is important enough to warrant its own chapter. Chapter 11, "BusyBox," covers BusyBox in detail.

This is the purpose of a Linux *distribution* as the term has come to be used. A typical Linux distribution comes with several CD-ROMs full of useful programs, libraries, tools, utilities, and documentation. Installation of a distribution typically leaves the user with a fully functional system based on a reasonable set of default configuration options, which can be tailored to suit a particular set of requirements. You may be familiar with one of the popular desktop Linux distributions, such as RedHat or Suse.

A Linux distribution for embedded targets differs in several significant ways. First, the executable target binaries from an embedded distribution will not run on your PC, but are targeted to the architecture and processor of your embedded system. (Of course, if your embedded Linux distribution targets the x86 architecture, this statement does not apply.) A desktop Linux distribution tends to have many GUI tools aimed at the typical desktop user, such as fancy graphical clocks, calculators, personal time-management tools, email clients and more. An embedded Linux distribution typically omits these components in favor of specialized tools aimed at developers, such as memory analysis tools, remote debug facilities, and many more.

Another significant difference between desktop and embedded Linux distributions is that an embedded distribution typically contains cross-tools, as opposed to native tools. For example, the `gcc` toolchain that ships with an embedded Linux distribution runs on your x86 desktop PC, but produces binary code that runs on your target system. Many of the other tools in the toolchain are similarly configured: They run on the development host (usually an x86 PC) but operate on foreign architectures such as ARM or PowerPC.

2.4.1 Commercial Linux Distributions

There are several vendors of commercial *embedded* Linux distributions. The leading embedded Linux vendors have been shipping embedded Linux distributions for some years. *Linuxdevices.com*, a popular embedded Linux news and information portal, has compiled a comprehensive list of commercially available embedded Linux distributions. It is somewhat dated but is still a very useful starting point. You can find their compilation at www.linuxdevices.com/articles/AT9952405558.html.

2.4.2 Do-It-Yourself Linux Distributions

You can choose to assemble all the components you need for your embedded project on your own. You will have to decide whether the risks are worth the effort. If you find yourself involved with embedded Linux purely for the pleasure of it, such as for a hobby or college project, this approach might be a good one. However, plan to spend a significant amount of time assembling all the tools and utilities your project needs, and making sure they all interoperate together.

For starters, you will need a toolchain. `Gcc` and `binutils` are available from www.fsf.org and other mirrors around the world. Both are required to compile the kernel and user-space applications for your project. These are distributed primarily in source code form, and you must compile the tools to suit your particular cross-development environment. Patches are often required to the most recent "stable" source trees of these utilities, especially when they will be used beyond the x86/IA32 architecture. The patches can usually be found at the same location as the base packages. The challenge is to discover which patch you need for your particular problem and/or architecture.

2.5 Chapter Summary

This chapter covered many subjects in a broad-brush fashion. Now you have a proper perspective for the material to follow in subsequent chapters. In later chapters, this perspective will be expanded to develop the skills and knowledge required to be successful in your next embedded project.

- Embedded systems share some common attributes. Often resources are limited, and user interfaces are simple or nonexistent, and are often designed for a specific purpose.

- The bootloader is a critical component of a typical embedded system. If your embedded system is based on a custom-designed board, you must provide a bootloader as part of your design. Often this is just a porting effort of an existing bootloader.

- Several software components are required to boot a custom board, including the bootloader and the kernel and file system image.

- Flash memory is widely used as a storage medium in embedded Linux systems. We introduced the concept of Flash memory and expand on this coverage in Chapters 9 and 10.

- An application program, also called a process, lives in its own virtual memory space assigned by the kernel. Application programs are said to run in user space.

- A properly equipped and configured cross-development environment is crucial to the embedded developer. We devote an entire chapter to this important subject in Chapter 12.

- You need an embedded Linux distribution to begin development of your embedded target. Embedded distributions contain many components, compiled and optimized for your chosen architecture.

2.5.1 Suggestions for Additional Reading

Linux Kernel Development, 2nd Edition
Robert Love
Novell Press, 2005

Understanding the Linux Kernel
Daniel P. Bovet & Marco Cesati
O'Reilly & Associates, Inc., 2002

Understanding the Linux Virtual Memory Manager
Bruce Perens
Prentice Hall, 2004

Chapter 3

Processor Basics

In this chapter

I n this chapter, we present some basic information to help you navigate the huge sea of embedded processor choices. We look at some of the processors on the market and the types of features they contain. Stand-alone processors are highlighted first. These tend to be the most powerful processors and require external chipsets to form complete systems. Next we present some of the many integrated processors that are supported under Linux. Finally, we look at some of the common hardware platforms in use today.

Literally dozens of embedded processors are available to choose from in a given embedded design. For the purposes of this chapter, we limit the available discussion to those that contain a hardware memory-management unit and, of course, to those that are supported under Linux. One of the fundamental architectural design aspects of Linux is that it is a virtual memory operating system.[1] Employing Linux on a processor that does not contain an MMU gives up one of the more valuable architectural features of the kernel and is beyond the scope of this book.

3.1 Stand-alone Processors

Stand-alone processors refer to processor chips that are dedicated solely to the processing function. As opposed to integrated processors, stand-alone processors require additional support circuitry for their basic operation. In many cases, this means a *chipset* or custom logic surrounding the processor to handle functions such as DRAM controller, system bus addressing configuration, and external peripheral devices such as keyboard controllers and serial ports. Stand-alone processors often offer the highest overall CPU performance.

Numerous processors exist in both 32-bit and 64-bit implementations[2] that have seen widespread use in embedded systems. These include the IBM PowerPC 970FX, the Intel Pentium M, and the Freescale MPC74xx Host Processors, among others.

---

[1] Linux has support for some basic processors that do not contain MMUs, but this is not considered a mainstream use of Linux.

[2] *32-bit* and *64-bit* refer to the native width of the processor's main facilities, such as its execution units, register file and address bus.

Here we present a sample from each of the major manufactures of stand-alone processors. These processors are well supported under Linux and have been used in many embedded Linux designs.

3.1.1 IBM 970FX

The IBM 970FX processor core is a high-performance 64-bit capable stand-alone processor. The 970FX is a *superscalar* architecture. This means the core is capable of fetching, issuing, and obtaining results from more than one instruction at a time. This is done through a pipelining architecture, which provides the effect of multiple streams of instruction simultaneously. The IBM 970FX contains up to 25 stages of pipelining, depending on the instruction stream and operations contained therein.

Some of the key features of the 970FX are as follows:

- A 64-bit implementation of the popular PowerPC architecture
- Deeply pipelined design, for very-high-performance computing applications
- Static and dynamic power-management features
- Multiple sleep modes, to minimize power requirements and maximize battery life
- Dynamically adjustable clock rates, supporting lower-power modes
- Optimized for high-performance, low-latency storage management

The IBM 970FX has been incorporated into a number of high-end server blades and computing platforms, including IBM's own Blade Server platform.

3.1.2 Intel Pentium M

Certainly one of the most popular architectures, x86 in both 32- and 64-bit flavors (more properly called IA32 and IA64, respectively) has been employed for embedded devices in a variety of applications. In the most common form, these platforms are based on a variety of commercial off-the-shelf (COTS) hardware implementations. Numerous manufacturers supply x86 single-board computers and complete platforms in a variety of form factors. See Section 3.2, "Integrated

Processors: Systems on Chip," later in this chapter for a discussion of the more common platforms in use today.

The Intel Pentium M has been used in a wide variety of laptop computers and has found a niche in embedded products. Like the IBM 970FX processor, the Pentium M is a superscalar architecture. These characteristics make it attractive in embedded applications:

- The Pentium M is based on the popular x86 architecture, and thus is widely supported by a large ecosystem of hardware and software vendors.

- It consumes less power than other x86 processors.

- Advanced power-management features enable low-power operating modes and multiple sleep modes.

- Dynamic clock speed capability enhances battery-powered operations such as standby.

- On chip thermal monitoring enables automatic transition to lower power modes, to reduce power consumption in overtemperature conditions.

- Multiple frequency and voltage operating points (dynamically selectable) are designed to maximize battery life in portable equipment.

Many of these features are especially useful for embedded applications. It is not uncommon for embedded products to require portable or battery-powered configurations. The Pentium M has enjoyed popularity in this application space because of its power- and thermal-management features.

3.1.3 Freescale MPC7448

The Freescale MPC7448 contains what is referred to as a fourth-generation PowerPC core, commonly called G4.[3] This high-performance 32-bit processor is commonly found in networking and telecommunications applications. Several companies manufacture blades that conform to an industry-standard platform specification, including this and other similar stand-alone Freescale processors. We examine these platforms in Section 3.3, "Hardware Platforms," later in this chapter.

---

[3] Freescale literature now refers to the G4 core as the e600 core.

The MPC7448 has enjoyed popularity in a wide variety of signal-processing and networking applications because of the advanced feature set highlighted here:

- Operating clock rates in excess of 1.5GHz

- 1MB onboard L2 cache

- Advanced power-management capabilities, including multiple sleep modes

- Advanced AltiVec vector-execution unit

- Voltage scaling for reduced-power configurations

The MPC7448 contains a Freescale technology called AltiVec to enable very fast algorithmic computations and other data-crunching applications. The AltiVec unit consists of a register file containing 32 very wide (128-bit) registers. Each value within one of these AltiVec registers can be considered a vector of multiple elements. AltiVec defines a set of instructions to manipulate this vector data effectively in parallel with core CPU instruction processing. AltiVec operations include such computations as sum-across, multiply-sum, simultaneous data distribute (store), and data gather (load) instructions.

Programmers have used the AltiVec hardware to enable very fast software computations commonly found in signal-processing and network elements. Examples include fast Fourier Transform, digital signal processing such as filtering, MPEG video coding and encoding, and fast generation of encryption protocols such as DES, MD5, and SHA1.

Other chips in the Freescale lineup of stand-alone processors include the MPC7410, MPC7445, MPC7447, MPC745x, and MPC7xx family.

3.1.4 Companion Chipsets

Stand-alone processors such as those just described require support logic to connect to and enable external peripheral devices such as main system memory (DRAM), ROM or Flash memory, system busses such as PCI, and other peripherals, such as keyboard controllers, serial ports, IDE interfaces, and the like. This support logic is often accomplished by companion *chipsets,* which may even be purpose-designed specifically for a family of processors.

For example, the Pentium M is supported by one such chipset, called the 855GM. The 855GM chipset is the primary interface to graphics and memory—thus, the suffix–GM. The 855GM has been optimized as a companion to the Pentium M. Figure 3-1 illustrates the relationship between the processor and chipsets in this type of hardware design.

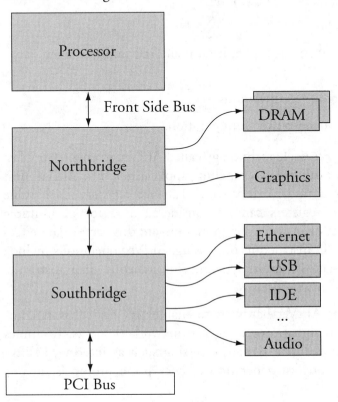

FIGURE 3-1
Processor/chipset relationship

Note the terminology that has become common for describing these chipsets. The Intel 855GM is an example of what is commonly referred to as a *northbridge* chip because it is directly connected to the processor's high-speed front side bus (FSB). Another companion chip that provides I/O and PCI bus connectivity is similarly referred to as the *southbridge* chip because of its position in the architecture. The southbridge chip (actually, an I/O controller) in these hardware architectures is responsible for providing interfaces such as those shown in Figure 3-1, including Ethernet, USB, IDE, audio, keyboard, and mouse controllers.

On the PowerPC side, the Tundra Tsi110 Host Bridge for PowerPC is an example of a chipset that supports the stand-alone PowerPC processors. The Tsi110 supports several interface functions for many common stand-alone PowerPC processors. The Tundra chip supports the Freescale MPC74xx and the IBM PPC 750xx family of processors. The Tundra chip can be used by these processors to provide direct interfaces to the following peripherals:

- DDR DRAM, integrated memory controller
- Ethernet (the Tundra provides four gigabit Ethernet ports)
- PCI Express (supports 2 PCI Express ports)
- PCI/X (PCI 2.3, PCI-X, and Compact PCI [cPCI])
- Serial ports
- I2C
- Programmable interrupt controller
- Parallel port

Many manufacturers of chipsets exist, including VIA Technologies, Marvell, Tundra, nVidia, Intel, and others. Marvell and Tundra primarily serve the PowerPC market, whereas the others specialize in Intel architectures. Hardware designs based on one of the many stand-alone processors, such as Intel x86, IBM, or Freescale PowerPC, need to have a companion chipset to interface to system devices.

One of the advantages of Linux as an embedded OS is rapid support of new chipsets. Linux currently has support for those chipsets mentioned here, as well as many others. Consult the Linux source code and configuration utility for information on your chosen chipset.

3.2 Integrated Processors: Systems on Chip

In the previous section, we highlighted stand-alone processors. Although they are used for many applications, including some high-horsepower processing engines, the vast majority of embedded systems employ some type of integrated processor, or system on chip (SOC). Literally scores, if not hundreds, exist to choose from. We examine a few from the industry leaders and look at some of the features that set each group apart. As in the section on stand-alone processors, we focus only on those integrated processors with strong Linux support.

Several major processor architectures exist, and each architecture has examples of integrated SOCs. PowerPC has been a traditional leader in many networking- and telecommunications-related embedded applications, while MIPS might have the market lead in lower-end consumer-grade equipment.[4] ARM is used in many cellular phones. These represent the major architectures in widespread use in embedded Linux systems. However, as you will see in Chapter 4, "The Linux Kernel: A Different Perspective," Linux supports more than 20 different hardware architectures today.

3.2.1 PowerPC

PowerPC is a Reduced Instruction Set Computer (RISC) architecture jointly designed by engineers from Apple, IBM, and Motorola's semiconductor division (now an independent entity spun off as Freescale Semiconductor). Many good documents describe the PowerPC architecture in great detail. Consult the "Suggestions for Additional Reading" at the end of this chapter as a starting point.

PowerPC processors have found their way into embedded products of every description. From automotive, consumer, and networking applications to the largest data and telecommunications switches, PowerPC is one of the most popular architectures for embedded applications. Because of this popularity, there exists a large array of hardware and software solutions from numerous manufacturers targeted at PowerPC.

3.2.2 AMCC PowerPC

Some of the examples later in this book are based on the AMCC PowerPC 440EP Embedded Processor. The 440EP is a popular integrated processor found in many networking and communications products. The following list highlights some of the features of the 440EP:

- On-chip dual-data-rate (DDR) SDRAM controller
- Integrated NAND Flash controller
- PCI bus interface
- Dual 10/100Mbps Ethernet ports
- On-chip USB 2.0 interface
- Up to four user-configurable serial ports
- Dual I²C controllers
- Programmable Interrupt Controller
- Serial Peripheral Interface (SPI) controller

---

[4] These are the author's own opinions based on market observation and not based on any scientific data.

- Programmable timers

- JTAG interface for debugging

This is indeed a complete system on chip (SOC). Figure 3-2 is a block diagram of the AMCC PowerPC 440EP Embedded Processor. With the addition of memory chips and physical I/O hardware, a complete high-end embedded system can be built around this integrated microprocessor with minimal interface circuitry required.

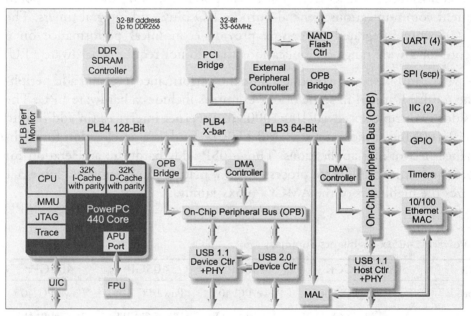

FIGURE 3-2
AMCC PPC 440EP Embedded Processor
(Courtesy AMCC Corporation)

Many manufacturers offer reference hardware platforms to enable a developer to explore the capabilities of the processor or other hardware. The examples later in this book (Chapters 14, "Kernel Debugging Techniques"; and 15, "Debugging Embedded Linux Applications") were executed on the AMCC Yosemite board, which is the company's reference platform containing the 440EP shown in Figure 3-2.

Numerous product configurations are available with PowerPC processors. As demonstrated in Figure 3-2, the AMCC 440EP contains sufficient I/O interfaces for many common products, with very little additional circuitry. Because this processor contains an integrated floating-point unit (FPU), it is ideally suited for products such as network-attached imaging systems, general industrial control, and networking equipment.

AMCC's PowerPC product lineup includes several configurations powered by two proven cores. Their 405 core products are available in configurations with and without Ethernet controllers. All 405 core configurations include integrated SDRAM controllers, dual UARTs for serial ports, I²C for low-level onboard management communications, general-purpose I/O pins, and integral timers. The AMCC 405 core integrated processors provide economical performance on a proven core for a wide range of applications that do not require a hardware FPU.

The AMCC 440-based core products raise the performance level and add peripherals. The 440EP featured in some of our examples includes a hardware FPU. The 440GX adds two triple-speed 10/100/1000MB Ethernet interfaces (in addition to the two 10/100Mbps Ethernet ports) and TCP/IP hardware acceleration for high-performance networking applications. The 440SP adds hardware acceleration for RAID 5/6 applications. All these processors have mature Linux support. Table 3-1 summarizes the highlights of the AMCC 405xx family.

TABLE 3-1
AMCC PowerPC 405xx Highlights Summary

Feature	405CR	405EP	405GP	405GPr
Core/speeds	PowerPC 405	PowerPC 405	PowerPC 405	PowerPC 405
	133–266MHz	133–333MHz	133–266MHz	266–400MHz
DRAM controller	SDRAM/133	SDRAM/133	SDRAM/133	SDRAM/133
Ethernet 10/100	N	2	1	1
GPIO lines	23	32	24	24
UARTs	2	2	2	2
DMA controller	4 channel	4 channel	4 channel	4 channel
I²C controller	Y	Y	Y	Y
PCI host controller	N	Y	Y	Y
Interrupt controller	Y	Y	Y	Y

See the AMCC website, at www.amcc.com/embedded, for complete details.

Table 3-2 summarizes the features of the AMCC 440xx family of processors.

TABLE 3-2
AMCC PowerPC 440xx Highlights Summary

Feature	440EP	440GP	440GX	440SP
Core/speeds	PowerPC 440 333–667MHz	PowerPC 440 400–500MHz	PowerPC 440 533–800MHz	PowerPC 440 533–667MHz
DRAM controller	DDR	DDR	DDR	DDR
Ethernet 10/100	2	2	2	via GigE
Gigabit Ethernet	N	N	2	1
GPIO lines	64	32	32	32
UARTs	4	2	2	3
DMA controller	4 channel	4 channel	4 channel	3 channel
I²C controller	2	2	2	2
PCI host controller	Y	PCI-X	PCI-X	three PCI-X
SPI controller	Y	N	N	N
Interrupt controller	Y	Y	Y	Y

3.2.3 Freescale PowerPC

Freescale Semiconductor has a large range of PowerPC processors with integrated peripherals. The manufacturer is currently advertising its PowerPC product portfolio centered on three broad vertical-market segments: networking, automotive, and industrial. Freescale PowerPC processors have enjoyed enormous success in the networking market segment. This lineup of processors has wide appeal in a large variety of network equipment, from the low end to the high end of the product space.

In a recent press release, Freescale Semiconductor announced that it had shipped more than 200 million integrated communications processors.[5] Part of this success is based around the company's PowerQUICC product line. The PowerQUICC architecture has been shipping for more than a decade. It is based on a PowerPC core integrated with a QUICC engine (also called a communications processor module or CPM in the Freescale literature). The QUICC engine is an independent RISC processor designed to offload the communications processing from the main PowerPC core, thus freeing up the PowerPC core to focus on control and management applications. The QUICC engine is a complex but highly flexible communications peripheral controller.

In its current incarnation, PowerQUICC encompasses four general families. For convenience, as we discuss these PowerQUICC products, we refer to it as PQ.

The PQ I family includes the original PowerPC-based PowerQUICC implementations and consists of the MPC8xx family of processors. These integrated communications processors operate at 50–133MHz and feature the embedded PowerPC 8xx core. The PQ I family has been used for ATM and Ethernet edge devices such as routers for the home and small office (SOHO) market, residential gateways, ASDL and cable modems, and similar applications.

The CPM or QUICC engine incorporates two unique and powerful communications controllers. The Serial Communication Controller (SCC) is a flexible serial interface capable of implementing many serial-based communications protocols, including Ethernet, HDLC/SDLC, AppleTalk, synchronous and asynchronous UARTs, IrDA, and other bit stream data.

The Serial Management Controller (SMC) is a module capable of similar serial-communications protocols, and includes support for ISDN, serial UART, and SPI protocols.

Using a combination of these SCCs and SMCs, it is possible to create very flexible I/O combinations. An internal time-division multiplexer even allows these interfaces to implement channelized communications such as T1 and E1 I/O.

---

[5] On the Freescale website, navigate to Media Center, Press Releases. This one was dated 10/31/2005 from Austin, Texas.

Table 3-3 summarizes a small sampling of the PQ I product line.

TABLE 3-3
Freescale Select PowerQUICC I Highlights

Feature	MPC850	MPC860	MPC875	MPC885
Core/speeds	PowerPC 8xx	PowerPC 8xx	PowerPC 8xx	PowerPC 8xx
	Up to 80MHz	Up to 80MHz	Up to 133MHz	Up to 133MHz
DRAM controller	Y	Y	Y	Y
USB	Y	N	Y	Y
SPI controller	Y	Y	Y	Y
I²C controller	Y	Y	Y	Y
SCC controllers	2	4	1	3
SMC controllers	2	2	1	1
Security engine	N	N	Y	Y
Dedicated Fast Ethernet controller	N	N	2	2

The next step up in the Freescale PowerPC product line is PowerQUICC II. PQ II incorporates the company's G2 PowerPC core derived from the 603e embedded PowerPC core. These integrated communications processors operate at 133–450MHz and feature multiple 10/100Mbps Ethernet interfaces, security engines, and ATM and PCI support, among many others. The PQ II encompasses the MPC82xx products.

PQ II adds two new types of controllers to the QUICC engine. The FCC is a full-duplex fast serial communications controller. The FCC supports high-speed communications such as 100Mbps Ethernet and T3/E3 up to 45Mbps. The MCC is a multichannel controller capable of 128KB × 64KB channelized data.

Table 3-4 summarizes the highlights of selected PowerQUICC II processors.

TABLE 3-4
Freescale Select PowerQUICC II Highlights

Feature	MPC8250	MPC8260	MPC8272	MPC8280
Core/speeds	G2/603e	G2/603e	G2/603e	G2/603e
	150–200MHz	100–300MHz	266–400MHz	266–400MHz
DRAM controller	Y	Y	Y	Y
USB	N	N	Y	Via SCC4
SPI controller	Y	Y	Y	Y
I^{2}C controller	Y	Y	Y	Y
SCC controllers	4	4	3	4
SMC controllers	2	2	2	2
FCC controllers	3	3	2	3
MCC controllers	1	2	0	2

Based on the Freescale PowerPC e300 core (evolved from the G2/603e), the PowerQUICC II Pro family operates at 266–667MHz and features support for Gigabit Ethernet, dual data rate (DDR) SDRAM controllers, PCI, high-speed USB, security acceleration, and more. These are the MPC83xx family of processors. The PQ II and PQ II Pro families of processors have been designed into a wide variety of equipment, such as LAN and WAN switches, hubs and gateways, PBX systems, and many other systems with similar complexity and performance requirements.

The PowerQUICC II Pro contains three family members without the QUICC engine, and two that are based on an updated version of the QUICC engine. The MPC8358E and MPC8360E both add a new Universal Communications Controller, which supports a variety of protocols.

Table 3-5 summarizes the highlights of select members of the PQ II Pro family.

TABLE 3-5
Freescale Select PowerQUICC II Pro Highlights

Feature	MPC8343E	MPC8347E	MPC8349E	MPC8360E
Core/speeds	e300	e300	e300	e300
	266–400MHz	266–667MHz	400–667MHz	266–667MHz
DRAM controller	Y-DDR	Y-DDR	Y-DDR	Y-DDR
USB	Y	2	2	Y
SPI controller	Y	Y	Y	Y
I²C controller	2	2	2	2
Ethernet 10/100/1000	2	2	2	Via UCC
UART	2	2	2	2
PCI controller	Y	Y	Y	Y
Security engine	Y	Y	Y	Y
MCC	0	0	0	1
UCC	0	0	0	8

At the top of the PowerQUICC family are the PQ III processors. These operate between 600MHz and 1.5GHz. They are based on the e500 core and support Gigabit Ethernet, DDR SDRAM, RapidIO, PCI and PCI/X, ATM, HDLC, and more. This family incorporates the MPC85xx product line. These processors have found their way into high-end products such as wireless base station controllers, optical edge switches, central office switches, and similar equipment.

Table 3-6 highlights some of the PQ III family members.

TABLE 3-6
Freescale Select PowerQUICC III Highlights

Feature	MPC8540	MPC8548E	MPC8555E	MPC8560
Core/speeds	e500	e500	e500	e500
	Up to 1.0GHz	Up to 1.5GHz	Up to 1.0GHz	Up to 1.0GHz
DRAM controller	Y-DDR	Y-DDR	Y-DDR	Y-DDR
USB	N	N	Via SCC	N
SPI controller	N	N	Y	Y
I²C controller	Y	Y	Y	Y
Ethernet 10/100	1	Via GigE	Via SCC	Via SCC
Gigabit Ethernet	2	4	2	2
UART	2	2	2	Via SCC
PCI controller	PCI/PCI-X	PCI/PCI-X	PCI	PCI/PCI-X
Rapid IO	Y	Y	N	Y
Security engine	N	Y	Y	N
SCC	—	—	3	4
FCC	—	—	2	3
SMC	—	—	2	0
MCC	—	—	0	2

3.2.4 MIPS

You might be surprised to learn that 32-bit processors based on the MIPS architecture have been shipping for more than 20 years. The MIPS architecture was designed in 1981 by a Stanford University engineering team led by Dr. John Hennessey, who later went on to form MIPS Computer Systems, Inc. That company has morphed into the present-day MIPS Technologies, whose primary role is the design and subsequent licensing of MIPS architecture and cores.

The MIPS core has been licensed by many companies, several of which have become powerhouses in the embedded processor market. MIPS is a Reduced

Instruction Set Computing (RISC) architecture with both 32-bit and 64-bit implementations shipping in many popular products. MIPS processors are found in a large variety of products, from high-end to consumer devices. It is public knowledge that MIPS processors power many popular well-known consumer products, such as Sony high definition television sets, Linksys wireless access points, and the popular Sony PlayStation 2 game console.[6]

The MIPS Technology website lists 73 licensees who are currently engaged in manufacturing products using MIPS processor cores. Some of these companies are household names, as with Sony, Texas Instruments, Cisco's Scientific Atlanta (a leading manufacturer of cable TV set-top boxes), Motorola, and others. Certainly, one of the largest and most successful of these is Broadcom Corporation.

3.2.5 Broadcom MIPS

Broadcom is a leading supplier of SOC solutions for markets such as cable TV set-top boxes, cable modems, HDTV, wireless networks, Gigabit Ethernet, and Voice over IP (VoIP). Broadcom's SOCs have been very popular in these markets. We mentioned earlier that you likely have Linux in your home even if you don't know it. Chances are, if you do, it is running on a Broadcom MIPS–based SOC.

In 2000, Broadcom acquired SiByte Inc., which resulted in the communications processor product lineup the company is currently marketing. These processors currently ship in single-core, dual-core, and quad-core configurations. The company still refers to them as SiByte processors.

The single-core SiByte processors include the BCM1122 and BCM1125H. They are both based on the MIPS64 core and operate at clock speeds at 400–900MHz. They include on-chip peripheral controllers such as DDR SDRAM controller, 10/100Mbps Ethernet, and PCI host controller. Both include SMBus serial configuration interface, PCMCIA, and two UARTs for serial port connections. The BCM1125H includes a triple-speed 10/100/1000Mbps Ethernet controller. One of the more striking features of these processors is their power dissipation. Both feature a 4W operating budget at 400MHz operation.

The dual-core SiByte processors include the BCM1250, BCM1255, and BCM1280. Also based on the MIPS64 core, these processors operate at clock rates

---

[6] Source: www.mips.com/content/PressRoom/PressReleases/2003-12-22

from 600MHz (BCM1250) to as high as 1.2GHz (BCM1255 and BCM1280). These dual-core chips include integrated peripheral controllers such as DDR SDRAM controllers, various combinations of Gigabit Ethernet controllers, 64-bit PCI-X interfaces, and SMBus, PCMCIA, and multiple UART interfaces. Like their single-core cousins, these dual-core implementations also feature low power dissipation. For example, the BCM1255 features a 13W power budget at 1GHz operation.

The quad-core SiByte processors include the BCM1455 and BCM1480 communications processors. As with the other SiByte processors, these are based on the MIPS64 core. The cores can be run from 800MHz to 1.2GHz. These SOCs include integrated DDR SDRAM controllers, four separate Gigabit Ethernet MAC controllers, and 64-bit PCI-X host controllers, and also contain SMBus, PCMCIA, and four serial UARTs.

Table 3-7 summarizes select Broadcom SiByte processors.

TABLE 3-7
Broadcom Select SiByte Processor Highlights

Feature	BCM1125H	BCM1250	BCM1280	BCM1480
Core/speeds	SB-1 MIPS64 400–900MHz	Dual SB-1 MIPS64 600–1000MHz	Dual SB-1 MIPS64 800–1200MHz	Quad SB-1 MIPS64 800–1200MHz
DRAM controller	Y-DDR	Y-DDR	Y-DDR	Y-DDR
Serial interface	2–55Mbps	2–55Mbps	4 UART	4 UART
SMBus interface	2	2	2	2
PCMCIA	Y	Y	Y	Y
Gigabit Ethernet (10/100/1000Mbps)	2	3	4	4
PCI controller	Y	Y	Y PCI/PCI-X	Y PCI/PCI-X
Security engine	N	N	N	
High-speed I/O (HyperTransport)	1	1	3	3

3.2.6 AMD MIPS

Advanced Micro Devices also plays a significant role in the embedded MIPS controller market. The company's 2002 acquisition of Alchemy Semiconductor garnered several popular single-chip integrated SOCs based on the MIPS32 core and architecture. The Alchemy line from AMD is based on the popular MIPS32 core. All feature relatively low power dissipation and a high level of onboard system integration.

The Au1000 and Au1100 operate at clock rates of 266–500MHz. Both feature onboard SDRAM controllers and separate bus controllers for attachment to external devices such as Flash and PCMCIA. Table 3-8 summarizes the current Alchemy product line.

TABLE 3-8
AMD Alchemy MIPS Highlights Summary

Feature*	Au1000	Au1100	Au1200	Au1500	Au1550
Core/speeds	MIPS32	MIPS32	MIPS32	MIPS32	MIPS32
	266–500MHz	333–500MHz	333–500MHz	333–500MHz	333–500MHz
DRAM controller	SDRAM	SDRAM	DDR SDRAM	SDRAM	DDR SDRAM
Ethernet 10/100	2	1	—	2	2
GPIO lines	32	48	48	39	43
UARTs	4	3	2	2	3
USB 1.1	Host + device	Host + device	USB 2.0	Host + device	Host + device
AC-97 audio	1	1	Via SPC	1	Via SPC
I²S controller	1	1	Via SPC	—	Via SPC
SD/MMC	N	2	2	N	N

*Other peripherals include IrDA controller, LCD controller, 2 SPCs, Power management, DMA engine, RTC, Camera interface, LCD controller, h/w hardware acceleration of encryption/decryption, PCI host controller, 4 SPCs, and Security engine.

3.2.7 Other MIPS

As we pointed out earlier, nearly 100 current MIPS licensees are shown on the MIPS Technologies licensees web page, at www.mips.com/content/Licensees/ ProductCatalog/licensees. Unfortunately, it is not possible in the space provided here to cover them all. Start your search at the MIPS technologies website for a good cross-section of the MIPS processor vendors.

For example, ATI Technologies uses a MIPS core in its Xilleon set-top box family of chipsets. Cavium Network's Octeon family uses MIPS64 cores in a variety of multicore processor implementations. Integrated Device Technology, Inc., (IDT) has a family of integrated communications processors called Interprise, based on the MIPS architecture. PMC-Sierra, NEC, Toshiba, and others have integrated processors based on MIPS. All of these and more are well supported under Linux.

3.2.8 ARM

The ARM architecture has achieved a very large market share in the consumer electronics marketplace. Many popular and now ubiquitous products contain ARM cores. Some well-known examples include the Sony PlayStation Portable (PSP), Apple iPod Nano,[7] Nintendo Game Boy Micro and DS, TomTom GO 300 GPS, and the Motorola E680i Mobile Phone, which features embedded Linux. Processors containing ARM cores power a majority of the world's digital cellular phones, according to the ARM Corporate Backgrounder at www.arm.com/miscPDFs/ 3822.pdf.

The ARM architecture is developed by ARM Holdings, plc and licensed to semiconductor manufacturers around the globe. Many of the world's leading semiconductor companies have licensed ARM technology and are currently shipping integrated processors based on one of the several ARM cores.

3.2.9 TI ARM

Texas Instruments uses ARM cores in the OMAP family of integrated processors. These processors contain many integrated peripherals intended to be used as single-chip solutions for various consumer products, such as cellular handsets, PDAs, and similar multimedia platforms. In addition to the interfaces commonly found on

---

[7] Reported by ARM to be the top-selling toy during the Christmas 2005 shopping season in the United States.

integrated processors, such as UARTs and I²C, the OMAP devices contain a wide range of special-purpose interfaces, including the following:

- LCD screen and backlight controllers
- Buzzer driver
- Camera interface
- MMC/SD card controller
- Battery-management hardware
- USB client/host interfaces
- Radio modem interface logic
- Integrated 2D or 3D graphics accelerators
- Integrated security accelerator
- S-Video outputs
- IrDA controller
- DACs for direct TV (PAL/NTSC) video output
- Integrated DSPs for video and audio processing

Many popular cellular handsets and PDA devices have been marketed based on the TI OMAP platform. Because they are based on an ARM core, these processors are supported by Linux today. Table 3-9 compares some of the more recent members of the TI OMAP family.

TABLE 3-9
TI ARM OMAP Highlights Summary

Feature	OMAP1710	OMAP2420	OMAP2430	OMAP3430
Core/speeds	ARM926 TEJ	ARM11	ARM1136	ARM Cortex A8
	Up to 200MHz	330MHz	330MHz	550MHz
DRAM controller	Y	Y	Y	Y
UARTs	Y	Y	Y	Y
USB	Client + host	Client + host	Client + host	Client + host

(continues)

TABLE 3-9 (Continued)

Feature	OMAP1710	OMAP2420	OMAP2430	OMAP3430
I²C controller	Y	Y	Y	Y
MMC-SD interface	Y	Y	Y	Y
Keypad controller	Y	Y	Y	Y
Camera interface	Y	Y	Y	Y
Graphics accelerator	2D	2D/3D	2D/3D	Y
Integrated DSP	TM320C55x	TM320C55x	N	N
Video acceleration hardware	N	Imaging Video Accelerator (IVA)	Imaging Video Accelerator (IVA 2)	Imaging Video Accelerator (IVA 2+)
Security accelerator	Y	Y	Y	Y
Audio codec support	Y	Y	Y	Y
Bluetooth & RF modem support interface	Y	Y	Y	Y
LCD controller	Y	Y	Y	Y
Display controllers	N	PAL/NTSC VGA/QVGA	PAL/NTSC VGA/QVGA	PAL/NTSC QVGA/XGA

3.2.10 Freescale ARM

The success of the ARM architecture is made more evident by the fact that leading manufacturers of competing architectures have licensed ARM technology. As a prime example, Freescale Semiconductor has licensed ARM technology for its line of i.MX application processors. These popular ARM-based integrated processors have achieved widespread industry success in multimedia consumer devices such as portable game platforms, PDAs, and cellular handsets.

The Freescale ARM product portfolio includes the i.MX21 and i.MX31 application processors. The i.MX21 features an ARM9 core, and the i.MX31 has an ARM11 core. Like their TI counterparts, these SOCs contain many integrated peripherals required by portable consumer electronics devices with multimedia requirements. The i.MX21/31 contain some of the following integrated interfaces:

- Graphics accelerator
- MPEG-4 encoder
- Keypad and LCD controllers
- Camera interface
- Audio multiplexer
- IrDA infrared I/O
- SD/MMC interface
- Numerous external I/O, such as PCMCIA, USB, DRAM controllers, and UARTs for serial port connection

3.2.11 Intel ARM XScale

Intel manufactures and markets several integrated processors based on the ARM v5TE architecture. Intel uses the XScale name for the architecture. These products are grouped into several application categories. Table 3-10 summarizes the XScale families by application type.

TABLE 3-10
Intel XScale Processor Summary

Category	Application	Example Processors
Application processors	Cellular handsets and PDAs	PXA27x, PXA29x
I/O processors	High-speed data processing used in storage, printing, telematics, and so on	IOP331/332/333
Network processors	Networking and communications data plane processing, fast packet processing, and so on	IXP425, IXP465 IXP2350, IXP2855

Many consumer and networking products have been developed using Intel XScale architecture processors. Some well-known examples include the GPS iQue M5 from

Garmin, the iPAQ by Hewlett-Packard, smart phones from Palm (Treo) and Motorola (A760), and many others. Linux currently supports all these processors.

Intel's network processors are found in high-performance networking equipment where requirements exist for fast data-path processing. Examples include deep packet inspection, data encryption/decryption, packet filtering, and signal processing. These network processors each contain an ARM core coupled with one or more dedicated processing engines, called a network processing engine (NPE). These NPEs are dedicated to specific data-path manipulation in real time at wire speeds. The NPE is a microprocessor, in the sense that it can execute microcoded algorithms in parallel with the thread of execution in the ARM core. Refer to the Intel website, at www.intel.com, for additional information on this powerful family of integrated processors.

3.2.12 Other ARM

More than 100 semiconductor companies are developing integrated solutions based on ARM technology—far too many to list here. Many offer specialized application processors serving vertical markets such as the handset market, storage area networking, network processing, and the automotive market, as well as many more. These companies include Altera, PMC-Sierra, Samsung Electronics, Philips Semiconductor, Fujitsu, and more. See the ARM Technologies website at www.arm.com for additional ARM licensees and information.

3.2.13 Other Architectures

We have covered the major architectures in widespread use in embedded Linux systems. However, for completeness, you should be aware of other architectures for which support exists in Linux. A recent Linux snapshot revealed 25 architecture branches (subdirectories). In some instances, the 64-bit implementation of an architecture is separated from its 32-bit counterpart. In other cases, ports are not current or are no longer maintained.

The Linux source tree contains ports for Sun Sparc and Sparc64, the Xtensa from Tensilica, and the v850 from NEC, to name a few. Spend a few minutes looking through the architecture branches of the Linux kernel to see the range of architectures for which Linux has been ported. Beware, however, that not all these architectures might be up-to-date in any given snapshot. You can be reasonably certain that the major architectures are fairly current, but the only way to be certain is to follow the development in the Linux community or consult with your favorite embedded Linux vendor. Appendix E, "Open Source Resources," contains a list of resources you can consult to help you stay current with Linux developments.

3.3 Hardware Platforms

The idea of a common hardware reference platform is not new. The venerable PC/104 and VMEbus are two examples of hardware platforms that have withstood the test of time in the embedded market.[8] More recent successful platforms include CompactPCI and its derivatives.

3.3.1 CompactPCI

The CompactPCI (cPCI) hardware platform is based on PCI electrical standards and Eurocard physical specifications. cPCI has the following general features:

- Vertical cards of 3U or 6U heights
- Latch system for securing and ejecting cards
- Front- or rear-panel I/O connections supported
- High-density backplane connector
- Staggered power pins for hot-swap support
- Support by many vendors
- Compatibility with standard PCI chipsets

You can view highlights of and obtain specifications for the cPCI architecture at the PCI Industrial Computer Manufacturers Group (PICMG) cPCI web page, at www.picmg.org/compactpci.stm.

3.3.2 ATCA

A successor to the successful cPCI, Advanced Telecommunications Computing Architecture is the name given to the architecture and platforms designed around the PICMG 3.x series of specifications. Many top-tier hardware manufacturers are

---

[8] VMEbus isn't really a hardware reference platform, per se, but based on Eurocard physical standards, the level of compatibility among multiple vendors qualifies it for the label.

shipping or developing new ATCA-based platforms. The primary applications for ATCA platforms are carrier-class telecommunications switching and transport equipment, and high-end data-center server and storage equipment.

ATCA platforms are leading the industry trend away from in-house proprietary hardware and software platforms. Many of the largest equipment manufacturers in the telecommunications and networking markets have been slowly moving away from the custom, in-house-designed hardware platforms. This trend is also evident in the software platforms, from operating systems to so-called middleware such as high-availability and protocol stack solutions. Downsizing and time-to-market pressures are two key factors driving this trend.

ATCA is defined by several PICMG specifications. Table 3-11 summarizes these specifications.

TABLE 3-11
ATCA PICMG 3.x Specification Summary

Specification	Summary
PICMG 3.0	Mechanical specifications, including interconnects, power, cooling, and base system management
PICMG 3.1	Ethernet and Fiber Channel switching fabric interface
PICMG 3.2	Infiniband switching fabric interface
PICMG 3.3	StarFabric interface
PICMG 3.4	PCI Express interface
PICMG 3.5	RapidIO Interface

The platforms described in this section are the most relevant in any discussion of embedded Linux platforms today. Especially with ATCA, the industry is increasingly moving toward commercial off-the-shelf (COTS) technology. Both ATCA and Linux play increasingly important roles in this industry trend.

3.4 Chapter Summary

- Many stand-alone processors are supported under Linux. The most widely supported of these are IA32/IA64 and PowerPC architectures. These stand-alone processors are used as building blocks to build very-high-performance computing engines. We presented several examples from Intel, IBM, and Freescale.

- Integrated processors, or systems on chip (SOCs), dominate the embedded Linux landscape. Many vendors and several popular architectures are used in embedded Linux designs. Several of the most popular are presented in this chapter by architecture and manufacturer.

- An increasingly popular trend is to move away from proprietary hardware and software platforms, toward commercial off-the-shelf (COTS) solutions. Two popular platforms in widespread use in embedded Linux systems: cPCI and ATCA.

3.4.1 Suggestions For Additional Reading

PowerPC 32-bit architecture reference manual:
Programming Environments Manual for 32-Bit Implementations of the PowerPC Architecture—Revision 2
Freescale Semiconductor, Inc.
www.freescale.com/files/product/doc/MPCFPE32B.pdf

PowerPC 64-bit architecture reference:
The Programming Environments Manual for 64-Bit Microprocessors—Version 3.0
International Business Machines, Inc.

Short summary of PowerPC architecture:
A Developer's Guide to the POWER Architecture
Brett Olsson, Processor Architect, IBM Corp.
Anthony Marsala, Software Engineer, IBM Corp.
www-128.ibm.com/developerworks/linux/library/l-powarch/

Intel XScale summary page
www.intel.com/design/intelxscale/

The Linux Kernel—A Different Perspective

If you want to learn about kernel internals, many good books are available on kernel design and operation. Several are presented in Section 4.5.1, "Suggestions for Additional Reading," in this and other chapters throughout the book. However, very little has been written about how the kernel is organized and structured from a project perspective. What if you're looking for the right place to add some custom support for your new embedded project? How do you know which files are important for your architecture?

At first glance, it might seem an almost impossible task to understand the Linux kernel and how to configure it for a specific platform or application. In a recent Linux kernel snapshot, the Linux kernel source tree consists of more than 20,000 files that contain more than six million lines—and that's just the beginning. You still need tools, a root file system, and many Linux applications to make a usable system.

This chapter introduces the Linux kernel and covers how the kernel is organized and how the source tree is structured. We then examine the components that make up the kernel image and discuss the kernel source tree layout. Following this, we present the details of the kernel build system and the files that drive the kernel configuration and build system. This chapter concludes by examining what is required for a complete embedded Linux system.

4.1 Background

Linus Torvalds wrote the original version of Linux while he was a student at the University of Helsinki in Finland. His work began in 1991. In August of that year, Linus posted this now-famous announcement on `comp.os.minix`:

```
From: torvalds@klaava.Helsinki.FI (Linus Benedict Torvalds)
Newsgroups: comp.os.minix
Subject: What would you like to see most in minix?
Summary: small poll for my new operating system
Message-ID: <1991Aug25.205708.9541@klaava.Helsinki.FI>
Date: 25 Aug 91 20:57:08 GMT
Organization: University of Helsinki


Hello everybody out there using minix -
```

```
I'm doing a (free) operating system (just a hobby, won't be big and professional
like gnu) for 386(486) AT clones.  This has been brewing since april, and is
starting to get ready.  I'd like any feedback on things people like/dislike in
minix, as my OS resembles it somewhat(same physical layout of the file-system
(due to practical reasons)among other things).

I've currently ported bash(1.08) and gcc(1.40), and things seem to work. This
implies that I'll get something practical within a few months, and I'd like to
know what features most people would want.  Any suggestions are welcome, but I
won't promise I'll implement them :-)

            Linus (torvalds@kruuna.helsinki.fi)

PS.  Yes - it's free of any minix code, and it has a multi-threaded fs.
It is NOT protable (uses 386 task switching etc), and it probably never
will support anything other than AT-harddisks, as that's all I have :-(.
```

Since that initial release, Linux has matured into a full-featured operating system with robustness, reliability, and high-end features that rival those of the best commercial operating systems. By some estimates, more than half of the Internet servers on the Web are powered by Linux servers. It is no secret that the online search giant Google uses a large collection of low-cost PCs running a fault-tolerant version of Linux to implement its popular search engine.

4.1.1 Kernel Versions

You can obtain the source code for a Linux kernel and complementary components in numerous places. Your local bookstore might have several versions as companion CD-ROMs in books about Linux. You also can download the kernel itself or even complete Linux distributions from numerous locations on the Internet. The official home for the Linux kernel is found at www.kernel.org. You will often hear the terms *mainline source* or *mainline kernel* referring to the source trees found at kernel.org.

As this book is being written, Linux Version 2.6 is the current version. Early in the development cycle, the developers chose a numbering system designed to differentiate between kernel source trees intended for development and experimentation and source trees intended to be stable, production-ready kernels. The numbering scheme contains a major version number, a minor version number, and then a sequence number. Before Linux Version 2.6, if the minor version number is even, it denotes a production kernel; if it is odd, it denotes a development kernel. For example:

- **Linux 2.4.*x***—Production kernel

- **Linux 2.5.*x***—Experimental (development)

- **Linux 2.6.*x***—Production kernel

Currently, there is no separate development branch of the Linux 2.6 kernel. All new features, enhancements, and bug fixes are funneled through a series of gate-keepers who ultimately filter and push changes up to the top-level Linux source trees maintained by Andrew Morton and Linus Torvalds.

It is easy to tell what kernel version you are working with. The first few lines of the top-level *makefile*[1] in a kernel source tree detail the exact kernel version represented by a given instance. It looks like this for the 2.6.14 production kernel:

```
VERSION = 2
PATCHLEVEL = 6
SUBLEVEL = 14
EXTRAVERSION =
NAME=Affluent Albatross
```

Later in the same makefile, these macros are used to form a version-level macro, like this:

```
KERNELRELEASE=$(VERSION).$(PATCHLEVEL).$(SUBLEVEL)$(EXTRAVERSION)
```

This macro is used in several places in the kernel source tree to indicate the kernel version. In fact, version information is used with sufficient frequency that the kernel developers have dedicated a set of macros derived from the version macros in the makefile. These macros are found in .../include/linux/version.h[2] in the Linux kernel source tree. They are reproduced here as Listing 4-1.

Listing 4-1

Kernel include File: .../include/linux/version.h

```
#define UTS_RELEASE "2.6.14"
#define LINUX_VERSION_CODE 132622
#define KERNEL_VERSION(a,b,c) (((a) << 16) + ((b) << 8) + (c))
```

You can check the kernel version from a command prompt on a running Linux system like this:

```
$ cat /proc/version
Linux version 2.6.13 (chris@pluto) (gcc version 4.0.0 (DENX ELDK 4.0 4.0.0)) #2
Thu Feb 16 19:30:13 EST 2006
```

One final note about kernel versions: You can make it easy to keep track of the kernel version in your own kernel project by customizing the EXTRAVERSION field.

---

[1] We talk about the kernel build system and makefiles shortly.

[2] Throughout this book, three dots preceding any path are used to indicate whatever path it might take on your system to reach the top-level Linux source tree.

For example, if you were developing enhancements for some new kernel feature, you might set EXTRAVERSION to something like this:

```
EXTRAVERSION=-foo
```

Later, when you use `cat /proc/version`, you would see `Linux version 2.6.13-foo`, and this would help you distinguish between development versions of your own kernel.

4.1.2 Kernel Source Repositories

The official home for the kernel source code is www.kernel.org. There you can find both current and historical versions of the Linux kernel, as well as numerous patches. The primary FTP repository found at `ftp.kernel.org` contains subdirectories going all the way back to Linux Version 1.0. This site is the primary focus for the ongoing development activities within the Linux kernel.

If you download a recent Linux kernel from kernel.org, you will find files in the source tree for 25 different architectures and subarchitectures. Several other development trees support the major architectures. One of the reasons is simply the sheer volume of developers and changes to the kernel. If every developer on every architecture submitted patches to kernel.org, the maintainers would be inundated with changes and patch management, and would never get to do any feature development. As anyone involved with kernel development will tell you, it's already very busy!

Several other public source trees exist outside the mainline kernel.org source, mostly for architecture-specific development. For example, a developer working on the MIPS architecture might find a suitable kernel at www.linux-mips.org. Normally, work done in an architecture tree is eventually submitted to the kernel.org kernel. Most architecture developers try to sync up to the mainline kernel often, to keep up with new developments whenever possible. However, it is not always straightforward to get one's patches included in the mainline kernel, and there will always be a lag. Indeed, differences in the architecture kernel trees exist at any given point in time.

If you are wondering how to find a kernel for your particular application, the best way to proceed is to obtain the latest stable Linux source tree. Check to see if support for your particular processor exists, and then search the Linux kernel mailing lists for any patches or issues related to your application. Also find the mailing list that most closely matches your interest, and search that archive also.

Appendix E, "Open Source Resources," contains several good references and sources of information related to kernel source repositories, mailing lists, and more.

4.2 Linux Kernel Construction

In the next few sections, we explore the layout, organization, and construction of the Linux kernel. Armed with this knowledge, you will find it much easier to navigate this large, complex source code base. Over time, there have been significant improvements in the organization of the source tree, especially in the architecture branch, which contains support for numerous architectures and specific machines. As this book is being written, an effort is underway to collapse the `ppc` and `ppc64` architecture branches into a single common `powerpc` branch. When the dust settles, there will be many improvements, including elimination of duplicate code, better organization of files, and partitioning of functionality.

4.2.1 Top-Level Source Directory

We make frequent reference to the *top-level source directory* throughout the book. In every case, we are referring to the highest-level directory contained in the kernel source tree. On any given machine, it might be located anywhere, but on a desktop Linux workstation, it is often found in `/usr/src/linux-x.y.z`, where `x.y.z` represents the kernel version. Throughout the book, we use the shorthand `.../` to represent the top-level kernel source directory.

The top-level kernel source directory contains the following subdirectories. (We have omitted the nondirectory entries in this listing, as well as directories used for source control for clarity and brevity.)

arch	crypto	Documentation	drivers fs		include
init	ipc	kernel	lib	mm	net
scripts	security	sound	usr		

Many of these subdirectories contain several additional levels of subdirectories containing source code, makefiles, and configuration files. By far the largest branch of the Linux kernel source tree is found under `.../drivers`. Here you can find support for Ethernet network cards, USB controllers, and the numerous hardware devices that the Linux kernel supports. As you might imagine, the `.../arch` subdirectory is the next largest, containing support for more than 20 unique processor architectures.

Additional files found in the top-level Linux subdirectory include the top-level makefile, a hidden configuration file (*dot-config*, introduced in Section 4.3.1, "The Dot-Config") and various other informational files not involved in the build itself. Finally, two important build targets are found in the top-level kernel source tree after a successful build: `System.map` and the kernel proper, `vmlinux`. Both are described shortly.

4.2.2 Compiling the Kernel

Understanding a large body of software such as Linux can be a daunting task. It is too large to simply "step through" the code to follow what is happening. Multithreading and preemption add to the complexity of analysis. In fact, even locating the entry point (the first line of code to be executed upon entry to the kernel) can be challenging. One of the more useful ways to understand the structure of a large binary image is to examine its built components.

The output of the kernel build system produces several common files, as well as one or more architecture-specific binary modules. Common files are always built regardless of the architecture. Two of the common files are `System.map` and `vmlinux`, introduced earlier. The former is useful during kernel debug and is particularly interesting. It contains a human-readable list of the kernel symbols and their respective addresses. The latter is an architecture-specific *ELF*[3] file in executable format. It is produced by the top-level kernel makefile for every architecture. If the kernel was compiled with symbolic debug information, it will be contained in the `vmlinux` image. In practice, although it is an ELF executable, this file is usually *never* booted directly, as you will see shortly.

Listing 4-2 is a snippet of output resulting from executing `make` in a recent kernel tree configured for the ARM XScale architecture. The kernel source tree was configured for the ADI Engineering Coyote reference board based on the Intel IXP425 network processor using the following command:

```
make ARCH=arm CROSS_COMPILE=xscale_be- ixp4xx_defconfig
```

This command does not build the kernel; it prepares the kernel source tree for the XScale architecture including an initial default configuration for this architecture and processor. It builds a default configuration (the dot-config file) that drives

---

[3] Executable and Linking Format, a de-facto standard format for binary executable files.

the kernel build, based on the defaults found in the `ixp4xx_defconfig` file. We have more to say about the configuration process later, in Section 4.3, "Kernel Build System."

Listing 4-2 shows the command that builds the kernel. Only the first few and last few lines of the build output are shown for this discussion.

Listing 4-2

Kernel Build Output

```
$ make ARCH=arm CROSS_COMPILE=xscale_be- zImage
  CHK       include/linux/version.h
  HOSTCC    scripts/basic/fixdep
  .
  . <hundreds of lines of output omitted here>
  .
  LD        vmlinux
  SYSMAP    System.map
  SYSMAP    .tmp_System.map
  OBJCOPY   arch/arm/boot/Image
  Kernel:   arch/arm/boot/Image is ready
  AS        arch/arm/boot/compressed/head.o
  GZIP      arch/arm/boot/compressed/piggy.gz
  AS        arch/arm/boot/compressed/piggy.o
  CC        arch/arm/boot/compressed/misc.o
  AS        arch/arm/boot/compressed/head-xscale.o
  AS        arch/arm/boot/compressed/big-endian.o
  LD        arch/arm/boot/compressed/vmlinux
  OBJCOPY   arch/arm/boot/zImage
  Kernel:   arch/arm/boot/zImage is ready
  Building modules, stage 2.
  ...
```

To begin, notice the invocation of the build. Both the desired architecture (`ARCH=arm`) and the toolchain (`CROSS_COMPILE=xscale_be-`) were specified on the command line. This forces `make` to use the XScale toolchain to build the kernel image and to use the arm-specific branch of the kernel source tree for architecture-dependent portions of the build. We also specify a target called *zImage*. This target is common to many architectures and is described in Chapter 5, "Kernel Initialization."

The next thing you might notice is that the actual commands used for each step have been hidden and replaced with a shorthand notation. The motivation behind this was to clean up the build output to draw more attention to intermediate build issues, particularly compiler warnings. In earlier kernel source trees, each compilation or link command was output to the console verbosely, which often required several lines for each step. The end result was virtually unreadable, and compiler warnings slipped by unnoticed in the noise. The new system is definitely an improvement because any anomaly in the build process is easily spotted. If you want or need to see the complete build step, you can force verbose output by defining V=1 on the make command line.

We have omitted most of the actual compilation and link steps in Listing 4-2, for clarity. (This particular build has more than 900 individual compile and link commands in the build. That would have made for a long listing, indeed.) After all the intermediate files and library archives have been built and compiled, they are put together in one large ELF build target called vmlinux. Although it is architecture specific, this vmlinux target is a common target—it is produced for all supported Linux architectures.

4.2.3 The Kernel Proper: vmlinux

Notice this line in Listing 4-2:

```
LD /arch/arm/boot/compressed/vmlinux
```

The vmlinux file is the actual *kernel proper*. It is a fully stand-alone, monolithic image. No unresolved external references exist within the vmlinux binary. When caused to execute in the proper context (by a bootloader designed to boot the Linux kernel), it boots the board on which it is running, leaving a completely functional kernel.

In keeping with the philosophy that to understand a system one must first understand its parts, let's look at the construction of the vmlinux kernel object.

Listing 4-3 reproduces the actual link stage of the build process that resulted in the `vmlinux` ELF object. We have formatted it with line breaks (indicated by the UNIX line-continuation character, '\') to make it more readable, but otherwise it is the exact output produced by the `vmlinux` link step in the build process from Listing 4-2. If you were building the kernel by hand, this is the link command you would issue from the command line.

Listing 4-3

Link Stage: vmlinux

```
xscale_be-ld -EB  -p --no-undefined -X -o vmlinux   \
-T arch/arm/kernel/vmlinux.lds                      \
arch/arm/kernel/head.o                              \
arch/arm/kernel/init_task.o                         \
init/built-in.o                                     \
--start-group                                       \
usr/built-in.o                                      \
arch/arm/kernel/built-in.o                          \
arch/arm/mm/built-in.o                              \
arch/arm/common/built-in.o                          \
arch/arm/mach-ixp4xx/built-in.o                     \
arch/arm/nwfpe/built-in.o                           \
kernel/built-in.o                                   \
mm/built-in.o                                       \
fs/built-in.o                                       \
ipc/built-in.o                                      \
security/built-in.o                                 \
crypto/built-in.o                                   \
lib/lib.a                                           \
arch/arm/lib/lib.a                                  \
lib/built-in.o                                      \
arch/arm/lib/built-in.o                             \
drivers/built-in.o                                  \
sound/built-in.o                                    \
net/built-in.o                                      \
--end-group                                         \
.tmp_kallsyms2.o
```

4.2.4 Kernel Image Components

From Listing 4-3, you can see that the vmlinux image consists of several composite binary images. Right now, it is not important to understand the purpose of each component. What is important is to understand the top-level view of what components make up the kernel. The first line of the link command in Listing 4-3 specifies the output file (-o vmlinux.) The second line specifies the *linker script* file (-T vmlinux.lds), a detailed recipe for how the kernel binary image should be linked.[4]

The third and subsequent lines from Listing 4-3 specify the object modules that form the resulting binary image. Notice that the first object specified is head.o. This object was assembled from /arch/arm/kernel/head.S, an architecture-specific assembly language source file that performs very low-level kernel initialization. If you were searching for the first line of code to be executed by the kernel, it would make sense to start your search here because it will ultimately be the first code found in the binary image created by this link stage. We examine kernel initialization in detail in Chapter 5.

The next object, init_task.o, sets up initial thread and task structures that the kernel requires. Following this is a large collection of object modules, each having a common name: built-in.o. You will notice, however, that each built-in.o object comes from a specific part of the kernel source tree, as indicated by the path component preceding the built-in.o object name. These are the binary objects that are included in the kernel image. An illustration might make this clearer.

---

[4] The linker script file has a peculiar syntax. The details can be found in the documentation for the GNU linker.

Figure 4-1 illustrates the binary makeup of the vmlinux image. It contains a section for each line of the link stage. It's not to scale because of space considerations, but you can see the relative sizes of each functional component.

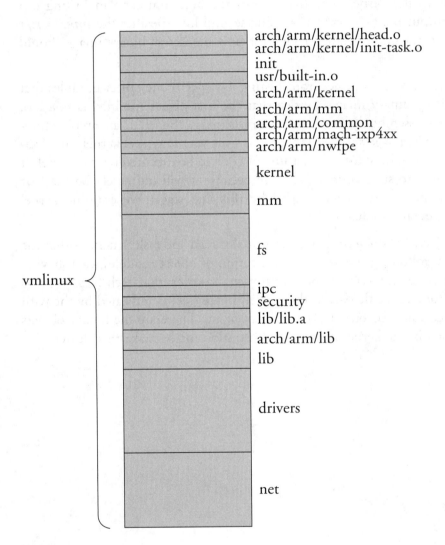

FIGURE 4-1
vmlinux image components

It might come as no surprise that the three largest binary components are the file system code, the network code, and all the built-in drivers. If you take the kernel code and the architecture-specific kernel code together, this is the next-largest binary component. Here you find the scheduler, process and thread management, timer management, and other core kernel functionality. Naturally, the kernel contains some architecture-specific functionality, such as low-level context switching, hardware-level interrupt and timer processing, processor exception handling, and more. This is found in .../arch/arm/kernel.

Bear in mind that we are looking at a specific example of a kernel build. In this particular example, we are building a kernel specific to the ARM XScale architecture and, more specifically, the Intel IXP425 network processor on the ADI Engineering reference board. You can see the machine-specific binary components in Figure 4-1 as arch/arm/mach-ixp4xx. Each architecture and machine type (processor/reference board) has different elements in the architecture-specific portions of the kernel, so the makeup of the vmlinux image is slightly different. When you understand one example, you will find it easy to navigate others.

To help you understand the breakdown of functionality in the kernel source tree, Table 4-1 lists each component in Figure 4-1, together with a short description of each binary element that makes up the vmlinux image.

TABLE 4-1
vmlinux Image Components Description

Component	Description
arch/arm/kernel/head.o	Kernel architecture-specific startup code.
init_task.o	Initial thread and task structs required by kernel.
init/built-in.o	Main kernel-initialization code. See Chapter 5.
usr/built-in.o	Built-in initramfs image. See Chapter 5.
arch/arm/kernel/built-in.o	Architecture-specific kernel code.
arch/arm/mm/built-in.o	Architecture-specific memory-management code.
arch/arm/common/built-in.o	Architecture-specific generic code. Varies by architecture.

(continues)

TABLE 4-1 (Continued)

Component	Description
`arch/arm/mach-ixp4xx/built-in.o`	Machine-specific code, usually initialization.
`arch/arm/nwfpe/built-in.o`	Architecture-specific floating point–emulation code.
`kernel/built-in.o`	Common components of the kernel itself.
`mm/built-in.o`	Common components of memory-management code.
`ipc/built-in.o`	Interprocess communications, such as SysV IPC.
`security/built-in.o`	Linux security components.
`lib/lib.a`	Archive of miscellaneous helper functions.
`arch/arm/lib/lib.a`	Architecture-specific common facilities. Varies by architecture.
`lib/built-in.o`	Common kernel helper functions.
`drivers/built-in.o`	All the built-in drivers—not loadable modules.
`sound/built-in.o`	Sound drivers.
`net/built-in.o`	Linux networking.
`.tmp_kallsyms2.o`	Symbol table.

When we speak of the kernel proper, this `vmlinux` image is being referenced. As mentioned earlier, very few platforms boot this image directly. For one thing, it is almost universally compressed. At a bare minimum, a bootloader must decompress the image. Many platforms require some type of stub bolted onto the image to perform the decompression. Later in Chapter 5, you will learn how this image is packaged for different architectures, machine types, and bootloaders, and the requirements for booting it.

4.2.5 Subdirectory Layout

Now that you've seen how the build system controls the kernel image, let's take a look at a representative kernel subdirectory. Listing 4-4 details the contents of the `mach-ixp425` subdirectory. This directory exists under the `.../arch/arm` architecture-specific branch of the source tree.

Listing 4-4

Kernel Subdirectory

```
$ ls -l linux-2.6/arch/arm/mach-ixp425
total 92
-rw-rw-r--  1 chris    chris    11892 Oct 10 14:53 built-in.o
-rw-rw-r--  1 chris    chris     6924 Sep 29 15:39 common.c
-rw-rw-r--  1 chris    chris     3525 Oct 10 14:53 common.o
-rw-rw-r--  1 chris    chris    13062 Sep 29 15:39 common-pci.c
-rw-rw-r--  1 chris    chris     7504 Oct 10 14:53 common-pci.o
-rw-rw-r--  1 chris    chris     1728 Sep 29 15:39 coyote-pci.c
-rw-rw-r--  1 chris    chris     1572 Oct 10 14:53 coyote-pci.o
-rw-rw-r--  1 chris    chris     2118 Sep 29 15:39 coyote-setup.c
-rw-rw-r--  1 chris    chris     2180 Oct 10 14:53 coyote-setup.o
-rw-rw-r--  1 chris    chris     2042 Sep 29 15:39 ixdp425-pci.c
-rw-rw-r--  1 chris    chris     3656 Sep 29 15:39 ixdp425-setup.c
-rw-rw-r--  1 chris    chris     2761 Sep 29 15:39 Kconfig
-rw-rw-r--  1 chris    chris      259 Sep 29 15:39 Makefile
-rw-rw-r--  1 chris    chris     3102 Sep 29 15:39 prpmc1100-pci.c
```

The directory contents in Listing 4-4 have common components found in many kernel source subdirectories: `Makefile` and `Kconfig`. These two files drive the kernel configuration-and-build process. Let's look at how that works.

4.3 Kernel Build System

The Linux kernel configuration and build system is rather complicated, as one would expect of software projects containing more than six million lines of code! In this section, we cover the foundation of the kernel build system for developers who need to customize the build environment.

A recent Linux kernel snapshot showed more than 800 makefiles[5] in the kernel source tree. This might sound like a large number, but it might not seem so large

---

[5] Not all these makefiles are directly involved in building the kernel. Some, for example, build documentation files.

when you understand the structure and operation of the build system. The Linux kernel build system has been significantly updated since the days of Linux 2.4 and earlier. For those of you familiar with the older kernel build system, we're sure you will find the new *Kbuild* system to be a huge improvement. We limit our discussion in this section to this and later kernel versions based on `Kbuild`.

4.3.1 The Dot-Config

Introduced earlier, the dot-config file is the configuration blueprint for building a Linux kernel image. You will likely spend significant effort at the start of your Linux project building a configuration that is appropriate for your embedded platform. Several editors, both text based and graphical, are designed to edit your kernel configuration. The output of this configuration exercise is written to a configuration file named `.config`, located in the top-level Linux source directory that drives the kernel build.

You have likely invested significant time perfecting your kernel configuration, so you will want to protect it. Several `make` commands delete this configuration file without warning. The most common is `make  mrproper`. This `make` target is designed to return the kernel source tree to its pristine, unconfigured state. This includes removing all configuration data from the source tree—and, yes, it deletes your `.config`.

As you might know, any filename in Linux preceded by a dot is a hidden file in Linux. It is unfortunate that such an important file is marked hidden; this has brought considerable grief to more than one developer. If you execute `make` `mrproper` without having a backup copy of your `.config` file, you, too, will share our grief. (You have been warned—back up your `.config` file!)

The .config file is a collection of definitions with a simple format. Listing 4.5 shows a snippet of a .config from a recent Linux kernel release.

Listing 4-5

Snippet from Linux 2.6 .config

```
...
# USB support
#
CONFIG_USB=m
# CONFIG_USB_DEBUG is not set

# Miscellaneous USB options
#
CONFIG_USB_DEVICEFS=y
# CONFIG_USB_BANDWIDTH is not set
# CONFIG_USB_DYNAMIC_MINORS is not set

# USB Host Controller Drivers
#
CONFIG_USB_EHCI_HCD=m
# CONFIG_USB_EHCI_SPLIT_ISO is not set
# CONFIG_USB_EHCI_ROOT_HUB_TT is not set
CONFIG_USB_OHCI_HCD=m
CONFIG_USB_UHCI_HCD=m
...
```

To understand the .config file, you need to understand a fundamental aspect of the Linux kernel. Linux has a monolithic structure. That is, the entire kernel is compiled and linked as a single statically linked executable. However, it is possible to compile and *incrementally link*[6] a set of sources into a single object module suitable for dynamic insertion into a running kernel. This is the usual method for supporting most common device drivers. In Linux, these are called *loadable modules*. They are also generically called device drivers. After the kernel is booted, a special application program is invoked to insert the loadable module into a running kernel.

Armed with that knowledge, let's look again at Listing 4-5. This snippet of the configuration file (.config) shows a portion of the USB subsystem configuration. The first configuration option, CONFIG_USB=m, declares that the USB subsystem is to be included in this kernel configuration and that it will be compiled as a *dynamically loadable module* (=m), to be loaded sometime after the kernel has booted. The other

---

[6] Incremental linking is a technique used to generate an object module that is intended to be linked again into another object. In this way, unresolved symbols that remain after incremental linking do not generate errors—they are resolved at the next link stage.

choice would have been =y, in which case the USB module would be compiled and statically linked as part of the kernel image itself. It would end up in the `.../drivers/built-in.o` composite binary that you saw in Listing 4-3 and Figure 4-1. The astute reader will realize that if a driver is configured as a loadable module, its code is not included in the kernel proper, but rather exists as a stand-alone object module, a *loadable module*, to be inserted into the running kernel after boot.

Notice in Listing 4-5 the CONFIG_USB_DEVICEFS=y declaration. This configuration option behaves in a slightly different manner. In this case, USB_DEVICEFS (as configuration options are commonly abbreviated) is not a stand-alone module, but rather a feature to be enabled or disabled in the USB driver. It does not necessarily result in a module that is compiled into the kernel proper (=y); instead, it enables one or more features, often represented as additional object modules to be included in the overall USB device driver module. Usually, the help text in the configuration editor, or the hierarchy presented by the configuration editor, makes this distinction clear.

4.3.2 Configuration Editor(s)

Early kernels used a simple command line driven script to configure the kernel. This was cumbersome even for early kernels, in which the number of configuration parameters was much smaller. This command line style interface is still supported, but using it is tedious, to say the least. A typical configuration from a recent kernel requires answering more than 600 questions from the command line, entering your choice followed by the Enter key for each query from the script. Furthermore, if you make a mistake, there is no way to back up; you must start from the beginning again. That can be profoundly frustrating if you make a mistake on the 599th entry!

In some situations, such as building a kernel on an embedded system without graphics, using the command line configuration utility is unavoidable, but this author would go to great lengths to find a way around it.

The kernel-configuration subsystem uses several graphical front ends. In fact, a recent Linux kernel release included 10 such configuration targets. They are summarized here, from text taken directly from the output of make help:

- config—Update current config using a line-oriented program
- menuconfig—Update current config using a menu-based program
- xconfig—Update current config using a QT-based front end
- gconfig—Update current config using a GTK-based front end

- oldconfig—Update current config using a provided .config as the base
- randconfig—New config with random answer to all options
- defconfig—New config with default answer to all options
- allmodconfig—New config that selects modules, when possible
- allyesconfig—New config in which all options are accepted with yes
- allnoconfig—New minimal config

The first four of these makefile configuration targets invoke a form of configuration editor, as described in the list. Because of space considerations, we focus our discussion in this chapter and others only on the GTK-based graphical front end. Realize that you can use the configuration editor of your choice with the same results.

The configuration editor is invoked by entering the command make gconfig from the top-level kernel directory.[7] Figure 4-2 shows the top-level configuration menu presented to the developer when gconfig is run. From here, every available configuration parameter can be accessed to generate a custom kernel configuration.

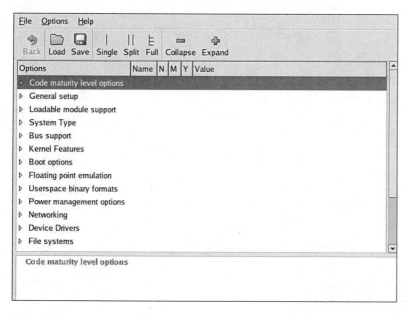

FIGURE 4-2
Top-level kernel configuration

---

[7] As mentioned, you can use the configuration editor of your choice, such as make xconfig or make menuconfig.

When the configuration editor is exited, you are prompted to save your changes. If you elect to save your changes, the global configuration file .config is updated (or created, if it does not already exist). This .config file, introduced earlier, drives the kernel build via the top-level makefile. You will notice in this makefile that the .config file is read directly by an include statement.

Most kernel software modules also read the configuration indirectly via the .config file as follows. During the build process, the .config file is processed into a C header file found in the .../include/linux directory, called autoconf.h. This is an automatically generated file and should never be edited directly because edits are lost each time a configuration editor is run. Many kernel source files include this file directly using the #include preprocessor directive. Listing 4-6 reproduces a section of this header file that corresponds to the earlier USB example above. Note that, for each entry in the .config file snippet in Listing 4-5, a corresponding entry is created in autoconf.h. This is how the source files in the kernel source tree reference the kernel configuration.

Listing 4-6

Linux autoconf.h

```
/*
 * USB support
 */
#define CONFIG_USB_MODULE 1
#undef CONFIG_USB_DEBUG

/*
 * Miscellaneous USB options
 */
#define CONFIG_USB_DEVICEFS 1
#undef CONFIG_USB_BANDWIDTH
#undef CONFIG_USB_DYNAMIC_MINORS

/*
 * USB Host Controller Drivers
 */
#define CONFIG_USB_EHCI_HCD_MODULE 1
#undef CONFIG_USB_EHCI_SPLIT_ISO
#undef CONFIG_USB_EHCI_ROOT_HUB_TT
#define CONFIG_USB_OHCI_HCD_MODULE 1
#define CONFIG_USB_UHCI_HCD_MODULE 1
```

If you haven't already done so, execute `make gconfig` in your top-level kernel source directory, and poke around this configuration utility to see the large number of subsections and configuration options available to the Linux developer. As long as you don't explicitly save your changes, they are lost upon exiting the configuration editor and you can safely explore without modifying your kernel configuration.[8] Many configuration parameters contain helpful explanation text, which can add to your understanding of the different configuration options.

4.3.3 Makefile Targets

If you type `make help` at the top-level Linux source directory, you are presented with a list of targets that can be generated from the source tree. The most common use of `make` is to specify no target. This generates the kernel ELF file `vmlinux` and is the default binary image for your chosen architecture (for example, `bzImage` for x86). Specifying `make` with no target also builds all the device-driver modules (kernel-loadable modules) specified by the configuration.

Many architectures and machine types require binary targets specific to the architecture and bootloader in use. One of the more common architecture-specific targets is `zImage`. In many architectures, this is the default target image that can be loaded and run on the target embedded system. One of the common mistakes that newcomers make is to specify `bzImage` as the `make` target. The `bzImage` target is specific to the x86/PC architecture. Contrary to popular myth, the `bzImage` is not a `bzip2`-compressed image. It is a big `zImage`. Without going into the details of legacy PC architecture, it is enough to know that a `bzImage` is suitable only for PC-compatible machines with an industry-standard PC-style BIOS.

---

[8] Better yet, make a backup copy of your `.config` file.

Listing 4-7 contains the output from make help from a recent Linux kernel. You can see from the listing that many targets are available in the top-level Linux kernel makefile. Each is listed along with a short description of its use. It is important to realize that even the help make target (as in make help) is architecture specific. You get a different list of architecture-specific targets depending on the architecture you pass on the make invocation. Listing 4-7 illustrates an invocation that specifies the ARM architecture, as you can see from the make command line.

Listing 4-7

Makefile Targets

```
$ make ARCH=arm help
Cleaning targets:
  clean            - remove most generated files but keep the config
  mrproper         - remove all generated files + config + various backup files

Configuration targets:
  config           - Update current config utilising a line-oriented program
  menuconfig       - Update current config utilising a menu based program
  xconfig          - Update current config utilising a QT based front-end
  gconfig          - Update current config utilising a GTK based front-end
  oldconfig        - Update current config utilising a provided .config as base
  randconfig       - New config with random answer to all options
  defconfig        - New config with default answer to all options
  allmodconfig     - New config selecting modules when possible
  allyesconfig     - New config where all options are accepted with yes
  allnoconfig      - New minimal config

Other generic targets:
  all              - Build all targets marked with [*]
* vmlinux          - Build the bare kernel
* modules          - Build all modules
  modules_install  - Install all modules
  dir/             - Build all files in dir and below
  dir/file.[ois]   - Build specified target only
  dir/file.ko      - Build module including final link
  rpm              - Build a kernel as an RPM package
  tags/TAGS        - Generate tags file for editors
  cscope           - Generate cscope index
  kernelrelease    - Output the release version string

Static analysers
  buildcheck       - List dangling references to vmlinux discarded sections and
                     init sections from non-init sections
  checkstack       - Generate a list of stack hogs
  namespacecheck   - Name space analysis on compiled kernel

Kernel packaging:
  rpm-pkg          - Build the kernel as an RPM package
  binrpm-pkg       - Build an rpm package containing the compiled kernel and
                     modules
```

```
      deb-pkg              - Build the kernel as an deb package
      tar-pkg              - Build the kernel as an uncompressed tarball
      targz-pkg            - Build the kernel as a gzip compressed tarball
      tarbz2-pkg           - Build the kernel as a bzip2 compressed tarball

Documentation targets:
  Linux kernel internal documentation in different formats:
  xmldocs (XML DocBook), psdocs (Postscript), pdfdocs (PDF)
  htmldocs (HTML), mandocs (man pages, use installmandocs to install)

Architecture specific targets (arm):
* zImage              - Compressed kernel image (arch/arm/boot/zImage)
  Image               - Uncompressed kernel image (arch/arm/boot/Image)
* xipImage            - XIP kernel image, if configured (arch/arm/boot/xipImage)
  bootpImage          - Combined zImage and initial RAM disk
                        (supply initrd image via make variable INITRD=<path>)
  install             - Install uncompressed kernel
  zinstall            - Install compressed kernel
                        Install using (your) ~/bin/installkernel or
                        (distribution) /sbin/installkernel or
                        install to $(INSTALL_PATH) and run lilo


      assabet_defconfig         - Build for assabet
      badge4_defconfig          - Build for badge4
      bast_defconfig            - Build for bast
      cerfcube_defconfig        - Build for cerfcube
      clps7500_defconfig        - Build for clps7500
      collie_defconfig          - Build for collie
      corgi_defconfig           - Build for corgi
      ebsa110_defconfig         - Build for ebsa110
      edb7211_defconfig         - Build for edb7211
      enp2611_defconfig         - Build for enp2611
      ep80219_defconfig         - Build for ep80219
      epxa10db_defconfig        - Build for epxa10db
      footbridge_defconfig      - Build for footbridge
      fortunet_defconfig        - Build for fortunet
      h3600_defconfig           - Build for h3600
      h7201_defconfig           - Build for h7201
      h7202_defconfig           - Build for h7202
      hackkit_defconfig         - Build for hackkit
      integrator_defconfig      - Build for integrator
      iq31244_defconfig         - Build for iq31244
      iq80321_defconfig         - Build for iq80321
      iq80331_defconfig         - Build for iq80331
      iq80332_defconfig         - Build for iq80332
      ixdp2400_defconfig        - Build for ixdp2400
      ixdp2401_defconfig        - Build for ixdp2401
      ixdp2800_defconfig        - Build for ixdp2800
      ixdp2801_defconfig        - Build for ixdp2801
      ixp4xx_defconfig          - Build for ixp4xx
      jornada720_defconfig      - Build for jornada720
      lart_defconfig            - Build for lart
      lpd7a400_defconfig        - Build for lpd7a400
      lpd7a404_defconfig        - Build for lpd7a404
      lubbock_defconfig         - Build for lubbock
```

```
lusl7200_defconfig      - Build for lusl7200
mainstone_defconfig     - Build for mainstone
mx1ads_defconfig        - Build for mx1ads
neponset_defconfig      - Build for neponset
netwinder_defconfig     - Build for netwinder
omap_h2_1610_defconfig  - Build for omap_h2_1610
pleb_defconfig          - Build for pleb
poodle_defconfig        - Build for poodle
pxa255-idp_defconfig    - Build for pxa255-idp
rpc_defconfig           - Build for rpc
s3c2410_defconfig       - Build for s3c2410
shannon_defconfig       - Build for shannon
shark_defconfig         - Build for shark
simpad_defconfig        - Build for simpad
smdk2410_defconfig      - Build for smdk2410
spitz_defconfig         - Build for spitz
versatile_defconfig     - Build for versatile

make V=0|1 [targets] 0 => quiet build (default), 1 => verbose build
make O=dir [targets] Locate all output files in "dir", including .config
make C=1   [targets] Check all c source with $CHECK (sparse)
make C=2   [targets] Force check of all c source with $CHECK (sparse)

Execute "make" or "make all" to build all targets marked with [*]
For further info see the ./README file
```

Many of these targets you might never use. However, it is useful to know that they exist. As you can see from Listing 4-7, the targets listed with an asterisk are built by default. Notice the numerous default configurations, listed as *_defconfig. Recall from Section 4.2.2, "Compiling the Kernel," the command we used to preconfigure a pristine kernel source tree: We invoked make with an architecture and a default configuration. The default configuration was ixp4xx_defconfig, which appears in this list of ARM targets. This is a good way to discover all the default configurations available for a particular kernel release and architecture.

4.3.4 Kernel Configuration

Kconfig (or a file with a similar root followed by an extension, such as Kconfig.*ext*) exists in almost 300 kernel subdirectories. Kconfig drives the configuration process for the features contained within its subdirectory. The contents of Kconfig are parsed by the configuration subsystem, which presents configuration choices to the user, and contains help text associated with a given configuration parameter.

The configuration utility (such as gconf, presented earlier) reads the Kconfig files starting from the arch subdirectory's Kconfig file. It is invoked from the

`Kconfig` makefile with an entry that looks like this:

```
gconfig: $(obj)/gconf
         $< arch/$(ARCH)/Kconfig
```

Depending on which architecture you are building, `gconf` reads this architecture-specific `Kconfig` as the top-level configuration definition. Contained within `Kconfig` are a number of lines that look like this:

```
source  "drivers/pci/Kconfig"
```

This directive tells the configuration editor utility to read in another `Kconfig` file from another location within the kernel source tree. Each architecture contains many such `Kconfig` files; taken together, these determine the complete set of menu options presented to the user when configuring the kernel. Each `Kconfig` file is free to source additional `Kconfig` files in different parts of the source tree. The configuration utility—gconf, in this case, recursively reads the `Kconfig` file chain and builds the configuration menu structure.

Listing 4-8 is a partial tree view of the `Kconfig` files associated with the ARM architecture. In a recent Linux 2.6 source tree from which this example was taken, the kernel configuration was defined by 170 separate `Kconfig` files. This listing omits most of those, for the sake of space and clarity—the idea is to show the overall structure. To list them all in this tree view would take several pages of this text.

Listing 4-8

Partial Listing of Kconfig for ARM Architecture

```
arch/arm/Kconfig <<<<<< (top level Kconfig)
 |->   init/Kconfig
 |   ...
 |->   arch/arm/mach-iop3xx/Kconfig
 |->   arch/arm/mach-ixp4xx/Kconfig
 |      ...
 |->   net/Kconfig
 |     |-->   net/ipv4/Kconfig
 |     |        |-->   net/ipv4/ipvs/Kconfig
 |     ...
 |->   drivers/char/Kconfig
 |     |-->   drivers/serial/Kconfig
 |     ...
 |->   drivers/usb/Kconfig
 |     |-->   drivers/usb/core/Kconfig
 |     |-->   drivers/usb/host/Kconfig
 | ...
 |->   lib/Kconfig
```

Looking at Listing 4-8, the file `arch/arm/Kconfig` would contain a line like this:

```
source "net/Kconfig"
```

The file `net/Kconfig` would contain a line like this:

```
source "net/ipv4/Kconfig"
```

. . . and so on.

As mentioned earlier, these `Kconfig` files taken together determine the configuration menu structure and configuration options presented to the user during kernel configuration. Figure 4-3 is an example of the configuration utility (`gconf`) for the ARM architecture compiled from the example in Listing 4-8.

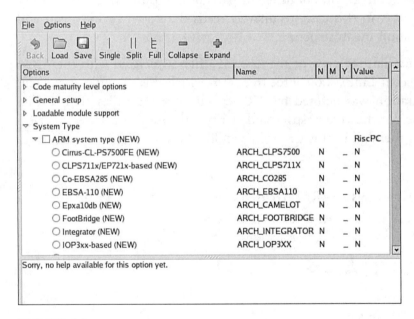

FIGURE 4-3
gconf configuration screen

4.3.5 Custom Configuration Options

Many embedded developers add feature support to the Linux kernel to support their particular custom hardware. One of the most common examples of this is multiple versions of a given hardware platform, each of which requires some compile-time options to be configured in the kernel source tree. Instead of having a separate version of the kernel source tree for each hardware version, a developer can add configuration options to enable his custom features.

The configuration management architecture described in the previous paragraphs makes it easy to customize and add features. A quick peek into a typical `Kconfig` file shows the structure of the configuration script language. As an example, assume that you have two hardware platforms based on the IXP425 network processor, and that your engineering team had dubbed them Vega and Constellation. Each board has specialized hardware that must be initialized early during the kernel boot phase. Let's see how easy it is to add these configuration options to the set of choices presented to the developer during kernel configuration. Listing 4-9 is a snippet from the top-level ARM `Kconfig` file.

Listing 4-9

Snippet from …/arch/arm/Kconfig

```
source "init/Kconfig"

menu "System Type"

choice
        prompt "ARM system type"
        default ARCH_RPC

config ARCH_CLPS7500
        bool "Cirrus-CL-PS7500FE"

config ARCH_CLPS711X
        bool "CLPS711x/EP721x-based"

...

source "arch/arm/mach-ixp4xx/Kconfig"
```

In this `Kconfig` snippet taken from the top-level ARM architecture `Kconfig`, you see the menu item System Type being defined. After the `ARM System type` prompt, you see a list of choices related to the ARM architecture. Later in the file, you see the inclusion of the IXP4*xx*-specific `Kconfig` definitions. In this file, you add your custom configuration switches. Listing 4-10 reproduces a snippet of this file. Again, for readability and convenience, we've omitted irrelevant text, as indicated by the ellipsis.

Listing 4-10

File Snippet: arch/arm/mach-ixp4xx/Kconfig

```
menu "Intel IXP4xx Implementation Options"

comment "IXP4xx Platforms"

config ARCH_AVILA
        bool "Avila"
        help
          Say 'Y' here if you want your kernel to support…

config ARCH_ADI_COYOTE
        bool "Coyote"
        help
          Say 'Y' here if you want your kernel to support
          the ADI Engineering Coyote…

# (These are our new custom options)
config ARCH_VEGA
        bool "Vega"
        help
          Select this option for "Vega" hardware support

config ARCH_CONSTELLATION
        bool "Constellation"
        help
          Select this option for "Constellation"
          hardware support
  . . .
```

Figure 4-4 illustrates the result of these changes as it appears when running the gconf utility (via make ARCH=arm gconfig). As a result of these simple changes, the configuration editor now includes options for our two new hardware platforms.[9] Shortly, you'll see how you can use this configuration information in the source tree to conditionally select objects that contain support for your new boards.

---

[9] We have intentionally removed many options under ARM system type and Intel IXP4*xx* Implementation Options to fit the picture on the page.

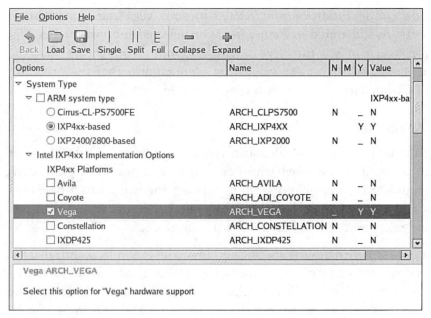

FIGURE 4-4
Custom configuration options

After the configuration editor (`gconf`, in these examples) is run and you select support for one of your custom hardware platforms, the `.config` file introduced earlier contains macros for your new options. As with all kernel-configuration options, each is preceded with `CONFIG_` to identify it as a kernel-configuration option. As a result, two new configuration options have been defined, and their state has been recorded in the `.config` file. Listing 4-11 shows the new `.config` file with your new configuration options.

Listing 4-11

Customized .config File Snippet

```
...
#
# IXP4xx Platforms
#
# CONFIG_ARCH_AVILA is not set
# CONFIG_ARCH_ADI_COYOTE is not set
CONFIG_ARCH_VEGA=y
# CONFIG_ARCH_CONSTELLATION is not set
# CONFIG_ARCH_IXDP425 is not set
# CONFIG_ARCH_PRPMC1100 is not set
...
```

Notice two new configuration options related to your Vega and Constellation hardware platforms. As illustrated in Figure 4-4, you selected support for Vega; in the `.config` file, you can see the new `CONFIG_` option representing that the Vega board is selected and set to the value `'y'`. Notice also that the `CONFIG_` option related to Constellation is present but not selected.

4.3.6 Kernel Makefiles

When building the kernel, the Makefiles scan the configuration and decide what subdirectories to descend into and what source files to compile for a given configuration. To complete the example of adding support for two custom hardware platforms, Vega and Constellation, let's look at the makefile that would read this configuration and take some action based on customizations.

Because you're dealing with hardware specific options in this example, assume that the customizations are represented by two hardware-setup modules called `vega_setup.c` and `constellation_setup.c`. We've placed these C source files in the `.../arch/arm/mach-ixp4xx` subdirectory of the kernel source tree. Listing 4-12 contains the complete makefile for this directory from a recent Linux release.

Listing 4-12

Makefile from .../arch/arm/mach-ixp4xx Kernel Subdirectory

```
#
# Makefile for the linux kernel.
#

obj-y    += common.o common-pci.o

obj-$(CONFIG_ARCH_IXDP4XX)     += ixdp425-pci.o ixdp425-setup.o
obj-$(CONFIG_MACH_IXDPG425)    += ixdpg425-pci.o coyote-setup.o
obj-$(CONFIG_ARCH_ADI_COYOTE)  += coyote-pci.o coyote-setup.o
obj-$(CONFIG_MACH_GTWX5715)    += gtwx5715-pci.o gtwx5715-setup.o
```

You might be surprised by the simplicity of this makefile. Much work has gone into the development of the kernel build system for just this reason. For the average developer who simply needs to add support for his custom hardware, the design of the kernel build system makes these kinds of customizations very straightforward.[10]

---

[10] In actuality, the kernel build system is very complicated, but most of the complexity is cleverly hidden from the average developer. As a result, it is relatively easy to add, modify, or delete configurations without having to be an expert.

Looking at this makefile, it might be obvious what must be done to introduce new hardware setup routines conditionally based on your configuration options. Simply add the following two lines at the bottom of the makefile, and you're done:

```
obj-$(CONFIG_ARCH_VEGA)      += vega_setup.o
obj-$(CONFIG_ARCH_CONSTELLATION)   += costellation_setup.o
```

These steps complete the simple addition of setup modules specific to the hypothetical example custom hardware. Using similar logic, you should now be able to make your own modifications to the kernel configuration/build system.

4.3.7 Kernel Documentation

A wealth of information is available in the Linux source tree itself. It would be difficult indeed to read it all because there are nearly 650 documentation files in 42 subdirectories in the . . . /Documentation directory. Be cautious in reading this material: Given the rapid pace of kernel development and release, this documentation tends to become outdated quickly. Nonetheless, it often provides a great starting point from which you can form a foundation on a particular kernel subsystem or concept.

Do not neglect the Linux Documentation Project, found at www.tldp.org, where you might find the most up-to-date version of a particular document or man page.[11] The list of suggested reading at the end of this chapter duplicates the URL for the Linux Documentation Project, for easy reference. Of particular interest to the previous discussion is the Kbuild documentation found in the kernel .../Documentation/kbuild subdirectory.

No discussion of Kernel documentation would be complete without mentioning Google. One day soon, *Googling* will appear in Merriam Webster's as a verb! Chances are, many problems and questions you might ask have already been asked and answered before. Spend some time to become proficient in searching the Internet for answers to questions. You will discover numerous mailing lists and other information repositories full of useful information related to your specific project or problem. Appendix E contains a useful list of open-source resources.

---

[11] Always assume that features advance faster than the corresponding documentation, so treat the docs as a guide rather than indisputable facts.

4.4 Obtaining a Linux Kernel

In general, you can obtain an embedded Linux kernel for your hardware platform in three ways: You can purchase a suitable commercial embedded Linux distribution; you can download a free embedded distribution, if you can find one suitable for your particular architecture and processor; or you can find the closest open-source Linux kernel to your application and port it yourself. We discuss Linux porting in Chapter 16, "Porting Linux."

Although porting an open source kernel to your custom board is not necessarily difficult, it represents a significant investment in engineering/development resources. This approach gives you access to free software, but deploying Linux in your development project is far from free, as we discussed in Chapter 1, "Introduction." Even for a small system with minimal application requirements, you need many more components than just a Linux kernel.

4.4.1 What Else Do I Need?

This chapter has focused on the layout and construction of the Linux kernel itself. As you might have already discovered, Linux is only a small component of an embedded system based on Linux. In addition to the Linux kernel, you need the following components to develop, test, and launch your embedded Linux widget:

* Bootloader ported to and configured for your specific hardware platform

* Cross-compiler and associated toolchain for your chosen architecture

* File system containing many packages—binary executables and libraries compiled for your native hardware architecture/processor

* Device drivers for any custom devices on your board

* Development environment, including host tools and utilities

* Linux kernel source tree enabled for your particular processor and board

These are the components of an embedded Linux distribution.

4.5 Chapter Summary

- The Linux kernel is more than 10 years old and has become a mainstream, well-supported operating system for many architectures.

- The Linux open source home is found at www.kernel.org. Virtually every release version of the kernel is available there, going all the way back to Linux 1.0.

- We leave it to other great books to describe the theory and operation of the Linux kernel. Here we discussed how it is built and identified the components that make up the image. Breaking up the kernel into understandable pieces is the key to learning how to navigate this large software project.

- This chapter covered the kernel build system and the process of modifying the build system to facilitate modifications.

- Several kernel configuration editors exist. We chose one and examined how it is driven and how to modify the menus and menu items within. These concepts apply to all the graphical front ends.

- The kernel itself comes with an entire directory structure full of useful kernel documentation. This is a helpful resource for understanding and navigating the kernel and its operation.

- This chapter concluded with a brief introduction to the options available for obtaining an embedded Linux distribution.

4.5.1 Suggestions for Additional Reading

Linux Kernel HOWTO:
www.tldp.org/HOWTO/Kernel-HOWTO

Kernel Kbuild documentation:
http://sourceforge.net/projects/kbuild/

The Linux Documentation Project:
www.tldp.org/

Tool Interface Standard (TIS) Executable and Linking Format (ELF) Specification,
Version 1.2
TIS Committee, May 1995

Linux kernel source tree:
.../Documentation/kbuild/makefiles.txt

Linux kernel source tree:
.../Documentation/kbuild/kconfig-language.txt

Linux Kernel Development, 2nd Edition
Rovert Love
Novell Press, 2005

# Chapter 5

Kernel Initialization

In this chapter

Whenthe power is applied to an embedded Linux system, a complex sequence of events is started. After a few seconds, the Linux kernel is operational and has spawned a series of application programs as specified by the system *init scripts*. A significant portion of these activities are governed by system configuration and are under the control of the embedded developer.

This chapter examines the initial sequence of events in the Linux kernel. We take a detailed look at the mechanisms and processes used during kernel initialization. We describe the Linux *kernel command line* and its use to customize the Linux environment on startup. With this knowledge, you will be able to customize and control the initialization sequence to meet the requirements of your particular embedded system.

5.1 Composite Kernel Image: Piggy and Friends

At power-on, the bootloader in an embedded system is first to get processor control. After the bootloader has performed some low-level hardware initialization, control is passed to the Linux kernel. This can be a manual sequence of events to facilitate the development process (for example, the user types interactive load/boot commands at the bootloader prompt), or an automated startup sequence typical of a production environment. We have dedicated Chapter 7, "Bootloaders," to this subject, so we defer any detailed bootloader discussion to that chapter.

In Chapter 4, "The Linux Kernel: A Different Perspective," we examined the components that make up the Linux kernel image. Recall that one of the common files built for every architecture is the ELF binary named vmlinux. This binary file is the monolithic kernel itself, or what we have been calling the *kernel proper*. In fact, when we looked at its construction in the link stage of vmlinux, we pointed out where we might look to see where the first line of code might be found. In most architectures, it is found in an assembly language source file called head.s or similar. In the PowerPC (ppc) branch of the kernel, several versions of head.s are present, depending on the processor. For example, the AMCC 440 series processors are initialized from a file called head_44x.s.

Some architectures and bootloaders are capable of directly booting the vmlinux kernel image. For example, platforms based on PowerPC architecture and the

U-Boot bootloader can usually boot the vmlinux image directly[1] (after conversion from ELF to binary, as you will shortly see). In other combinations of architecture and bootloader, additional functionality might be needed to set up the proper context and provide the necessary utilities for loading and booting the kernel.

Listing 5-1 details the final sequence of steps in the kernel build process for a hardware platform based on the ADI Engineering Coyote Reference Platform, which contains an Intel IXP425 network processor. This listing uses the quiet form of output from the kernel build system, which is the default. As pointed out in Chapter 4, it is a useful shorthand notation, allowing more focus on errors and warnings during the build.

Listing 5-1

Final Kernel Build Sequence: ARM/IXP425 (Coyote)

```
$ make ARCH=arm CROSS_COMPILE=xscale_be- zImage
...    < many build steps omitted for clarity>
  LD        vmlinux
  SYSMAP    System.map
  OBJCOPY   arch/arm/boot/Image
  Kernel:   arch/arm/boot/Image is ready
  AS        arch/arm/boot/compressed/head.o
  GZIP      arch/arm/boot/compressed/piggy.gz
  AS        arch/arm/boot/compressed/piggy.o
  CC        arch/arm/boot/compressed/misc.o
  AS        arch/arm/boot/compressed/head-xscale.o
  AS        arch/arm/boot/compressed/big-endian.o
  LD        arch/arm/boot/compressed/vmlinux
  OBJCOPY   arch/arm/boot/zImage
  Kernel:   arch/arm/boot/zImage is ready
  Building  modules, stage 2.
...
```

In the third line of Listing 5-1, the vmlinux image (the kernel proper) is linked. Following that, a number of additional object modules are processed. These include head.o, piggy.o,[2] and the architecture-specific head-xscale.o, among others. (The tags identify what is happening on each line. For example, AS indicates that the assembler is invoked, GZIP indicates compression, and so on.) In general, these

---

[1] The kernel image is nearly always stored in compressed format, unless boot time is a critical issue. In this case, the image might be called uImage, a compressed vmlinux file with a U-Boot header. See Chapter 7, "Bootloaders."

[2] The term *piggy* was originally used to describe a "piggy-back" concept. In this case, the binary kernel image is piggy-backed onto the bootstrap loader to produce the composite kernel image.

object modules are specific to a given architecture (ARM/XScale, in this example) and contain low-level utility routines needed to boot the kernel on this particular architecture. Table 5-1 details the components from Listing 5-1.

TABLE 5-1
ARM/XScale Low-Level Architecture Objects

Component	Function/Description
vmlinux	Kernel proper, in ELF format, including symbols, comments, debug info (if compiled with -g) and architecture-generic components.
System.map	Text-based kernel symbol table for vmlinux module.
Image	Binary kernel module, stripped of symbols, notes, and comments.
head.o	ARM-specific startup code generic to ARM processors. It is this object that is passed control by the bootloader.
piggy.gz	The file Image compressed with gzip.
piggy.o	The file piggy.gz in assembly language format so it can be linked with a subsequent object, misc.o (see the text).
misc.o	Routines used for decompressing the kernel image (piggy.gz), and the source of the familiar boot message: "Uncompressing Linux . . . Done" on some architectures.
head-xscale.o	Processor initialization specific to the XScale processor family.
big-endian.o	Tiny assembly language routine to switch the XScale processor into big-endian mode.
vmlinux	Composite kernel image. Note this is an unfortunate choice of names, because it duplicates the name for the kernel proper; the two are not the same. This binary image is the result when the kernel proper is linked with the objects in this table. See the text for an explanation.
zImage	Final composite kernel image loaded by bootloader. See the following text.

An illustration will help you understand this structure and the following discussion. Figure 5-1 shows the image components and their metamorphosis during the build process leading up to a bootable kernel image. The following sections describe the components and process in detail.

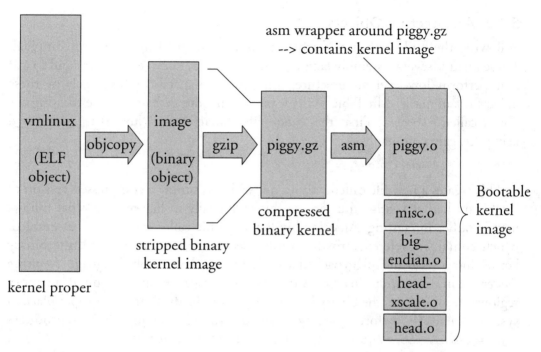

FIGURE 5-1
Composite kernel image construction

5.1.1 The Image Object

After the `vmlinux` kernel ELF file has been built, the kernel build system continues to process the targets described in Table 5-1. The `Image` object is created from the `vmlinux` object. `Image` is basically the `vmlinux` ELF file stripped of redundant sections (notes and comments) and also stripped of any debugging symbols that might have been present. The following command is used for this:

```
xscale_be-objcopy -O binary -R .note -R .comment -S \
vmlinux arch/arm/boot/Image
```

In the previous `objcopy` command, the `-O` option tells `objcopy` to generate a binary file, the `-R` option removes the ELF sections named `.note` and `.comment`, and the `-S` option is the flag to strip debugging symbols. Notice that `objcopy` takes the `vmlinux` ELF image as input and generates the target binary file called `Image`. In summary, `Image` is nothing more than the kernel proper in binary form stripped of debug symbols and the `.note` and `.comment` ELF sections.

5.1.2 Architecture Objects

Following the build sequence further, a number of small modules are compiled. These include several assembly language files (`head.o`, `head-xscale.o`, and so on) that perform low-level architecture and processor-specific tasks. Each of these objects is summarized in Table 5-1. Of particular note is the sequence creating the object called `piggy.o`. First, the `Image` file (binary kernel image) is compressed using this gzip command:

```
gzip -f -9 < Image > piggy.gz
```

This creates a new file called `piggy.gz`, which is simply a compressed version of the binary kernel `Image`. You can see this graphically in Figure 5-1. What follows next is rather interesting. An assembly language file called `piggy.S` is assembled, which contains a reference to the compressed `piggy.gz`. In essence, the binary kernel image is being piggybacked into a low-level assembly language *bootstrap loader*.[3] This bootstrap loader initializes the processor and required memory regions, decompresses the binary kernel image, and loads it into the proper place in system memory before passing control to it. Listing 5-2 reproduces `.../arch/arm/boot/compressed/piggy.S` in its entirety.

Listing 5-2

Assembly File `Piggy.S`

```
    .section .piggydata,#alloc
    .globl    input_data
input_data:
    .incbin   "arch/arm/boot/compressed/piggy.gz"
    .globl    input_data_end
input_data_end:
```

This small assembly language file is simple yet produces a complexity that is not immediately obvious. The purpose of this file is to cause the compressed, binary kernel image to be emitted by the assembler as an ELF section called `.piggydata`. It is triggered by the `.incbin` assembler preprocessor directive, which can be viewed as the assembler's version of a `#include` file. In summary, the net result of this assembly language file is to contain the compressed binary kernel image as a

---

[3] Not to be confused with the bootloader, a bootstrap loader can be considered a second-stage loader, where the bootloader itself can be thought of as a first-stage loader.

payload within another image—the bootstrap loader. Notice the labels `input_data` and `input_data_end`. The bootstrap loader uses these to identify the boundaries of the binary payload, the kernel image.

5.1.3 Bootstrap Loader

Not to be confused with a bootloader, many architectures use a *bootstrap loader* (or second-stage loader) to load the Linux kernel image into memory. Some bootstrap loaders perform checksum verification of the kernel image, and most perform decompression and relocation of the kernel image. The difference between a bootloader and a bootstrap loader in this context is simple: The bootloader controls the board upon power-up and does not rely on the Linux kernel in any way. In contrast, the bootstrap loader's primary purpose in life is to act as the *glue* between a board-level bootloader and the Linux kernel. It is the bootstrap loader's responsibility to provide a proper context for the kernel to run in, as well as perform the necessary steps to decompress and relocate the kernel binary image. It is similar to the concept of a primary and secondary loader found in the PC architecture.

Figure 5-2 makes this concept clear. The bootstrap loader is concatenated to the kernel image for loading.

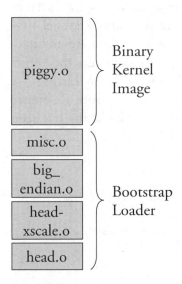

FIGURE 5-2
Composite kernel image for ARM XScale

In the example we have been studying, the bootstrap loader consists of the binary images shown in Figure 5-2. The functions performed by this bootstrap loader include the following:

- Low-level assembly processor initialization, which includes support for enabling the processor's internal instruction and data caches, disabling interrupts, and setting up a C runtime environment. These include `head.o` and `head-xscale.o`.

- Decompression and relocation code, embodied in `misc.o`.

- Other processor-specific initialization, such as `big-endian.o`, which enables the big endian mode for this particular processor.

It is worth noting that the details we have been examining in the preceding sections are specific to the ARM/XScale kernel implementation. Each architecture has different details, although the concepts are similar. Using a similar analysis to that presented here, you can learn the requirements of your own architecture.

5.1.4 Boot Messages

Perhaps you've seen a PC workstation booting a desktop Linux distribution such as Red Hat or SUSE Linux. After the PC's own BIOS messages, you see a flurry of console messages being displayed by Linux as it initializes the various kernel subsystems. Significant portions of the output are common across disparate architectures and machines. Two of the more interesting early boot messages are the kernel version string and the *kernel command line,* which is detailed shortly. Listing 5-3 reproduces the kernel boot messages for the ADI Engineering Coyote Reference Platform booting Linux on the Intel XScale IXP425 processor. The listing has been formatted with line numbers for easy reference.

Listing 5-3

Linux Boot Messages on IPX425

```
1 Uncompressing Linux... done, booting the kernel.
2 Linux version 2.6.14-clh (chris@pluto) (gcc version 3.4.3 (MontaVista 3.4.3-
L 25.0.30.0501131 2005-07-23)) #11 Sat Mar 25 11:16:33 EST 2006
3 CPU: XScale-IXP42x Family [690541c1] revision 1 (ARMv5TE)
4 Machine: ADI Engineering Coyote
5 Memory policy: ECC disabled, Data cache writeback
6 CPU0: D VIVT undefined 5 cache
```

```
7  CPU0: I cache: 32768 bytes, associativity 32, 32 byte lines, 32 sets
8  CPU0: D cache: 32768 bytes, associativity 32, 32 byte lines, 32 sets
9  Built 1 zonelists
10 Kernel command line: console=ttyS0,115200 ip=bootp root=/dev/nfs
11 PID hash table entries: 512 (order: 9, 8192 bytes)
12 Console: colour dummy device 80x30
13 Dentry cache hash table entries: 16384 (order: 4, 65536 bytes)
14 Inode-cache hash table entries: 8192 (order: 3, 32768 bytes)
15 Memory: 64MB = 64MB total
16 Memory: 62592KB available (1727K code, 339K data, 112K init)
17 Mount-cache hash table entries: 512
18 CPU: Testing write buffer coherency: ok
19 softlockup thread 0 started up.
20 NET: Registered protocol family 16
21 PCI: IXP4xx is host
22 PCI: IXP4xx Using direct access for memory space
23 PCI: bus0: Fast back to back transfers enabled
24 dmabounce: registered device 0000:00:0f.0 on pci bus
25 NetWinder Floating Point Emulator V0.97 (double precision)
26 JFFS2 version 2.2. (NAND) (C) 2001-2003 Red Hat, Inc.
27 Serial: 8250/16550 driver $Revision: 1.90 $ 2 ports, IRQ sharing disabled
28 ttyS0 at MMIO 0xc8001000 (irq = 13) is a XScale
29 io scheduler noop registered
30 io scheduler anticipatory registered
31 io scheduler deadline registered
32 io scheduler cfq registered
33 RAMDISK driver initialized: 16 RAM disks of 8192K size 1024 blocksize
34 loop: loaded (max 8 devices)
35 eepro100.c:v1.09j-t 9/29/99 Donald Becker
↳ http://www.scyld.com/network/eepro100.html
36 eepro100.c: $Revision: 1.36 $ 2000/11/17 Modified by Andrey V. Savochkin
↳ <saw@saw.sw.com.sg> and others
37 eth0: 0000:00:0f.0, 00:0E:0C:00:82:F8, IRQ 28.
38   Board assembly 741462-016, Physical connectors present: RJ45
39   Primary interface chip i82555 PHY #1.
40   General self-test: passed.
41   Serial sub-system self-test: passed.
42   Internal registers self-test: passed.
43   ROM checksum self-test: passed (0x8b51f404).
44 IXP4XX-Flash.0: Found 1 x16 devices at 0x0 in 16-bit bank
45  Intel/Sharp Extended Query Table at 0x0031
46 Using buffer write method
47 cfi_cmdset_0001: Erase suspend on write enabled
48 Searching for RedBoot partition table in IXP4XX-Flash.0 at offset 0xfe0000
49 5 RedBoot partitions found on MTD device IXP4XX-Flash.0
50 Creating 5 MTD partitions on "IXP4XX-Flash.0":
51 0x00000000-0x00060000 : "RedBoot"
52 0x00100000-0x00260000 : "MyKernel"
53 0x00300000-0x00900000 : "RootFS"
54 0x00fc0000-0x00fc1000 : "RedBoot config"
```

```
55 mtd: partition "RedBoot config" doesn't end on an erase block -- force
∟ read-only0x00fe0000-0x01000000 : "FIS directory"
56 NET: Registered protocol family 2
57 IP route cache hash table entries: 1024 (order: 0, 4096 bytes)
58 TCP established hash table entries: 4096 (order: 2, 16384 bytes)
59 TCP bind hash table entries: 4096 (order: 2, 16384 bytes)
60 TCP: Hash tables configured (established 4096 bind 4096)
61 TCP reno registered
62 TCP bic registered
63 NET: Registered protocol family 1
64 Sending BOOTP requests . OK
65 IP-Config: Got BOOTP answer from 192.168.1.10, my address is 192.168.1.141
66 IP-Config: Complete:
67      device=eth0, addr=192.168.1.141, mask=255.255.255.0, gw=255.255.25
∟ 5.255,
68      host=192.168.1.141, domain=, nis-domain=(none),
69      bootserver=192.168.1.10, rootserver=192.168.1.10,
∟ rootpath=/home/chris/sandbox/coyote-target
70 Looking up port of RPC 100003/2 on 192.168.1.10
71 Looking up port of RPC 100005/1 on 192.168.1.10
72 VFS: Mounted root (nfs filesystem).
73 Freeing init memory: 112K
74 Mounting proc
75 Starting system loggers
76 Configuring lo
77 Starting inetd
78 / #
```

The kernel produces much useful information during startup, as shown in Listing 5-3. We study this output in some detail in the next few sections. Line 1 is produced by the bootstrap loader we presented earlier in this chapter. This message was produced by the decompression loader found in `.../arch/arm/boot/compressed/misc.c`.

Line 2 of Listing 5-3 is the kernel version string. It is the first line of output from the kernel itself. One of the first lines of C code executed by the kernel (in `.../init/main.c`) upon entering `start_kernel()` is as follows:

```
printk(linux_banner);
```

This line produces the output just described—the kernel version string, Line 2 of Listing 5-3. This version string contains a number of pertinent data points related to the kernel image:

- Kernel version: Linux version 2.6.10-clh

- Username/machine name where kernel was compiled

- Toolchain info: gcc version 3.4.3, supplied by MontaVista Software
- Build number
- Date and time compiled

This is useful information both during development and later in production. All but one of the entries are self-explanatory. The *build number* is simply a tool that the developers added to the version string to indicate that something more substantial than the date and time changed from one build to the next. It is a way for developers to keep track of the build in a generic and automatic fashion. You will notice in this example that this was the eleventh build in this series, as indicated by the #11 on line 2 of Listing 5-3. The version string is stored in a hidden file in the top-level Linux directory and is called .version. It is automatically incremented by a build script found in .../scripts/mkversion and by the top-level makefile. In short, it is a version string that is automatically incremented whenever anything substantial in the kernel is rebuilt.

5.2 Initialization Flow of Control

Now that we have an understanding of the structure and components of the composite kernel image, let's examine the flow of control from the bootloader to the kernel in a complete boot cycle. As we discussed in Chapter 2, "Your First Embedded Experience," the bootloader is the low-level component resident in system nonvolatile memory (Flash or ROM) that takes control immediately after the power has been applied. It is typically a small, simple set of routines designed primarily to do low-level initialization, boot image loading, and system diagnostics. It might contain memory dump and fill routines for examining and modifying the contents of memory. It might also contain low-level board self-test routines, including memory and I/O tests. Finally, a bootloader contains logic for loading and passing control to another program, usually an operating system such as Linux.

The ARM XScale platform used as a basis for the examples in this chapter contains the Redboot bootloader. When power is first applied, this bootloader is invoked and proceeds to load the operating system (OS). When the bootloader locates and loads the OS image (which could be resident locally in Flash, on a hard drive, or via a local area network or other device), control is passed to that image.

On this particular XScale platform, the bootloader passes control to our `head.o` module at the label `start` in the bootstrap loader. This is illustrated in Figure 5-3.

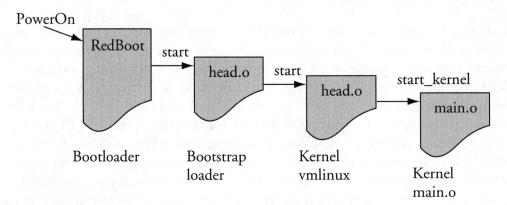

FIGURE 5-3
ARM boot control flow

As detailed earlier, the bootstrap loader prepended to the kernel image has a single primary responsibility: to create the proper environment to decompress and relocate the kernel, and pass control to it. Control is passed from the bootstrap loader directly to the kernel proper, to a module called `head.o` for most architectures. It is an unfortunate historical artifact that both the bootstrap loader and the kernel proper contain a module called `head.o` because it is a source of confusion to the new embedded Linux developer. The `head.o` module in the bootstrap loader might be more appropriately called `kernel_bootstrap_loader_head.o`, although I doubt that the kernel developers would accept this patch. In fact, a recent Linux 2.6 source tree contains no fewer than 37 source files named `head.S`. This is another reason why you need to know your way around the kernel source tree.

Refer back to Figure 5-3 for a graphical view of the flow of control. When the bootstraploader has completed its job, control is passed to the kernel proper's `head.o`, and from there to `start_kernel()` in `main.c`.

5.2.1 Kernel Entry Point: head.o

The intention of the kernel developers was to keep the architecture-specific head.o module very generic, without any specific machine[4] dependencies. This module, derived from the assembly language file head.S, is located at .../arch/<ARCH>/kernel/head.S, where <ARCH> is replaced by the given architecture. The examples in this chapter are based on the ARM/XScale, as you have seen, with <ARCH>=arm.

The head.o module performs architecture- and often CPU-specific initialization in preparation for the main body of the kernel. CPU-specific tasks are kept as generic as possible across processor families. Machine-specific initialization is performed elsewhere, as you will discover shortly. Among other low-level tasks, head.o performs the following tasks:

- Checks for valid processor and architecture
- Creates initial page table entries
- Enables the processor's memory management unit (MMU)
- Establishes limited error detection and reporting
- Jumps to the start of the kernel proper, main.c

These functions contain some hidden complexities. Many novice embedded developers have tried to single-step through parts of this code, only to find that the debugger becomes hopelessly lost. Although a discussion of the complexities of assembly language and the hardware details of virtual memory is beyond the scope of this book, a few things are worth noting about this complicated module.

When control is first passed to the kernel's head.o from the bootstrap loader, the processor is operating in what we used to call real mode in x86 terminology. In effect, the logical address contained in the processor's *program counter*[5] (or any other register, for that matter) is the actual physical address driven onto the processor's electrical memory address pins. Soon after the processor's registers and kernel data structures are initialized to enable memory translation, the processor's memory management unit (MMU) is turned on. Suddenly, the address space as seen by the processor is yanked from beneath it and replaced by an arbitrary virtual addressing scheme determined by the kernel developers. This creates a complexity that can

---

[4] The term *machine* as used here refers to a specific hardware reference platform.

[5] Often called Instruction Pointer, the register which holds the address of the next machine instruction in memory.

really be understood only by a detailed analysis of both the assembly language constructs and logical flow, as well as a detailed knowledge of the CPU and its hardware address translation mechanism. In short, physical addresses are replaced by
logical addresses the moment the MMU is enabled. That's why a debugger can't
single-step through this portion of code as with ordinary code.

The second point worth noting is the limited available mapping at this early stage
of the kernel boot process. Many developers have stumbled into this limitation
while trying to modify `head.o` for their particular platform.[6] One such scenario
might go like this. Let's say you have a hardware device that needs a firmware load
very early in the boot cycle. One possible solution is to compile the necessary
firmware statically into the kernel image and then reference it via a pointer to download it to your device. However, because of the limited memory mapping done at
this point, it is quite possible that your firmware image will exist beyond the range
that has been mapped at this early stage in the boot cycle. When your code executes,
it generates a page fault because you have attempted to access a memory region for
which no valid mapping has been created inside the processor. Worse yet, a page
fault handler has not yet been installed at this early stage, so all you get is an unex-
plained system crash. At this early stage in the boot cycle, you are pretty much guaranteed *not* to have any error messages to help you figure out what's wrong.

You are wise to consider delaying any custom hardware initialization until after the
kernel has booted, if at all possible. In this manner, you can rely on the well-known
device driver model for access to custom hardware instead of trying to customize the
much more complicated assembly language startup code. Numerous undocumented
techniques are used at this level. One common example of this is to work around
hardware errata that may or may not be documented. A much higher price will be
paid in development time, cost, and complexity if you must make changes to the
early startup assembly language code. Hardware and software engineers should discuss these facts during early stages of hardware development, when often a minor
hardware change can lead to significant savings in software development time.

It is important to recognize the constraints placed upon the developer in a virtual memory environment. Many experienced embedded developers have little or no
experience in this environment, and the scenario presented earlier is but one small
example of the pitfalls that await the developer new to virtual memory

---

[6] Modifying `head.S` for your custom platform is highly discouraged. There is almost always a better way.
See Chapter 16, "Porting Linux," for additional information.

architectures. Nearly all modern 32-bit and larger microprocessors have memory-management hardware used to implement virtual memory architectures. One of the most significant advantages of virtual memory machines is that they help separate teams of developers write large complex applications, while protecting other software modules, and the kernel itself, from programming errors.

5.2.2 Kernel Startup: main.c

The final task performed by the kernel's own `head.o` module is to pass control to the primary kernel startup file written in C. We spend a good portion of the rest of this chapter on this important file.

For each architecture, there is a different syntax and methodology, but every architecture's `head.o` module has a similar construct for passing control to the kernel proper. For the ARM architecture it looks as simple as this:

```
b       start_kernel
```

For PowerPC, it looks similar to this:

```
lis     r4,start_kernel@h
ori     r4,r4,start_kernel@l
lis     r3,MSR_KERNEL@h
ori     r3,r3,MSR_KERNEL@l
mtspr   SRR0,r4
mtspr   SRR1,r3
rfi
```

Without going into details of the specific assembly language syntax, both of these examples result in the same thing. Control is passed from the kernel's first object module (`head.o`) to the C language routine `start_kernel()` located in `.../init/main.c`. Here the kernel begins to develop a life of its own.

The file `main.c` should be studied carefully by anyone seeking a deeper understanding of the Linux kernel, what components make it up, and how they are initialized and/or instantiated. `main.c` does all the startup work for the Linux kernel, from initializing the first kernel thread all the way to mounting a root file system and executing the very first *user space* Linux application program.

The function `start_kernel()` is by far the largest function in `main.c`. Most of the Linux kernel initialization takes place in this routine. Our purpose here is to highlight those particular elements that will prove useful in the context of embedded systems development. It is worth repeating: Studying `main.c` is a great way to spend your time if you want to develop a better understanding of the Linux kernel as a system.

5.2.3 Architecture Setup

Among the first few things that happen in `.../init/main.c` in the `start_kernel()` function is the call to `setup_arch()`. This function takes a single parameter, a pointer to the *kernel command line* introduced earlier and detailed in the next section.

```
setup_arch(&command_line);
```

This statement calls an architecture-specific setup routine responsible for performing initialization tasks common across each major architecture. Among other functions, `setup_arch()` calls functions that identify the specific CPU and provides a mechanism for calling high-level CPU-specific initialization routines. One such function, called directly by `setup_arch()`, is `setup_processor()`, found in `.../arch/arm/kernel/setup.c`. This function verifies the CPU ID and revision, calls CPU-specific initialization functions, and displays several lines of information on the console during boot.

An example of this output can be found in Listing 5-3, lines 3 through 8. Here you can see the CPU type, ID string, and revision read directly from the processor core. This is followed by details of the processor cache type and size. In this example, the IXP425 has a 32KB I (instruction) cache and 32KB D (data) cache, along with other implementation details of the internal processor cache.

One of the final actions of the architecture setup routines is to perform any machine-dependent initialization. The exact mechanism for this varies across different architectures. For ARM, you will find machine-specific initialization in the `.../arch/arm/mach-*` series of directories, depending on your machine type. MIPS architecture also contains directories specific to supported reference platforms. For PowerPC, there is a machine-dependent structure that contains pointers to many common setup functions. We examine this in more detail in Chapter 16, "Porting Linux."

5.3 Kernel Command Line Processing

Following the architecture setup, `main.c` performs generic early kernel initialization and then displays the kernel command line. Line 10 of Listing 5-3 is reproduced here for convenience.

```
Kernel command line: console=ttyS0,115200 ip=bootp root=/dev/nfs
```

In this simple example, the kernel being booted is instructed to open a console device on serial port device `ttyS0` (usually the first serial port) at a baud rate of

115Kbps. It is being instructed to obtain its initial IP address information from a BOOTP server and to mount a root file system via the NFS protocol. (We cover BOOTP later in Chapter 12, "Embedded Development Environment," and NFS in Chapters 9, "File Systems," and 12. For now, we limit the discussion to the kernel command line mechanism.)

Linux is typically launched by a bootloader (or bootstrap loader) with a series of parameters that have come to be called the *kernel command line*. Although we don't actually invoke the kernel using a command prompt from a shell, many bootloaders can pass parameters to the kernel in a fashion that resembles this well-known model. On some platforms whose bootloaders are not Linux aware, the kernel command line can be defined at compile time and becomes hard coded as part of the kernel binary image. On other platforms (such as a desktop PC running Red Hat Linux), the command line can be modified by the user without having to recompile the kernel. The bootstrap loader (Grub or Lilo in the desktop PC case) builds the kernel command line from a configuration file and passes it to the kernel during the boot process. These command line parameters are a boot mechanism to set initial configuration necessary for proper boot on a given machine.

Numerous command line parameters are defined throughout the kernel. The `.../Documentation` subdirectory in the kernel source contains a file called `kernel-parameters.txt` containing a list of kernel command line parameters in dictionary order. Remember the previous warning about kernel documentation: The kernel changes far faster than the documentation. Use this file as a guide, but not a definitive reference. More than 400 distinct kernel command line parameters are documented in this file, and it cannot be considered a comprehensive list. For that, you must refer directly to the source code.

The basic syntax for kernel command line parameters is fairly simple and mostly evident from the example in line 10 of Listing 5-3. Kernel command line parameters can be either a single text word, a key=value pair, or a key= value1, value2, ... key and multivalue format. It is up to the consumer of this information to process the data as delivered. The command line is available globally and is processed by many modules as needed. As noted earlier, `setup_arch()` in `main.c` is called with the kernel command line as its only argument. This is to pass architecture-specific parameters and configuration directives to the relevant portions of architecture- and machine-specific code.

Device driver writers and kernel developers can add additional kernel command-line parameters for their own specific needs. Let's take a look at the mechanism.

Unfortunately, some complications are involved in using and processing kernel command line parameters. The first of these is that the original mechanism is being deprecated in favor of a much more robust implementation. The second complication is that we need to comprehend the complexities of a *linker script file* to fully understand the mechanism.[7]

5.3.1 The __setup Macro

As an example of the use of kernel command line parameters, consider the specification of the console device. We want this device to be initialized early in the boot cycle so that we have a destination for console messages during boot. This initialization takes place in a kernel object called `printk.o`. The C source file for this module is found in `.../kernel/printk.c`. The console initialization routine is called `console_setup()` and takes the kernel command line parameter string as its only argument.

The challenge is to communicate the console parameters specified on the kernel command line to the setup and device driver routines that require this data in a modular and general fashion. Further complicating the issue is that typically the command line parameters are required early, before (or in time for) those modules that need them. The startup code in `main.c`, where the main processing of the kernel command line takes place, cannot possibly know the destination functions for each of hundreds of kernel command line parameters without being hopelessly polluted with knowledge from every consumer of these parameters. What is needed is a flexible and generic way to pass these kernel command line parameters to their consumers.

In Linux 2.4 and earlier kernels, developers used a simple macro to generate a not-so-simple sequence of code. Although it is being deprecated, the __setup macro is still in widespread use throughout the kernel. We next use the kernel command line from Listing 5-3 to demonstrate how the __setup macro works.

From the previous kernel command line (line 10 of Listing 5-3), this is the first complete command line parameter passed to the kernel:

```
console=ttyS0,115200
```

For the purposes of this example, the actual meaning of the parameters is irrelevant. Our goal here is to illustrate the mechanism, so don't be concerned if you don't understand the argument or its values.

---

[7] It's not necessarily all that complex, but most of us never need to understand a linker script file. The embedded engineer does. It is well documented in the GNU LD manual referenced at the end of this chapter.

Listing 5-4 is a snippet of code from .../`kernel/printk.c`. The body of the function has been stripped because it is not relevant to the discussion. The most relevant part of Listing 5-4 is the last line, the invocation of the __setup macro. This macro expects two arguments; in this case, it is passed a string literal and a function pointer. It is no coincidence that the string literal passed to the __setup macro is the same as the first eight characters of the kernel command line related to the console: `console=`.

Listing 5-4

Console Setup Code Snippet

```
/*
 *      Setup a list of consoles. Called from init/main.c
 */
static int __init console_setup(char *str)
{
    char name[sizeof(console_cmdline[0].name)];
    char *s, *options;
    int idx;

    /*
     * Decode str into name, index, options.
     */


    return 1;
}

__setup("console=", console_setup);
```

You can think of this macro as a registration function for the kernel command-line console parameter. In effect, it says: When the console= string is encountered on the kernel command line, invoke the function represented by the second __setup macro argument—in this case, the console_setup() function. But how is this information communicated to the early setup code, outside this module, which has no knowledge of the console functions? The mechanism is both clever and somewhat complicated, and relies on lists built by the linker.

The details are hidden in a set of macros designed to conceal the syntactical tedium of adding *section attributes* (and other attributes) to a portion of object code. The objective is to build a static list of string literals associated with function pointers. This list is emitted by the compiler in a separately named ELF section in the final vmlinux ELF image. It is important to understand this technique; it is used in several places within the kernel for special-purpose processing.

Let's now examine how this is done for the __setup macro case. Listing 5-5 is a portion of code from the header file .../include/linux/init.h defining the __setup family of macros.

Listing 5-5

Family of __setup Macro Definitions from init.h

```
. . .
#define __setup_param(str, unique_id, fn, early)              \
        static char __setup_str_##unique_id[] __initdata = str; \
        static struct obs_kernel_param __setup_##unique_id    \
                __attribute_used__                            \
                __attribute__((__section__(".init.setup")))   \
                __attribute__((aligned((sizeof(long)))))      \
                = { __setup_str_##unique_id, fn, early }

#define __setup_null_param(str, unique_id)                    \
        __setup_param(str, unique_id, NULL, 0)

#define __setup(str, fn)                                      \
        __setup_param(str, fn, fn, 0)
. . .
```

Listing 5-5 is the author's definition of syntactical tedium! Recall from Listing 5.4 that our invocation of the original __setup macro looked like this:

```
__setup("console=", console_setup);
```

With some slight simplification, here is what the compiler's preprocessor produces after macro expansion:

```
static char __setup_str_console_setup[] __initdata = "console=";
static struct obs_kernel_param __setup_console_setup  \
__attribute__((__section__(".init.setup"))) =
    { __setup_str_console_setup, console_setup, 0};
```

To make this more readable, we have split the second and third lines, as indicated by the UNIX line-continuation character \.

We have intentionally left out two compiler attributes whose description does not add any insight to this discussion. Briefly, the __attribute_used__ (itself a macro hiding further syntactical tedium) tells the compiler to emit the function or variable, even if the optimizer determines that it is unused.[8] The __attribute__ (aligned) tells the compiler to align the structures on a specific boundary, in this case sizeof(long).

---

[8] Normally, the compiler will complain if a variable is defined static and never referenced in the compilation unit. Because these variables are not explicitly referenced, the warning would be emitted without this directive.

What we have left after simplification is the heart of the mechanism. First, the compiler generates an array of characters called __setup_str_console_ setup[] initialized to contain the string console=. Next, the compiler generates a structure that contains three members: a pointer to the kernel command line string (the array just declared), the pointer to the setup function itself, and a simple flag. The key to the magic here is the section attribute attached to the structure. This attribute instructs the compiler to emit this structure into a special *section* within the ELF object module, called .init.setup. During the link stage, all the structures defined using the __setup macro are collected and placed into this .init.setup section, in effect creating an array of these structures. Listing 5-6, a snippet from .../init/main.c, shows how this data is accessed and used.

Listing 5-6

Kernel Command Line Processing

```
1 extern struct obs_kernel_param __setup_start[], __setup_end[];
2
3 static int __init obsolete_checksetup(char *line)
4 {
5          struct obs_kernel_param *p;
6
7          p = __setup_start;
8          do {
9                  int n = strlen(p->str);
10                 if (!strncmp(line, p->str, n)) {
11                         if (p->early) {
12                                 /* Already done in parse_early_param?
⌐ (Needs
13                                  * exact match on param part) */
14                                 if (line[n] == '\0' || line[n] == '=')
15                                         return 1;
16                         } else if (!p->setup_func) {
17                                 printk(KERN_WARNING "Parameter %s is
⌐ obsolete,"
18                                        " ignored\n", p->str);
19                                 return 1;
20                         } else if (p->setup_func(line + n))
21                                 return 1;
22                 }
23                 p++;
24         } while (p < __setup_end);
25         return 0;
26 }
```

Examination of this code should be fairly straightforward, with a couple of explanations. The function is called with a single command line argument, parsed elsewhere within `main.c`. In the example we've been discussing, `line` would point to the string `console=ttyS0,115200`, which is one component from the kernel command line. The two external structure pointers `__setup_start` and `__setup_end` are defined in a linker script file, not in a C source or header file. These labels mark the start and end of the array of `obs_kernel_param` structures that were placed in the `.init.setup` section of the object file.

The code in Listing 5-6 scans all these structures via the pointer `p` to find a match for this particular kernel command line parameter. In this case, the code is searching for the string `console=` and finds a match. From the relevant structure, the function pointer element returns a pointer to the `console_setup()` function, which is called with the balance of the parameter (the string `ttyS0,115200`) as its only argument. This process is repeated for every element in the kernel command line until the kernel command line has been completely exhausted.

The technique just described, collecting objects into lists in uniquely named ELF sections, is used in many places in the kernel. Another example of this technique is the use of the `__init` family of macros to place one-time initialization routines into a common section in the object file. Its cousin `__initdata`, used to mark one-time-use data items, is used by the `__setup` macro. Functions and data marked as initialization using these macros are collected into a specially named ELF section. Later, after these one-time initialization functions and data objects have been used, the kernel frees the memory occupied by these items. You might have seen the familiar kernel message near the final part of the boot process saying, "Freeing init memory: 296K." Your mileage may vary, but a third of a megabyte is well worth the effort of using the `__init` family of macros. This is exactly the purpose of the `__initdata` macro in the earlier declaration of `__setup_str_ console_setup[]`.

You might have been wondering about the use of symbol names preceded with `obsolete_`. This is because the kernel developers are replacing the kernel command line processing mechanism with a more generic mechanism for registering both boot time and loadable module parameters. At the present time, hundreds of parameters are declared with the `__setup` macro. However, new development is expected to use the family of functions defined by the kernel header file `.../include/linux/moduleparam.h`, most notably, the family of `module_param*` macros. These are explained in more detail in Chapter 8, "Device Driver Basics," when we introduce device drivers.

The new mechanism maintains backward compatibility by including an `unknown` function pointer argument in the parsing routine. Thus, parameters that are unknown to the `module_param*` infrastructure are considered unknown, and the processing falls back to the old mechanism under control of the developer. This is easily understood by examining the well-written code in `.../kernel/params.c` and the `parse_args()` calls in `.../init/main.c`.

The last point worth mentioning is the purpose of the flag member of the `obs_kernel_param` structure created by the `__setup` macro. Examination of the code in Listing 5-6 should make it clear. The flag in the structure, called `early`, is used to indicate whether this particular command line parameter was already consumed earlier in the boot process. Some command line parameters are intended for consumption very early in the boot process, and this flag provides a mechanism for an early parsing algorithm. You will find a function in `main.c` called `do_early_param()` that traverses the linker-generated array of `__setup`-generated structures and processes each one marked for early consumption. This gives the developer some control over when in the boot process this processing is done.

5.4 Subsystem Initialization

Many kernel subsystems are initialized by the code found in `main.c`. Some are initialized explicitly, as with the calls to `init_timers()` and `console_init()`, which need to be called very early. Others are initialized using a technique very similar to that described earlier for the `__setup` macro. In short, the linker builds lists of function pointers to various initialization routines, and a simple loop is used to execute each in turn. Listing 5-7 shows how this works.

Listing 5-7

Example Initialization Routine

```
static int __init customize_machine(void)
{
    /* customizes platform devices, or adds new ones */
    if (init_machine)
        init_machine();
    return 0;
}
arch_initcall(customize_machine);
```

This code snippet comes from .../arch/arm/kernel/setup.c. It is a simple routine designed to provide a customization hook for a particular board.

5.4.1 The *__initcall Macros

Notice two important things about the initialization routine in Listing 5-7. First, it is defined with the __init macro. As we saw earlier, this macro applies the *section* attribute to declare that this function gets placed into a section called .init.text in the vmlinux ELF file. Recall that the purpose of placing this function into a special section of the object file is so the memory space that it occupies can be reclaimed when it is no longer needed.

The second thing to notice is the macro immediately following the definition of the function: arch_initcall(customize_machine). This macro is part of a family of macros defined in .../include/linux/init.h. These macros are reproduced here as Listing 5-8.

Listing 5-8

initcall Family of Macros

```
#define __define_initcall(level,fn) \
    static initcall_t __initcall_##fn __attribute_used__ \
    __attribute__((__section__(".initcall" level ".init"))) = fn

#define core_initcall(fn)           __define_initcall("1",fn)
#define postcore_initcall(fn)       __define_initcall("2",fn)
#define arch_initcall(fn)           __define_initcall("3",fn)
#define subsys_initcall(fn)         __define_initcall("4",fn)
#define fs_initcall(fn)             __define_initcall("5",fn)
#define device_initcall(fn)         __define_initcall("6",fn)
#define late_initcall(fn)           __define_initcall("7",fn)
```

In a similar fashion to the __setup macro previously detailed, these macros declare a data item based on the name of the function, and use the *section* attribute to place this data item into a uniquely named section of the vmlinux ELF file. The benefit of this approach is that main.c can call an arbitrary initialization function for a subsystem that it has no knowledge of. The only other option, as mentioned earlier, is to pollute main.c with knowledge of every subsystem in the kernel.

As you can see from Listing 5-8, the name of the section is .initcallN.init, where N is the level defined between 1 and 7. The data item is assigned the address of the function being named in the macro. In the example defined by Listings 5-7 and 5-8, the data item would be as follows (simplified by omitting the section attribute):

```
static initcall_t __initcall_customize_machine = customize_machine;
```

This data item is placed in the kernel's object file in a section called `.initcall1.init`.

The level (*N*) is used to provide an ordering of initialization calls. Functions declared using the `core_initcall()` macro are called before all others. Functions declared using the `postcore_initcall()` macros are called next, and so on, while those declared with `late_initcall()` are the last initialization functions to be called.

In a fashion similar to the `__setup` macro, you can think of this family of `*_initcall` macros as registration functions for kernel subsystem initialization routines that need to be run once at kernel startup and then never used again. These macros provide a mechanism for causing the initialization routine to be executed during system startup, and a mechanism to discard the code and reclaim the memory after the routine has been executed. The developer is also provided up to seven levels of *when* to perform the initialization routines. Therefore, if you have a subsystem that relies on another being available, you can enforce this ordering using these levels. If you `grep` the kernel for the string `[a-z]*_initcall`, you will see that this family of macros is used extensively.

One final note about the `*_initcall` family of macros: The use of multiple levels was introduced during the development of the 2.6 kernel series. Earlier kernel versions used the `__initcall()` macro for this purpose. This macro is still in widespread use, especially in device drivers. To maintain backward compatibility, this macro has been defined to `device_initcall()`, which has been defined as a level 6 `initcall`.

5.5 The init Thread

The code found in `.../init/main.c` is responsible for bringing the kernel to life. After `start_kernel()` performs some basic kernel initialization, calling early initialization functions explicitly by name, the very first kernel thread is spawned. This thread eventually becomes the kernel thread called `init()`, with a *process id* (PID) of 1. As you will learn, `init()` becomes the parent of all Linux processes in user space. At this point in the boot sequence, two distinct threads are running: that represented by `start_kernel()` and now `init()`. The former goes on to become the idle process, having completed its work. The latter becomes the init process. This can be seen in Listing 5-9.

Listing 5-9

Creation of Kernel `init` Thread

```
static void noinline rest_init(void)
        __releases(kernel_lock)
{
        kernel_thread(init, NULL, CLONE_FS | CLONE_SIGHAND);
        numa_default_policy();
        unlock_kernel();
        preempt_enable_no_resched();

        /*
         * The boot idle thread must execute schedule()
         * at least one to get things moving:
         */
        schedule();

        cpu_idle();
}
```

The `start_kernel()` function calls `rest_init()`, reproduced in Listing 5-9. The kernel's `init` process is spawned by the call to `kernel_thread()`. `init` goes on to complete the rest of the system initialization, while the thread of execution started by `start_kernel()` loops forever in the call to `cpu_idle()`.

The reason for this structure is interesting. You might have noticed that `start_kernel()`, a relatively large function, was marked with the __init macro. This means that the memory it occupies will be reclaimed during the final stages of kernel initialization. It is necessary to exit this function and the address space that it occupies before reclaiming its memory. The answer to this was for `start_kernel()` to call `rest_init()`, shown in Listing 5-9, a much smaller piece of memory that becomes the idle process.

5.5.1 Initialization via initcalls

When `init()` is spawned, it eventually calls `do_initcalls()`, which is the function responsible for calling all the initialization functions registered with the `*_initcall` family of macros. The code is reproduced in Listing 5-10 in simplified form.

Listing 5-10

Initialization via initcalls

```
static void __init do_initcalls(void)
{
    initcall_t *call;

    for (call = &__initcall_start; call < &__initcall_end; call++) {

        if (initcall_debug) {
            printk(KERN_DEBUG "Calling initcall 0x%p", *call);
            print_symbol(": %s()", (unsigned long) *call);
            printk("\n");
        }

        (*call)();

    }
}
```

This code is self-explanatory, except for the two labels marking the loop boundaries: `__initcall_start` and `__initcall_end`. These labels are not found in any C source or header file. They are defined in the linker script file used during the link stage of `vmlinux`. These labels mark the beginning and end of the list of initialization functions populated using the `*_initcall` family of macros. You can see each of the labels by looking at the `System.map` file in the top-level kernel directory. They all begin with the string `__initcall`, as described in Listing 5-8.

In case you were wondering about the debug print statements in `do_initcalls()`, you can watch these calls being executed during bootup by setting the kernel command line parameter `initcall_debug`. This command line parameter enables the printing of the debug information shown in Listing 5-10. Simply start your kernel with the kernel command line parameter `initcall_debug` to enable this diagnostic output.[9]

---

[9] You might have to lower the default loglevel on your system to see these debug messages. This is described in many references about Linux system administration. In any case, you should see them in the kernel log file.

Here is an example of what you will see when you enable these debug statements:

```
...
Calling initcall 0xc00168f4: tty_class_init+0x0/0x3c()
Calling initcall 0xc000c32c: customize_machine+0x0/0x2c()
Calling initcall 0xc000c4f0: topology_init+0x0/0x24()
Calling initcall 0xc000e8f4: coyote_pci_init+0x0/0x20()
PCI: IXP4xx is host
PCI: IXP4xx Using direct access for memory space
...
```

Notice the call to `customize_machine()`, the example of Listing 5-7. The debug output includes the virtual kernel address of the function (0xc000c32c, in this case) and the size of the function (0x2c here.) This is a useful way to see the details of kernel initialization, especially the order in which various subsystems and modules get called. Even on a modestly configured embedded system, dozens of these initialization functions are invoked in this manner. In this example taken from an ARM XScale embedded target, there are 92 such calls to various kernel-initialization routines.

5.5.2 Final Boot Steps

Having spawned the `init()` thread and all the various initialization calls have completed, the kernel performs its final steps in the boot sequence. These include freeing the memory used by the initialization functions and data, opening a system console device, and starting the first userspace process. Listing 5-11 reproduces the last steps in the kernel's `init()` from `main.c`.

Listing 5-11

Final Kernel Boot Steps from `main.c`

```
if (execute_command) {
        run_init_process(execute_command);
        printk(KERN_WARNING "Failed to execute %s.  Attempting "
                            "defaults...\n", execute_command);
}

run_init_process("/sbin/init");
run_init_process("/etc/init");
run_init_process("/bin/init");
run_init_process("/bin/sh");

panic("No init found.  Try passing init= option to kernel.");
```

Notice that if the code proceeds to the end of the `init()` function, a kernel *panic* results. If you've spent any time experimenting with embedded systems or custom root file systems, you've undoubtedly encountered this very common error message as the last line of output on your console. It is one of the most frequently asked questions (FAQs) on a variety of public forums related to Linux and embedded systems.

One way or another, one of these `run_init_process()` commands must proceed without error. The `run_init_process()` function does not return on successful invocation. It overwrites the calling process with the new one, effectively replacing the current process with the new one. It uses the familiar `execve()` system call for this functionality. The most common system configurations spawn `/sbin/init` as the userland[10] initialization process. We study this functionality in depth in the next chapter.

One option available to the embedded system developer is to use a custom userland initialization program. That is the purpose of the conditional statement in the previous code snippet. If `execute_command` is non-null, it points to a string containing a custom user-supplied command to be executed in user space. The developer specifies this command on the kernel command line, and it is set via the `__setup` macro we examined earlier in this chapter. An example kernel command line incorporating several concepts discussed in this chapter might look like this:

```
initcall_debug init=/sbin/myinit console=ttyS1,115200 root=/dev/hda1
```

This kernel command line instructs the kernel to display all the initialization routines as encountered, configures the initial console device as `/dev/ttyS1` at 115 kbps, and executes a custom user space initialization process called `myinit`, located in the `/sbin` directory on the root file system. It directs the kernel to mount its root file system from the device `/dev/hda1`, which is the first IDE hard drive. Note that, in general, the order of parameters given on the kernel command line is irrelevant. The next chapter covers the details of user space system initialization.

---

[10] Userland is an often-used term for any program, library, script, or anything else in user space.

5.6 Chapter Summary

- The Linux kernel project is large and complex. Understanding the structure and composition of the final image is key to learning how to customize your own embedded project.

- Many architectures concatenate an architecture-specific *bootstrap loader* onto the kernel binary image to set up the proper execution environment required by the Linux kernel. We presented the bootstrap loader build steps to differentiate this functionality from the kernel proper.

- Understanding the initialization flow of control will help deepen your knowledge of the Linux kernel and provide insight into how to customize for your particular set of requirements.

- We found the kernel entry point in `head.o` and followed the flow of control into the first kernel C file, `main.c`. We looked at a booting system and the messages it produced, along with an overview of many of the important initialization concepts.

- The kernel command line processing and the mechanisms used to declare and process kernel command line parameters was presented. This included a detailed look at some advanced coding techniques for calling arbitrary unknown setup routines using linker-produced tables.

- The final kernel boots steps produce the first userspace processes. Understanding this mechanism and its options will enable you to customize and troubleshoot embedded Linux startup issues.

5.6.1 Suggestions for Additional Reading

GNU Compiler Collection documentation:
http://gcc.gnu.org/onlinedocs/gcc[11]

Using LD, the GNU linker
http://www.gnu.org/software/binutils/manual/ld-2.9.1/ld.html

Kernel documentation:
`.../Documentation/kernel-parameters.txt`

---

[11] Especially the sections on function attributes, type attributes, and variable attributes.

Chapter 6

System Initialization

In this chapter

129

In Chapter 2, "Your First Embedded Experience," we pointed out that the Linux kernel itself is but a small part of any embedded Linux system. After the kernel has initialized itself, it must mount a root file system and execute a set of developer-defined initialization routines. In this chapter, we examine the details of post-kernel system initialization.

We begin by looking at the root file system and its layout. Next we develop and study a minimal system configuration. Later in this chapter, we add functionality to the minimal system configuration to produce useful example embedded system configurations. We complete the coverage of system initialization by introducing the *initial ramdisk,* or `initrd`, and its operation and use. The chapter concludes with a brief look at Linux shutdown logic.

6.1 Root File System

In Chapter 5, "Kernel Initialization," we examined the Linux kernel's behavior during the initialization process. We made several references to mounting a *root file system.* Linux, like many other advanced operating systems, requires a root file system to realize the benefits of its services. Although it is certainly possible to use Linux in an environment without a file system, it makes little sense because most of the features and value of Linux would be lost. It would be similar to putting your entire system application into an overbloated device driver or kernel thread.

The root file system refers to the file system mounted at the base of the file system hierarchy, designated simply as /. As you will discover in Chapter 9, "File Systems," even a small embedded Linux system typically mounts several file systems on different locations in the file system hierarchy. The `proc` file system, introduced in Chapter 9, is an example. It is a special-purpose file system mounted at /proc under the root file system. The root file system is simply the first file system mounted at the base of the file system hierarchy.

As you will shortly see, the root file system has special requirements for a Linux system. Linux expects the root file system to contain programs and utilities to boot a system, initialize services such as networking and a system console, load device drivers, and mount additional file systems.

6.1.1 FHS: File System Hierarchy Standard

Several kernel developers authored a standard governing the organization and layout of a UNIX file system. The File System Hierarchy Standard (FHS) establishes a minimum baseline of compatibility between Linux distributions and application programs. You'll find a reference to this standard in Section 6.7.1 "Suggestions for Additional Reading" at the end of this chapter. You are encouraged to review the FHS standard for a better background on the layout and rationale of UNIX file system organization.

Many Linux distributions have directory layouts closely matching that described in the FHS standard. The standard exists to provide one element of a common base between different UNIX and Linux distributions. The FHS standard allows your application software (and developers) to predict where certain system elements, including files and directories, can be found on the file system.

6.1.2 File System Layout

Where space is a concern, many embedded systems developers create a very small root file system on a bootable device (such as Flash memory) and later mount a larger file system from another device, perhaps a hard disk or network NFS server. In fact, it is not uncommon to mount a larger root file system right on top of the original small one. You'll see an example of that when we examine the *initial ramdisk* (initrd) later in this chapter.

A simple Linux root file system might contain the following top-level directory entries:

```
.
|
|--bin
|--dev
|--etc
|--lib
|--sbin
|--usr
|--var
|--tmp
```

Table 6-1 details the most common contents of each of these root directory entries.

TABLE 6-1
Top-Level Directories

Directory	Contents
bin	Binary executables, usable by all users on the system[1]
dev	Device nodes (see Chapter 8, "Device Driver Basics")
etc	Local system-configuration files
lib	System libraries, such as the standard C library and many others
sbin	Binary executables usually reserved for superuser accounts on the system
usr	A secondary file system hierarchy for application programs, usually read-only
var	Contains variable files, such as system logs and temporary configuration files
tmp	Temporary files

The very top of the Linux file system hierarchy is referenced by the forward slash character (/) by itself. For example, to list the contents of the root directory, one would type this:

```
$ ls /
```

This produces a listing similar to the following:

```
root@coyote:/# ls /
bin  dev  etc  home  lib  mnt  opt  proc  root  sbin  tmp  usr  var
root@coyote:/#
```

This directory listing contains directory entries for additional functionality, including /mnt and /proc. Notice that we reference these directory entries preceded by the forward slash, indicating that the path to these top-level directories starts from the root directory.

6.1.3 Minimal File System

To illustrate the requirements of the root file system, we have created a minimal root file system. This example was produced on the ADI Engineering Coyote Reference

---

[1] Often embedded systems do not have user accounts other than a single root user.

board using an XScale processor. Listing 6-1 is the output from the `tree` command on this minimal root file system.

Listing 6-1

Contents of Minimal Root File System

```
.
|-- bin
|   |-- busybox
|   '-- sh -> busybox
|-- dev
|   '-- console
|-- etc
|   '-- init.d
|       '-- rcS
'-- lib
    |-- ld-2.3.2.so
    |-- ld-linux.so.2 -> ld-2.3.2.so
    |-- libc-2.3.2.so
    '-- libc.so.6 -> libc-2.3.2.so

5 directories, 8 files
```

This root configuration makes use of `busybox`, a popular and aptly named toolkit for embedded systems. In short, `busybox` is a stand-alone binary that provides support for many common Linux command line utilities. `busybox` is so pertinent for embedded systems that we devote Chapter 11, "BusyBox," to this flexible utility.

Notice in our example minimum file system in Listing 6-1 that there are only eight files in five directories. This tiny root file system boots and provides the user with a fully functional command prompt on the serial console. Any commands that have been enabled in `busybox`[2] are available to the user.

Starting from /bin, we have the `busybox` executable and a soft link called `sh` pointing back to `busybox`. You will see shortly why this is necessary. The file in /dev is a *device node*[3] required to open a console device for input and output. Although it is not strictly necessary, the `rcS` file in the /etc/init.d directory is the default initialization script processed by `busybox` on startup. Including `rcS` silences the warning message issued by `busybox` if `rcS` is missing.

---

[2] BusyBox commands are covered in Chapter 11.

[3] Device nodes are explained in detail in Chapter 8.

The final directory entry and set of files required are the two libraries, GLIBC (`libc-2.3.2.so`) and the Linux dynamic loader (`ld-2.3.2.so`). GLIBC contains the standard C library functions, such as `printf()` and many others that most application programs depend on. The Linux dynamic loader is responsible for loading the binary executable into memory and performing the dynamic linking required by the application's reference to shared library functions. Two additional soft links are included, `ld-linux.so.2` pointing back to `ld-2.3.2.so` and `libc.so.6` referencing `libc-2.3.2.so`. These links provide version immunity and backward compatibility for the libraries themselves, and are found on all Linux systems.

This simple root file system produces a fully functional system. On the ARM/XScale board on which this was tested, the size of this small root file system was about 1.7MB. It is interesting to note that more than 80 percent of that size is contained within the C library itself. If you need to reduce its size for your embedded system, you might want to investigate the Library Optimizer Tool at http://libraryopt.sourceforge.net/.

6.1.4 The Root FS Challenge

The challenge of a root file system for an embedded device is simple to explain. It is not so simple to overcome. Unless you are lucky enough to be developing an embedded system with a reasonably large hard drive or large Flash storage on board, you might find it difficult to fit your applications and utilities onto a single Flash memory device. Although costs continue to come down for Flash storage, there will always be competitive pressure to reduce costs and speed time to market. One of the single largest reasons Linux continues to grow in popularity as an embedded OS is the huge and growing body of Linux application software.

Trimming a root file system to fit into a given storage space requirement can be daunting. Many packages and subsystems consist of dozens or even hundreds of files. In addition to the application itself, many packages include configuration files, libraries, configuration utilities, icons, documentation files, locale files related to internationalization, database files, and more. The Apache web server from the Apache Software Foundation is an example of a popular application often found in embedded systems. The base Apache package from one popular embedded Linux distribution contains 254 different files. Furthermore, they aren't all simply copied into a single directory on your file system. They need to be populated in several different locations on the file system for the Apache application to function without modification.

These concepts are some of the fundamental aspects of *distribution engineering,* and they can be quite tedious. Linux distribution companies such as Red Hat (in the desktop and enterprise market segments) and Monta Vista Software (in the embedded market segment) spend considerable engineering resources on just this: packaging a collection of programs, libraries, tools, utilities, and applications that together make up a Linux distribution. By necessity, building a root file system employs elements of distribution engineering on a smaller scale.

6.1.5 Trial-and-Error Method

Until recently, the only way to populate the contents of your root file system was to use the trial-and-error method. Perhaps the process can be automated by creating a set of scripts for this purpose, but the knowledge of which files are required for a given functionality still had to come from the developer. Tools such as Red Hat Package Manager (rpm) can be used to install packages on your root file system. rpm has reasonable dependency resolution within given packages, but it is complex and involves a steep learning curve. Furthermore, using rpm does not lend itself easily to building small root file systems because it has limited capability to strip unnecessary files from the installation, such as documentation and unused utilities in a given package.

6.1.6 Automated File System Build Tools

The leading vendors of embedded Linux distributions ship very capable tools designed to automate the task of building root file systems in Flash or other devices. These tools are usually graphical in nature, enabling the developer to select files by application or functionality. They have features to strip unnecessary files such as documentation and other unneeded files from a package, and many have the capability to select at the individual file level. These tools can produce a variety of file system formats for later installation on your choice of device. Contact your favorite embedded Linux distribution vendor for details on these powerful tools.

6.2 Kernel's Last Boot Steps

In the previous chapter, we introduced the steps the kernel takes in the final phases of system boot. The final snippet of code from `.../init/main.c` is reproduced in Listing 6-2 for convenience.

Listing 6-2

Final Boot Steps from `main.c`

```
...
  if (execute_command) {
          run_init_process(execute_command);
          printk(KERN_WARNING "Failed to execute %s.  Attempting "
                              "defaults...\n", execute_command);
  }

  run_init_process("/sbin/init");
  run_init_process("/etc/init");
  run_init_process("/bin/init");
  run_init_process("/bin/sh");

  panic("No init found.  Try passing init= option to kernel.");
```

This is the final sequence of events for the kernel thread called `init` spawned by the kernel during the final stages of boot. The `run_init_process()` is a small wrapper around the `execve()` function, which is a kernel system call with a rather interesting behavior. The `execve()` function never returns if no error conditions are encountered in the call. The memory space in which the calling thread is executing is overwritten by the called program's memory image. In effect, the called program directly replaces the calling thread, including inheriting its Process ID (PID).

The structure of this initialization sequence has been unchanged for a long time in the development of the Linux kernel. In fact, Linux version 1.0 contained similar constructs. Essentially, this is the start of user space[4] processing. As you can see from Listing 6-2, unless the Linux kernel is successful in executing one of these processes, the kernel will halt, displaying the message passed in the `panic()` system call. If you have been working with embedded systems for any length of time, and

---

[4] In actuality, modern Linux kernels create a userspace-like environment earlier in the boot sequence for specialized activities, which are beyond the scope of this book.

especially if you have experience working on root file systems, you are more than familiar with this kernel `panic()` and its message! If you search on Google for this `panic()` error message, you will find page after page of hits for this FAQ. When you complete this chapter, you will be an expert at troubleshooting this common failure.

Notice a key ingredient of these processes: They are all programs that are expected to reside on a root file system that has a similar structure to that presented in Listing 6-1. Therefore we know that we must at least satisfy the kernel's requirement for an `init` process that is capable of executing within its own environment.

In looking at Listing 6-2, this means that at least one of the `run_init_process()` function calls must succeed. You can see that the kernel tries to execute one of four programs in the order in which they are encountered. As you can see from the listing, if none of these four programs succeeds, the booting kernel issues the dreaded `panic()` function call and dies right there. Remember, this snippet of code from `.../init/main.c` is executed only once on bootup. If it does not succeed, the kernel can do little but complain and halt, which it does through the `panic()` function call.

6.2.1 First User Space Program

On most Linux systems, `/sbin/init` is spawned by the kernel on boot. This is why it is attempted first from Listing 6-2. Effectively, this becomes the first user space program to run. To review, this is the sequence:

1.   Mount the root file system

2.   Spawn the first user space program, which, in this discussion, becomes `init`

In our example minimal root file system from Listing 6-2, the first three attempts at spawning a user space process would fail because we did not provide an executable file called `init` anywhere on the file system. Recall from Listing 6-1 that we had a soft link called `sh` that pointed back to `busybox`. You should now realize the purpose for that soft link: It causes `busybox` to be executed by the kernel as the initial process, while also satisfying the common requirement for a shell executable from userspace.[5]

---

[5] When `busybox` is invoked via the `sh` symbolic link, it spawns a shell. We cover this in detail in Chapter 11.

6.2.2 Resolving Dependencies

It is not sufficient to simply include an executable such as init on your file system and expect it to boot. For every process you place on your root file system, you must also satisfy its dependencies. Most processes have two categories of dependencies: those that are needed to resolve unresolved references within a dynamically linked executable, and external configuration or data files that an application might need. We have a tool to find the former, but the latter can be supplied only by at least a cursory understanding of the application in question.

An example will help make this clear. The init process is a dynamically linked executable. To run init, we need to satisfy its library dependencies. A tool has been developed for this purpose: ldd. To understand what libraries a given application requires, simply run your cross-version of ldd on the binary:

```
$ ppc_4xxFP-ldd init
        libc.so.6 => /opt/eldk/ppc_4xxFP/lib/libc.so.6
        ld.so.1 => /opt/eldk/ppc_4xxFP/lib/ld.so.1
$
```

From this ldd output, we can see that the PowerPC init executable in this example is dependent on two libraries. These are the standard C library (libc.so.6) and the Linux dynamic loader (ld.so.1).

To satisfy the second category of dependencies for an executable, the configuration and data files that it might need, there is little substitute for some knowledge about how the subsystem works. For example, init expects to read its operational configuration from a data file called inittab located on /etc. Unless you are using a tool that has this knowledge built in, such as those described in the earlier Section 6.1.6, "Automated File System Build Tools," you must supply that knowledge.

6.2.3 Customized Initial Process

It is worth noting that the developer can control which initial process is executed at startup. This is done by a kernel command line parameter. It is hinted at in Listing 6-2 by the text contained within the panic() function call. Building on our kernel command line from Chapter 5, here is how it might look with a developer-specified init process:

```
console=ttyS0,115200 ip=bootp root=/dev/nfs init=/sbin/myinit
```

Specifying `init=` in the kernel command line in this way, you must provide a binary executable on your root file system in the `/sbin` directory called `myinit`. This would be the first process to gain control at the completion of the kernel's boot process.

6.3 The Init Process

Unless you are doing something highly unusual, you will never need to provide a customized initial process because the capabilities of the standard `init` process are very flexible. The `init` program, together with a family of startup scripts that we examine shortly, implement what is commonly called *System V Init*, from the original UNIX System V that used this schema. We now examine this powerful system configuration and control utility.

We saw in the previous section that `init` is the first user space process spawned by the kernel after completion of the boot process. As you will learn, every process in a running Linux system has a child-parent relationship with another process running in the system. `init` is the ultimate parent of all user space processes in a Linux system. Furthermore, `init` provides the default set of environment parameters for all other processes to inherit, including such things as `PATH` and `CONSOLE`.

Its primary role is to spawn additional processes under the direction of a special configuration file. This configuration file is usually stored as `/etc/inittab`. `init` has the concept of a *runlevel*. A runlevel can be thought of as a system state. Each runlevel is defined by the services enabled and programs spawned upon entry to that runlevel.

`init` can exist in a single runlevel at any given time. Runlevels used by `init` include runlevels from 0 to 6 and a special runlevel called `s`. Runlevel 0 instructs `init` to halt the system, while runlevel 6 results in a system reboot. For each runlevel, a set of startup and shutdown scripts is usually provided that define the action a system should take for each runlevel. Actions to perform for a given runlevel are determined by the `/etc/inittab` configuration file, described shortly.

Several of the runlevels have been reserved for specific purposes in many distributions. Table 6-2 details the runlevels and their purpose in common use in many Linux distributions.

TABLE 6-2
Runlevels

Runlevel	Purpose
0	System shutdown (halt)
1	Single-user system configuration for maintenance
2	User defined
3	General purpose multiuser configuration
4	User defined
5	Multiuser with graphical user interface on startup
6	System restart (reboot)

The runlevel scripts are commonly found under a directory called `/etc/rc.d/init.d`. Here you will find most of the scripts that enable and disable individual services. Services can be configured manually, by invoking the script and passing one of the appropriate arguments to the script, such as `start`, `stop`, or `restart`. Listing 6-3 displays an example of restarting the `nfs` service.

Listing 6-3

NFS Restart

```
$ /etc/rc.d/init.d/nfs restart
Shutting down NFS mountd:                          [   OK   ]
Shutting down NFS daemon:                          [   OK   ]
Shutting down NFS quotas:                          [   OK   ]
Shutting down NFS services:                        [   OK   ]
Starting NFS services:                             [   OK   ]
Starting NFS quotas:                               [   OK   ]
Starting NFS daemon:                               [   OK   ]
Starting NFS mountd:                               [   OK   ]
```

If you have spent any time with a desktop Linux distribution such as Red Hat or Fedora, you have undoubtedly seen lines like this during system startup.

A runlevel is defined by the services that are enabled at that runlevel. Most Linux distributions contain a directory structure under `/etc` that contains symbolic links to the service scripts in `/etc/rc.d/init.d`. These runlevel directories are typically rooted at `/etc/rc.d`. Under this directory, you will find a series of runlevel directories that contain startup and shutdown specifications for each runlevel. `init` simply executes these scripts upon entry and exit from a runlevel. The scripts define the system state, and `inittab` instructs `init` on which scripts to associate with a given runlevel. Listing 6-4 contains the directory structure beneath `/etc/rc.d` that drives the runlevel startup and shutdown behavior upon entry to or exit from the specified runlevel, respectively.

Listing 6-4

Runlevel Directory Structure

```
$ ls -l /etc/rc.d
total 96
drwxr-xr-x  2 root  root   4096 Oct 20 10:19 init.d
-rwxr-xr-x  1 root  root   2352 Mar 16  2004 rc
drwxr-xr-x  2 root  root   4096 Mar 22  2005 rc0.d
drwxr-xr-x  2 root  root   4096 Mar 22  2005 rc1.d
drwxr-xr-x  2 root  root   4096 Mar 22  2005 rc2.d
drwxr-xr-x  2 root  root   4096 Mar 22  2005 rc3.d
drwxr-xr-x  2 root  root   4096 Mar 22  2005 rc4.d
drwxr-xr-x  2 root  root   4096 Mar 22  2005 rc5.d
drwxr-xr-x  2 root  root   4096 Mar 22  2005 rc6.d
-rwxr-xr-x  1 root  root    943 Dec 31 16:36 rc.local
-rwxr-xr-x  1 root  root  25509 Jan 11  2005 rc.sysinit
```

Each of the runlevels is defined by the scripts contained in the `rcN.d`, where *N* is the runlevel. Inside each `rcN.d` directory, you will find numerous symlinks arranged in a specific order. These symbolic links start with either a *K* or an *S*. Those beginning with *S* point to service scripts, which are invoked with startup instructions; those starting with a *K* point to service scripts that are invoked with shutdown instructions. An example with a very small number of services might look like Listing 6-5.

Listing 6-5

Example Runlevel Directory

```
lrwxrwxrwx  1 root  root  17 Nov 25  2004 S10network -> ../init.d/network
lrwxrwxrwx  1 root  root  16 Nov 25  2004 S12syslog  -> ../init.d/syslog
lrwxrwxrwx  1 root  root  16 Nov 25  2004 S56xinetd  -> ../init.d/xinetd
lrwxrwxrwx  1 root  root  16 Nov 25  2004 K50xinetd  -> ../init.d/xinetd
lrwxrwxrwx  1 root  root  16 Nov 25  2004 K88syslog  -> ../init.d/syslog
lrwxrwxrwx  1 root  root  17 Nov 25  2004 K90network -> ../init.d/network
```

In this example, we are instructing the startup scripts to start three services upon entry to this fictitious runlevel: `network`, `syslog`, and `xinetd`. Because the `S*` scripts are ordered with a numeric tag, they will be started in this order. In a similar fashion, when exiting this runlevel, three services will be terminated: `xinetd`, `syslog`, and `network`. In a similar fashion, these services will be terminated in the order presented by the two-digit number following the `K` in the symlink filename. In an actual system, there would undoubtedly be many more entries. You can include your own entries for your own custom applications, too.

The top-level script that executes these service startup and shutdown scripts is defined in the `init` configuration file, which we now examine.

6.3.1 inittab

When `init` is started, it reads the system configuration file `/etc/inittab`. This file contains directives for each runlevel, as well as directives that apply to all runlevels. This file and `init`'s behavior are well documented in man pages on most Linux workstations, as well as by several books covering system administration. We do not attempt to duplicate those works; we focus on how a developer might configure `inittab` for an embedded system. For a detailed explanation of how `inittab` and `init` work together, view the man page on most Linux workstations by typing **man init** and **man inittab**.

Let's take a look at a typical `inittab` for a simple embedded system. Listing 6-6 contains a simple `inittab` example for a system that supports a single runlevel as well as shutdown and reboot.

Listing 6-6

Simple Example inittab

```
# /etc/inittab

# The default runlevel (2 in this example)
id:2:initdefault:

# This is the first process (actually a script) to be run.
si::sysinit:/etc/rc.sysinit

# Execute our shutdown script on entry to runlevel 0
10:0:wait:/etc/init.d/sys.shutdown
```

```
# Execute our normal startup script on entering runlevel 2
l2:2:wait:/etc/init.d/runlvl2.startup

# This line executes a reboot script (runlevel 6)
l6:6:wait:/etc/init.d/sys.reboot

# This entry spawns a login shell on the console
# Respawn means it will be restarted each time it is killed
con:2:respawn:/bin/sh
```

This very simple[6] inittab script describes three individual runlevels. Each runlevel is associated with a script, which must be created by the developer for the desired actions in each runlevel. When this file is read by init, the first script to be executed is /etc/rc.sysinit. This is denoted by the sysinit tag. Then init enters runlevel 2, and executes the script defined for runlevel 2. From this example, this would be /etc/init.d/runlvl2.startup. As you might guess from the :wait: tag in Listing 6-6, init waits until the script completes before continuing. When the runlevel 2 script completes, init spawns a shell on the console (through the /bin/sh symbolic link), as shown in the last line of Listing 6-6. The respawn keyword instructs init to restart the shell each time it detects that it has exited. Listing 6-7 shows what it looks like during boot.

Listing 6-7

Example Startup Messages

```
...
VFS: Mounted root (nfs filesystem).
Freeing init memory: 304K
INIT: version 2.78 booting
This is rc.sysinit
INIT: Entering runlevel: 2
This is runlvl2.startup

#
```

The startup scripts in this example do nothing except announce themselves for illustrative purposes. Of course, in an actual system, these scripts enable features and services that do useful work! Given the simple configuration in this example, you would enable the services and applications for your particular widget in the /etc/init.d/runlvl2.startup script and do the reverse—disable your

---

[6] This inittab is a nice example of a small, purpose-built embedded system.

applications, services, and devices—in your shutdown and/or reboot scripts. In the next section, we look at some typical system configurations and the required entries in the startup scripts to enable these configurations.

6.3.2 Example Web Server Startup Script

Although simple, this example startup script is designed to illustrate the mechanism and guide you in designing your own system startup and shutdown behavior. This example is based on `busybox`, which has a slightly different initialization behavior than `init`. These differences are covered in detail in Chapter 11.

In a typical embedded appliance that contains a web server, we might want several servers available for maintenance and remote access. In this example, we enable servers for HTTP and Telnet access (via inetd). Listing 6-8 contains a simple `rc.sysinit` script for our hypothetical web server appliance.

Listing 6-8

Web Server `rc.sysinit`

```
#!/bin/sh

echo "This is rc.sysinit"

busybox mount -t proc none /proc

# Load the system loggers
syslogd
klogd

# Enable legacy PTY support for telnetd
busybox mkdir /dev/pts
busybox mknod /dev/ptmx c 5 2
busybox mount -t devpts devpts /dev/pts
```

In this simple initialization script, we first enable the `proc` file system. The details of this useful subsystem are covered in Chapter 9. Next we enable the system loggers so that we can capture system information during operation. This is especially useful when things go wrong. The last entries enable support for the UNIX PTY subsystem, which is required for the implementation of the Telnet server used for this example.

Listing 6-9 contains the commands in the runlevel 2 startup script. This script contains the commands to enable any services we want to have operational for our appliance.

Listing 6-9

Example Runlevel 2 Startup Script

```
#!/bin/sh

echo "This is runlvl2.startup"

echo "Starting Internet Superserver"
inetd

echo "Starting web server"
webs &
```

Notice how simple this runlevel 2 startup script actually is. First we enable the so-called Internet superserver `inetd`, which intercepts and spawns services for common TCP/IP requests. In our example, we enabled Telnet services through a configuration file called `/etc/inetd.conf`. Then we execute the web server, here called `webs`. That's all there is to it. Although minimal, this is a working configuration for Telnet and web services.

To complete this configuration, you might supply a shutdown script (refer back to Listing 6-6), which, in this case, would terminate the web server and the Internet superserver before system shutdown. In our example scenario, that is sufficient for a clean shutdown.

6.4 Initial RAM Disk

The Linux kernel contains a mechanism to mount an early root file system to perform certain startup-related system initialization and configuration. This mechanism is known as the *initial RAM disk,* or simply *initrd.* Support for this functionality must be compiled into the kernel. This kernel configuration option is found under Block Devices, RAM disk support in the kernel configuration utility. Figure 6-1 shows an example of the configuration for initrd.

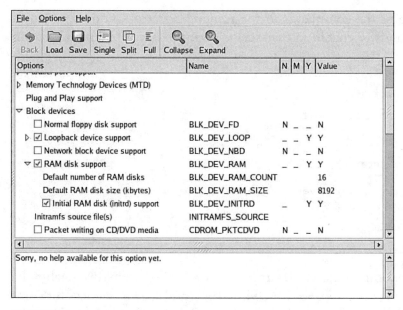

FIGURE 6-1
Linux kernel configuration utility

6.4.1 Initial RAM Disk Purpose

The initial RAM disk is a small self-contained root file system that usually contains directives to load specific device drivers before the completion of the boot cycle. In Linux workstation distributions such as Red Hat and Fedora Core, an initial RAM disk is used to load the device drivers for the EXT3 file system before mounting the real root file system. An initrd is frequently used to load a device driver that is required in order to access the real root file system.

6.4.2 Booting with initrd

To use the initrd functionality, the bootloader gets involved on most architectures to pass the initrd image to the kernel. A common scenario is that the bootloader loads a compressed kernel image into memory and then loads an initrd image into another section of available memory. In doing so, it becomes the bootloader's responsibility to pass the load address of the initrd image to the kernel before passing control to it. The exact mechanism differs depending on the architecture, bootloader, and platform implementation. However, the kernel must know where the initrd image is located so it can load it.

Some architectures and platforms construct a single composite binary image. This scheme is used when the bootloader does not have specific Linux support for loading `initrd` images. In this case, the kernel and `initrd` image are simply concatenated together. You will find reference to this type of composite image in the kernel makefiles as `bootpImage`. Presently, this is used only for `arm` architecture.

So how does the kernel know where to find the `initrd` image? Unless there is some special magic in the bootloader, it is usually sufficient simply to pass the `initrd` image start address and size to the kernel via the kernel command line. Here is an example of a kernel command line for a popular ARM-based reference board containing the TI OMAP 5912 processor.

```
console=ttyS0,115200 root=/dev/nfs                          \
   nfsroot=192.168.1.9:/home/chris/sandbox/omap-target      \
   initrd=0x10800000,0x14af47
```

The previous kernel command line has been separated into several lines to fit in the space provided. In actual practice, it is a single line, with the individual elements separated by spaces. This kernel command line defines the following kernel behavior:

- Specify a single console on device `ttyS0` at 115 kilobaud

- Mount a root file system via NFS, the network file system

- Find the NFS root file system on host 192.168.1.9
  (from directory `/home/chris/sandbox/omap-target`)

- Load and mount an initial ramdisk from physical memory location 0x10800000, which has a size of 0x14AF47 (1,355,591 bytes)

One additional note regarding this example: Almost universally, the `initrd` image is compressed. The size specified on the kernel command line is the size of the compressed image.

6.4.3 Bootloader Support for initrd

Let's look at a simple example based on the popular U-Boot bootloader running on an ARM processor. This bootloader has been designed with Linux kernel support. Using U-Boot, it is easy to include an `initrd` image with the kernel image. Listing 6-10 examines a typical boot sequence containing an initial ramdisk image.

Listing 6-10

Booting Kernel with Ramdisk Support

```
# tftpboot 0x10000000 kernel-uImage
...
Load address: 0x10000000
Loading: ########################## done
Bytes transferred = 1069092 (105024 hex)

# tftpboot 0x10800000 initrd-uboot
...
Load address: 0x10800000
Loading: ############################################ done
Bytes transferred = 282575 (44fcf hex)

# bootm 0x10000000 0x10800040
Uncompressing kernel................done.
...
RAMDISK driver initialized: 16 RAM disks of 16384K size 1024 blocksize
...
RAMDISK: Compressed image found at block 0
VFS: Mounted root (ext2 filesystem).
Greetings: this is linuxrc from Initial RAMDisk
Mounting /proc filesystem

BusyBox v1.00 (2005.03.14-16:37+0000) Built-in shell (ash)
Enter 'help' for a list of built-in commands.

# (<<<< Busybox command prompt)
```

Here in Listing 6-10, we get a glimpse of the U-Boot bootloader, which we examine in more detail in the next chapter. The tftpboot command causes U-Boot to download the kernel image from a tftp server. The kernel image is downloaded and placed into the base of this target system's memory at the 256MB address (0x10000000 hex[7]). Then a second image, the initial ramdisk image, is downloaded from a tftp server into memory at a higher memory address (256MB + 8MB, in this example). Finally, we issue the U-Boot bootm command, which is the "boot from memory" command. The bootm command takes two arguments: the address of the Linux kernel image, optionally followed by an address representing the location of the initial ramdisk image.

---

[7] It just so happens that on this particular board, our physical SDRAM starts at 256MB.

Take special note of one feature of the U-Boot bootloader. It fully supports loading kernel and ramdisk images over an Ethernet connection. This is a very useful development configuration. You can get a kernel and ramdisk image onto your board in other ways as well. You can flash them into your Flash memory using a hardware-based flash programming tool, or you can use a serial port and download the kernel and file system images via RS-232. However, because these images are typically large (a kernel can be about a megabyte, and a ramdisk can be tens of megabytes), you will save a significant amount of engineering time if you invest in this Ethernet-based tftp download method. Whatever bootloader you choose, make sure it supports network download of development images.

6.4.4 initrd Magic: linuxrc

When the kernel boots, it detects the presence of the initrd image, and copies the compressed binary file from the specified physical location in RAM into a proper kernel ramdisk and mounts it as the root file system. The magic of the initrd comes from the contents of a special file within the initrd image. When the kernel mounts the initial ramdisk, it looks for a specific file called linuxrc. It treats this file as a script file and proceeds to execute the commands contained therein. This mechanism enables the system designer to specify the behavior of initrd. Listing 6-11 contains a sample linuxrc file.

Listing 6-11

Example linuxrc File

```
#!/bin/sh

echo 'Greetings: this is 'linuxrc' from Initial Ramdisk'
echo 'Mounting /proc filesystem'
mount -t proc /proc /proc

busybox sh
```

In practice, this file would contain directives required before we mount the real root file system. One example might be to load CompactFlash drivers to obtain a real root file system from a CompactFlash device. For purposes of this example, we simply spawn a busybox shell and halt the boot process for examination. You can see the # command prompt from Listing 6-10 resulting from this busybox shell. If one were to type the exit command here, the kernel would continue its boot process until complete.

After the kernel copies the ramdisk from physical memory into a kernel ramdisk, it returns this physical memory back to the available memory pool. You can think of this as transferring the `initrd` image from physical memory at the hard-coded address into the kernel's own virtual memory (in the form of a kernel ramdisk device).

One last comment about Listing 6-11: The `mount` command in which the `/proc` file system is mounted seems redundant in its use of the word `proc`. This command would also work:

```
mount -t proc none /proc
```

Notice that the device field of the `mount` command has been changed to `none`. The `mount` command ignores the device field because no physical device is associated with the `proc` file system. The `-t proc` is enough to instruct `mount` to mount the `/proc` file system on the `/proc` mount point. I use the former invocation as a mental reminder that we are actually mounting the kernel pseudo device (the `/proc` file system) on `/proc`. The `mount` command ignores this argument. Use the method that you prefer.

6.4.5 The initrd Plumbing

As part of the Linux boot process, the kernel must locate and mount a root file system. Late in the boot process, the kernel decides what and where to mount in a function called `prepare_namespace()`. If `initrd` support is enabled in the kernel, as illustrated in Figure 6-1, and the kernel command line is so configured, the kernel decompresses the compressed `initrd` image from physical memory and eventually copies the contents of this file into a ramdisk device (`/dev/ram`). At this point, we have a proper file system on a kernel ramdisk. After the file system has been read into the ramdisk, the kernel effectively mounts this ramdisk device as its root file system. Finally, the kernel spawns a kernel thread to execute the `linuxrc` file on the `initrd` image.[8]

When the `linuxrc` script has completed execution, the kernel unmounts the `initrd` and proceeds with the final stages of system boot. If the real root device has a directory called `/initrd`, Linux mounts the `initrd` file system on this path (in

---

[8] Out of necessity (space), this is a very simplified description of the sequence of events. The actual mechanism is similar in concept, but several significant details are omitted for clarity. You are encouraged to consult the kernel source code for more details. See `.../init/main.c` and `.../init/do_mounts*.c`.

this context, called a *mount point*). If this directory does not exist in the final root file system, the initrd image is simply discarded.

If the kernel command line contains a root= parameter specifying a ramdisk (root=/dev/ram0, for example), the previously described initrd behavior changes in two important ways. First, the processing of the linuxrc executable is skipped. Second, no attempt is made to mount another file system as root. This means that you can have a Linux system with initrd as the only root file system. This is useful for minimal system configurations in which the only root file system is the ramdisk. Placing /dev/ram0 on the kernel command line allows the full system initialization to complete with the initrd as the final root file system.

6.4.6 Building an initrd Image

Constructing a suitable root file system image is one of the more challenging aspects of embedded systems. Creating a proper initrd image is even more challenging because it needs to be small and specialized. For this section, we examine initrd requirements and file system contents.

Listing 6-12 was produced by running the tree utility on our example initrd image from this chapter.

Listing 6-12

Contents of Example initrd

```
.
|-- bin
|   |-- busybox
|   |-- echo -> busybox
|   |-- mount -> busybox
|   '-- sh -> busybox
|-- dev
|   |-- console
|   |-- ram0
|   '-- ttyS0
|-- etc
|-- linuxrc
'-- proc

4 directories, 8 files
```

As you can see, it is very small indeed; it takes up a little more than 500KB in uncompressed form. Since it is based on `busybox`, it has many capabilities. Because `busybox` is statically linked, it has no dependencies on any system libraries. You will learn more about `busybox` in Chapter 11.

6.5 Using initramfs

`initramfs` is a relatively new (Linux 2.6) mechanism for executing early user space programs. It is conceptually similar to `initrd`, as described in the previous section. Its purpose is also similar: to enable loading of drivers that might be required before mounting the real root file system. However, it differs in significant ways from the `initrd` mechanism.

The technical implementation details differ significantly between `initrd` and `initramfs`. For example, `initramfs` is loaded before the call to `do_basic_setup()`,[9] which provides a mechanism for loading firmware for devices before its driver has been loaded. For more details, the Linux kernel documentation for this subsystem is relatively up-to-date. See `.../Documentation/filesystems/ramfs-rootfs-initramfs.txt`.

From a practical perspective, `initramfs` is much easier to use. `initramfs` is a `cpio` archive, whereas `initrd` is a gzipped file system image. This simple difference contributes to the easy of use of `initramfs`. It is integrated into the Linux kernel source tree and is built automatically when you build the kernel image. Making changes to it is far easier than building and loading a new `initrd` image. Listing 6-13 shows the contents of the Linux kernel `.../usr` directory, where the `initramfs` image is built. The contents of Listing 6-13 are shown after a kernel has been built.

---

[9] `do_basic_setup` is called from `.../init/main.c` and calls `do_initcalls()`. This causes driver module initialization routines to be called. This was described in detail in Chapter 5 and shown in Listing 5-10.

Listing 6-13

Kernel `initramfs` Build Directory

```
$ ls -l
total 56
-rw-rw-r--  1 chris chris   834 Mar 25 11:13 built-in.o
-rwxrwxrwx-x 1 chris chris 11512 Mar 25 11:13 gen_init_cpio
-rw-rw-r--  1 chris chris 10587 Oct 27  2005 gen_init_cpio.c
-rw-rw-r--  1 chris chris   512 Mar 25 11:13 initramfs_data.cpio
-rw-rw-r--  1 chris chris   133 Mar 25 11:13 initramfs_data.cpio.gz
-rw-rw-r--  1 chris chris   786 Mar 25 11:13 initramfs_data.o
-rw-rw-r--  1 chris chris  1024 Oct 27  2005 initramfs_data.S
-rw-rw-r--  1 chris chris   113 Mar 25 11:13 initramfs_list
-rw-rw-r--  1 chris chris  1619 Oct 27  2005 Kconfig
-rw-rw-r--  1 chris chris  2048 Oct 27  2005 Makefile
```

The file `initramfs_list` contains a list of files that will be included in the `initramfs` archive. The default for recent Linux kernels looks like this:

```
dir /dev 0755 0 0
nod /dev/console 0600 0 0 c 5 1
dir /root 0700 0 0
```

This produces a small default directory structure containing the `/root` and `/dev` top-level directories, as well as a single device node representing the console. Add to this file to build your own `initramfs`. You can also specify a source for your `initramfs` files via the kernel-configuration facility. Enable `INITRAMFS_SOURCE` in your kernel configuration and point it to a location on your development workstation; the kernel build system will use those files as the source for your `initramfs` image.

The final output of this build directory is the `initramfs_data_cpio.gz` file. This is a compressed archive containing the files you specified (either through the `initramfs_list` or via the `INITRAMFS_SOURCE` kernel-configuration option). This archive is linked into the final kernel image. This is another advantage of `initramfs` over `initrd`: There is no need to load a separate `initrd` image at boot time, as is the case with `initrd`.

6.6 Shutdown

Orderly shutdown of an embedded system is often overlooked in a design. Improper shutdown can affect startup times and can even corrupt certain file system types. One of the more common complaints using the EXT2 file system (the default in many desktop Linux distributions for several years) is the time it takes for an `fsck` (file system check) on startup after unplanned power loss. Servers with large disk systems can take on the order of hours to properly `fsck` through a collection of large EXT2 partitions.

Each embedded project will likely have its own shutdown strategy. What works for one might or might not work for another. The scale of shutdown can range from a full System V shutdown scheme, to a simple script to halt or reboot. Several Linux utilities are available to assist in the shutdown process, including the `shutdown`, `halt`, and `reboot` commands. Of course, these must be available for your chosen architecture.

A shutdown script should terminate all userspace processes, which results in closing any open files used by those processes. If `init` is being used, issuing the command `init 0` halts the system. In general, the shutdown process first sends all processes the `SIGTERM` signal, to notify them that the system is shutting down. A short delay ensures that all processes have the opportunity to perform their shutdown actions, such as closing files, saving state, and so on. Then all processes are sent the `SIGKILL` signal, which results in their termination. The shutdown process should attempt to unmount any mounted file systems and call the architecture-specific halt or reboot routines. The Linux `shutdown` command in conjunction with `init` exhibits this behavior.

6.7 Chapter Summary

- A root file system is required for all Linux systems. They can be difficult to build from scratch because of complex dependencies by each application.

- The File System Hierarchy standard provides guidance to developers for laying out a file system for maximum compatibility and flexibility.

- We presented a minimal file system as an example of how root file systems are created.

- The Linux kernel's final boot steps define and control a Linux system's startup behavior. Several mechanisms are available depending on your embedded Linux system's requirements.

- The `init` process was presented in detail. This powerful system-configuration and control utility can serve as the basis for your own embedded Linux system. System initialization based on `init` was presented, along with example startup script configurations.

- Initial ramdisk is a Linux kernel feature to allow further startup behavior customization before mounting a final root file system and spawning `init`. We presented the mechanism and example configuration for using this powerful feature.

- `initramfs` simplifies the initial ramdisk mechanism, while providing similar early startup facilities. It is easier to use, does not require loading a separate image, and is built automatically during each kernel build.

6.7.1 Suggestions for Additional Reading

File System Hierarchy Standard
Maintained by freestandards.org
www.pathname.com/fhs/

Boot Process, Init and Shutdown
Linux Documentation Project
http://tldp.org/LDP/intro-linux/html/sect_04_02.html

Init man page
Linux Documentation Project
http://tldp.org/LDP/sag/html/init.html

A brief description of System V init
http://docs.kde.org/en/3.3/kdeadmin/ksysv/what-is-sysv-init.html

Booting Linux: The History and the Future
Werner Almesberger
www.almesberger.net/cv/papers/ols2k-9.ps

Chapter 7

Bootloaders

In this chapter

P revious chapters have made reference to and even provided examples of bootloader operations. A critical component of an embedded system, the bootloader provides the foundation from which the other system software is spawned. This chapter starts by examining the bootloader's role in a system. We follow this with an introduction to some common features of bootloaders. Armed with this background, we take a detailed look at a popular bootloader used for embedded systems. We conclude this chapter by introducing a few of the more popular bootloaders.

Numerous bootloaders are in use today. It would be impractical in the given space to cover much detail on even the most popular ones. Therefore, we have chosen to explain concepts and use examples based on one of the more popular bootloaders in the open source community for PowerPC, MIPS, ARM, and other architectures: the U-Boot bootloader.

7.1 Role of a Bootloader

When power is first applied to a processor board, many elements of hardware must be initialized before even the simplest program can run. Each architecture and processor has a set of predefined actions and configurations, which include fetching some initialization code from an on-board storage device (usually Flash memory). This early initialization code is part of the bootloader and is responsible for breathing life into the processor and related hardware components.

Most processors have a default address from which the first bytes of code are fetched upon application of power and release of reset. Hardware designers use this information to arrange the layout of Flash memory on the board and to select which address range(s) the Flash memory responds to. This way, when power is first applied, code is fetched from a well-known and predictable address, and software control can be established.

The bootloader provides this early initialization code and is responsible for initializing the board so that other programs can run. This early initialization code is almost always written in the processor's native assembly language. This fact alone presents many challenges, some of which we examine here.

Of course, after the bootloader has performed this basic processor and platform initialization, its primary role becomes booting a full-blown operating system. It is responsible for locating, loading, and passing execution to the primary operating system. In addition, the bootloader might have advanced features, such as the capability to validate an OS image, the capability to upgrade itself or an OS image, and the capability to choose from among several OS images based on a developer-defined policy. Unlike the traditional PC-BIOS model, when the OS takes control, the bootloader is overwritten and ceases to exist.[1]

7.2 Bootloader Challenges

Even a simple "Hello World" program written in C requires significant hardware and software resources. The application developer does not need to know or care much about these details because the C runtime environment transparently provides this infrastructure. A bootloader developer has no such luxury. Every resource that a bootloader requires must be carefully initialized and allocated before it is used. One of the most visible examples of this is Dynamic Random Access Memory (DRAM).

7.2.1 DRAM Controller

DRAM chips cannot be directly read from or written to like other microprocessor bus resources. They require specialized hardware controllers to enable read and write cycles. To further complicate matters, DRAM must be constantly refreshed or the data contained within will be lost. Refresh is accomplished by sequentially reading each location in DRAM in a systematic manner and within the timing specifications set forth by the DRAM manufacturer. Modern DRAM chips support many modes of operation, such as burst mode and dual data rate for high-performance applications. It is the DRAM controller's responsibility to configure DRAM, keep it refreshed within the manufacturer's timing specifications, and respond to the various read and write commands from the processor.

Setting up a DRAM controller is the source of much frustration for the newcomer to embedded development. It requires detailed knowledge of DRAM architecture, the controller itself, the specific DRAM chips being used, and the overall hardware design. Though this is beyond the scope of this book, the interested

---

[1] Some embedded designs protect the bootloader and provide callbacks to bootloader routines, but this is almost never a good design approach. Linux is far more capable than bootloaders, so there is often little point in doing so.

reader can learn more about this important concept by referring to the references at the end of this chapter. Appendix D, "SDRAM Interface Considerations," provides more background on this important topic.

Very little can happen in an embedded system until the DRAM controller and DRAM itself have been properly initialized. One of the first things a bootloader must do is to enable the memory subsystem. After it is initialized, memory can be used as a resource. In fact, one of the first actions many bootloaders perform after memory initialization is to copy themselves into DRAM for faster execution.

7.2.2 Flash Versus RAM

Another complexity inherent in bootloaders is that they are required to be stored in nonvolatile storage but are usually loaded into RAM for execution. Again, the complexity arises from the level of resources available for the bootloader to rely on. In a fully operational computer system running an operating system such as Linux, it is relatively easy to compile a program and invoke it from nonvolatile storage. The runtime libraries, operating system, and compiler work together to create the infrastructure necessary to load a program from nonvolatile storage into memory and pass control to it. The aforementioned "Hello World" program is a perfect example. When compiled, it can be loaded into memory and executed simply by typing the name of the executable (`hello`) on the command line (assuming, of course, that the executable exists somewhere on your PATH).

This infrastructure does not exist when a bootloader gains control upon power-on. Instead, the bootloader must create its own operational context and move itself, if required, to a suitable location in RAM. Furthermore, additional complexity is introduced by the requirement to execute from a read-only medium.

7.2.3 Image Complexity

As application developers, we do not need to concern ourselves with the layout of a binary executable file when we develop applications for our favorite platform. The compiler and binary utilities are preconfigured to build a binary executable image containing the proper components needed for a given architecture. The linker places startup (prologue) and shutdown (epilogue) code into the image. These objects set up the proper execution context for your application, which typically starts at `main()` in your application.

This is absolutely not the case with a typical bootloader. When the bootloader gets control, there is no context or prior execution environment. In a typical system, there might not be any DRAM until the bootloader initializes the processor and related hardware. Consider what this means. In a typical C function, any local variables are stored on the stack, so a simple function like the one in Listing 7-1 is unusable.

Listing 7-1

Simple C function

```
int setup_memory_controller(board_info_t *p)
    {
    unsigned int *dram_controller_register = p->dc_reg;
...
```

When a bootloader gains control on power-on, there is no stack and no stack pointer. Therefore, a simple C function similar to Listing 7-1 will likely crash the processor because the compiler will generate code to create and initialize the pointer `dram_controller_register` on the stack, which does not yet exist. The bootloader must create this execution context before any C functions are called.

When the bootloader is compiled and linked, the developer must exercise complete control over how the image is constructed and linked. This is especially true if the bootloader is to relocate itself from Flash to RAM. The compiler and linker must be passed a handful of parameters defining the characteristics and layout of the final executable image. Two primary characteristics conspire to add complexity to the final binary executable image.

The first characteristic that presents complexity is the need to organize the startup code in a format compatible with the processor's boot sequence. The first bytes of executable code must be at a predefined location in Flash, depending on the processor and hardware architecture. For example, the AMCC PowerPC 405GP processor seeks its first machine instructions from a hard-coded address of 0xFFFF_FFFC. Other processors use similar methods with different details. Some processors are configurable at power-on to seek code from one of several predefined locations, depending on hardware configuration signals.

How does a developer specify the layout of a binary image? The linker is passed a *linker description file,* also called a *linker command script.* This special file can be thought of as a recipe for constructing a binary executable image. Listing 7-2 contains a snippet from an existing linker description file in use in a popular bootloader, which we discuss shortly.

Listing 7-2

Linker Command Script—Reset Vector Placement

```
SECTIONS
{
  .resetvec 0xFFFFFFFC :
  {
    *(.resetvec)
  } = 0xffff
...
```

A complete description of linker command scripts syntax is beyond the scope of this book. The interested reader is directed to the GNU LD manual referenced at the end of this chapter. Looking at Listing 7-2, we see the beginning of the definition for the output section of the binary ELF image. It directs the linker to place the section of code called .resetvec at a fixed address in the output image, starting at location 0xFFFF_FFFC. Furthermore, it specifies that the rest of this section shall be filled with all ones (0xFFFF.) This is because an erased Flash memory array contains all ones. This technique not only saves wear and tear on the Flash memory, but it also significantly speeds up programming of that sector.

Listing 7-3 is the complete assembly language file from a recent U-Boot distribution that defines the .resetvec code section. It is contained in an assembly language file called .../cpu/ppc4xx/resetvec.S. Notice that this code section cannot exceed 4 bytes in length in a machine with only 32 address bits. This is because only a single instruction is defined in this section, no matter what configuration options are present.

Listing 7-3

Source Definition of `.resetvec`

```
/* Copyright MontaVista Software Incorporated, 2000 */
#include <config.h>
      .section .resetvec,"ax"
#if defined(CONFIG_440)
      b _start_440
#else
#if defined(CONFIG_BOOT_PCI) && defined(CONFIG_MIP405)
      b _start_pci
#else
      b _start
#endif
#endif
```

This assembly language file is very easy to understand, even if you have no assembly language programming experience. Depending on the particular configuration (as specified by the CONFIG_* macros), an unconditional branch instruction (b in PowerPC assembler syntax) is generated to the appropriate start location in the main body of code. This branch location is a 4-byte PowerPC instruction, and as we saw in the snippet from the linker command script in Listing 7-2, this simple branch instruction is placed in the absolute Flash address of 0xFFFF_FFFC in the output image. As mentioned earlier, the PPC 405GP processor fetches its first instruction from this hard-coded address. This is how the first sequence of code is defined and provided by the developer for this particular architecture and processor combination.

7.2.4 Execution Context

The other primary reason for bootloader image complexity is the lack of execution context. When the sequence of instructions from Listing 7-3 starts executing (recall that these are the first machine instructions after power-on), the resources available to the running program are nearly zero. Default values designed into the hardware ensure that fetches from Flash memory work properly and that the system clock has some default values, but little else can be assumed.[2] The reset state of each processor is usually well defined by the manufacturer, but the reset state of a board is defined by the hardware designers.

Indeed, most processors have no DRAM available at startup for temporary storage of variables or, worse, for a stack that is required to use C program calling conventions. If you were forced to write a "Hello World" program with no DRAM and, therefore, no stack, it would be quite different from the traditional "Hello World" example.

This limitation places significant challenges on the initial body of code designed to initialize the hardware. As a result, one of the first tasks the bootloader performs on startup is to configure enough of the hardware to enable at least some minimal amount of RAM. Some processors designed for embedded use have small amounts of on-chip static RAM available. This is the case with the PPC 405GP we've been discussing. When RAM is available, a stack can be allocated using part of that

---

[2] The details differ, depending upon architecture, processor, and details of the hardware design.

RAM, and a proper context can be constructed to run higher-level languages such as C. This allows the rest of the processor and platform initialization to be written in something other than assembly language.

7.3 A Universal Bootloader: Das U-Boot

Many open-source and commercial bootloaders are available, and many more one-of-a-kind home-grown designs are in widespread use today. Most of these have some level of commonality of features. For example, all of them have some capability to load and execute other programs, particularly an operating system. Most interact with the user through a serial port. Support for various networking subsystems (such as Ethernet) is less common but a very powerful feature.

Many bootloaders are specific to a particular architecture. The capability of a bootloader to support a wide variety of architectures and processors can be an important feature to larger development organizations. It is not uncommon for a single development organization to have multiple processors spanning more than one architecture. Investing in a single bootloader across multiple platforms ultimately results in lower development costs.

In this section, we study an existing bootloader that has become very popular in the embedded Linux community. The official name for this bootloader is Das U-Boot. It is maintained by Wolfgang Denk and hosted on SourceForge at http://u-boot.sourceforge.net/. U-Boot has support for multiple architectures and has a large following of embedded developers and hardware manufacturers who have adopted it for use in their projects and have contributed to its development.

7.3.1 System Configuration: U-Boot

For a bootloader to be useful across many processors and architectures, some method of configuring the bootloader is necessary. As with the Linux kernel itself, configuration of a bootloader is done at compile time. This method significantly reduces the complexity of the bootloader, which, in itself, is an important characteristic.

In the case of U-Boot, board-specific configuration is driven by a single header file specific to the target platform, and a few soft links in the source tree that select the correct subdirectories based on target board, architecture, and CPU. When configuring U-Boot for one of its supported platforms, issue this command:

```
$ make <platform>_config
```

Here, `platform` is one of the many platforms supported by U-Boot. These platform-configuration targets are listed in the top level U-Boot makefile. For example, to configure for the Spectrum Digital OSK, which contains a TI OMAP 5912 processor, issue this command:

```
$ make omap5912osk_config
```

This configures the U-Boot source tree with the appropriate soft links to select ARM as the target architecture, the ARM926 core, and the 5912 OSK as the target platform.

The next step in configuring U-Boot for this platform is to edit the configuration file specific to this board. This file is found in the U-Boot `../include/configs` subdirectory and is called `omap5912osk.h`. The README file that comes with the U-Boot distribution describes the details of configuration and is the best source for this information.

Configuration of U-Boot is done using configuration variables defined in a board-specific header file. Configuration variables have two forms. Configuration *options* are selected using macros in the form of `CONFIG_XXXX`. Configuration *settings* are selected using macros in the form of `CFG_XXXX`. In general, configuration options (`CONFIG_XXX`) are user configurable and enable specific U-Boot operational features. Configuration settings (`CFG_XXX`) are usually hardware specific and require detailed knowledge of the underlying processor and/or hardware platform. Board-specific U-Boot configuration is driven by a header file dedicated to that specific platform that contains configuration options and settings appropriate for the underlying platform. The U-Boot source tree includes a directory where these board-specific configuration header files reside. They can be found in `.../include/configs` from the top-level U-Boot source directory.

Numerous features and modes of operation can be selected by adding definitions to the board-configuration file. Listing 7-4 contains a partial configuration header file for a fictitious board based on the PPC 405GP processor.

Listing 7-4

Partial U-Boot Board-Configuration Header File

```
#define CONFIG_405GP            /* Processor definition */
#define CONFIG_4XX              /* Sub-arch specification, 4xx family */

#define CONFIG_SYS_CLK_FREQ    33333333 /* PLL Frequency  */
#define CONFIG_BAUDRATE          9600
#define CONFIG_PCI              /* Enable support for PCI */
...
#define CONFIG_COMMANDS         (CONFIG_CMD_DFL | CFG_CMD_DHCP)
...
#define CFG_BASE_BAUD            691200

/* The following table includes the supported baudrates */
#define CFG_BAUDRATE_TABLE    \
    {1200, 2400, 4800, 9600, 19200, 38400, 57600, 115200, 230400}

#define CFG_LOAD_ADDR           0x100000    /* default load address */
...
/* Memory Bank 0 (Flash Bank 0) initialization */
#define CFG_EBC_PB0AP           0x9B015480
#define CFG_EBC_PB0CR           0xFFF18000

#define CFG_EBC_PB1AP           0x02815480
#define CFG_EBC_PB1CR           0xF0018000
...
```

Listing 7-4 gives an idea of how U-Boot itself is configured for a given board. An actual board-configuration file can contain hundreds of lines similar to those found here. In this example, you can see the definitions for the CPU, CPU family (4xx), PLL clock frequency, serial port baud rate, and PCI support. We have included examples of configuration variables (CONFIG_XXX) and configuration settings (CFG_XXX). The last few lines are actual processor register values required to initialize the external bus controller for memory banks 0 and 1. You can see that these values can come only from a detailed knowledge of the board and processor.

Many aspects of U-Boot can be configured using these mechanisms, including what functionality will be compiled into U-Boot (support for DHCP, memory tests, debugging support, and so on). This mechanism can be used to tell U-Boot how much and what kind of memory is on a given board, and where that memory is mapped. The interested reader can learn much more by looking at the U-Boot code directly, especially the excellent README file.

7.3.2 U-Boot Command Sets

U-Boot supports more than 60 standard command sets that enable more than 150 unique commands using CFG_* macros. A command set is enabled in U-Boot through the use of configuration setting (CFG_*) macros. For a complete list from a recent U-Boot snapshot, consult Appendix B, "U-Boot Configurable Commands." Here are just a few, to give you an idea of the capabilities available:

Command Set	Commands
CFG_CMD_FLASH	Flash memory commands
CFG_CMD_MEMORY	Memory dump, fill, copy, compare, and so on
CFG_CMD_DHCP	DHCP Support
CFG_CMD_PING	Ping support
CFG_CMD_EXT2	EXT2 File system support

The following line of Listing 7-4 defines the commands enabled in a given U-Boot configuration, as driven by the board-specific header file:

```
#define CONFIG_COMMANDS     (CONFIG_CMD_DFL | CFG_CMD_DHCP)
```

Instead of typing out each individual CFG_* macro in your own board-specific configuration header, you can start from a default set of commands predefined in the U-Boot source. The macro CONFIG_CMD_DFL defines this default set of commands. CONFIG_CMD_DFL specifies a list of default U-Boot command sets such as tftpboot (boot an image from a tftpserver), bootm (boot an image from memory), memory utilities such as md (display memory), and so on. To enable your specific combination of commands, you can start with the default and add and subtract as necessary. The example from Listing 7-4 adds the DHCP command set to the default. You can subtract in a similar fashion:

```
#define CONFIG_COMMANDS     (CONFIG_CMD_DFL & ~CFG_CMD_NFS)
```

Take a look at any board-configuration header file in .../include/ configs/ for examples.

7.3.3 Network Operations

Many bootloaders include support for Ethernet interfaces. In a development environment, this is a huge time saver. Loading even a modest kernel image over a serial port can take minutes versus a few seconds over a 10Mbps Ethernet link. Furthermore, serial links are more prone to errors from poorly behaved serial terminals.

Some of the more important features to look for in a bootloader include support for the BOOTP, DHCP, and TFTP protocols. For those unfamiliar with these, BOOTP (Bootstrap Protocol) and DHCP (Dynamic Host Control Protocol) are protocols that enable a target device with an Ethernet port to obtain an IP address and other network-related configuration information from a central server. TFTP (Trivial File Transfer Protocol) allows the target device to download files (such as a Linux kernel image) from a TFTP server. References to these protocol specifications are listed at the end of this chapter. Servers for these services are described in Chapter 12", "Embedded Development Environment."

Figure 7-1 illustrates the flow of information between the target device and a BOOTP server. The client (U-Boot, in this case) initiates a broadcast packet searching for a BOOTP server. The server responds with a reply packet that includes the client's IP address and other information. The most useful data includes a filename used to download a kernel image.

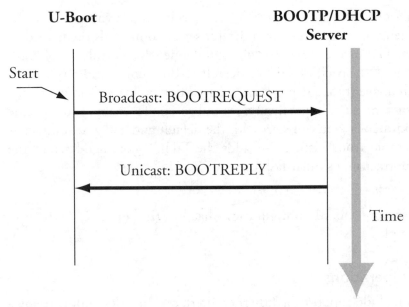

FIGURE 7-1
BOOTP client/server handshake

In practice, dedicated BOOTP servers no longer exist as stand-alone servers. DHCP servers included with your favorite Linux distribution also support BOOTP protocol packets.

The DHCP protocol builds upon BOOTP. It can supply the target with a wide variety of configuration information. In practice, the information exchange is often limited by the target/bootloader DHCP client implementation. Listing 7-5 contains an example of a DHCP server configuration block identifying a single target device. This is a snippet from a DHCP configuration file from the Fedora Core 2 DHCP implementation.

Listing 7-5

DHCP Target Specification

```
host coyote {
        hardware ethernet 00:0e:0c:00:82:f8;
        netmask 255.255.255.0;
        fixed-address 192.168.1.21;
        server-name 192.168.1.9;
        filename "coyote-zImage";
        option root-path "/home/chris/sandbox/coyote-target";
}
...
```

When this DHCP server receives a packet from a device matching the hardware Ethernet address contained in Listing 7-5, it responds by sending that device the parameters in this target specification. Table 7-1 describes the fields in the target specification.

TABLE 7-1
DHCP Target Parameters

DHCP Target Parameter	Purpose	Comments
host	Hostname	Symbolic label from DHCP configuration file
hardware ethernet	Ethernet hardware address	Low-level Ethernet hardware address of the target's Ethernet interface
fixed-address	Target IP address	The IP address that the target will assume

(continues)

TABLE 7-1 (Continued)

DHCP Target Parameter	Purpose	Comments
`netmask`	Target netmask	The IP netmask that the target will assume
`server-name`	TFTP server IP address	The IP address to which the target will direct requests for file transfers, root file system, and so on
`filename`	TFTP filename	The filename that the boot-loader can use to boot a secondary image (usually a Linux kernel)

When the bootloader on the target board has completed the BOOTP or DHCP exchange, the parameters described previously are used for further configuration. For example, the bootloader uses the target IP address to bind its Ethernet port with this IP address. The bootloader then uses the `server-name` field as a destination IP address to request the file contained in the `filename` field, which, in most cases, represents a Linux kernel image. Although this is the most common use, this same scenario could be used to download and execute manufacturing test and diagnostics firmware.

It should be noted that the DHCP protocol supports many more parameters than those detailed in Table 7-1. These are simply the more common parameters you might encounter for embedded systems. See the DHCP specification referenced at the end of this chapter for complete details.

7.3.4 Storage Subsystems

Many bootloaders support the capability of booting images from a variety of non-volatile storage devices in addition to the usual Flash memory. The difficulty in supporting these types of devices is the relative complexity in both hardware and software. To access data on a hard drive, for example, the bootloader must have device driver code for the IDE controller interface, as well as knowledge of the underlying partition scheme and file system. This is not trivial and is one of the tasks more suited to full-blown operating systems.

Even with the underlying complexity, methods exist for loading images from this class of device. The simplest method is to support the hardware only. In this scheme, no knowledge of the file system is assumed. The bootloader simply rawloads from absolute sectors on the device. This scheme can be used by dedicating an unformatted partition from sector 0 on an IDE-compatible device (such as CompactFlash) and loading the data found there without any structure imposed on the data. This is an ideal configuration for loading a kernel image or other binary image. Additional partitions on the device can be formatted for a given file system and can contain complete file systems. After the kernel boots, device drivers can be used to access the additional partitions.

U-Boot can load an image from a specified raw partition or from a partition with a file system structure. Of course, the board must have a supported hardware device (an IDE subsystem) and U-Boot must be so configured. Adding CFG_CMD_IDE to the board-specific configuration file enables support for an IDE interface, and adding CFG_CMD_BOOTD enables support for booting from a raw partition. If you are porting U-Boot to a custom board, you will have to modify U-Boot to understand your particular hardware.

7.3.5 Booting from Disk: U-Boot

As described in the previous section, U-Boot supports several methods for booting a kernel image from a disk subsystem. This simple command illustrates one of the supported methods:

```
=> diskboot 0x400000 0:0
```

To understand this syntax, you must first understand how U-Boot numbers disk devices. The 0:0 in this example specifies the device and partition. In this simple example, U-Boot performs a raw binary load of the image found on the first IDE device (IDE device 0) from the first partition found on this device. The image is loaded into system memory at physical address 0x400000.

After the kernel image has been loaded into memory, the U-Boot bootm command (boot from memory) is used to boot the kernel:

```
=> bootm 0x400000
```

7.4 Porting U-Boot

One of the reasons U-Boot has become so popular is the ease in which new plat-forms can be supported. Each board port must supply a subordinate makefile that supplies board-specific definitions to the build process. These files are all given the name `config.mk` and exist in the `.../board/xxx` subdirectory under the U-Boot top-level source directory, where xxx specifies a particular board.

As of a recent U-Boot 1.1.4 snapshot, more than 240 different board configura-tion files are named `config.mk` under the `.../boards` subdirectory. In this same U-Boot version, 29 different CPU configurations are supported (counted in the same manner). Note that, in some cases, the CPU configuration covers a family of chips, such as `ppc4xx`, which has support for several processors in the PowerPC 4xx family. U-Boot supports a large variety of popular CPUs and CPU families in use today, and a much larger collection of reference boards based on these processors.

If your board contains one of the supported CPUs, porting U-Boot is quite straightforward. If you must add a new CPU, plan on significantly more effort. The good news is that someone before you has probably done the bulk of the work. Whether you are porting to a new CPU or a new board based on an existing CPU, study the existing source code for specific guidance. Determine what CPU is clos-est to yours, and clone the functionality found in that CPU-specific directory. Finally, modify the resulting sources to add the specific support for your new CPU's requirements.

7.4.1 EP405 U-Boot Port

The same logic applies to porting U-Boot to a new board. Let's look at an example. We will use the Embedded Planet EP405 board, which contains the AMCC PowerPC 405GP processor. The particular board used for this example was pro-vided courtesy of Embedded Planet and came with 64MB of SDRAM and 16MB of on-board Flash. Numerous other devices complete the design.

The first step is to see how close we can come to an existing board. Many boards in the U-Boot source tree support the 405GP processor. A quick `grep` of the board-configuration header files narrows the choices to those that support the 405GP processor:

```
$ cd .../u-boot/include/configs$ grep -l CONFIG_405GP *
```

In a recent U-Boot snapshot, 25 board configuration files are configured for 405GP. After examining a few, the AR405.h configuration is chosen as a baseline. It contains support for the LXT971 Ethernet transceiver, which is also on the EP405. The goal is to minimize any development work by borrowing from others in the spirit of open source. Let's tackle the easy steps first. Copy the board-configuration file to a new file with a name appropriate for your board. We'll call ours EP405.h. These commands are issued from the top-level U-Boot source tree.

```
$ cp .../include/configs/AR405.h .../include/configs/EP405.h
```

Then create the board-specific directory and make a copy of the AR405 board files. We don't know yet whether we need all of them. That step comes later. After copying the files to your new board directory, edit the filenames appropriately for your board name.

```
$ cd board    <<< from top level U-Boot source directory
$ mkdir ep405
$ cp esd/ar405/* ep405
```

Now comes the hard part. Jerry Van Baren, a developer and U-Boot contributor, detailed a humorous though realistic process for porting U-Boot in an e-mail posting to the U-Boot mailing list. His complete process, documented in C, can be found in the U-Boot README file. The following summarizes the hard part of the porting process in Jerry's style and spirit:

```
while (!running) {
    do {
        Add / modify source code
    } until (compiles);
    Debug;
...
}
```

Jerry's process, as summarized here, is the simple truth. When you have selected a baseline from which to port, you must add, delete, and modify source code until it compiles, and then debug it until it is running without error! There is no magic formula. Porting any bootloader to a new board requires knowledge of many areas of hardware and software. Some of these disciplines, such as setting up SDRAM controllers, are rather specialized and complex. Virtually all of this work involves a detailed knowledge of the underlying hardware. The net result: Be prepared to spend many entertaining hours poring over your processor's hardware reference manual, along with the data sheets of numerous other components that reside on your board.

7.4.2 U-Boot Makefile Configuration Target

Now that we have a code base to start from, we must make some modifications to the top-level U-Boot makefile to add the configuration steps for our new board. Upon examining this makefile, we find a section for configuring the U-Boot source tree for the various supported boards. We now add support for our new one so we can build it. Because we derived our board from the ESD AR405, we will use that rule as the template for building our own. If you follow along in the U-Boot source code, you will see that these rules are placed in the makefile in alphabetical order of their configuration name. We shall be good open-source citizens and follow that lead. We call our configuration target `EP405_config`, again in concert with the U-Boot conventions.

```
EBONY_config:      unconfig
      @./mkconfig $(@:_config=) ppc ppc4xx ebony

+EP405_config:     unconfig
+      @./mkconfig $(@:_config=) ppc ppc4xx ep405
+
ERIC_config:       unconfig
      @./mkconfig $(@:_config=) ppc ppc4xx eric
```

Our new configuration rule has been inserted as shown in the three lines preceded with the + character (unified `diff` format).

Upon completing the steps just described, we have a U-Boot source tree that represents a *starting point.* It probably will not even compile cleanly, and that should be our first step. At least the compiler can give us some guidance on where to start.

7.4.3 EP405 Processor Initialization

The first task that your new U-Boot port must do correctly is to initialize the processor and the memory (DRAM) subsystems. After reset, the 405GP processor core is designed to fetch instructions starting from 0xFFFF_FFFC. The core attempts to execute the instructions found here. Because this is the top of the memory range, the instruction found here must be an unconditional branch instruction.

This processor core is also hard-coded to configure the upper 2MB memory region so that it is accessible without programming the external bus controller, to which Flash memory is usually attached. This forces the requirement to branch to a location within this address space because the processor is incapable of addressing memory anywhere else until our bootloader code initializes additional memory regions. We must branch to somewhere at or above 0xFFE0_0000. How did we know all this? Because we read the 405GP user's manual!

The behavior of the 405GP processor core, as described in the previous paragraph, places requirements on the hardware designer to ensure that, on power-up, nonvolatile memory (Flash) is mapped to the required upper 2MB memory region. Certain attributes of this initial memory region assume default values on reset. For example, this upper 2MB region will be configured for 256 wait states, three cycles of address-to-chip select delay, three cycles of chip select to output enable delay, and seven cycles of hold time.[3] This allows maximum freedom for the hardware designer to select appropriate devices or methods of getting instruction code to the processor directly after reset.

We've already seen how the reset vector is installed to the top of Flash in Listing 7-2. When configured for the 405GP, our first lines of code will be found in the file .../cpu/ppc4xx/start.s. The U-Boot developers intended this code to be *processor generic*. In theory, there should be no need for board-specific code in this file. You will see how this is accomplished.

We don't need to understand PowerPC assembly language in any depth to understand the logical flow in start.s. Many frequently asked questions (FAQs) have been posted to the U-Boot mailing list about modifying low-level assembly code. In nearly all cases, it is not necessary to modify this code if you are porting to one of the many supported processors. It is mature code, with many successful ports running on it. You need to modify the board-specific code (at a bare minimum) for your port. If you find yourself troubleshooting or modifying the early startup assembler code for a processor that has been around for a while, you are most likely heading down the wrong road.

Listing 7-6 reproduces a portion of start.s for the *4xx architecture*.

Listing 7-6

U-Boot 4xx startup code

```
...
#if defined(CONFIG_405GP) || defined(CONFIG_405CR) ||
 defined(CONFIG_405) || defined(CONFIG_405EP)
    /*-------------------------------- */
```

---

[3] This data was taken directly from the 405GP user's manual, referenced at the end of this chapter.

```
/* Clear and set up some registers. */
/*------------------------------ */
addi    r4,r0,0x0000
mtspr   sgr,r4
mtspr   dcwr,r4
mtesr   r4              /* clear Exception Syndrome Reg */
mttcr   r4              /* clear Timer Control Reg */
mtxer   r4              /* clear Fixed-Point Exception Reg */
mtevpr  r4            /* clear Exception Vector Prefix Reg */
addi    r4,r0,0x1000   /* set ME bit (Machine Exceptions) */
oris    r4,r4,0x0002            /* set CE bit (Critical Exceptions) */
mtmsr   r4                      /* change MSR */
addi    r4,r0,(0xFFFF-0x10000)  /* set r4 to 0xFFFFFFFF (status in the */
                        /* dbsr is cleared by setting bits to 1) */
mtdbsr  r4                      /* clear/reset the dbsr */


/*------------------------------ */
/* Invalidate I and D caches. Enable I cache for defined memory regions */
/* to speed things up. Leave the D cache disabled for now. It will be */
/* enabled/left disabled later based on user selected menu options. */
/* Be aware that the I cache may be disabled later based on the menu */
/* options as well. See miscLib/main.c. */
/*------------------------------ */
bl      invalidate_icache
bl      invalidate_dcache


/*------------------------------ */
/* Enable two 128MB cachable regions.    */
/*------------------------------     */
addis   r4,r0,0x8000
addi    r4,r4,0x0001
mticcr  r4                      /* instruction cache */
isync

addis   r4,r0,0x0000
addi    r4,r4,0x0000
mtdccr  r4                      /* data cache */
```

The first code to execute in start.s for the 405GP processor starts about a third of the way into the source file, where a handful of processor registers are cleared or set to sane initial values. The instruction and data caches are then invalidated, and the instruction cache is enabled to speed up the initial load. Two 128MB cacheable regions are set up, one at the high end of memory (the Flash region) and the other at the bottom (normally the start of system DRAM). U-Boot eventually is copied to RAM in this region and executed from there. The reason for this is performance: Raw reads from RAM are an order of magnitude (or more) faster than reads from Flash. However, for the *4xx* CPU, there is another subtle reason for enabling the instruction cache, as we shall soon discover.

7.4.4 Board-Specific Initialization

The first opportunity for any board-specific initialization comes in .../cpu/ppc4xx/start.S just after the cacheable regions have been initialized. Here we find a call to an external assembler language routine called ext_bus_cntlr_init.

```
bl ext_bus_cntlr_init   /* Board specific bus cntrl init */
```

This routine is defined in .../board/ep405/init.S, in the new board-specific directory for our board. It provides a hook for very early hardware-based initialization. This is one of the files that has been customized for our EP405 platform. This file contains the board-specific code to initialize the 405GP's external bus controller for our application. Listing 7-7 contains the meat of the functionality from this file. This is the code that initializes the 405GP's external bus controller.

Listing 7-7

External Bus Controller Initialization

```
    .globl  ext_bus_cntlr_init
ext_bus_cntlr_init:
    mflr    r4              /* save link register          */
    bl      ..getAddr
..getAddr:
    mflr    r3              /* get _this_ address          */
    mtlr    r4              /* restore link register       */
    addi    r4,0,14         /* prefetch 14 cache lines...  */
    mtctr   r4              /* ...to fit this function     */
                            /* cache (8x14=112 instr)      */
..ebcloop:
    icbt    r0,r3           /* prefetch cache line for [r3] */
    addi    r3,r3,32        /* move to next cache line     */
    bdnz    ..ebcloop       /* continue for 14 cache lines */

    /*------------------------------------------------ */
    /* Delay to ensure all accesses to ROM are complete */
    /* before changing  bank 0 timings              */
    /* 200usec should be enough.                    */
    /* 200,000,000 (cycles/sec) X .000200 (sec) =   */
```

```
    /* 0x9C40 cycles                                        */
    /*-------------------------------------------------- */

    addis    r3,0,0x0
    ori      r3,r3,0xA000 /* ensure 200usec have passed t */
    mtctr    r3

..spinlp:
    bdnz     ..spinlp      /* spin loop                    */

    /*--------------------------------------------------*/
    /* Now do the real work of this function            */
    /* Memory Bank 0 (Flash and SRAM) initialization    */
    /*--------------------------------------------------*/

    addi    r4,0,pb0ap            /* *ebccfga = pb0ap;    */
    mtdcr   ebccfga,r4
    addis   r4,0,EBC0_B0AP@h    /* *ebccfgd = EBC0_B0AP;  */
    ori     r4,r4,EBC0_B0AP@l
    mtdcr   ebccfgd,r4

    addi    r4,0,pb0cr            /* *ebccfga = pb0cr;    */
    mtdcr   ebccfga,r4
    addis   r4,0,EBC0_B0CR@h    /* *ebccfgd = EBC0_B0CR;  */
    ori     r4,r4,EBC0_B0CR@l
    mtdcr   ebccfgd,r4

    /*--------------------------------------------------*/
    /* Memory Bank 4 (NVRAM & BCSR) initialization      */
    /*--------------------------------------------------*/

    addi    r4,0,pb4ap            /* *ebccfga = pb4ap;    */
    mtdcr   ebccfga,r4
    addis   r4,0,EBC0_B4AP@h    /* *ebccfgd = EBC0_B4AP;  */
    ori     r4,r4,EBC0_B4AP@l
    mtdcr   ebccfgd,r4

    addi    r4,0,pb4cr            /* *ebccfga = pb4cr;    */
    mtdcr   ebccfga,r4
    addis   r4,0,EBC0_B4CR@h    /* *ebccfgd = EBC0_B4CR;  */
    ori     r4,r4,EBC0_B4CR@l
    mtdcr   ebccfgd,r4

    blr                          /* return               */
```

The example in Listing 7-7 was chosen because it is typical of the subtle complexities involved in low-level processor initialization. It is important to realize the context in which this code is running. It is executing from Flash, before any DRAM is available. There is no stack. This code is preparing to make fundamental changes to the controller that governs access to the very Flash it is executing from. It is well documented for this particular processor that executing code from Flash while modifying the external bus controller to which the Flash is attached can lead to errant reads and a resulting processor crash.

The solution is shown in this assembly language routine. Starting at the label `..getAddr`, and for the next seven assembly language instructions, the code essentially prefetches itself into the instruction cache, using the `icbt` instruction. When the entire subroutine has been successfully read into the instruction cache, it can proceed to make the required changes to the external bus controller without fear of a crash because it is executing directly from the internal instruction cache. Subtle, but clever! This is followed by a short delay to make sure all the requested i-cache reads have completed.

When the prefetch and delay have completed, the code proceeds to configure Memory Bank 0 and Memory Bank 4 appropriately for our board. The values come from a detailed knowledge of the underlying components and their interconnection on the board. The interested reader can consult the "Suggestions for Additional Reading" at the end of the chapter for all the details of PowerPC assembler and the 405GP processor from which this example was derived.

Consider making a change to this code without a complete understanding of what is happening here. Perhaps you added a few lines and increased its size beyond the range that was prefetched into the cache. It would likely crash (worse, it might crash only sometimes), but stepping through this code with a debugger would not yield a single clue as to why.

The next opportunity for board-specific initialization comes after a temporary stack has been allocated from the processor's data cache. This is the branch to initialize the SDRAM controller around line 727 of `.../cpu/ppc4xx/start.S`:

```
bl sdram_init
```

The execution context now includes a stack pointer and some temporary memory for local data storage—that is, a partial C context, allowing the developer to use C for the relatively complex task of setting up the system SDRAM controller and other initialization tasks. In our EP405 port, the `sdram_init()` code resides in `.../board/ep405/ep405.c` and was customized for this particular board and DRAM configuration. Because this board does not use a commercially available memory SIMM, it is not possible to determine the configuration of the DRAM dynamically, like so many other boards supported by U-Boot. It is hard-coded in `sdram_init`.

Many off-the-shelf memory DDR modules have a SPD (Serial Presence Detect) PROM containing parameters defining the memory module. These parameters can be read under program control via I2C and can be used as input to determine proper parameters for the memory controller. U-Boot has support for this technique but might need to be modified to work with your specific board. Many examples of its use can be found in the U-Boot source code. The configuration option `CONFIG_SPD_EEPROM` enables this feature. You can `grep` for this option to find examples of its use.

7.4.5 Porting Summary

By now, you can appreciate some of the difficulties of porting a bootloader to a hardware platform. There is simply no substitute for a detailed knowledge of the underlying hardware. Of course, we'd like to minimize our investment in time required for this task. After all, we usually are not paid based on how well we understand every hardware detail of a given processor, but rather on our ability to deliver a working solution in a timely manner. Indeed, this is one of the primary reasons open source has flourished. We just saw how easy it was to port U-Boot to a new hardware platform—not because we're world-class experts on the processor, but because many before us have done the bulk of the hard work already.

Listing 7-8 is the complete list of new or modified files that complete the basic EP405 port for U-Boot. Of course, if there had been new hardware devices for which no support exists in U-Boot, or if we were porting to a new CPU that is not yet supported in U-Boot, this would have been a much more significant effort. The point to be made here, at the risk of sounding redundant, is that there is simply no substitute for a detailed knowledge of both the hardware (CPU and subsystems) and the underlying software (U-Boot) to complete a port successfully in a reasonable time frame. If you start the project from that frame of mind, you will have a successful outcome.

Listing 7-8

New or Changed Files for U-Boot EP405 Port

```
$ diff -purN u-boot u-boot-ep405/ | grep +++
+++ u-boot-ep405/board/ep405/config.mk
+++ u-boot-ep405/board/ep405/ep405.c
+++ u-boot-ep405/board/ep405/ep405.h
+++ u-boot-ep405/board/ep405/flash.c
+++ u-boot-ep405/board/ep405/init.S
+++ u-boot-ep405/board/ep405/Makefile
+++ u-boot-ep405/board/ep405/u-boot.lds
+++ u-boot-ep405/include/config.h
+++ u-boot-ep405/include/config.mk
+++ u-boot-ep405/include/configs/EP405.h
+++ u-boot-ep405/include/ppc405.h
+++ u-boot-ep405/Makefile
```

Recall that we derived all the files in the . . ./board/ep405 directory from another directory. Indeed, we didn't create any files from scratch for this port. We borrowed from the work of others and customized where necessary to achieve our goals.

7.4.6 U-Boot Image Format

Now that we have a working bootloader for our EP405 board, we can load and run programs on it. Ideally, we want to run an operating system such as Linux. To do this, we need to understand the image format that U-Boot requires. U-Boot expects a small header on the image file that identifies several attributes of the image. U-Boot uses the mkimage tool (part of the U-Boot source code) to build this image header.

Recent Linux kernel distributions have built-in support for building images directly bootable by U-Boot. Both the ARM and PPC branches of the kernel source tree have support for a target called uImage. Let's look at the PPC case. The following snippet from the Linux kernel PPC makefile .../arch/ppc/boot/images/Makefile contains the rule for building the U-Boot target called uImage:

```
quiet_cmd_uimage = UIMAGE  $@
      cmd_uimage = $(CONFIG_SHELL) $(MKIMAGE) -A ppc \
    -O linux -T kernel -C gzip -a 00000000 -e 00000000 \
    -n 'Linux-$(KERNELRELEASE)' -d $< $@
```

Ignoring the syntactical complexity, understand that this rule calls a shell script identified by the variable $(MKIMAGE). The shell script executes the U-Boot mkimage utility with the parameters shown. The mkimage utility creates the U-Boot header and prepends it to the supplied kernel image. The parameters are defined as follows:

-A   Specifies the target image architecture

-O   Species the target image OS—in this case, Linux

-T   Specifies the target image type—a kernel, in this case

-C   Specifies the target image compression type—here, gzip

-a   Sets the U-Boot *loadaddress* to the value specified—in this case, 0

-e   Sets the U-Boot image entry point to the supplied value

-n   A text field used to identify the image to the human user

-d   The executable image file to which the header is prepended

Several U-Boot commands use this header data both to verify the integrity of the image (U-Boot also puts a CRC signature in the header) and to instruct various commands what to do with the image. U-Boot has a command called iminfo that reads the image header and displays the image attributes from the target image. Listing 7-9 contains the results of loading a uImage (bootable Linux kernel image formatted for U-Boot) to the EP405 board via U-Boot's tftpboot command and executing the iminfo command on the image.

Listing 7-9

U-Boot iminfo Command

```
=> tftpboot 400000 uImage-ep405
ENET Speed is 100 Mbps - FULL duplex connection
TFTP from server 192.168.1.9; our IP address is 192.168.1.33
Filename 'uImage-ep405'.
Load address: 0x400000
Loading: ##########  done
Bytes transferred = 891228 (d995c hex)
=> iminfo

## Checking Image at 00400000 ...
   Image Name:    Linux-2.6.11.6
   Image Type:    PowerPC Linux Kernel Image (gzip compressed)
   Data Size:     891164 Bytes = 870.3 kB
   Load Address:  00000000
   Entry Point:   00000000
   Verifying Checksum ... OK
=>
```

7.5 Other Bootloaders

Here we introduce the more popular bootloaders, describe where they might be used, and give a summary of their features. This is not intended to be a thorough tutorial because to do so would require a book of its own. The interested reader can consult the "Suggestions for Additional Reading" at the end of this chapter for further study.

7.5.1 Lilo

The Linux Loader, or Lilo, was widely used in commercial Linux distributions for desktop PC platforms; as such, it has its roots in the Intel x86/IA32 architecture. Lilo has several components. It has a primary bootstrap program that lives on the first sector of a bootable disk drive.[4] The primary loader is limited to a disk sector size, usually 512 bytes. Therefore, its primary purpose is simply to load and pass control to a secondary loader. The secondary loader can span multiple partitions and does most of the work of the bootloader.

Lilo is driven by a configuration file and utility that is part of the `lilo` executable. This configuration file can be read or written to only under control of the host operating system. That is, the configuration file is not referenced by the early boot code in either the primary or secondary loaders. Entries in the configuration file are read and processed by the `lilo` configuration utility during system installation or administration. Listing 7-10 is an example of a simple `lilo.conf` configuration file describing a typical dual-boot Linux and Windows installation.

Listing 7-10

Example Lilo Configuration: `lilo.conf`

```
# This is the global lilo configuration section
# These settings apply to all the "image" sections

boot = /dev/hda
timeout=50
default=linux
```

---

[4] This is mostly for historical reasons. From the early days of PCs, BIOS programs loaded only the first sector of a disk drive and passed control to it.

```
# This  describes the primary kernel boot image
# Lilo will display it with the label 'linux'
image=/boot/myLinux-2.6.11.1
        label=linux
        initrd=/boot/myInitrd-2.6.11.1.img
        read-only
        append="root=LABEL=/"

# This is the second OS in a dual-boot configuration
# This entry will boot a secondary image from /dev/hda1
other=/dev/hda1
        optional
        label=that_other_os
```

This configuration file instructs the Lilo configuration utility to use the master boot record of the first hard drive (/dev/hda). It contains a delay instruction to wait for the user to press a key before the timeout (5 seconds, in this case). This gives the system operator the choice to select from a list of OS images to boot. If the system operator presses the Tab key before the timeout, Lilo presents a list to choose from. Lilo uses the label tag as the text to display for each image.

The images are defined with the image tag in the configuration file. In the example presented in Listing 7-10, the primary (default) image is a Linux kernel image with a file name of myLinux-2.6.11.1. Lilo loads this image from the hard drive. It then loads a second file to be used as an initial ramdisk. This is the file myInitrd-2.6.11.1.img. Lilo constructs a kernel command line containing the string "root=LABEL=/" and passes this to the Linux kernel upon execution. This instructs Linux where to get its root file system after boot.

7.5.2 GRUB

Many current commercial Linux distributions now ship with the GRUB bootloader. GRUB, or GRand Unified Bootloader, is a GNU project. It has many enhanced features not found in Lilo. The biggest difference between GRUB and Lilo is GRUB's capability to understand file systems and kernel image formats. Furthermore, GRUB can read and modify its configuration at boot time. GRUB also supports booting across a network, which can be a tremendous asset in an embedded environment. GRUB offers a command line interface at boot time to modify the boot configuration.

Like Lilo, GRUB is driven by a configuration file. Unlike Lilo's static configuration however, the GRUB bootloader reads this configuration at boot time. This means that the configured behavior can be modified at boot time for different system configurations.

Listing 7-11 is an example GRUB configuration file. This is the configuration file from the PC on which this manuscript is being written. The GRUB configuration file is called `grub.conf` and is usually placed in a small partition dedicated to storing boot images. On the machine from which this example is taken, that directory is called `/boot`.

Listing 7-11

Example GRUB Configuration File: `grub.conf`

```
default=0
timeout=3
splashimage=(hd0,1)/grub/splash.xpm.gz

title Fedora Core 2 (2.6.9)
        root (hd0,1)
        kernel /bzImage-2.6.9 ro root=LABEL=/ rhgb proto=imps quiet
        initrd /initrd-2.6.9.img

title Fedora Core (2.6.5-1.358)
        root (hd0,1)
        kernel /vmlinuz-2.6.5-1.358 ro root=LABEL=/ rhgb quiet

title That Other OS
        rootnoverify (hd0,0)
        chainloader +1
```

GRUB first presents the user with a list of images that are available to boot. The `title` entries from Listing 7-11 are the image names presented to the user. The `default` tag specifies which image to boot if no keys have been pressed in the timeout period, which is 3 seconds in this example. Images are counted starting from zero.

Unlike Lilo, GRUB can actually read a file system on a given partition to load an image from. The `root` tag specifies the root partition from which all filenames in the `grub.conf` configuration file are rooted. In this example configuration, the root is partition number 1 on the first hard disk drive, specified as `root(hd0,1)`. Partitions are numbered from zero; this is the second partition on the first hard disk.

The images are specified as filenames relative to the specified root. In Listing 7-11, the default boot image is a Linux 2.6.9 kernel with a matching initial ramdisk image called `initrd-2.6.9.img`. Notice that the GRUB syntax has the kernel command line parameters on the same line as the kernel file specification.

7.5.3 Still More Bootloaders

Numerous other bootloaders have found their way into specific niches. For example, Redboot is another open-source bootloader that Intel and the XScale community have adopted for use on various evaluation boards based on the Intel IXP and PXA processor families. Micromonitor is in use by board vendors such as Cogent and others. YAMON has found popularity in MIPs circles.[5] LinuxBIOS is used primarily in X86 environments. In general, when you consider a boot loader, you should consider some important factors up front:

- Does it support my chosen processor?

- Has it been ported to a board similar to my own?

- Does it support the features I need?

- Does it support the hardware devices I intend to use?

- Is there a large community of users where I might get support?

- Are there any commercial vendors from which I can purchase support?

These are some of the questions you must answer when considering what bootloader to use in your embedded project. Unless you are doing something on the "bleeding edge" of technology using a brand-new processor, you are likely to find that someone has already done the bulk of the hard work in porting a bootloader to your chosen platform. Use the resources at the end of this chapter to help make your final decisions.

7.6 Chapter Summary

- The bootloader's role in an embedded system cannot be overstated. It is the first piece of software that takes control upon applying power.

---

[5] In an acknowledgment of the number of bootloaders in existence, the YAMON user's guide bills itself as Yet Another MONitor.

- This chapter examined the role of the bootloader and discovered the limited execution context in which a bootloader must exist.

- Das U-Boot has become a popular universal bootloader for many processor architectures. It supports a large number of processors, reference hardware platforms, and custom boards.

- U-Boot is configured using a series of configuration variables in a board-specific header file. Appendix B contains a list of all the standard U-Boot command sets supported in a recent U-Boot release.

- Porting U-Boot to a new board based on a supported processor is relatively straightforward. In this chapter, we walked through the steps of a typical port to a board with similar support in U-Boot.

- There is no substitute for detailed knowledge of your processor and hardware platform when bootloader modification or porting must be accomplished.

- We briefly introduced additional bootloaders in use today so you can make an informed choice for your particular requirements.

7.6.1 Suggestions for Additional Reading

Application Note: Introduction to Synchronous DRAM
Maxwell Technologies
www.maxwell.com/pdf/me/app_notes/Intro_to_SDRAM.pdf

Using LD, the GNU linker
Free Software Foundation
www.gnu.org/software/binutils/manual/ld-2.9.1/ld.html

The DENX U-Boot and Linux Guide (DLUG) for TQM8xxL
Wolfgang Denx et al., Denx Software Engineering
www.denx.de/twiki/bin/view/DULG/Manual

RFC 793, "Trivial File Transfer Protocol"
The Internet Engineering Task Force
www.ietf.org/rfc/rfc783.txt

RFC 951, "Bootstrap Protocol"
The Internet Engineering Task Force
www.ietf.org/rfc/rfc951.txt

RFC 1531, "Dynamic Host Control Protocol"
The Internet Engineering Task Force
www.ietf.org/rfc/rfc1531.txt

PowerPC 405GP Embedded Processor user's manual
International Business Machines, Inc.

Programming Environments Manual for 32-bit Implementations
of the PowerPC Architecture
Freescale Semiconductor, Inc.

Lilo Bootloader
www.tldp.org/HOWTO/LILO.html

GRUB Bootloader
www.gnu.org/software/grub/

Chapter 8

Device Driver Basics

In this chapter

application ⟷ device driver

Oﾠne of the more challenging aspects of system design is partitioning functionality in a rational manner. The familiar device driver model found in UNIX and Linux provides a natural partitioning of functionality between your application code and hardware or kernel devices. In this chapter, we develop an understanding of this model and the basics of Linux device driver architecture. After reading this chapter, you will have a solid foundation for continuing your study of device drivers using one of the excellent texts listed at the end of this chapter.

This chapter begins by presenting Linux device driver concepts and the build system for drivers within the kernel source tree. We examine the Linux device driver architecture and present a simple working example driver. We introduce the user space utilities for loading and unloading kernel modules.[1] We present a simple application to illustrate the interface between applications and device drivers. We conclude this chapter with a discussion of device drivers and the GNU Public License.

8.1 Device Driver Concepts

Many experienced embedded developers struggle at first with the concepts of device drivers in a virtual memory operating system. This is because many popular legacy real-time operating systems do not have a similar architecture. The introduction of virtual memory and kernel space versus user space frequently introduces complexity that is not familiar to experienced embedded developers.

One of the fundamental purposes of a device driver is to isolate the user's programs from ready access to critical kernel data structures and hardware devices. Furthermore, a well-written device driver hides the complexity and variability of the hardware device from the user. For example, a program that wants to write data to the hard disk need not care if the disk drive uses 512-byte or 1024-byte sectors. The user simply opens a file and issues a write command. The device driver handles the details and isolates the user from the complexities and perils of hardware device programming. The device driver provides a consistent user interface to a large variety of hardware devices. It provides the basis for the familiar UNIX/Linux convention that everything must be represented as a file.

---

[1] The terms *module* and *device driver* are used here interchangeably.

8.1.1 Loadable Modules

Unlike some other operating systems, Linux has the capability to add and remove kernel components at runtime. Linux is structured as a monolithic kernel with a well-defined interface for adding and removing device driver modules dynamically after boot time. This feature not only adds flexibility to the user, but it has proven invaluable to the device driver development effort. Assuming that your device driver is reasonably well behaved, you can insert and remove the device driver from a running kernel at will during the development cycle instead of rebooting the kernel every time a change occurs.

Loadable modules have particular importance to embedded systems. Loadable modules enhance field upgrade capabilities; the module itself can be updated in a live system without the need for a reboot. Modules can be stored on media other than the root (boot) device, which can be space constrained.

Of course, device drivers can also be statically compiled into the kernel, and, for many drivers, this is completely appropriate. Consider, for example, a kernel configured to mount a root file system from a network-attached NFS server. In this scenario, you configure the network-related drivers (TCP/IP and the network interface card driver) to be compiled into the main kernel image so they are available during boot for mounting the remote root file system. You can use the initial ramdisk functionality as described in Chapter 6, "System Initialization," as an alternative to having these drivers compiled statically as part of the kernel proper. In this case, the necessary modules and a script to load them would be included in the initial ramdisk image.

Loadable modules are installed after the kernel has booted. Startup scripts can load device driver modules, and modules can also be "demand loaded" when needed. The kernel has the capability to request a module when a service is requested that requires a particular module.

Terminology has never been standardized when discussing kernel modules. Many terms have been and continue to be used interchangeably when discussing loadable kernel modules. Throughout this and later chapters, the terms *device driver, loadable kernel module (LKM), loadable module,* and *module* are all used to describe a loadable kernel device driver module.

8.1.2 Device Driver Architecture

The basic Linux device driver model is familiar to UNIX/Linux system developers. Although the device driver model continues to evolve, some fundamental constructs have remained nearly constant over the course of UNIX/Linux evolution. Device drivers are broadly classified into two basic categories: *character devices* and *block devices*. Character devices can be thought of as serial streams of sequential data. Examples of character devices include serial ports and keyboards. Block devices are characterized by the capability to read and write blocks of data to and from random locations on an addressable medium. Examples of block devices include hard drives and floppy disk drives.

8.1.3 Minimal Device Driver Example

Because Linux supports loadable device drivers, it is relatively easy to demonstrate a simple device driver skeleton. Listing 8-1 illustrates a loadable device driver module that contains the bare minimum structure to be loaded and unloaded by a running kernel.

Listing 8-1

Minimal Device Driver

```
/* Example Minimal Character Device Driver */
#include <linux/module.h>

static int __init hello_init(void)
{
    printk("Hello Example Init\n");

    return 0;
}

static void __exit hello_exit(void)
{
    printk("Hello Example Exit\n");
}

module_init(hello_init);
module_exit(hello_exit);

MODULE_AUTHOR("Chris Hallinan");
MODULE_DESCRIPTION("Hello World Example");
MODULE_LICENSE("GPL");
```

The skeletal driver in Listing 8-1 contains enough structure for the kernel to load and unload the driver, and to invoke the initialization and exit routines. Let's look at how this is done because it illustrates some important high-level concepts that are useful for device driver development.

A device driver is a special kind of binary module. Unlike a stand-alone binary executable application, a device driver cannot be simply executed from a command prompt. The 2.6 kernel series requires that the binary be in a special "kernel object" format. When properly built, the device driver binary module contains a `.ko` suffix. The build steps and compiler options required to create the `.ko` module object can be quite complex. Here we outline a set of steps to harness the power of the Linux kernel build system without requiring you to become an expert in it, which is beyond the scope of this book.

8.1.4 Module Build Infrastructure

A device driver must be compiled against the kernel on which it will execute. Although it is possible to load and execute kernel modules built against a different kernel version, it is risky to do so unless you are certain that the module does not rely on any features of your new kernel. The easiest way to do this is to build the module within the kernel's own source tree. This ensures that as the developer changes the kernel configuration, his custom driver is automatically rebuilt with the correct kernel configuration. It is certainly possible to build your drivers outside of the kernel source tree. However, in this case, you are responsible for making sure that your device driver build configuration stays in sync with the kernel you want to run your driver on. This typically includes compiler switches, location of kernel header files, and kernel configuration options.

For the example driver introduced in Listing 8-1, the following changes were made to the stock Linux kernel source tree to enable building this example driver. We explain each step in detail.

1. Starting from the top-level Linux source directory, create a directory under `.../drivers/char` called `examples`.

2. Add a menu item to the kernel configuration to enable building `examples` and to specify built-in or loadable kernel module.

3. Add the new `examples` subdirectory to the `.../drivers/char/Makefile` conditional on the menu item created in step 2.

4. Create a makefile for the new `examples` directory, and add the
    `hello1.o` module object to be compiled conditional on the menu
    item created in step 2.

5. Finally, create the driver `hello1.c` source file from Listing 8.1.

Adding the `examples` directory under the `.../drivers/char` subdirectory is
self-explanatory. After this directory is created, two files are created in this directory:
the module source file itself from Listing 8-1 and the makefile for the `examples`
directory. The makefile for `examples` is quite trivial. It will contain this single line:

```
obj-$(CONFIG_EXAMPLES) += hello1.o
```

Adding the menu item to the kernel configuration utility is a little more
involved. Listing 8-2 contains a patch that, when applied to the
`.../drivers/char/Kconfig` file from a recent Linux release, adds the configuration menu item to enable our `examples` configuration option. For those readers
not familiar with the `diff`/`patch` format, each line in Listing 8-1 preceded by a
single plus (+) character is inserted in the file between the indicated lines (those
without the leading + character).

Listing 8-2

Kconfig Patch for Examples

```
diff -u ~/base/linux-2.6.14/drivers/char/Kconfig
./drivers/char/Kconfig
--- ~/base/linux-2.6.14/drivers/char/Kconfig
+++ ./drivers/char/Kconfig
@@ -4,6 +4,12 @@

 menu "Character devices"

+config EXAMPLES
+        tristate "Enable Examples"
+        default M
+        ---help---
+        Enable compilation option for driver examples
+
 config VT
        bool "Virtual terminal" if EMBEDDED
        select INPUT
```

When applied to `Kconfig` in the `.../drivers/char` subdirectory of a recent
Linux kernel, this patch results in a new kernel configuration option called

CONFIG_EXAMPLES. As a reminder from our discussion on building the Linux kernel in Chapter 4, "The Linux Kernel—A Different Perspective," the configuration utility is invoked as follows (this example assumes the ARM architecture):

```
$ make ARCH=ARM CROSS_COMPILE=xscale_be- gconfig
```

After the configuration utility is invoked using a command similar to the previous one, our new Enable Examples configuration option appears under the Character devices menu, as indicated in the patch. Because it is defined as type tristate, the kernel developer can choose from three choices:

(N)   No. Do not compile examples.

"√" (Y)   Yes. Compile examples and link with final kernel image.

"_" (M)   Module. Compile examples as dynamically loadable module.

Figure 8-1 shows the resulting gconfig screen with the new configuration option added. The dash (–) in the check box selects (M)odule, as indicated in the M column on the right. A check mark in the check box selects (Y)es, indicating that the driver module should be compiled as part of the kernel proper. An empty check box indicates that the option is not selected.

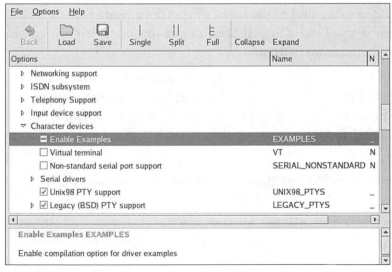

FIGURE 8-1
Kernel configuration with Examples module

Now that we have added the configuration option to enable compiling our `examples` device driver module, we need to modify the makefile in `.../drivers/char` to instruct the build system to descend into our new `examples` subdirectory if the configuration option `CONFIG_EXAMPLES` is present in our configuration. Listing 8-3 contains the patch for this against the makefile in a recent Linux release.

Listing 8-3

Makefile Patch for `Examples`

```
diff -u ~/base/linux-2.6.14/drivers/char/Makefile
./drivers/char/Makefile
--- ~/base/linux-2.6.14/drivers/char/Makefile
+++ ./drivers/char/Makefile
@@ -88,6 +88,7 @@
 obj-$(CONFIG_DRM) += drm/
 obj-$(CONFIG_PCMCIA) += pcmcia/
 obj-$(CONFIG_IPMI_HANDLER) += ipmi/
+obj-$(CONFIG_EXAMPLES) += examples/

 obj-$(CONFIG_HANGCHECK_TIMER) += hangcheck-timer.o
```

The patch in Listing 8-3 adds the single line (preceded by the + character) to the makefile found in `.../drivers/char`. The additional lines of context are there so that the patch utility can determine where to insert the new line. Our new `examples` directory was added to the end of the list of directories already being searched in this makefile, which seemed like a logical place to put it. Other than for consistency and readability, the location is irrelevant.

Having completed the steps in this section, the infrastructure is now in place to build the example device driver. The beauty of this approach is that the driver is built automatically whenever a kernel build is invoked. As long as the configuration option defined in Listing 8-3 is selected (either M or Y), the driver module is included in the build.

Building for an arbitrary ARM system, the command line for building modules might look like this:

```
$ make ARCH=arm CROSS_COMPILE=xscale_be- modules
```

Listing 8-4 shows the build output after a typical editing session on the module (all other modules have already been built in this kernel source tree.)

Listing 8-4

Module Build Output

```
$ make ARCH=arm CROSS_COMPILE=xscale_be- modules
  CHK      include/linux/version.h
make[1]: 'arch/arm/kernel/asm-offsets.s' is up to date.
make[1]: 'include/asm-arm/mach-types.h' is up to date.
  CC [M]  drivers/char/examples/hello1.o
  Building modules, stage 2.
  MODPOST
  LD [M]  drivers/char/examples/hello1.ko
```

8.1.5 Installing Your Device Driver

Now that this driver is built, we can load and unload it on a running kernel to observe its behavior. Before we can load the module, we need to copy it to an appropriate location on our target system. Although we could put it anywhere we want, a convention is in place for kernel modules and where they are populated on a running Linux system. As with module compilation, it is easiest to let the kernel build system do that for us. The makefile target `modules_install` automatically places modules in the system in a logical layout. You simply need to supply the desired location as a prefix to the default path.

In a standard Linux workstation installation, you might already know that the device driver modules live in `/lib/modules/<kernel-version>/...` ordered in a manner similar to the device driver directory hierarchy in the Linux kernel tree.[2] The `<kernel-version>` string is produced by executing the command `uname -r` on your target Linux system. If you do not provide an installation prefix to the kernel build system, by default, your modules are installed in your own workstation's `/lib/modules/...` directory. This is probably not what you had intended. You can point to a temporary location in your home directory and manually copy the modules to your target's file system. Alternatively, if your target embedded system uses NFS root mount to a directory on your local development

---

[2] This path is used by Red Hat and Fedora distributions, and is also required by the File System Hierarchy Standard referenced at the end of this chapter. Other distributions might use different locations in the file system for kernel modules.

workstation, you can install the modules directly to the target file system. The following example assumes the latter.

```
$ make ARCH=arm CROSS_COMPILE=xscale_be-              \
    INSTALL_MOD_PATH=/home/chris/sandbox/coyote-target  \
    modules_install
```

This places all your modules in the directory `coyote-target`, which on this example system is exported via NFS and mounted as root on the target system.[3]

8.1.6 Loading Your Module

Having completed all the steps necessary, we are now in a position to load and test the device driver module. Listing 8-5 shows the output resulting from loading and subsequently unloading the device driver on the embedded system.

Listing 8-5

Loading and Unloading a Module

```
$ modprobe hello1              <<< Load the driver
Hello Example Init
$ modprobe -r hello1           <<< Unload the driver
Hello Example Exit
$
```

You should be able to correlate the output with our device driver source code found in Listing 8-1. The module does no work other than printing messages to the kernel log system via `printk()`, which we see on our console.[4] When the module is loaded, the module-initialization function is called. We specify the initialization function that will be executed on module insertion using the `module_init()` macro. We declared it as follows:

```
module_init(hello_init);
```

In our initialization function, we simply print the obligatory hello message and return. In a real device driver, this is where you would perform any initial resource allocation and hardware device initialization. In a similar fashion, when we unload the module (using the `modprobe -r` command), our module exit routine is called.

---

[3] Hosting a target board and NFS root mount are covered in detail in Chapter 12, "Embedded Development Environment".

[4] If you don't see the messages on the console, either disable your syslogd logger or lower the console loglevel. We describe how to do this in Chapter 14, "Kernel Debugging Techniques".

As shown in Listing 8-1, the exit routine is specified using the `module_exit()` macro.

That's all there is to a skeletal device driver capable of live insertion in an actual kernel. In the sections to follow, we introduce additional functionality to our loadable device driver module that illustrates how a user space program would interact with a device driver module.

8.2 Module Utilities

We had a brief introduction to module utilities in Listing 8-5. There we used the module utility modprobe to insert and remove a device driver module from a Linux kernel. A number of small utilities are used to manage device driver modules. This section introduces them. You are encouraged to refer to the man page for each utility, for complete details. In fact, those interested in a greater knowledge of Linux loadable modules should consult the source code for these utilities. Section 8.6.1, "Suggestions for Additional Reading" at the end of this chapter contains a reference for where they can be found.

8.2.1 insmod

The insmod utility is the simplest way to insert a module into a running kernel. You supply a complete pathname, and insmod does the work. For example:

```
$ insmod /lib/modules/2.6.14/kernel/drivers/char/examples/hello1.ko
```

This loads the module `hello1.ko` into the kernel. The output would be the same as shown in Listing 8-5—namely, the `Hello` message. The insmod utility is a simple program that does not require or accept any options. It requires a full pathname because it has no logic for searching for the module. Most often, you will use modprobe, described shortly, because it has many more features and capabilities.

8.2.2 Module Parameters

Many device driver modules can accept parameters to modify their behavior. Examples include enabling debug mode, setting verbose reporting, or specifying module-specific options. The insmod utility accepts parameters (also called *options* in some contexts) by specifying them after the module name. Listing 8-6 shows our modified `hello1.c` example, adding a single module parameter to enable debug mode.

Listing 8-6

Example Driver with Parameter

```
/* Example Minimal Character Device Driver */
#include <linux/module.h>

static int debug_enable = 0;          /* Added driver parameter */
module_param(debug_enable, int, 0);   /* and these 2 lines */
MODULE_PARM_DESC(debug_enable, "Enable module debug mode.");

static int __init hello_init(void)
{
    /* Now print value of new module parameter */
    printk("Hello Example Init - debug mode is %s\n",
            debug_enable ? "enabled" : "disabled")

    return 0;
}

static void __exit hello_exit(void)
{
    printk("Hello Example Exit\n");
}

module_init(hello_init);
module_exit(hello_exit);

MODULE_AUTHOR("Chris Hallinan");
MODULE_DESCRIPTION("Hello World Example");
MODULE_LICENSE("GPL");
```

added (marginal note pointing to the three static/module_param/MODULE_PARM_DESC lines)

modified (marginal note pointing to the printk line)

Three lines have been added to our example device driver module. The first declares a static integer to hold our debug flag. The second line is a macro defined in `.../include/linux/moduleparam.h` that registers the module parameter with the kernel module subsystem. The third new line is a macro that registers a string description associated with the parameter with the kernel module subsystem. The purpose of this will become clear when we examine the `modinfo` command later in this chapter.

If we now use insmod to insert our example module, and add the debug_enable option, we should see the resulting output, based on our modified hello1.c module in Listing 8-6.

```
$ insmod /lib/modules/.../examples/hello1.ko debug_enable=1
  Hello Example Init - debug mode is enabled
```

Or, if we omit the optional module parameter:

```
$ insmod /lib/modules/.../examples/hello1.ko
  Hello Example Init - debug mode is disabled
```

8.2.3 lsmod

The lsmod utility is also quite trivial. It simply displays a formatted list of the modules that are inserted into the kernel. Recent versions take no parameters and simply format the output of /proc/modules.[5] Listing 8-7 is an example of the output from lsmod.

Listing 8-7

lsmod Example Output Format

```
$ lsmod
Module                  Size  Used by
ext3                  121096  0
jbd                    49656  1 ext3
loop                   12712  0
hello1                  1412  0
$
```

Notice the rightmost column labeled Used by. This column indicates that the device driver module is in use and shows the dependency chain. In this example, the jbd module (journaling routines for journaling file systems) is being used by the ext3 module, the default journaling file system for many popular Linux desktop distributions. This means that the ext3 device driver depends on the presence of jbd.

8.2.4 modprobe

This is where the cleverness of modprobe comes into play. In Listing 8-7, we see the relationship between the ext3 and jbd modules. The ext3 module depends on the

---

[5] /proc/modules is part of the proc file system, which is introduced in Chapter 9, "File Systems".

jbd module. The modprobe utility can discover this relationship and load the dependent modules in the proper order. The following command loads both the jbd.ko and ext3.ko driver modules:

```
$ modprobe ext3
```

The modprobe utility has several command line options that control its behavior. As we saw earlier, modprobe can be used to remove modules, including the modules upon which a given module depends. Here is an example of module removal that removes both jbd.ko and ext3.ko:

```
$ modprobe -r ext3
```

The modprobe utility is driven by a configuration file called modprobe.conf. This enables a system developer to associate devices with device drivers. For a simple embedded system, modprobe.conf might be empty or might contain very few lines. The modprobe utility is compiled with a set of default rules that establish the defaults in the absence of a valid modprobe.conf. Invoking modprobe with only the -c option displays the set of default rules used by modprobe.

Listing 8-8 represents a typical modprobe.conf, which might be found on a system containing two Ethernet interfaces; one is a wireless adapter based on the Prism2 chipset, and the other is a typical PCI Ethernet card. This system also contains a sound subsystem based on an integrated Intel sound chipset.

Listing 8-8

Typical `modprobe.conf` File

```
$ cat /etc/modprobe.conf
alias eth1 orinoci_pci
options eth1 orinoco_debug=9
alias eth0 e100
alias snd-card-0 snd-intel8x0
options snd-card-0 index=0
$
```

When the kernel boots and discovers the wireless chipset, this configuration file instructs modprobe to load the orinoco_pci device driver, bound to kernel device eth1, and pass the optional module parameter orinoco_debug=9 to the device driver. The same action is taken upon discovery of the sound card hardware. Notice the optional parameters associated with the sound driver snd-intel8x0.

8.2.5 depmod

How does modprobe know about the dependencies of a given module? The depmod utility plays a key role in this process. When modprobe is executed, it searches for a file called `modules.dep` in the same location where the modules are installed. The depmod utility creates this module-dependency file.

This file contains a list of all the modules that the kernel build system is configured for, along with dependency information for each. It is a simple file format: Each device driver module occupies one line in the file. If the module has dependencies, they are listed in order following the module name. For example, from Listing 8-7, we saw that the `ext3` module had a dependency on the `jbd` module. The dependency line in `modules.dep` would look like this:

```
ext3.ko: jbd.ko
```

In actual practice, each module name is preceded by its absolute path in the file system, to avoid ambiguity. We have omitted the path information for readability. A more complicated dependency chain, such as sound drivers, might look like this:

```
snd-intel8x0.ko: snd-ac97-codec.ko snd-pcm.ko snd-timer.ko \
    snd.ko soundcore.ko snd-page-alloc.ko
```

Again, we have removed the leading path components for readability. Each module filename in the `modules.dep` file is an absolute filename, with complete path information, and exists on a single line. The previous example has been truncated to two lines, to fit in the space on this page.

Normally, depmod is run automatically during a kernel build. However, in a cross-development environment, you must have a cross-version of depmod that knows how to read the modules that are compiled in the native format of your target architecture. Alternatively, most embedded distributions have a method and `init` script entries to run depmod on each boot, to guarantee that the module dependencies are kept up-to-date.

8.2.6 rmmod

This utility is also quite trivial. It simply removes a module from a running kernel. Pass it the module name as a parameter. There is no need to include a pathname or file extension. For example:

```
$ rmmod hello1
   Hello Example Exit
```

The only interesting point to understand here is that when you use rmmod, it executes the module's *_exit() function, as shown in the previous example, from our hello1.c example of Listings 8-1 and 8-6.

It should be noted that, unlike modprobe, rmmod does not remove dependent modules. Use modprobe -r for this.

8.2.7 modinfo

You might have noticed the last three lines of the skeletal driver in Listing 8-1, and later in Listing 8-6. These macros are there to place tags in the binary module to facilitate their administration and management. Listing 8-9 is the result of modinfo executed on our hello1.ko module.

Listing 8-9

modinfo Output

```
$ modinfo hello1
filename:        /lib/modules/.../char/examples/hello1.ko
author:          Chris Hallinan
description:     Hello World Example
license:         GPL
vermagic:        2.6.14 ARMv5 gcc-3.3
depends:
parm:            debug_enable:Enable module debug mode. (int)
$
```

The first field is obvious: It is the full filename of the device driver module. For readability in this listing, we have truncated the path again. The next lines are a direct result of the descriptive macros found at the end of Listing 8-6—namely, the filename, author, and license information. These are simply tags for use by the module utilities and do not affect the behavior of the device driver itself. You can learn more about modinfo from its man page and the modinfo source itself.

One very useful feature of modinfo is to learn what parameters the module supports. From Listing 8-9, you can see that this module supports just one parameter. This was the one we added in Listing 8-6, debug_enable. The listing gives the name, type (in this case, an int), and descriptive text field we entered with the MODULE_PARM_DESC() macro. This can be very handy, especially for modules in which you might not have easy access to the source code.

8.3 Driver Methods

We've covered much ground in our short treatment of module utilities. In the remaining sections of this chapter, we describe the basic mechanism for communicating with a device driver from a user space program (your application code).

   We have introduced the two fundamental methods responsible for one-time initialization and exit processing of the module. Recall from Listing 8-1 that these are `module_init()` and `module_exit()`. We discovered that these routines are invoked at the time the module is inserted into or removed from a running kernel. Now we need some methods to interface with our device driver from our application program. After all, two of the more important reasons we use device drivers are to isolate the user from the perils of writing code in kernel space and to present a unified method to communicate with hardware or kernel-level devices.

8.3.1 Driver File System Operations

After the device driver is loaded into a live kernel, the first action we must take is to prepare the driver for subsequent operations. The `open()` method is used for this purpose. After the driver has been opened, we need routines for reading and writing to the driver. A `release()` routine is provided to clean up after operations when complete (basically, a close call). Finally, a special system call is provided for nonstandard communication to the driver. This is called `ioctl()`. Listing 8-10 adds this infrastructure to our example device driver.

Listing 8-10

Adding File System Ops to `Hello.c`

```
#include <linux/module.h>
#include <linux/fs.h>

#define HELLO_MAJOR 234

static int debug_enable = 0;
module_param(debug_enable, int, 0);
MODULE_PARM_DESC(debug_enable, "Enable module debug mode.");

struct file_operations hello_fops;

static int hello_open(struct inode *inode, struct file *file)
{
    printk("hello_open: successful\n");
    return 0;
}
```

```c
static int hello_release(struct inode *inode, struct file *file)
{
    printk("hello_release: successful\n");
    return 0;
}

static ssize_t hello_read(struct file *file, char *buf, size_t count,
            loff_t *ptr)
{
    printk("hello_read: returning zero bytes\n");
    return 0;
}

static ssize_t hello_write(struct file *file, const char *buf,
            size_t count, loff_t * ppos)
{
    printk("hello_read: accepting zero bytes\n");
    return 0;
}

static int hello_ioctl(struct inode *inode, struct file *file,
            unsigned int cmd, unsigned long arg)
{
    printk("hello_ioctl: cmd=%ld, arg=%ld\n", cmd, arg);
    return 0;
}

static int __init hello_init(void)
{
    int ret;
    printk("Hello Example Init - debug mode is %s\n",
            debug_enable ? "enabled" : "disabled");
    ret = register_chrdev(HELLO_MAJOR, "hello1", &hello_fops);
        if (ret < 0) {
            printk("Error registering hello device\n");
            goto hello_fail1;
        }
    printk("Hello: registered module successfully!\n");

    /* Init processing here... */

    return 0;

hello_fail1:
    return ret;
}

static void __exit hello_exit(void)
{
    printk("Hello Example Exit\n");
}
```

```
struct file_operations hello_fops = {
    owner:    THIS_MODULE,
    read:     hello_read,
    write:    hello_write,
    ioctl:    hello_ioctl,
    open:     hello_open,
    release:  hello_release,
};

module_init(hello_init);
module_exit(hello_exit);

MODULE_AUTHOR("Chris Hallinan");
MODULE_DESCRIPTION("Hello World Example");
MODULE_LICENSE("GPL");
```

This expanded device driver example includes many new lines. From the top, we've had to add a new kernel header file to get the definitions for the file system operations. We've also defined a major number for our device driver. (*Note to device driver authors:* This is <u>not</u> the proper way to allocate a device driver major number. Refer to the Linux kernel documentation (.../Documentation/devices.txt) or one of the excellent texts on device drivers for guidance on the allocation of major device numbers. For this simple example, we simply choose one that we know isn't in use on our system.)

Next we see definitions for four new functions, our open, close, read, and write methods. In keeping with good coding practices, we've adopted a consistent naming scheme that will not collide with any other subsystems in the kernel. Our new methods are called `hello_open()`, `hello_release()`, `hello_read()`, and `hello_write()`, respectively. For purposes of this simple exercise, they are do-nothing functions that simply print a message to the kernel log subsystem.

Notice that we've also added a new function call to our `hello_init()` routine. This line registers our device driver with the kernel. With that registration call, we pass a structure containing pointers to the required methods. The kernel uses this structure, of type `struct file_operations`, to bind our specific device functions with the appropriate requests from the file system. When an application opens a device represented by our device driver and requests a `read()` operation, the file system associates that generic `read()` request with our module's `hello_read()` function. The following sections examine this process in detail.

8.3.2 Device Nodes and mknod

To understand how an application binds its requests to a specific device represented by our device driver, we must understand the concept of a device node. A device node is a special file type in Linux that represents a device. Virtually all Linux distributions keep device nodes in a common location (specified by the Filesystem Hierarchy Standard[6]), in a directory called `/dev`. A dedicated utility is used to create a device node on a file system. This utility is called mknod.

An example of node creation is the best way to illustrate its functionality and the information it conveys. In keeping with our simple device driver example, let's create the proper device node to exercise it:

```
$ mknod /dev/hello1 c 234 0
```

After executing this command on our target embedded system, we end up with a new file called `/dev/hello1` that represents our device driver module. If we list this file to the console, it looks like this:

```
$ ls -l /dev/hello1
crw-r--r--   1 root   root   234, 0 Jul 14 2005 /dev/hello1
```

The parameters we passed to mknod include the name, type, and major and minor numbers for our device driver. The name we chose, of course, was hello1. Because we are demonstrating the use of a character driver, we use c to indicate that. The major number is 234, the number we chose for this example, and the minor number is 0.

By itself, the device node is just another file on our file system. However, because of its special status as a device node, we use it to bind to an installed device driver. If an application process issues an open() system call with our device node as the path parameter, the kernel searches for a valid device driver registered with a major number that matches the device node—in our case, 234. This is the mechanism by which the kernel associates our particular device to the device node.

As most C programmers know, the open() system call, or any of its variants, returns a reference (file descriptor) that our applications use to issue subsequent file system operations, such as read, write, and close. This reference is then passed to the various file system operations, such as read, write, or their variants.

---

[6] Reference to this standard is found in the "Suggestions for Additional Reading," at the end of this chapter.

For those curious about the purpose of the minor number, it is a mechanism for handling multiple devices or subdevices with a single device driver. It is not used by the operating system; it is simply passed to the device driver. The device driver can use the minor number in any way it sees fit. As an example, with a multiport serial card, the major number would specify the driver. The minor number might specify one of the multiple ports handled by the same driver on the multiport card. Interested readers are encouraged to consult one of the excellent texts on device drivers for further details.

8.4 Bringing It All Together

Now that we have a skeletal device driver, we can load it and exercise it. Listing 8-11 is a simple user space application that exercises our device driver. We've already seen how to load the driver. Simply compile it and issue the `make modules_ install` command to place it on your file system, as previously described.

Listing 8-11

Exercising Our Device Driver

```
#include <stdio.h>
#include <stdlib.h>
#include <sys/types.h>
#include <sys/stat.h>
#include <fcntl.h>
#include <unistd.h>

int main(int argc, char **argv)
{
    /* Our file descriptor */
    int fd;
    int rc = 0;
    char *rd_buf[16];

    printf("%s: entered\n", argv[0]);

    /* Open the device */
    fd = open("/dev/hello1", O_RDWR);
    if ( fd == -1 ) {
        perror("open failed");
        rc = fd;
        exit(-1);
    }
    printf("%s: open: successful\n", argv[0]);
```

```
    /* Issue a read */
    rc = read(fd, rd_buf, 0);
    if ( rc == -1 ) {
        perror("read failed");
        close(fd);
        exit(-1);
    }
    printf("%s: read: returning %d bytes!\n", argv[0], rc);

    close(fd);
    return 0;
}
```

This simple file, compiled on an ARM XScale system, demonstrates the binding of application to device driver, through the device node. Like the device driver, it doesn't do any useful work, but it does demonstrate the concepts as it exercises some of the methods we introduced in the device driver of Listing 8-10.

First we issue an open() system call[7] on our device node created earlier. If the open succeeds, we indicate that with a message to the console. Next we issue a read() command and again print a message to the console on success. Notice that a read of 0 bytes is perfectly acceptable as far as the kernel is concerned and, in actual practice, indicates an end-of-file or out-of-data condition. Your device driver defines that special condition. When complete, we simply close the file and exit. Listing 8-12 captures the output of running this example application on an ARM XScale target:

Listing 8-12

Using the Example Driver

```
$ modprobe hello1
Hello Example Init - debug mode is disabled
Hello: registered module successfully!
$ ./use-hello
./use-hello: entered
./use-hello: open: successful
./use-hello: read: returning zero bytes!
$
```

---

[7] Actually, the open() call is a C library wrapper function around the Linux sys_open() system call.

8.5 Device Drivers and the GPL

Much discussion and debate surrounds the issue of device drivers and how the terms of the GNU Public License apply to device drivers. The first test is well understood: If your device driver (or any software, for that matter) is based, even in part, on existing GPL software, it is called a *derived work*. For example, if you start with a current Linux device driver and modify it to suit your needs, this is certainly considered a derived work, and you are obligated to license this modified device driver under the terms of the GPL, observing all its requirements.

This is where the debate comes in. First, the disclaimer. This is not a legal opinion, and the author is not a lawyer. Some of these concepts have not been tested in court as of this writing. The prevailing opinion of the legal and open source communities is that if a work can be proven[8] to be independently derived, and a given device driver does not assume "intimate knowledge" of the Linux kernel, the developers are free to license it in any way they see fit. If modifications are made to the kernel to accommodate a special need of the driver, it is considered a derived work and, therefore, is subject to the GPL.

A large and growing body of information exists in the open source community regarding these issues. It seems likely that, at some point in the future, these concepts will be tested in a court of law and precedent will be established. How long that might take is anyone's guess. If you are interested in gaining a better understanding of the legal issues surrounding Linux and open source, you might enjoy www.open-bar.org.

8.6 Chapter Summary

This chapter presented a high-level overview of device driver basics and how they fit into the architecture of a Linux system. Armed with the basics, readers new to device drivers can jump into one of the excellent texts devoted to device driver writers. Consult Section 8.6.1 for references.

- Device drivers enforce a rational separation between unprivileged user applications and critical kernel resources such as hardware and other devices, and present a well-known unified interface to applications.

---

[8] This practice is not unique to open source. Copyright and patent infringement is an ongoing concern for all developers.

- The minimum infrastructure to load a device driver is only a few lines of code. We presented this minimum infrastructure and built on the concepts to a simple shell of a driver module.

- Device drivers configured as loadable modules can be inserted into and removed from a running kernel after kernel boot.

- Module utilities are used to manage the insertion, removal, and listing of device driver modules. We covered the details of the module utilities used for these functions.

- Device nodes on your file system provide the glue between your userspace application and the device driver.

- Driver methods implement the familiar open, read, write, and close functionality commonly found in UNIX/Linux device drivers. This mechanism was explained by example, including a simple user application to exercise these driver methods.

- We concluded this chapter with an introduction to the relationship between kernel device drivers and the Open Source GNU Public License.

8.6.1 Suggestions for Additional Reading

Linux Device Drivers, 3rd Edition
Alessandro Rubini and Jonathan Corbet
O'Reilly Publishing, 2005

Filesystem Hierarchy Standard
Edited by Rusty Russel, Daniel Quinlan, and Christopher Yeoh
The File Systems Hierarchy Standards Group
www.pathname.com/fhs/

Rusty's Linux Kernel Page
Module Utilities for 2.6
Rusty Russell
http://kernel.org/pub/linux/kernel/people/rusty/

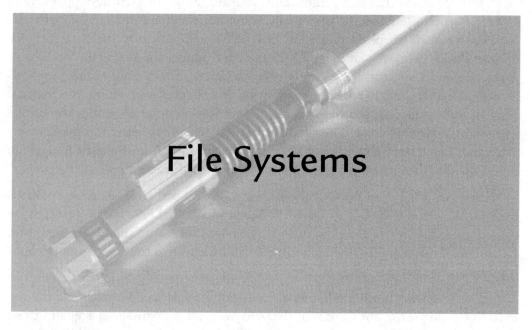

File Systems

In this chapter

Perhaps one of the most important decisions an embedded developer makes is which file system(s) to deploy. Some file systems optimize for performance, whereas others optimize for size. Still others optimize for data recovery after device or power failure. This chapter introduces the major file systems in use on Linux systems and examines the characteristics of each as they apply to embedded designs. It is not the intent of this chapter to examine the internal technical details of each file system. Instead, this chapter examines the operational characteristics and development issues related to each file system presented. References in Section 9.11.1, "Suggestions for Additional Reading," are provided at the end of the chapter for the interested reader.

Starting with the most popular file system in use on earlier Linux desktop distributions, we introduce concepts using the Second Extended File System (ext2) to lay some foundation for further discussion. Next we look at its successor, the Third Extended File System (ext3), which is the default file system for many popular desktop Linux distributions being shipped today.

After introducing some fundamentals, we examine a variety of specialized file systems, including those optimized for data recovery and for storage space, and those designed for use on Flash memory devices. The Network File System (NFS) is presented, followed by a discussion of the more important Pseudo File Systems, including the `proc` file system and `sysfs`.

9.1 Linux File System Concepts

Before delving into the details of the individual file systems, let's look at the big picture of how data is stored on a Linux system. In our study of device drivers in Chapter 8, "Device Driver Basics," we looked at the structure of a character device. In general, character devices store and retrieve data in serial streams. The most basic example of a character device is a serial port or magnetic tape drive. In contrast, block devices store and retrieve data in equal-sized chucks of data at a time. For example, a typical IDE hard disk controller can transfer 512 bytes of data at a time to and from a specific, addressable location on the physical media. File systems are based on block devices.

9.1.1 Partitions

Before we begin our discussion of file systems, we start by introducing partitions, the logical division of a physical device upon which a file system exists. At the highest level, data is stored on physical devices in partitions. A partition is a logical division of the physical medium (hard disk, Flash memory) whose data is organized following the specifications of a given partition type. A physical device can have a single partition covering all its available space, or it can be divided into multiple partitions to suit a particular task. A partition can be thought of as a logical disk onto which a complete file system can be written.

Figure 9-1 shows the relationship between partitions and file systems.

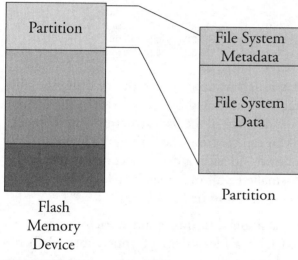

FIGURE 9-1
Partitions and file systems

Linux uses a utility called fdisk to manipulate partitions on block devices. A recent fdisk utility found on many Linux distributions has knowledge of more than 90 different partition types. In practice, only a few are commonly used on Linux systems. Some common partition types include Linux, FAT32, and Linux Swap.

Listing 9-1 displays the output of the fdisk utility targeting a CompactFlash device connected to a USB port. On this particular target system, the USB subsystem assigned the CompactFlash physical device to the device node /dev/sdb.

Listing 9-1

Displaying Partition Information Using fdisk

```
# fdisk /dev/sdb

Command (m for help): p

Disk /dev/sdb: 49 MB, 49349120 bytes
4 heads, 32 sectors/track, 753 cylinders
Units = cylinders of 128 * 512 = 65536 bytes

   Device Boot       Start         End      Blocks   Id  System
/dev/sdb1    *            1         180       11504   83  Linux
/dev/sdb2               181         360       11520   83  Linux
/dev/sdb3               361         540       11520   83  Linux
/dev/sdb4               541         753       13632   83  Linux
```

For this discussion, we have created four partitions on the device using the fdisk utility. One of them is marked bootable, as indicated by the asterisk in the column labeled Boot. This is simply the setting of a flag in the data structure that represents the partition table on the device. As you can see from the listing, the logical unit of storage used by fdisk is a cylinder.[1] On this device, a cylinder contains 64KB. On the other hand, Linux represents the smallest unit of storage as a logical block. You can deduce from this listing that a block is a unit of 1024 bytes.

After the CompactFlash has been partitioned in this manner, each device representing a partition can be formatted with a file system of your choice. When a partition is formatted with a given file system type, Linux can mount the corresponding file system from that partition.

9.2 ext2

Building on the example of Listing 9-1, we need to format the partitions created with fdisk. To do so, we use the Linux mke2fs utility. mke2fs is similar to the familiar DOS format command. This utility makes a file system of type ext2 on the specified partition. mke2fs is specific to the ext2 file system; other file systems have their own versions of these utilities. Listing 9-2 captures the output of this process.

---

[1] The term *cylinder* was borrowed from the unit of storage on a rotational media. It consists of the data under a group of heads on a given sector of a disk device. Here it is used for compatibility purposes with the existing file system utilities.

Listing 9-2

Formatting a Partition Using mke2fs

```
# mke2fs /dev/sdb1 -L CFlash_Boot_Vol
mke2fs 1.37 (21-Mar-2005)
Filesystem label=CFlash_Boot_Vol
OS type: Linux
Block size=1024 (log=0)
Fragment size=1024 (log=0)
2880 inodes, 11504 blocks
575 blocks (5.00%) reserved for the super user
First data block=1
Maximum filesystem blocks=11796480
2 block groups
8192 blocks per group, 8192 fragments per group
1440 inodes per group
Superblock backups stored on blocks:
        8193

Writing inode tables: done
Writing superblocks and filesystem accounting information: done

This filesystem will be automatically checked every 39 mounts or
180 days, whichever comes first.  Use tune2fs -c or -i to override.
#
```

Listing 9-2 contains a great deal of detail relating to the ext2 file system and provides an excellent way to begin to understand its operational characteristics. Note that this partition was formatted as type ext2 with a volume label of CFlash_Boot_Vol. It was created on a Linux partition (OS Type:) with a block size of 1024 bytes. Space was allocated for 2,880 inodes, occupying 11,504 blocks. An inode is the fundamental data structure representing a single file. For more detailed information about the internal structure of the ext2 file system, the reader is directed to Section 9.11.1 at the end of this chapter.

Looking at the output of mke2fs in Listing 9-2, we can ascertain certain characteristics of how the storage device is organized. We already know that the block size is 1024 bytes. If necessary for your particular application, mke2fs can be instructed to format an ext2 file system with different block sizes. Current implementations allow block sizes of 1,024, 2,048, and 4,096 blocks.

Block size is always a compromise for best performance. On one hand, large block sizes waste more space on disks with many files because each file must fit into an integral number of blocks. Any leftover fragment above block_size * n must occupy another full block, even if only 1 byte. On the other hand, very small block sizes increase the file system overhead of managing the metadata that describes the block-to-file mapping. Benchmark testing on your particular hardware implementation is the only way to be sure you have selected an optimum block size.

9.2.1 Mounting a File System

After a file system has been created, we can mount that file system on a running Linux system, provided that we have access to the hardware device and that the kernel has been compiled with support for our particular file system type, either as a compiled-in module or a dynamically loadable module. The following command mounts the previously created ext2 file system on a mount point that we specify:

```
# mount /dev/sdb1 /mnt/flash
```

This example assumes that we have a directory created on our target Linux machine called /mnt/flash. This is called the mount point because we are installing (mounting) the file system rooted at this point in our file system hierarchy. We are mounting the Flash device described earlier that the kernel assigned to the device /dev/sdb1. On a typical Linux desktop (development) machine, we need to have root privileges to execute this command.[2] The mount point is any place on your file system that you decide, which becomes the top level (root) of your newly mounted device. In the previous example, to reference any files on your Flash device, you must prefix the path with /mnt/flash.

The mount command is a powerful command, with many options. Many of the options that mount accepts depend on the target file system type of the mount operation. Most of the time, mount can determine the type of file system on a properly formatted file system known to the kernel. We provide additional usage examples for the mount command as we proceed through this chapter.

Listing 9-3 displays the directory contents of a Flash device configured for an arbitrary embedded system.

---

[2] File systems can be made mountable by nonroot users, as with cdrom.

Listing 9-3

Flash Device Listing

```
$ ls -l /mnt/flash
total 24
drwxr-xr-x  2 root root   1024 Jul 18 20:18 bin
drwxr-xr-x  2 root root   1024 Jul 18 20:18 boot
drwxr-xr-x  2 root root   1024 Jul 18 20:18 dev
drwxr-xr-x  2 root root   1024 Jul 18 20:18 etc
drwxr-xr-x  2 root root   1024 Jul 18 20:18 home
drwxr-xr-x  2 root root   1024 Jul 18 20:18 lib
drwx------  2 root root  12288 Jul 17 13:02 lost+found
drwxr-xr-x  2 root root   1024 Jul 18 20:18 proc
drwxr-xr-x  2 root root   1024 Jul 18 20:18 root
drwxr-xr-x  2 root root   1024 Jul 18 20:18 sbin
drwxr-xr-x  2 root root   1024 Jul 18 20:18 tmp
drwxr-xr-x  2 root root   1024 Jul 18 20:18 usr
drwxr-xr-x  2 root root   1024 Jul 18 20:18 var
$
```

Listing 9-3 is an example of what an embedded systems root file system might look like at the top (root) level. Chapter 6, "System Initialization," provides guidance and examples for how to determine the contents of the root file system.

9.2.2 Checking File System Integrity

The e2fsck command is used to check the integrity of an ext2 file system. A file system can become corrupted for several reasons, but by far the most common reason is an unexpected power failure or intentional power-down without first closing all open files and unmounting the file systems. Linux distributions perform these operations during the shutdown sequence (assuming an orderly shutdown of the system). However, when we are dealing with embedded systems, unexpected power-downs are common, and we need to provide some defensive measures against these cases. e2fsck is our first line of defense for unexpected power-down using the ext2 file system.

Listing 9.4 shows the output of e2fsck run on our CompactFlash from the previous examples. It has been formatted and properly unmounted; there should be no errors.

Listing 9-4

Clean File System Check

```
# e2fsck /dev/sdb1
e2fsck 1.37 (21-Mar-2005)
CFlash_Boot_Vol: clean, 23/2880 files, 483/11504 blocks
#
```

The e2fsck utility checks several aspects of the file system for consistency. If no issues are found, e2fsck issues a message similar to that shown in Listing 9-4. Note that e2fsck should be run only on an unmounted file system. Although it is possible to run it on a mounted file system, doing so can cause significant damage to internal file system structures on the disk or Flash device.

To create a more interesting example, Listing 9-5 was created by pulling the CompactFlash device out of its socket while still mounted. We intentionally created a file and editing session on that file before removing it from the system. This can result in corruption of the data structures describing the file, as well as the actual data blocks containing the file's data.

Listing 9-5

Corrupted File System Check

```
# e2fsck -y /dev/sdb1
e2fsck 1.37 (21-Mar-2005)
/dev/sdb1 was not cleanly unmounted, check forced.
Pass 1: Checking inodes, blocks, and sizes
Inode 13, i_blocks is 16, should be 8.  Fix? yes

Pass 2: Checking directory structure
Pass 3: Checking directory connectivity
Pass 4: Checking reference counts
Pass 5: Checking group summary information

/dev/sdb1: ***** FILE SYSTEM WAS MODIFIED *****
/dev/sdb1: 25/2880 files (4.0% non-contiguous), 488/11504 blocks
#
```

From Listing 9-5, you can see that e2fsck detected that the CompactFlash was not cleanly unmounted. Furthermore, you can see the processing on the file system during e2fsck checking. The e2fsck utility makes five passes over the file system, checking various elements of the internal file system's data structures. An error associated with a file, identified by inode[3] 13, was automatically fixed because the -y flag was included on the e2fsck command line.

Of course, in a real system, you might not be this lucky. Some types of file system errors are not repairable using e2fsck. Moreover, the embedded system designer should understand that if power has been removed without proper shutdown, the boot cycle can be delayed by the length of time it takes to scan your boot device and repair any errors. Indeed, if these errors are not repairable, the system boot is halted and manual intervention is indicated. Furthermore, it should be noted that if your file system is large, the file system check (fsck) can take minutes or even hours for large multigigabyte file systems.

Another defense against file system corruption is to ensure that writes are committed to disk immediately when written. The sync utility can be used to force all queued I/O requests to be committed to their respective devices. One strategy to minimize the window of vulnerability for data corruption from unexpected power loss or drive failure is to issue the sync command after every file write or strategically as needed by your application requirements. The trade-off here is, of course, a performance penalty. Deferring disk writes is a performance optimization used in all modern operating systems. Using sync effectively defeats this optimization.

The ext2 file system has matured as a fast, efficient, and robust file system for Linux systems. However, if you need the additional reliability of a journaling file system, or if boot time after unclean shutdown is an issue in your design, you should consider the ext3 file system.

9.3 ext3

The ext3 file system has become a powerful, high-performance, and robust journaling file system. It is currently the default file system for many popular desktop Linux distributions such as Red Hat and the Fedora Core series.

The ext3 file system is basically an extension of the ext2 file system with added journaling capability. Journaling is a technique in which each change to the file system is logged in a special file so that recovery is possible from known journaling points. One of the primary advantages of the ext3 file system is its capability to be mounted directly after an unclean shutdown. As stated in the previous section,

---

[3] A file on a file system is represented by an internal ext2 data structure called an inode.

when a system shuts down unexpectedly, such as during a power failure, the system forces a file system consistency check, which can be a lengthy operation. With ext3 file systems, there is no need for a consistency check because the journal can simply be played back to ensure consistency of the file system.

Without going into design details that are beyond the scope of this book, it is worth a quick explanation of how a journaling file system works. A journaling file system contains a special file, often hidden from the user, that is used to store file system metadata[4] and file data itself. This special file is referred to as the journal. Whenever the file system is subject to a change (such as a write operation) the changes are first written to the journal. The file system drivers make sure that this write is committed to the journal before the actual changes are posted and committed to the storage media (disk or Flash, for example). After the changes have been logged in the journal, the driver posts the changes to the actual file and metadata on the media. If a power failure occurs during the media write and a reboot occurs, all that is necessary to restore consistency to the file system is to replay the changes in the journal.

One of the most significant design goals for the ext3 file system was that it be both backward and forward compatible with the ext2 file system. It is possible to convert an ext2 file system to ext3 file system and back again without reformatting or rewriting all the data on the disk. Let's see how this is done.[5] Listing 9-6 details the procedure.

Listing 9-6

Converting ext2 File System to ext3 File System

```
# mount /dev/sdb1 /mnt/flash      <<< Mount the ext2 file system
# tune2fs -j /dev/sdb1            <<< Create the journal
tune2fs 1.37 (21-Mar-2005)
Creating journal inode: done
This filesystem will be automatically checked every 23 mounts or
180 days, whichever comes first.  Use tune2fs -c or -i to override.
#
```

Notice that we first mounted the file system on /mnt/flash for illustrative purposes only. Normally, we would execute this command on an unmounted ext2

---

[4] Metadata is data about the file, as opposed to the file's data itself. Examples include a file's date, time, size, blocks used, and so on.

[5] Converting a file system in this manner should be considered a development activity only.

partition. The design behavior for `tune2fs` when the file system is mounted is to create the journal file called `.journal`, a hidden file. A file in Linux preceded with the period (`.`) is considered a hidden file; most Linux command line file utilities silently ignore files of this type. From Listing 9-7, we can see that the `ls` command was invoked with the `-a` flag, which tells the ls utility to list all files.

Listing 9-7

ext3 Journal File

```
$ ls -al /mnt/flash
total 1063
drwxr-xr-x  15 root root     1024 Aug 25 19:25 .
drwxrwxrwx   5 root root     4096 Jul 18 19:49 ..
drwxr-xr-x   2 root root     1024 Aug 14 11:27 bin
drwxr-xr-x   2 root root     1024 Aug 14 11:27 boot
drwxr-xr-x   2 root root     1024 Aug 14 11:27 dev
drwxr-xr-x   2 root root     1024 Aug 14 11:27 etc
drwxr-xr-x   2 root root     1024 Aug 14 11:27 home
-rw-------   1 root root  1048576 Aug 25 19:25 .journal
drwxr-xr-x   2 root root     1024 Aug 14 11:27 lib
drwx------   2 root root    12288 Aug 14 11:27 lost+found
drwxr-xr-x   2 root root     1024 Aug 14 11:27 proc
drwxr-xr-x   2 root root     1024 Aug 14 11:27 root
drwxr-xr-x   2 root root     1024 Aug 14 11:27 sbin
drwxr-xr-x   2 root root     1024 Aug 14 11:27 tmp
drwxr-xr-x   2 root root     1024 Aug 14 11:27 usr
drwxr-xr-x   2 root root     1024 Aug 14 11:27 var
```

Now that we have created the journal file on our Flash module, it is effectively formatted as an ext3 file system. The next time the system is rebooted or the `e2fsck` utility is run on the partition containing the newly created ext3 file system, the journal file is automatically made invisible. Its metadata is stored in a reserved `inode` set aside for this purpose. As long as you can see the `.journal` file, it is dangerous to modify or delete this file.

It is possible and sometimes advantageous to create the journal file on a different device. For example, if you have more than one physical device on your system, you can place your ext3 journaling file system on the first drive and have the journal file on the second drive. This method works regardless of whether your physical storage is based on Flash or rotational media. To create the journaling file system from an existing ext2 file system with the journal file in a separate partition, invoke `tune2fs` in the following manner:

```
# tune2fs -J device=/dev/sda1 -j /dev/sdb1
```

For this to work, you must have already formatted the device where the journal is to reside with a journal file—it must be an ext3 file system.

9.4 ReiserFS

The ReiserFS file system has enjoyed popularity among some desktop distributions such as SuSE and Gentoo. As of this writing, Reiser4 is the current incarnation of this journaling file system. Like the ext3 file system, ReiserFS guarantees that either a given file system operation completes in its entirety or none of it completes. Unlike ext3, Reiser4 has introduced an API for system programmers to guarantee the atomicity of a file system transaction. Consider the following example:

A database program is busy updating records in the database. Several writes are issued to the file system. Power is lost after the first write but before the last one has completed. A journaling file system guarantees that the metadata changes have been stored to the journal file so that when power is again applied to the system, the kernel can at least establish a consistent state of the file system. That is, if file A was reported has having 16KB before the power failure, it will be reported as having 16KB afterward, and the directory entry representing this file (actually, the inode) properly records the size of the file. This does not mean, however, that the file data was properly written to the file; it indicates only that there are no errors on the file system. Indeed, it is likely that data was lost by the database program in the previous scenario, and it would be up to the database logic to recover the lost data if recovery is to occur at all.

Reiser4 implements high-performance "atomic" file system operations designed to protect both the state of the file system (its consistency) and the data involved in a file system operation. Reiser4 provides a user-level API to enable programs such as database managers to issue a file system write command that is guaranteed to either succeed in its entirety or fail in a similar manner, thus guaranteeing not only that file system consistency is maintained, but that no partial data or garbage data remains in files after system crash.

For more details and the actual software for ReiserFS, visit the home page referenced in Section 9.11.1 at the end of this chapter.

9.5 JFFS2

Flash memory has been used extensively in embedded products. Because of the nature of Flash memory technology, it is inherently less efficient and more prone to data corruption caused by power loss from much larger write times. The inefficiency stems from the block size. Block sizes of Flash memory devices are often measured in the tens or hundreds of kilobytes. Flash memory can be erased only a block at a time, although writes can usually be executed 1 byte or word at a time. To update a single file, an entire block must be erased and rewritten.

It is well known that the distribution of file sizes on any given Linux machine (or other OS) contains many more smaller files than larger files. The histogram in Figure 9-2, generated with gnuplot, illustrates the distribution of file sizes on a typical Linux development system.

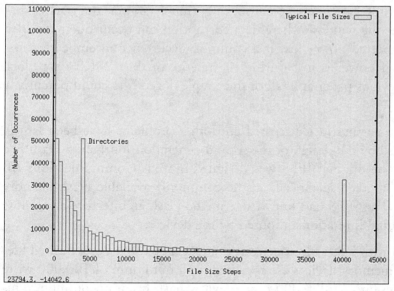

FIGURE 9-2
File sizes in bytes

From Figure 9-2, we can see that the bulk of the file sizes are well below approximately 10KB. The spike at 4096 represents directories. Directory entries (also files themselves) are exactly 4096 bytes in length, and there are many of them. The spike above 40,000 bytes is an artifact of the measurement. It is a count of the number of files greater than approximately 40KB, the end of the measurement quantum. It is interesting to note that the vast majority of files are very small.

Small file sizes present a unique challenge to the Flash file system designer. Because Flash memory must be erased one entire block at a time, and the size of a Flash block is often many multiples of the smaller file sizes, Flash is subject to time-consuming block rewriting. For example, assume that a 128KB block of Flash is being used to hold a couple dozen files of 4096 bytes or less. Now assume that one of those files needs to be modified. This causes the Flash file system to invalidate the entire 128KB block and rewrite every file in the block to a newly erased block. This can be a time-consuming process.

Because Flash writes can be time-consuming (much slower than hard disk writes), this increases the window where data corruption can occur due to sudden loss of power. Unexpected power loss is a common occurrence in embedded systems. For instance, if power is lost during the rewrite of the 128KB data block referenced in the previous paragraph, all of the couple dozen files could potentially be lost.

Enter JFFS2. These issues just discussed and other problems have been largely reduced or eliminated by the design of the second-generation Journaling Flash File System, or JFFS2. The original JFFS was designed by Axis Communications AB of Sweden and was targeted specifically at the commonly available Flash memory devices at the time. The JFFS had knowledge of the Flash architecture and, more important, architectural limitations imposed by the devices.

Another problem with Flash file systems is that Flash memory has a limited lifetime. Typical Flash memory devices are specified for a minimum of 100,000 write cycles, and, more recently, 1,000,000-cycle devices have become common. This specification is applicable to each block of the Flash device. This unusual limitation imposes the requirement to spread the writes evenly across the blocks of a Flash memory device. JFFS2 uses a technique called wear leveling to accomplish this function.

Building a JFFS2 image is relatively straightforward. As always, you must ensure that your kernel has support for JFFS2 and that your development workstation contains a compatible version of the `mkfs.jffs2` utility. JFFS2 images are built from a directory that contains the desired files on the file system image. Listing 9-8 shows a typical directory structure for a Flash device designed to be used as a root file system.

Listing 9-8

Directory Layout for JFFS2 File System

```
$ ls -l
total 44
drwxr-xr-x   2 root root 4096 Aug 14 11:27 bin
drwxr-xr-x   2 root root 4096 Aug 14 11:27 dev
drwxr-xr-x   2 root root 4096 Aug 14 11:27 etc
drwxr-xr-x   2 root root 4096 Aug 14 11:27 home
drwxr-xr-x   2 root root 4096 Aug 14 11:27 lib
drwxr-xr-x   2 root root 4096 Aug 14 11:27 proc
drwxr-xr-x   2 root root 4096 Aug 14 11:27 root
drwxr-xr-x   2 root root 4096 Aug 14 11:27 sbin
drwxr-xr-x   2 root root 4096 Aug 14 11:27 tmp
drwxr-xr-x   2 root root 4096 Aug 14 11:27 usr
drwxr-xr-x   2 root root 4096 Aug 14 11:27 var
$
```

When suitably populated with runtime files, this directory layout can be used as a template for the `mkfs.jffs2` command. The `mkfs.jffs2` command produces a properly formatted JFFS2 file system image from a directory tree such as that in Listing 9-8. Command line parameters are used to pass `mkfs.jffs2` the directory location as well as the name of the output file to receive the JFFS2 image. The default is to create the JFFS2 image from the current directory. Listing 9-9 shows the command for building the JFFS2 image.

Listing 9-9

`mkfs.jffs2` Command Example

```
# mkfs.jffs2 -d ./jffs2-image-dir -o jffs2.bin
# ls -l
total 4772
-rw-r--r--    1 root    root    1098640 Sep 17 22:03 jffs2.bin
drwxr-xr-x   13 root    root       4096 Sep 17 22:02 jffs2-image-dir
#
```

The directory structure and files from Listing 9-8 are in the `jffs2-image-dir` directory in our example. We arbitrarily execute the `mkfs.jffs2` command from the directory above our file system image. Using the `-d` flag, we tell the mkfs.jffs2 command where the file system template is located. We use the -o flag to name the output file to which the resulting JFFS2 image is written. The resulting image, jffs2.bin, is used in Chapter 10, "MTD Subsystem," when we examine the JFFS2 file together with the MTD subsystem.

It should be pointed out that any Flash-based file system that supports write operations is subject to conditions that can lead to premature failure of the underlying Flash device. For example, enabling system loggers (syslogd and klogd) configured to write their data to Flash-based file systems can easily overwhelm a Flash device with continuous writes. Some categories of program errors can also lead to continuous writes. Care must be taken to limit Flash writes to values within the lifetime of Flash devices.

9.6 cramfs

From the README file in the cramfs project, the goal of cramfs is to "cram a file system into a small ROM." The cramfs file system is very useful for embedded systems that contain a small ROM or FLASH memory that holds static data and programs. Borrowing again from the cramfs README file, "cramfs is designed to be simple and small, and compress things well."

The cramfs file system is read only. It is created with a command line utility called mkcramfs. If you don't have it on your development workstation, you can download it from the link at the end of this chapter. As with JFFS2, mkcramfs builds a file system image from a directory specified on the command line. Listing 9-10 details the procedure for building a cramfs image. We use the same file system structure from Listing 9-8 that we used to build the JFFS2 image.

Listing 9-10

mkcramfs Command Example

```
# mkcramfs
usage: mkcramfs [-h] [-v] [-b blksize] [-e edition] [-i file] [-n name]
dirname outfile
 -h          print this help
 -E          make all warnings errors (non-zero exit status)
 -b blksize  use this blocksize, must equal page size
 -e edition  set edition number (part of fsid)
 -i file     insert a file image into the filesystem (requires >= 2.4.0)
 -n name     set name of cramfs filesystem
 -p          pad by 512 bytes for boot code
```

```
-s          sort directory entries (old option, ignored)
-v          be more verbose
-z          make explicit holes (requires >= 2.3.39)
dirname     root of the directory tree to be compressed
outfile     output file
```

```
#
# mkcramfs . ../cramfs.image
warning: gids truncated to 8 bits (this may be a security concern)
# ls -l ../cramfs.image
-rw-rw-r--  1 chris chris 1019904 Sep 19 18:06 ../cramfs.image
```

The mkcramfs command was initially issued without any command line parameters to reproduce the usage message. Because there is no man page for this utility, this is the best way to understand its usage. We subsequently issued the command specifying the current directory,   ., as the source of the files for the cramfs file system, and a file called cramfs.image as the destination. Finally, we listed the file just created, and we see a new file called cramfs.image.

Note that if your kernel is configured with cramfs support, you can mount this file system image on your Linux development workstation and examine its contents. Of course, because it is a read-only file system, you cannot modify it. Listing 9-11 demonstrates mounting the cramfs file system on a mount point called /mnt/flash.

Listing 9-11

Examining the cramfs File System

```
# mount -o loop cramfs.image /mnt/flash
# ls -l /mnt/flash
total 6
drwxr-xr-x  1 root    root 704 Dec 31  1969 bin
drwxr-xr-x  1 root    root   0 Dec 31  1969 dev
drwxr-xr-x  1 root    root 416 Dec 31  1969 etc
drwxr-xr-x  1 root    root   0 Dec 31  1969 home
drwxr-xr-x  1 root    root 172 Dec 31  1969 lib
drwxr-xr-x  1 root    root   0 Dec 31  1969 proc
drws------  1 root    root   0 Dec 31  1969 root
drwxr-xr-x  1 root    root 272 Dec 31  1969 sbin
drwxrwxrwt  1 root    root   0 Dec 31  1969 tmp
drwxr-xr-x  1 root    root 124 Dec 31  1969 usr
drwxr-xr-x  1 root    root 212 Dec 31  1969 var
#
```

You might have noticed the warning message regarding group ID (GID) when the mkcramfs command was executed. The cramfs file system uses very terse meta-data to reduce file system size and increase the speed of execution. One of the "features" of the cramfs file system is that it truncates the group ID field to 8 bits. Linux uses 16-bit group ID field. The result is that files created with group IDs greater than 255 are truncated with the warning issued in Listing 9-10.

Although somewhat limited in terms of maximum file sizes, maximum number of files, and so on, the cramfs file system is ideal for boot ROMS, in which read-only operation and fast compression are ideally suited.

9.7 Network File System

Those of you who have developed in the UNIX environment will undoubtedly be familiar with the Network File System, or simply NFS. Properly configured, NFS enables you to export a directory on an NFS server and mount that directory on a remote client machine as if it were a local file system. This is useful in general for large networks of UNIX/Linux machines, and it can be a panacea to the embedded developer. Using NFS on your target board, an embedded developer can have access to a huge number of files, libraries, tools, and utilities during development and debugging, even if the target embedded system is resource constrained.

As with the other file systems, your kernel must be configured with NFS support, for both the server-side functionality and the client side. NFS server and client functionality is independently configured in the kernel configuration.

Detailed instructions for configuring and tuning NFS are beyond the scope of this book, but a short introduction helps to illustrate how useful NFS can be in the embedded environment. See Section 9.11.1 at the end of this chapter for a pointer to detailed information about NFS, including the complete NFS-Howto.

On your development workstation with NFS enabled, a file contains the names of each directory that you want to export via the Network File System. On Red Hat and other distributions, this file is located in the /etc directory and is named exports. Listing 9-12 illustrates a sample /etc/exports such as might be found on a development workstation used for embedded development.

Listing 9-12

Contents of `/etc/exports`

```
$ cat /etc/exports
# /etc/exports
/home/chris/sandbox/coyote-target *(rw,sync,no_root_squash)
/home/chris/workspace *(rw,sync,no_root_squash)
$
```

This file contains the names of two directories on a Linux development worksta-tion. The first directory contains a target file system for an ADI Engineering Coyote reference board. The second directory is a general workspace that contains projects targeted for an embedded system. This is arbitrary; you can set things up any way you choose.

On an embedded system with NFS enabled, the following command mounts the `.../workspace` directory exported by the NFS server on a mount point of our choosing:

```
$ mount -t nfs pluto:/home/chris/workspace /workspace
```

Notice some important points about this command. We are instructing the `mount` command to mount a remote directory (on a machine named pluto) onto a local mount point called `/workspace`. For this syntax to work, two requirements must be met on the embedded target. First, for the target to recognize the symbol-ic machine name pluto, it must be capable of resolving the symbolic name. The eas-iest way to do this is to place an entry in the `/etc/hosts` file on the target. This allows the networking subsystem to resolve the symbolic name to its corresponding IP address. The entry in the target's `/etc/hosts` file would look like this:

```
192.168.10.9        pluto
```

The second requirement is that the embedded target must have a directory in its root directory called `/workspace`. This is called a mount point. The previous mount command causes the contents of the NFS server's `/home/chris/workspace` directory to be available on the embedded system's `/workspace` path.

This is quite useful, especially in a cross-development environment. Let's say that you are working on a large project for your embedded device. Each time you make changes to the project, you need to move that application to your target so you can test and debug it. Using NFS in the manner just described, assuming that you are working in the NFS exported directory on your host, the changes are immediately available on your target embedded system without the need to upload the newly compiled project files. This can speed development considerably.

9.7.1 Root File System on NFS

Mounting your project workspace on your target embedded system is very useful for development and debugging because it facilitates rapid access to changes and source code for source-level debugging. This is especially useful when the target system is severely resource constrained. NFS really shines as a development tool when you mount your embedded system's root file system entirely from an NFS server. From Listing 9-12, notice the `coyote-target` entry. This directory on your development workstation could contain hundreds or thousands of files compatible with your target architecture.

The leading embedded Linux distributions targeted at embedded systems ship tens of thousands of files compiled and tested for the chosen target architecture. To illustrate this, Listing 9-13 contains a directory listing of the `coyote-target` directory referenced in Listing 9-12.

Listing 9-13

Target File System Example Summary

```
$ du -h --max-depth=1
724M    ./usr
4.0K    ./opt
39M     ./lib
12K     ./dev
27M     ./var
4.0K    ./tmp
3.6M    ./boot
4.0K    ./workspace
1.8M    ./etc
4.0K    ./home
4.0K    ./mnt
8.0K    ./root
29M     ./bin
32M     ./sbin
4.0K    ./proc
64K     ./share
855M    .
$
$ find -type f | wc -l
29430
```

This target file system contains just shy of a gigabyte worth of binary files targeted at the ARM architecture. As you can see from the listing, this is more than 29,000 binary, configuration and documentation files. This would hardly fit on the average Flash device found on an embedded system!

This is the power of an NFS root mount. For development purposes, it can only increase productivity if your embedded system is loaded with all the tools and utilities you are familiar with on a Linux workstation. Indeed, likely dozens of command line tools and development utilities that you have never seen can help you shave time off your development schedule. You will learn more about some of these useful tools in Chapter 13, "Development Tools."

To enable your embedded system to mount its root file system via NFS at boot time is relatively straightforward. First, you must configure your target's kernel for NFS support. There is also a configuration option to enable root mounting of an NFS remote directory. This is illustrated in Figure 9-3.

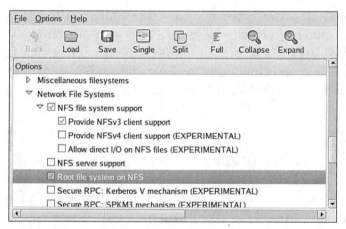

FIGURE 9-3
NFS kernel configuration

Notice that the NFS file system support has been selected, along with support for "Root file system on NFS." After these kernel-configuration parameters have been selected, all that remains is to somehow feed information to the kernel so that it knows where to look for the NFS server. Several methods can be used for this, and some depend on the chosen target architecture and choice of bootloader. At a minimum, the kernel can be passed the proper parameters on the kernel command line to configure its IP port and server information on power-up. A typical kernel command line might look like this:

```
console=ttyS0,115200 ip=bootp root=/dev/nfs
```

This tells the kernel to expect a root file system via NFS and to obtain the relevant parameters (server name, server IP address, and root directory to mount) from a BOOTP server. This is a common and tremendously useful configuration during the development phase of a project. If you are statically configuring your target's IP address, your kernel command line might look like this:

```
console=ttyS0,115200                                              \
ip=192.168.1.139:192.168.1.1:192.168.1.1:255.255.255.0:coyote1:eth0:off  \
   nfsroot=192.168.1.1:/home/chris/sandbox/coyote-target  \
   root=/dev/nfs
```

Of course, this would all be on one line. The `ip=` parameter is defined in `.../net/ipv4/ipconfig.c` and has the following syntax, all on one line:

```
ip=<client-ip>:<server-ip>:<gw-ip>:<netmask>:<hostname>:<device>:<PROTO>
```

Here, `client-ip` is the target's IP address; `server-ip` is the address of the NFS server; `gw-ip` is the gateway (router), in case the `server-ip` is on a different subnet; and `netmask` defines the class of IP addressing. `hostname` is a string that is passed as the target hostname; `device` is the Linux device name, such as eth0; and `PROTO` defines the protocol used to obtain initial IP parameters.

9.8 Pseudo File Systems

A number of file systems fall under the category of Pseudo File Systems in the kernel-configuration menu. Together they provide a range of facilities useful in a wide range of applications. For additional information, especially on the `proc` file system, spend an afternoon poking around this useful system facility. Where appropriate, references to additional reading material can be found in Section 9.11.1, at the end of this chapter.

9.8.1 Proc File System

The `/proc` file system took its name from its original purpose, an interface that allows the kernel to communicate information about each running process on a Linux system. Over the course of time, it has grown and matured to provide much more than process information. We introduce the highlights here; a complete tour of the /proc file system is left as an exercise for the reader.

The /proc file system has become a virtual necessity for all but the simplest of Linux systems, even embedded ones. Many user-level functions rely on the contents of the /proc file system to do their job. For example, the mount command, issued without any parameters, lists all the currently active mount points on a running system, from the information delivered by /proc/mounts. If the /proc file system is not available, the mount command silently returns. Listing 9-14 illustrates this on the ADI Engineering Coyote board.

Listing 9-14

Mount Dependency on /proc

```
# mount
rootfs on / type rootfs (rw)
/dev/root on / type nfs
(rw,v2,rsize=4096,wsize=4096,hard,udp,nolock,addr=192.168.1.19)
tmpfs on /dev/shm type tmpfs (rw)
/proc on /proc type proc (rw,nodiratime)

< Now unmount proc and try again ...>

# umount /proc
# mount
#
```

Notice in Listing 9-14 that /proc itself is listed as a mounted file system, as type proc mounted on /proc. This is not doublespeak; your system must have a mount point called /proc at the top-level directory tree as a destination for the /proc file system to be mounted on.[6] To mount the /proc file system, use the mount command as with any other file system:

```
$ mount -t proc /proc /proc
```

The general form of the mount command, from the man page, is mount [-t fstype] something somewhere. In the previous invocation, we could have substituted none for /proc, as follows:

```
$ mount -t proc none /proc
```

---

[6] It is certainly possible to mount /proc anywhere you like on your file system, but all the utilities (including mount) that require proc expect to find it mounted on /proc.

This looks somewhat less like doublespeak. The `something` parameter is not strictly necessary because `/proc` is a pseudo file system and not a real physical device. However, specifying `/proc` as in the earlier example helps remind us that we are mounting the `/proc` file system on the `/proc` directory (or, more appropriately, on the `/proc` mount point).

Of course, by this time, it might be obvious that to get `/proc` file system functionality, it must be enabled in the kernel configuration. This kernel-configuration option can be found in the File Systems submenu under the category Pseudo File Systems.

Each user process running in the kernel is represented by an entry in the `/proc` file system. For example, the `init` process introduced in Chapter 6 is always assigned the process id (PID) of 1. Processes in the `/proc` file system are represented by a directory that is given the PID number as its name. For example, the `init` process with a PID of 1 would be represented by a `/proc/1` directory. Listing 9-15 shows the contents of this directory on our embedded Coyote board.

Listing 9-15

`init` Process `/proc` Entries

```
# ls -l /proc/1
total 0
-r--------    1 root    root    0 Jan  1 00:25 auxv
-r--r--r--    1 root    root    0 Jan  1 00:21 cmdline
lrwxrwxrwx    1 root    root    0 Jan  1 00:25 cwd -> /
-r--------    1 root    root    0 Jan  1 00:25 environ
lrwxrwxrwx    1 root    root    0 Jan  1 00:25 exe -> /sbin/init
dr-x------    2 root    root    0 Jan  1 00:25 fd
-r--r--r--    1 root    root    0 Jan  1 00:25 maps
-rw-------    1 root    root    0 Jan  1 00:25 mem
-r--r--r--    1 root    root    0 Jan  1 00:25 mounts
-rw-r--r--    1 root    root    0 Jan  1 00:25 oom_adj
-r--r--r--    1 root    root    0 Jan  1 00:25 oom_score
lrwxrwxrwx    1 root    root    0 Jan  1 00:25 root -> /
-r--r--r--    1 root    root    0 Jan  1 00:21 stat
-r--r--r--    1 root    root    0 Jan  1 00:25 statm
-r--r--r--    1 root    root    0 Jan  1 00:21 status
dr-xr-xr-x    3 root    root    0 Jan  1 00:25 task
-r--r--r--    1 root    root    0 Jan  1 00:25 wchan
```

These entries, which are present in the `/proc` file system for each running process, contain much useful information, especially for analyzing and debugging a process. For example, the `cmdline` entry contains the complete command line used to invoke the process, including any arguments. The cwd and root directories contain the processes' view of the current working directory and the current root directory.

One of the more useful entries for system debugging is the maps entry. This contains a list of each virtual memory segment assigned to the program, along with attributes about each. Listing 9-16 is the output from /proc/1/maps in our example of the init process.

Listing 9-16

init Process Memory Segments from /proc

```
# cat /proc/1/maps
00008000-0000f000 r-xp 00000000 00:0a 9537567    /sbin/init
00016000-00017000 rw-p 00006000 00:0a 9537567    /sbin/init
00017000-0001b000 rwxp 00017000 00:00 0
40000000-40017000 r-xp 00000000 00:0a 9537183    /lib/ld-2.3.2.so
40017000-40018000 rw-p 40017000 00:00 0
4001f000-40020000 rw-p 00017000 00:0a 9537183    /lib/ld-2.3.2.so
40020000-40141000 r-xp 00000000 00:0a 9537518    /lib/libc-2.3.2.so
40141000-40148000 ---p 00121000 00:0a 9537518    /lib/libc-2.3.2.so
40148000-4014d000 rw-p 00120000 00:0a 9537518    /lib/libc-2.3.2.so
4014d000-4014f000 rw-p 4014d000 00:00 0
befeb000-bf000000 rwxp befeb000 00:00 0
#
```

The usefulness of this information is readily apparent. You can see the program segments of the init process itself in the first two entries. You can also see the memory segments used by the shared library objects being used by the init process. The format is as follows:

```
vmstart-vmend  attr  pgoffset  devname inode filename
```

Here, vmstart and vmend are the starting and ending virtual memory addresses, respectively; attr indicates memory region attributes, such as read, write, and execute, and tells whether this region is shareable; pgoffset is the page offset of the region (a kernel virtual memory parameter); and devname, displayed as xx:xx, is a kernel representation of the device ID associated with this memory region. The memory regions that are not associated with a file are also not associated with a device, thus the 00:00. The final two entries are the inode and file associated with the given memory region. Of course, if there is no file, there is no inode associated with it, and it displays with a zero. These are usually data segments.

Other useful entries are listed for each process. The status entry contains useful status information about the running process, including items such as the parent

PID, user and group IDs, virtual memory usage stats, signals, and capabilities. More details can be obtained from the references at the end of the chapter.

Some frequently used /proc entries are cpuinfo, meminfo, and version. The cpuinfo entry lists attributes that the kernel discovers about the processor(s) running on the system. The meminfo entry provides statistics on the total system memory. The version entry mirrors the Linux kernel version string, together with information on what compiler and machine were used to build the kernel.

Many more useful /proc entries are provided by the kernel; we have only scratched the surface of this useful subsystem. Many utilities have been designed for extracting and reporting information contained with the /proc file system. Two popular examples are top and ps, which every embedded Linux developer should be intimately familiar with. These are introduced in Chapter 13. Other utilities useful for interfacing with the /proc file system include free, pkill, pmap, and uptime. See the procps package for more details.

9.8.2 sysfs

Like the /proc file system, sysfs is not representative of an actual physical device. Instead, sysfs models specific kernel objects such as physical devices and provides a way to associate devices with device drivers. Some agents in a typical Linux distribution depend on the information on sysfs.

We can get some idea of what kinds of objects are exported by looking directly at the directory structure exported by sysfs. Listing 9-17 shows the top-level /sys directory on our Coyote board.

Listing 9-17

Top-Level /sys Directory Contents

```
# dir /sys
total 0
drwxr-xr-x    21 root     root     0 Jan  1 00:00 block
drwxr-xr-x     6 root     root     0 Jan  1 00:00 bus
drwxr-xr-x    10 root     root     0 Jan  1 00:00 class
drwxr-xr-x     5 root     root     0 Jan  1 00:00 devices
drwxr-xr-x     2 root     root     0 Jan  1 00:00 firmware
drwxr-xr-x     2 root     root     0 Jan  1 00:00 kernel
drwxr-xr-x     5 root     root     0 Jan  1 00:00 module
drwxr-xr-x     2 root     root     0 Jan  1 00:00 power
#
```

As you can see, sysfs provides a subdirectory for each major class of system device, including the system buses. For example, under the block subdirectory, each block device is represented by a subdirectory entry. The same holds true for the other directories at the top level.

Most of the information stored by sysfs is in a format more suitable for machines than humans to read. For example, to discover the devices on the PCI bus, one could look directly at the /sys/bus/pci subdirectory. On our Coyote board, which has a single PCI device attached (an Ethernet card), the directory looks like this:

```
# ls /sys/bus/pci/devices/
0000:00:0f.0 -> ../../../devices/pci0000:00/0000:00:0f.0
```

This entry is actually a symbolic link pointing to another node in the sysfs directory tree. We have formatted the output of ls here to illustrate this, while still fitting in a single line. The name of the symbolic link is the kernel's representation of the PCI bus, and it points to a devices subdirectory called pci0000:00 (the PCI bus representation), which contains a number of subdirectories and files representing attributes of this specific PCI device. As you can see, the data is rather difficult to discover and parse.

A useful utility exists to browse the sysfs file system directory structure. Called systool, it comes from the sysfsutils package found on sourceforge.net. Here is how systool would display the PCI bus from the previous discussion:

```
$ systool -b pci
  Bus = "pci"
    0000:00:0f.0 8086:1229
```

Again we see the kernel's representation of the bus and device (0f), but this time the tool displays the vendor ID (8086 = Intel) and device ID (1229 = eepro100 Ethernet card) obtained from the /sys/devices/pci0000:00 branch of /sys where these attributes are kept. Executed with no parameters, systool displays the top-level system hierarchy. Listing 9-18 is an example from our Coyote board.

Listing 9-18

Output from systool

```
$ systool
Supported sysfs buses:
        i2c
        ide
        pci
        platform
Supported sysfs classes:
        block
        i2c-adapter
        i2c-dev
        input
        mem
        misc
        net
        pci_bus
        tty
Supported sysfs devices:
        pci0000:00
        platform
        system
```

You can see from this listing the variety of system information available from `sysfs`. Many utilities use this information to determine the characteristics of system devices or to enforce system policies, such as power management and hot-plug capability.

9.9 Other File Systems

Numerous file systems are supported under Linux. Space does not permit coverage of all of them. However, you should be aware of some other important file systems frequently found in embedded systems.

The ramfs file system is best considered from the context of the Linux source code module that implements it. Listing 9-19 reproduces the first several lines of that file.

Listing 9-19

Linux ramfs Source Module Comments

```
/*
 * Resizable simple ram filesystem for Linux.
 *
 * Copyright (C) 2000 Linus Torvalds.
 *               2000 Transmeta Corp.
 *
 * Usage limits added by David Gibson, Linuxcare Australia.
 * This file is released under the GPL.
 */

/*
 * NOTE! This filesystem is probably most useful
 * not as a real filesystem, but as an example of
 * how virtual filesystems can be written.
 *
 * It doesn't get much simpler than this. Consider
 * that this file implements the full semantics of
 * a POSIX-compliant read-write filesystem.
```

This module was written primarily as an example of how virtual file systems can be written. One of the primary differences between this file system and the ramdisk facility found in modern Linux kernels is its capability to shrink and grow according to its use. A ramdisk does not have this property. This source module is compact and well written. It is presented here for its educational value. You are encouraged to study this good example.

The `tmpfs` file system is similar to and related to rams. Like ramfs, everything in `tmpfs` is stored in kernel virtual memory, and the contents of `tmpfs` are lost on power-down or reboot. The `tmpfs` file system is useful for fast temporary storage of files. I use `tmpfs` mounted on `/tmp` in a midi/audio application to speed up the creation and deletion of temporary objects required by the audio subsystem. This is also a great way to keep your `/tmp` directory clean—its contents are lost on every reboot. Mounting `tmpfs` is similar to any other virtual file system:

```
# mount -t tmpfs /tmpfs /tmp
```

As with other virtual file systems such as `/proc`, the first `/tmpfs` parameter in the previous mount command is a "no-op"—that is, it could be the word `none` and still function. However, it is a good reminder that you are mounting a virtual file system called `tmpfs`.

9.10 Building a Simple File System

It is straightforward to build a simple file system image. Here we demonstrate the use of the Linux kernel's loopback device. The loopback device enables the use of a regular file as a block device. In short, we build a file system image in a regular file and use the Linux loopback device to mount that file in the same way any other block device is mounted.

To build a simple root file system, start with a fixed-sized file containing all zeros:

```
# dd if=/dev/zero of=./my-new-fs-image bs=1k count=512
```

This command creates a file of 512KB containing nothing but zeros. We fill the file with zeros to aid in compression later and to have a consistent data pattern for uninitialized data blocks within the file system. Use caution with the dd command. Executing dd with no boundary (count=) or with an improper boundary can fill up your hard drive and possibly crash your system. dd is a powerful tool; use it with the respect it deserves. Simple typos in commands such as dd, executed as root, have destroyed countless file systems.

When we have the new image file, we actually format the file to contain the data structures defined by a given file system. In this example, we build an ext2 file system. Listing 9-20 details the procedure.

Listing 9-20

Creating an ext2 File System Image

```
# /sbin/mke2fs ./my-new-fs-image
mke2fs 1.35 (28-Feb-2004)
./my-new-fs-image is not a block special device.
Proceed anyway? (y,n) y
Filesystem label=
OS type: Linux
Block size=1024 (log=0)
Fragment size=1024 (log=0)
64 inodes, 512 blocks
25 blocks (4.88%) reserved for the super user
First data block=1
1 block group
8192 blocks per group, 8192 fragments per group
64 inodes per group

Writing inode tables: done
Writing superblocks and filesystem accounting information: done

This filesystem will be automatically checked every 24 mounts or
180 days, whichever comes first.  Use tune2fs -c or -i to override.
#
```

As with `dd`, the `mke2fs` command can destroy your system, so use it with care. In this example, we asked `mke2fs` to format a file rather than a hard drive partition (block device) for which it was intended. As such, `mke2fs` detected that fact and asked us to confirm the operation. After confirming, `mke2fs` proceeded to write an ext2 superblock and file system data structures into the file. We then can mount this file like any block device, using the Linux loopback device:

```
# mount -o loop ./my-new-fs-image /mnt/flash
```

This command mounts the file `my-new-fs-image` as a file system on the mount point named `/mnt/flash`. The mount point name is not important; you can mount it wherever you want, as long as the mount point exists. Use `mkdir` to create your mount point.

After the newly created image file is mounted as a file system, we are free to make changes to it. We can add and delete directories, make device nodes, and so on. We can use `tar` to copy files into or out of it. When the changes are complete, they are saved in the file, assuming that you didn't exceed the size of the device. Remember, using this method, the size is fixed at creation time and cannot be changed.

9.11 Chapter Summary

- Partitions are the logical division of a physical device. Numerous partition types are supported under Linux.

- A file system is mounted on a mount point in Linux. The root file system is mounted at the root of the file system hierarchy and referred to as `/`.

- The popular ext2 file system is mature and fast, and is often found on embedded and other Linux systems such as Red Hat and the Fedora Core series.

- The ext3 file system adds journaling on top of the ext2 file system, for better data integrity and system reliability.

- ReiserFS is another popular and high-performance journaling file system found on many embedded and other Linux systems.

- JFFS2 is a journaling file system optimized for use with Flash memory. It contains Flash-friendly features such as wear leveling for longer Flash memory lifetime.

- cramfs is a read-only file system perfect for small-system boot ROMs and other read-only programs and data.

- NFS is one of the most powerful development tools for the embedded developer. It can bring the power of a workstation to your target device. Learn how to use NFS as your embedded target's root file system. The convenience and time savings will be worth the effort.

- Many pseudo file systems are available on Linux. A few of the more important ones are presented here, including the proc file system and sysfs.

- The RAM-based tmpfs file system has many uses for embedded systems. Its most significant improvement over traditional ramdisks is the capability to resize itself dynamically to meet operational requirements.

9.11.1 Suggestions for Additional Reading

"Design and Implementation of the Second Extended Filesystem"
Rémy Card, Theodore Ts'o, and Stephen Tweedie
First published in the *Proceedings of the First Dutch
International Symposium on Linux*
Available on http://e2fsprogs.sourceforge.net/ext2intro.html

"A Non-Technical Look Inside the EXT2 File System"
Randy Appleton
www.linuxgazette.com/issue21/ext2.html

Whitepaper: *Red Hat's New Journaling File System: ext3*
Michael K. Johnson
www.redhat.com/support/wpapers/redhat/ext3/

ReiserFS Home Page
www.namesys.com/

"JFFS: The Journaling Flash File System"
David Woodhouse
http://sources.redhat.com/jffs2/jffs2.pdf

README file from cramfs project
Unsigned (assumed to be the project author)
http://sourceforge.net/projects/cramfs/

NFS home page
http://nfs.sourceforge.net

The /proc file system documentation
www.tldp.org/LDP/lkmpg/2.6/html/c712.htm

File System Performance: The Solaris OS, UFS, Linux ext3, and ReiserFS
A technical whitepaper
Dominic Kay
www.sun.com/software/whitepapers/solaris10/fs_performance.pdf

Chapter 10

MTD Subsystem

In this chapter

The Memory Technology Devices (MTD) subsystem grew out of the need to support a wide variety of memory-like devices such as Flash memory chips. Many different types of Flash chips are available, along with numerous methods to program them, partly because of the many specialized and high-performance modes that are supported. The MTD layer architecture enables the separation of the low-level device complexities from the higher-layer data organization and storage formats that use memory devices.

In this chapter, we introduce the MTD subsystem and provide some simple examples of its use. First we look at what is required of the kernel to support MTD services. We introduce some simple operations on a development workstation with MTD enabled, as a means to understand the basics of this subsystem. In this chapter, we integrate MTD and the JFFS2 file system.

We next introduce the concept of partitions as they relate to the MTD layer. We examine the details of building partitions from a bootloader and how they are detected by the Linux kernel. The chapter continues with a brief introduction to the MTD utilities. We conclude by putting it all together and booting a target board using an in-Flash JFFS2 file system image.

10.1 Enabling MTD Services

To use MTD services, your kernel must be configured with MTD enabled. Many configuration options exist for MTD, some of which can be confusing. The best way to understand the myriad choices is simply to begin working with them. To illustrate the mechanics of the MTD subsystem and how it fits in with the system, we begin with some very simple examples that you can perform on your Linux development workstation. Figure 10-1 shows the kernel configuration (invoked per the usual `make ARCH=<arch> gconfig`) necessary to enable the bare-minimum MTD functionality. Listing 10-1 displays the `.config` file entries resulting from the selections shown in Figure 10-1.

Listing 10-1

Basic MTD Configuration from `.config`

```
CONFIG_MTD=y
CONFIG_MTD_CHAR=y
CONFIG_MTD_BLOCK=y
CONFIG_MTD_MTDRAM=m
CONFIG_MTDRAM_TOTAL_SIZE=8192
CONFIG_MTDRAM_ERASE_SIZE=128
```

The MTD subsystem is enabled via the first configuration option, which is selected via the first check box shown in Figure 10-1, Memory Technology Device (MTD) Support. The next two entries from the configuration shown in Figure 10-1 enable special device-level access to the MTD devices, such as Flash memory, from user space. The first one (CONFIG_MTD_CHAR) enables character device mode access, essentially a sequential access characterized by byte-at-a-time sequential read and write access. The second (CONFIG_MTD_BLOCK) enables access to the MTD device in block device mode, the access method used for disk drives, in which blocks of multiple bytes of data are read or written at a time. These access modes allow the use of familiar Linux commands to read and write data to the Flash memory, as you shall shortly see.

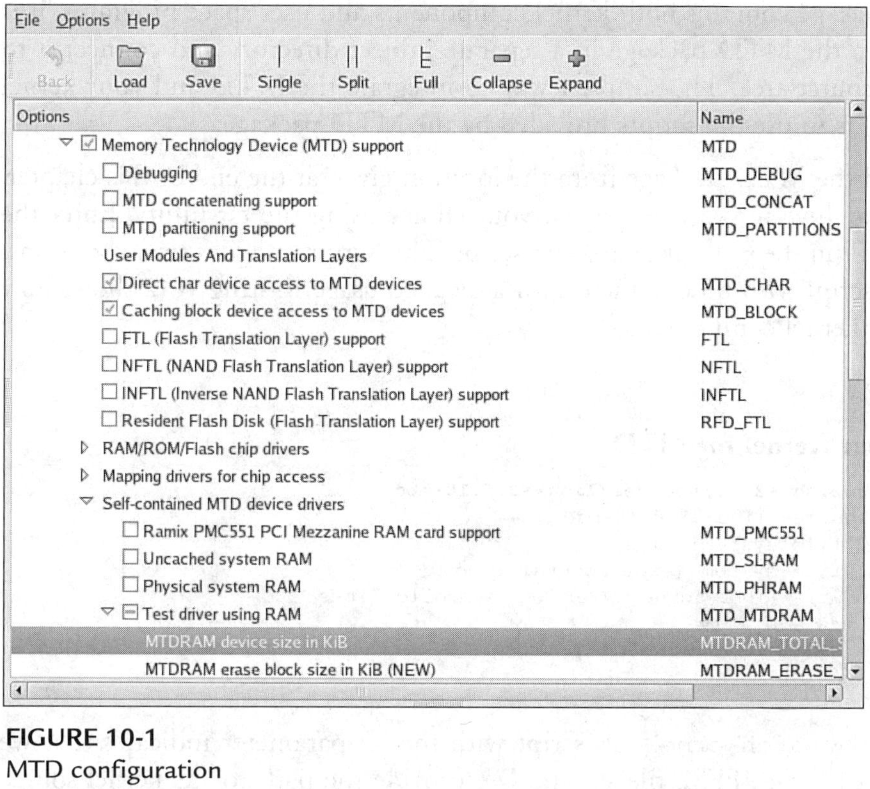

FIGURE 10-1
MTD configuration

The CONFIG_MTD_MTDRAM element enables a special test driver that enables us to examine the MTD subsystem even if we don't have any MTD devices (such as Flash memory) available. Coupled with this configuration selection are two parameters associated with the RAM-based test driver: the device size and the erase size. For this example, we have specified 8192KB total size and 128KB erase size. The objective of this test driver is to emulate a Flash device, primarily to facilitate MTD subsystem testing and development. Because Flash memory is architected using fixed-size erase blocks, the test driver also contains the concept of erase blocks. You will see how these parameters are used shortly.

10.1.1 Building MTD

MTD is included in any recent snapshot of the Linux kernel. However, if you need to take advantage of MTD features that have been added since your kernel version was released, you must download and build the MTD drivers and utilities. Because the MTD package contains both kernel components and user space programs, it is useful to keep the MTD package in a separate project directory and connect it to your kernel source tree. The simplest way to integrate the MTD and your kernel source tree(s) is to use the scripts provided by the MTD package.

Download the MTD package from the location given at the end of this chapter. Unpack the archive into a directory of your choice using the tar utility. Enter the directory and run the `patchkernel.sh` script. This script provides several options. Execute the script with no parameters for a detailed usage. Listing 10-2 shows how to install the kernel components.

Listing 10-2

Patching Your Kernel for MTD

```
$ ./patchkernel.sh -2 ../sources/linux-2.6.10-mtd
Patching ../sources/linux-2.6.10-mtd/
Include JFFS2 file system: jffs2
Include JFFS3 file system (experimental): no
Method: ln       << Will actually create symbolic links
Can we start now ? [y/N]y

$
```

Invoking the `patchkernel.sh` script with the -2 parameter indicates that we want support for the JFFS2 file system. We provide the path to the kernel source directory as `../sources/linux-2.6.10-mtd`. By default, `patchkernel.sh` does not copy any files into the kernel source directory. Instead, it creates symbolic links from the kernel source tree pointing into the MTD subdirectory itself. In this way, you can maintain a common source tree for MTD for any number of kernels that you happen to have on your development workstation. This allows the MTD kernel drivers to be built with the kernel build system, including information about your specific kernel configuration.

10.2 MTD Basics

Now that we have enabled a simple MTD configuration in our kernel, we can examine how this subsystem works on our Linux development workstation. Using the test RAM driver we just configured in the previous section, we can mount a JFFS2 image using an MTD device. Assuming that you created a JFFS2 image as detailed in Chapter 9, "File Systems," you might want to mount it and examine it. The Linux kernel does not support mounting a JFFS2 file system image directly on a loopback device, such as is possible with ext2 and other file system images. So we must use a different method. This can be achieved using the MTD RAM test driver on our development Linux workstation with MTD enabled, as in Figure 10-1. Listing 10-3 illustrates the steps.

Listing 10-3

Mounting JFFS2 on an MTD RAM Device

```
# modprobe jffs2
# modprobe mtdblock
# modprobe mtdram
# dd if=jffs2.bin of=/dev/mtdblock0
 4690+1 records in
 4690+1 records out
# mkdir /mnt/flash
# mount -t jffs2 /dev/mtdblock0 /mnt/flash
# ls -l /mnt/flash
total 0
drwxr-xr-x   2 root root  0 Sep 17 22:02 bin
drwxr-xr-x   2 root root  0 Sep 17 21:59 dev
drwxr-xr-x   7 root root  0 Sep 17 15:31 etc
drwxr-xr-x   2 root root  0 Sep 17 15:31 home
drwxr-xr-x   2 root root  0 Sep 17 22:02 lib
drwxr-xr-x   2 root root  0 Sep 17 15:31 proc
drws------   2 root root  0 Sep 17 15:31 root
drwxr-xr-x   2 root root  0 Sep 17 22:02 sbin
drwxrwxrwt   2 root root  0 Sep 17 15:31 tmp
drwxr-xr-x   9 root root  0 Sep 17 15:31 usr
drwxr-xr-x  14 root root  0 Sep 17 15:31 var
#
```

From Listing 10-3, first we install the loadable modules that the Linux kernel requires to support JFFS2 and the MTD subsystem. We load the JFFS2 module followed by the `mtdblock` and `mtdram` modules. After the necessary device drivers are loaded, we use the Linux `dd` command to copy our JFFS2 file system image into the MTD RAM test driver using the `mtdblock` device. In essence, we are using system RAM as a backing device to emulate an MTD block device.

After we have copied our JFFS2 file system image into the MTD block device, we can mount it using the `mount` command, in the manner shown in Listing 10-3. After the MTD pseudo-device has been mounted, we can work with the JFFS2 file system image in any way we choose. The only limitation using this method is that we can't enlarge the image. The size of the image is limited by two factors. First, when we configured the MTD RAM test device, we gave it a maximum size of 8MB.[1] Second, when we created the JFFS2 image, we fixed the size of the image using the mkfs.jffs2 utility. The image size was determined by the contents of the directory we specified when we created it. Refer back to Listing 9-9, in Chapter 9, to recall how our `jffs2.bin` image was built.

It is important to realize the limitations of using this method to examine the contents of a JFFS2 file system. Consider what we did: We copied the contents of a file (the JFFS2 file system binary image) into a kernel block device (`/dev/mtdblock0`). Then we mounted the kernel block device (`/dev/mtdblock`) as a JFFS2 file system. After we did this, we could use all the traditional file system utilities to examine and even modify the file system. Tools such as `ls`, `df`, `dh`, `mv`, `rm`, and `cp` can all be used to examine and modify the file system. However, unlike the loopback device, there is no connection between the file we copied and the mounted JFFS2 file system image. Therefore, if we unmount the file system after making changes, the changes will be lost. If you want to save the changes, you must copy them back into a file. One such method is the following:

```
# dd if=/dev/mtdblock0 of=./your-modified-fs-image.bin
```

This command creates a file called `your-modified-fs-image.bin` that is the same size as the `mtdblock0` device which was specified during configuration. In our

---

[1] The size was fixed in the kernel configuration when we enabled the MTD RAM test device in the Linux kernel configuration.

example, it would be 8MB. Lacking suitable JFFS2 editing facilities, this is a perfectly valid way to examine and modify a JFFS2 file system. More important, it illustrates the basics of the MTD subsystem on our development system without real Flash memory. Now let's look at some hardware that contains Flash physical devices.

10.2.1 Configuring MTD

To use MTD with the Flash memory on your board, you must have MTD configured correctly. The following list contains the requirements that must be satisfied to configure MTD for your board, Flash, and Flash layout.

- Specify the partitioning on your Flash device

- Specify the type of Flash and location

- Configure the proper Flash driver for your chosen chip

- Configure the kernel with the appropriate driver(s)

Each of these steps is explored in the following sections.

10.3 MTD Partitions

Most Flash devices on a given hardware platform are divided into several sections, called partitions, similar to the partitions found on a typical desktop workstation hard drive. The MTD subsystem provides support for such Flash partitions. The MTD subsystem must be configured for MTD partitioning support. Figure 10-2 illustrates the configuration options for MTD partitioning support.

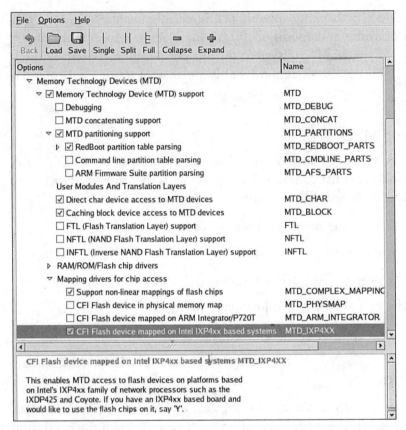

FIGURE 10-2
Kernel configuration for MTD partitioning support

Several methods exist for communicating the partition data to the Linux kernel. The following methods are currently supported. You can see the configuration options for each in Figure 10-2 under MTD Partitioning Support.

- Redboot partition table parsing

- Kernel command-line partition table definition

- Board-specific mapping drivers

MTD also allows configurations without partition data. In this case, MTD simply treats the entire Flash memory as a single device.

10.3.1 Redboot Partition Table Partitioning

One of the more common methods of defining and detecting MTD partitions stems from one of the original implementations: Redboot partitions. Redboot is a bootloader found on many embedded boards, especially ARM XScale boards such as the ADI Engineering Coyote Reference Platform.

The MTD subsystem defines a method for storing partition information on the Flash device itself, similar in concept to a partition table on a hard disk. In the case of the Redboot partitions, the developer reserves and specifies a Flash erase block that holds the partition definitions. A mapping driver is selected that calls the partition parsing functions during boot to detect the partitions on the Flash device. Figure 10-2 shows the mapping driver for our example board; it is the final highlighted entry defining `CONFIG_MTD_IXP4xx`.

As usual, taking a detailed look at an example helps to illustrate these concepts. We start by looking at the information provided by the Redboot bootloader for the Coyote platform. Listing 10-4 captures some of the output of the Redboot bootloader upon power-up.

Listing 10-4

Redboot Messages on Power-Up

```
Platform: ADI Coyote (XScale)
IDE/Parallel Port CPLD Version: 1.0
Copyright (C) 2000, 2001, 2002, Red Hat, Inc.

RAM: 0x00000000-0x04000000, 0x0001f960-0x03fd1000 available
FLASH: 0x50000000 - 0x51000000, 128 blocks of 0x00020000 bytes each.
...
```

This tells us that RAM on this board is physically mapped starting at address 0x00000000 and that Flash is mapped at physical address 0x50000000 through 0x51000000. We can also see that the Flash has 128 blocks of 0x00020000 (128KB) each.

Redboot contains a command to create and display partition information on the Flash. Listing 10-5 contains the output of the `fis list` command, part of the Flash Image System family of commands available in the Redboot bootloader.

Listing 10-5

Redboot Flash Partition List

```
RedBoot> fis list
Name                FLASH addr   Mem addr     Length       Entry point
RedBoot             0x50000000   0x50000000   0x00060000   0x00000000
RedBoot config      0x50FC0000   0x50FC0000   0x00001000   0x00000000
FIS directory       0x50FE0000   0x50FE0000   0x00020000   0x00000000
RedBoot>
```

From Listing 10-5, we see that the Coyote board has three partitions defined on the Flash. The partition named RedBoot contains the executable Redboot bootloader image. The partition named RedBoot config contains the configuration parameters maintained by the bootloader. The final partition named FIS directory holds information about the partition table itself.

When properly configured, the Linux kernel can detect and parse this partition table and create MTD partitions representing the physical partitions on Flash. Listing 10-6 reproduces a portion of the boot messages that are output from the aforementioned ADI Engineering Coyote board, booting a Linux kernel configured with support for detecting Redboot partitions.

Listing 10-6

Detecting Redboot Partitions on Linux Boot

```
...
IXP4XX-Flash0: Found 1 x16 devices at 0x0 in 16-bit bank
 Intel/Sharp Extended Query Table at 0x0031
Using buffer write method
cfi_cmdset_0001: Erase suspend on write enabled
Searching for RedBoot partition table in IXP4XX-Flash0 at offset 0xfe0000
3 RedBoot partitions found on MTD device IXP4XX-Flash0
Creating 3 MTD partitions on "IXP4XX-Flash0":
0x00000000-0x00060000 : "RedBoot"
0x00fc0000-0x00fc1000 : "RedBoot config"
0x00fe0000-0x01000000 : "FIS directory"
...
```

The first message in Listing 10-6 is printed when the Flash chip is detected, via the Common Flash Interface (CFI) driver, enabled via CONFIG_MTD_CFI. CFI is an industry-standard method for determining the Flash chip's characteristics, such as manufacturer, device type, total size, and erase block size. See Section 10.5.1, "Suggestions for Additional Reading," at the end of this chapter for a pointer to the CFI specification.

CFI is enabled via the kernel-configuration utility under the Memory Technology Devices (MTD) top-level menu. Select `Detect flash chips by Common Flash Interface (CFI) probe` under `RAM/ROM/Flash chip drivers`, as illustrated in Figure 10-3.

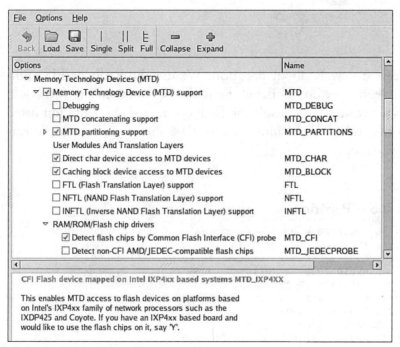

FIGURE 10-3
Kernel configuration for MTD CFI support

As shown in Listing 10-6, the Flash chip is detected via the CFI interface. Because we also enabled `CONFIG_MTD_REDBOOT_PARTS` (see Figure 10-2), MTD scans for the Redboot partition table on the Flash chip. Notice also that the chip has been enumerated with the device name `IXP4XX-Flash0`. You can see from Listing 10-6 that the Linux kernel has detected three partitions on the Flash chip, as enumerated previously using the `fis list` command in Redboot.

When the infrastructure is in place as described here, the Linux kernel automatically detects and creates kernel data structures representing the three Flash partitions. Evidence of these can be found in the `/proc` file system when the kernel has completed initialization, as shown in Listing 10-7.

Listing 10-7

Kernel MTD Flash Partitions

```
root@coyote:~# cat /proc/mtd
dev:    size   erasesize   name
mtd0: 00060000 00020000 "RedBoot"
mtd1: 00001000 00020000 "RedBoot config"
mtd2: 00020000 00020000 "FIS directory"
#
```

We can easily create a new Redboot partition. We use the Redboot FIS commands for this example, but we do not detail the Redboot commands in this book. However, the interested reader can consult the Redboot user documentation listed in Section 10.5.1 at the end of this chapter. Listing 10-8 shows the details of creating a new Redboot partition.

Listing 10-8

Creating a New Redboot Partition

```
RedBoot> load -r -v -b 0x01008000 coyote-40-zImage
Using default protocol (TFTP)
Raw file loaded 0x01008000-0x0114dccb, assumed entry at 0x01008000
RedBoot> fis create -b 0x01008000 -l 0x145cd0 -f 0x50100000 MyKernel
... Erase from 0x50100000-0x50260000: ...........
... Program from 0x01008000-0x0114dcd0 at 0x50100000: ...........
... Unlock from 0x50fe0000-0x51000000: .
... Erase from 0x50fe0000-0x51000000: .
... Program from 0x03fdf000-0x03fff000 at 0x50fe0000: .
... Lock from 0x50fe0000-0x51000000: .
```

First, we load the image we will use to create the new partition. We will use our kernel image for the example. We load it to memory address 0x01008000. Then we create the new partition using the Redboot `fis create` command. We have instructed Redboot to create the new partition in an area of Flash starting at 0x50100000. You can see the action as Redboot first erases this area of Flash and then programs the kernel image. In the final sequence, Redboot unlocks its directory area and updates the FIS Directory with the new partition information. Listing 10-9 shows the output of `fis list` with the new partition. Compare this with the output in Listing 10-5.

Listing 10-9

New Redboot Partition List

```
RedBoot> fis list
Name             FLASH addr   Mem addr    Length       Entry point
RedBoot          0x50000000   0x50000000  0x00060000   0x00000000
RedBoot config   0x50FC0000   0x50FC0000  0x00001000   0x00000000
FIS directory    0x50FE0000   0x50FE0000  0x00020000   0x00000000
MyKernel         0x50100000   0x50100000  0x00160000   0x01008000
```

Of course, when we boot the Linux kernel, it discovers the new partition and we can operate on it as we see fit. The astute reader might have realized the other benefit of this new partition: We can now boot the kernel from Flash instead of having to load it via `tftp` every time. The command is illustrated next. Simply pass the Redboot `exec` command the Flash starting address of the partition and the length of the image to transfer into RAM.

```
RedBoot> exec -b 0x50100000 -l 0x145cd0
    Uncompressing Linux.......... done, booting the kernel.
    ...
```

10.3.2 Kernel Command Line Partitioning

As detailed in Section 10.3, "MTD Partitions," the raw Flash partition information can be communicated to the kernel using other methods. Indeed, possibly the most straightforward, though perhaps not the simplest method is to manually pass the partition information directly on the kernel command line. Of course, as we have already learned, some bootloaders make that easy (for example U-Boot), whereas others do not have a facility to pass a kernel command line to the kernel upon boot. In these cases, the kernel command line must be configured at compile time and, therefore, is more difficult to change, requiring a recompile of the kernel itself each time the partitions are modified.

To enable command-line partitioning in the MTD subsystem, your kernel must be configured for this support. You can see this configuration option in Figure 10-2 under `MTD partitioning support`. Select the option for command-line partition table parsing, which defines the `CONFIG_MTD_CMDLINE_PARTS` option.

Listing 10-10 shows the format for defining a partition on the kernel command line (taken from `.../drivers/mtd/cmdlinepart.c`).

Listing 10-10

Kernel Command-Line MTD Partition Format

```
mtdparts=<mtddef>[;<mtddef]
 * <mtddef>   := <mtd-id>:<partdef>[,<partdef>]
 * <partdef>  := <size>[@offset][<name>][ro]
 * <mtd-id>   := unique name used in mapping driver/device (mtd->name)
 * <size>     := std linux memsize OR "-" to denote all remaining space
 * <name>     := '(' NAME ')'
```

Each `mtddef` parameter passed on the kernel command line defines a separate partition. As shown is Listing 10-10, each `mtddef` definition contains multiple parts. You can specify a unique ID, partition size, and offset from the start of the Flash. You can also pass the partition a name and, optionally, the read-only attribute. Referring back to our Redboot partition definitions in Listing 10-5, we could statically define these on the kernel command line as follows:

```
mtdparts=MainFlash:384K(Redboot),4K(config),128K(FIS),-(unused)
```

With this definition, the kernel would instantiate four MTD partitions, with an MTD ID of `MainFlash`, containing the sizes and layout matching that found in Listing 10-5.

10.3.3 Mapping Driver

The final method for defining your board-specific Flash layout is to use a dedicated board-specific mapping driver. The Linux kernel source tree contains many examples of mapping drivers, located in `.../drivers/mtd/maps`. Any one of these will provide good examples for how to create your own. The implementation details vary by architecture.

The mapping driver is a proper kernel module, complete with `module_init()` and `module_exit()` calls, as described in Chapter 8, "Device Driver Basics." A typical mapping driver is small and easy to navigate, often containing fewer than a couple dozen lines of C.

Listing 10-11 reproduces a section of `.../drivers/mtd/maps/pq2fads`. This mapping driver defines the Flash device on a Freescale PQ2FADS evaluation board that supports the MPC8272 and other processors.

Listing 10-11

PQ2FADs Flash Mapping Driver

```
...
static struct mtd_partition pq2fads_partitions[] = {
        {
#ifdef CONFIG_ADS8272
                .name      = "HRCW",
                .size      = 0x40000,
                .offset     = 0,
                .mask_flags = MTD_WRITEABLE,   /* force read-only */
        }, {
                .name      = "User FS",
                .size      = 0x5c0000,
                .offset     = 0x40000,
#else
                .name      = "User FS",
                .size      = 0x600000,
                .offset     = 0,
#endif
        }, {
                .name      = "uImage",
                .size      = 0x100000,
                .offset     = 0x600000,
                .mask_flags = MTD_WRITEABLE,   /* force read-only */
        }, {
                .name      = "bootloader",
                .size      = 0x40000,
                .offset     = 0x700000,
                .mask_flags = MTD_WRITEABLE,   /* force read-only */
        }, {
                .name      = "bootloader env",
                .size      = 0x40000,
                .offset          = 0x740000,
                .mask_flags = MTD_WRITEABLE,   /* force read-only */
        }
};

/* pointer to MPC885ADS board info data */
extern unsigned char __res[];

static int __init init_pq2fads_mtd(void)
{
        bd_t *bd = (bd_t *)__res;
        physmap_configure(bd->bi_flashstart, bd->bi_flashsize,
                        PQ2FADS_BANK_WIDTH, NULL);

        physmap_set_partitions(pq2fads_partitions,
                        sizeof (pq2fads_partitions) /
                        sizeof (pq2fads_partitions[0]));
```

(continues)

Listing 10-11 (continued)

```
     return 0;
}

static void __exit cleanup_pq2fads_mtd(void)
{
}

module_init(init_pq2fads_mtd);
module_exit(cleanup_pq2fads_mtd);
...
```

This simple but complete Linux device driver communicates the PQ2FADS Flash mapping to the MTD subsystem. Recall from Chapter 8 that when a function in a device driver is declared with the `module_init()` macro, it is automatically invoked during Linux kernel boot at the appropriate time. In this PQ2FADS mapping driver, the module initialization function `init_pq2fads_mtd()` performs just two simple calls:

- `physmap_configure()` passes to the MTD subsystem the Flash chip's physical address, size, and bank width, along with any special setup function required to access the Flash.

- `physmap_set_partitions()` passes the board's unique partition information to the MTD subsystem from the partition table defined in the `pq2fads_partitions[]` array found at the start of this mapping driver.

Following this simple example, you can derive a mapping driver for your own board.

10.3.4 Flash Chip Drivers

MTD has support for a wide variety of Flash chips and devices. Chances are very good that your chosen chip has also been supported. The most common Flash chips support the Common Flash Interface (CFI) mentioned earlier. Older Flash chips might have JEDEC support, which is an older Flash compatibility standard. Figure 10-4 shows the kernel configuration from a recent Linux kernel snapshot. This version supports many Flash types.

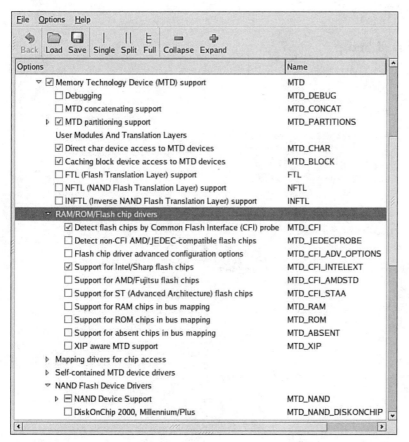

FIGURE 10-4
Flash device support

If your Flash chip is not supported, you must provide a device file yourself. Using one of the many examples in `.../drivers/mtd/chips` as a starting point, customize or create your own Flash device driver. Better yet, unless the chip was just introduced with some newfangled interface, chances are good that someone has already produced a driver.

10.3.5 Board-Specific Initialization

Along with a mapping driver, your board-specific (platform) setup must provide the underlying definitions for proper MTD Flash system operation. Listing 10-12 reproduces the relevant portions of `.../arch/arm/mach-ixp4xx/coyote-setup.c`.

Listing 10-12

Coyote-Specific Board Setup

```
static struct flash_platform_data coyote_flash_data = {
        .map_name    = "cfi_probe",
        .width       = 2,
};

static struct resource coyote_flash_resource = {
        .start            = COYOTE_FLASH_BASE,
        .end              = COYOTE_FLASH_BASE + COYOTE_FLASH_SIZE - 1,
        .flags            = IORESOURCE_MEM,
};

static struct platform_device coyote_flash = {
        .name        = "IXP4XX-Flash",
        .id          = 0,
        .dev         = {
              .platform_data = &coyote_flash_data,
        },
        .num_resources      = 1,
        .resource    = &coyote_flash_resource,
};

...

static struct platform_device *coyote_devices[] __initdata = {
        &coyote_flash,
        &coyote_uart
};

static void __init coyote_init(void)
{
        ...

        platform_add_devices(coyote_devices,
                             ARRAY_SIZE(coyote_devices));
}

...
```

In Listing 10-12, only the relevant portions of the coyote-setup.c platform
initialization file are reproduced. Starting from the bottom, the coyote_init()
function calls platform_add_devices(), specifying the Coyote-specific devices
defined earlier in this file. You'll notice that two devices are defined just above the
coyote_init() routine. The one we're interested in for this discussion is
coyote_flash. This structure of type struct platform_device contains all the
important details needed by the Linux kernel and MTD subsystem.

The `.name` member of the `coyote_flash` structure binds our platform-specific Flash resource to a mapping driver with the same name. You can see this in the mapping driver file `.../drivers/mtd/maps/ixp4xx.c`. The `.resource` member communicates the base address of the Flash on the board. The `.dev` member, which contains a `.platform_data` member, ties our Flash setup to a chip driver. In this case, we have specified that our board will use the CFI probe method, specified in the kernel configuration as `CONFIG_MTD_CFI`. You can see this configuration selection in Figure 10-4.

Depending on your own architecture and board, you can use a method similar to this to define the Flash support for your own board.

10.4 MTD Utilities

The MTD package contains a number of system utilities useful for setting up and managing your MTD subsystem. The utilities are built separately from the primary MTD subsystem, which should be built from within your Linux kernel source tree. The utilities can be built in a similar manner to any other cross-compiled user space code.

You must use caution when using these utilities because there is no protection from mistakes. A single-digit typo can wipe out the bootloader on your hardware platform, which can definitely ruin your day unless you've backed it up and know how to reprogram it using a JTAG Flash programmer.

In keeping with a common practice throughout this book, we cannot devote sufficient space to cover every MTD utility. We highlight the most common and useful ones, and leave it as an exercise for the reader to explore the rest. A recent MTD snapshot contained more than 20 binary utilities.

The `flash_*` family of utilities is useful for raw device operations on an MTD partition. These include flashcp, flash_erase, flash_info, flash_lock, flash_unlock, and others. Hopefully their names are descriptive enough to give some idea of their function. After partitions are defined and enumerated as kernel devices, any of these user space utilities can be run on a partition. We repeat the warning we issued earlier: If you execute `flash_erase` on the partition containing your bootloader, you'll be the proud owner of a silicon paperweight. If you intend to experiment like this, it's a good idea to have a backup of your bootloader image and know how to re-Flash it using a hardware JTAG emulator or other Flash programming tool.

Our new partition created in Listing 10-8 (MyKernel) shows up in the kernel running on the Coyote board, as detailed in Listing 10-13. Here you can see the new partition we created instantiated as the kernel device mtd1.

Listing 10-13

Kernel MTD Partition List

```
root@coyote:~# cat /proc/mtd
dev:    size   erasesize   name
mtd0: 00060000 00020000  "RedBoot"
mtd1: 00160000 00020000  "MyKernel"
mtd2: 00001000 00020000  "RedBoot config"
mtd3: 00020000 00020000  "FIS directory"
```

Using the MTD utilities, we can perform a number of operations on the newly created partition. The following shows the results of a flash_erase command on the partition:

```
# flash_erase /dev/mtd1
Erase Total 1 Units
Performing Flash Erase of length 131072 at offset 0x0 done
```

To copy a new kernel image to this partition, use the flashcp command:

```
root@coyote:~# flashcp /workspace/coyote-40-zImage /dev/mtd1
```

It gets a bit more interesting working with a root file system partition. We have the option of using the bootloader or the Linux kernel to place the initial image on the Redboot flash partition. First, we use Redboot to create the new partition that will hold our root file system. The following command creates a new partition on the Flash called RootFS starting at physical memory 0x50300000, with a length of 30 blocks. Remember, a block, generically called an erase unit, is 128KB on this Flash chip.

```
RedBoot> fis create -f 0x50300000 -l 0x600000 -n RootFS
```

Next, we boot the kernel and copy the root file system image into the new partition we have named RootFS. This is accomplished with the following command from a Linux command prompt on your target board. Note that this assumes you have already placed your file system image in a directory accessible to your board.

As mentioned many times throughout this book, NFS is your best choice for development.

```
root@coyote:~# flashcp /rootfs.ext2 /dev/mtd2
```

The file system can be anywhere from a couple megabytes up to the largest size we have allowed on this partition, so this can take some time. Remember, this operation involves programming (sometimes called flashing) the image into the Flash memory. After copying, we can mount the partition as a file system. Listing 10-14 displays the sequence.

Listing 10-14

Mounting MTD Flash Partition as ext2 File System

```
root@coyote:~# mount -t ext2 /dev/mtdblock2 /mnt/remote ro
root@coyote:~# ls -l /mnt/remote/
total 16
drwxr-xr-x  2 root root 1024 Nov 19  2005 bin
drwxr-xr-x  2 root root 1024 Oct 26  2005 boot
drwxr-xr-x  2 root root 1024 Nov 19  2005 dev
drwxr-xr-x  5 root root 1024 Nov 19  2005 etc
drwxr-xr-x  2 root root 1024 Oct 26  2005 home
drwxr-xr-x  3 root root 1024 Nov 19  2005 lib
drwxr-xr-x  3 root root 1024 Nov 19  2005 mnt
drwxr-xr-x  2 root root 1024 Oct 26  2005 opt
drwxr-xr-x  2 root root 1024 Oct 26  2005 proc
drwxr-xr-x  2 root root 1024 Oct 26  2005 root
drwxr-xr-x  2 root root 1024 Nov 19  2005 sbin
drwxr-xr-x  2 root root 1024 Oct 26  2005 srv
drwxr-xr-x  2 root root 1024 Oct 26  2005 sys
drwxr-xr-x  2 root root 1024 Oct 26  2005 tmp
drwxr-xr-x  6 root root 1024 Oct 26  2005 usr
drwxr-xr-x  2 root root 1024 Nov 19  2005 var
root@coyote:~#
```

Listing 10-14 has two important subtleties. Notice that we have specified /dev/mtdblock2 on the mount command line. This is the MTD block driver that enables us to access the MTD partition as a block device. Using /dev/mtd2 as a specifier instructs the kernel to use the MTD character driver. Both the mtdchar and mtdblock are pseudodrivers used to provide either character-based or block-oriented access to the underlying Flash partition. Because mount expects a block device, you must use the block-device specifier. Figure 10-1 shows the kernel configuration that enables these access methods. The respective kernel configuration macros are CONFIG_MTD_CHAR and CONFIG_MTD_BLOCK.

The second subtlety is the use of the read-only (ro) command-line switch on the `mount` command. It is perfectly acceptable to mount an ext2 image from Flash using the MTD block emulation driver for read-only purposes. However, there is no support for writing to an ext2 device using the `mtdblock` driver. This is because ext2 has no knowledge of Flash erase blocks. For write access to a Flash-based file system, we need to use a file system with Flash knowledge, such as JFFS2.

10.4.1 JFFS2 Root File System

Creating a JFFS2 root file system is a straightforward process. In addition to compression, JFFS2 supports wear leveling, a feature designed to increase Flash lifetime by fairly distributing the write cycles across the blocks of the device. As pointed out in Chapter 9, Flash memory is subject to a limited number of write cycles. Wear leveling should be considered a mandatory feature in any Flash-based file system you employ. As mentioned elsewhere in this book, you should consider Flash memory as a write-occasional medium. Specifically, you should avoid allowing any processes that require frequent writes to target the Flash file system. Be especially aware of any logging programs, such as syslogd.

We can build a JFFS2 image on our development workstation using the ext2 image we used on our Redboot `RootFS` partition. The compression benefits will be immediately obvious. The image we used in the previous `RootFS` example was an ext2 file system image. Here is the listing in long (-1) format:

```
# ls -l rootfs.ext2
-rw-r--r--  1 root root 6291456 Nov 19 16:21 rootfs.ext2
```

Now let's convert this file system image to JFFS2 using the mkfs.jffs2 utility found in the MTD package. Listing 10-15 shows the command and results.

Listing 10-15

Converting RootFS to JFFS2

```
# mount -o loop rootfs.ext2 /mnt/flash/
# mkfs.jffs2 -r /mnt/flash -e 128 -b -o rootfs.jffs2
# ls -l rootfs.jffs2
-rw-r--r--  1 root root 2401512 Nov 20 10:08 rootfs.jffs2
#
```

First we mount the ext2 file system image on a loopback device on an arbitrary mount point on our development workstation. Next we invoke the MTD utility mkfs.jffs2 to create the JFFS2 file system image. The -r flag tells mkfs.jffs2 where the root file system image is located. The -e instructs mkfs.jffs2 to build the image while assuming a 128KB block size. The default is 64KB. JFFS2 does not exhibit its most efficient behavior if the Flash device contains a different block size than the block size of the image. Finally, we display a long listing and discover that the resulting JFFS2 root file system image has been reduced in size by more than 60 percent. When you are working with limited Flash memory, this is a substantial reduction in precious Flash resource usage.

Take note of an important command-line flag passed to mkfs.jffs2 in Listing 10-15. The -b flag is the –big-endian flag. This instructs the mkfs.jffs2 utility to create a JFFS2 Flash image suitable for use on a big-endian target. Because we are targeting the ADI Engineering Coyote board, which contains an Intel IXP425 processor running in big-endian mode, this step is crucial for proper operation. If you fail to specify big endian, you will get several screens full of complaints from the kernel as it tries to negotiate the superblock of a JFFS2 file system that is essentially gibberish.[2] Anyone care to guess how I remembered this important detail?

In a similar manner to the previous example, we can copy this image to our Redboot RootFS Flash partition using the flashcp utility. Then we can boot the Linux kernel using a JFFS2 root file system. Listing 10-16 provides the details, running the MTD utilities on our target hardware.

Listing 10-16

Copying JFFS2 to RootFS Partition

```
root@coyote:~# cat /proc/mtd
dev:    size   erasesize  name
mtd0: 00060000 00020000 "RedBoot"
mtd1: 00160000 00020000 "MyKernel"
mtd2: 00600000 00020000 "RootFS"
mtd3: 00001000 00020000 "RedBoot config"
mtd4: 00020000 00020000 "FIS directory"
root@coyote:~# flash_erase /dev/mtd2
Erase Total 1 Units
Performing Flash Erase of length 131072 at offset 0x0 done
root@coyote:~# flashcp /rootfs.jffs2 /dev/mtd2
root@coyote:~#
```

---

[2] The kernel can be configured to operate with a wrong-endian MTD file system, at the cost of reduced performance. In some configurations (such as multiprocessor designs), this can be a useful feature.

It is important to note that you must have the JFFS2 file system enabled in your kernel configuration. Execute `make ARCH=<arch> gconfig` and select JFFS2 under File Systems, Miscellaneous File Systems. Another useful hint is to use the `-v` (verbose) flag on the MTD utilities. This provides progress updates and other useful information during the Flash operations.

We have already seen how to boot a kernel with the Redboot `exec` command. Listing 10-17 details the sequence of commands to load and boot the Linux kernel with our new JFFS2 file system as root.

Listing 10-17

Booting with JFFS2 as Root File System

```
RedBoot> load -r -v -b 0x01008000 coyote-zImage
Using default protocol (TFTP)
Raw file loaded 0x01008000-0x0114decb, assumed entry at 0x01008000
RedBoot> exec -c "console=ttyS0,115200 rootfstype=jffs2 root=/dev/mtdblock2"
Using base address 0x01008000 and length 0x00145ecc
Uncompressing Linux...... done, booting the kernel.
...
```

10.5 Chapter Summary

- The Memory Technology Devices (MTD) subsystem provides support for memory devices such as Flash memory in the Linux kernel.

- MTD must be enabled in your Linux kernel configuration. Several figures in this chapter detailed the configuration options.

- As part of the MTD kernel configuration, the proper Flash driver(s) for your Flash chips must be selected. Figure 10-4 presented the collection of chip drivers supported in a recent Linux kernel snapshot.

- Your Flash memory device can be managed as a single large device or can be divided into multiple partitions.

- Several methods are available for communicating the partition information to the Linux kernel. These include Redboot partition information, kernel command-line parameters, and mapping drivers.

- A mapping driver, together with definitions supplied by your architecture-specific board support, defines your Flash configuration to the kernel.

- MTD comes with a number of user space utilities to manage the images on your Flash devices.

- The Journaling Flash File System 2 (JFFS2) is a good companion to the MTD subsystem for small, efficient Flash-based file systems. In this chapter, we built a JFFS2 image and mounted it as root on our target device.

10.5.1 Suggestions for Additional Reading

MTD Linux home page
www.linux-mtd.infradead.org/

Redboot user documentation
http://ecos.sourceware.org/ecos/docs-latest/redboot/redboot-guide.html

Common Flash Memory Interface Specification
AMD Corporation
www.amd.com/us-en/assets/content_type/DownloadableAssets/
cfi_r20.pdf

Chapter 11

BusyBox

In this chapter

The man page for BusyBox declares that BusyBox is "The Swiss Army Knife of Embedded Linux." This is a fitting description, for BusyBox is a small and efficient replacement for a large collection of standard Linux command line utilities. It often serves as the foundation for a resource-limited embedded platform. This chapter introduces BusyBox and provides a good starting point for customizing your own BusyBox installation.

We previously alluded to BusyBox in multiple locations. In this chapter, we present the details of this useful package. After a brief introduction to BusyBox, we explore the BusyBox configuration utility. This is used to tailor BusyBox to your particular requirements. We then discuss the requirements for cross-compiling the BusyBox package.

BusyBox operational issues are considered, including how it is used in an embedded system. We examine the BusyBox initialization sequence and explain how this departs from the standard System V initialization. In this section, we also present an example initialization script. After seeing the steps for installing BusyBox on a target system, you will learn about some of the BusyBox commands and their limitations.

11.1 Introduction to BusyBox

BusyBox has gained tremendous popularity in the embedded Linux community. It is remarkably easy to configure, compile, and use, and it has the potential to significantly reduce the overall system resources required to support a wide collection of common Linux utilities. BusyBox provides compact replacements for many traditional full-blown utilities found on most desktop and embedded Linux distributions. Examples include the file utilities such as `ls`, `cat`, `cp`, `dir`, `head`, and `tail`; general utilities such as `dmesg`, `kill`, `halt`, `fdisk`, `mount`, `umount`; and many more. BusyBox also provides support for more complex operations, such as `ifconfig`, `netstat`, `route`, and other network utilities.

BusyBox is modular and highly configurable, and can be tailored to suit your particular requirements. The package includes a configuration utility similar to that used to configure the Linux kernel and will, therefore, seem quite familiar.

The commands in BusyBox are generally simpler implementations than their full-blown counterparts. In some cases, only a subset of the usual command line options is supported. In practice, however, you will find that the BusyBox subset of command functionality is more than sufficient for most general embedded requirements.

11.1.1 BusyBox is Easy

If you are able to configure and build the Linux kernel, you will find BusyBox very straightforward to configure, build, and install. The steps are similar:

1. Execute a configuration utility and enable your choice of features

2. Run `make dep` to build a dependency tree

3. Run `make` to build the package

4. Install the binary and a series of *symbolic links*[1] on your target system

You can build and install BusyBox on your development workstation or your target embedded system. BusyBox works equally well in both environments. However, you must take care when installing on your development workstation that you keep it isolated in a working directory, to avoid overwriting your system's startup files or primary utilities.

11.2 BusyBox Configuration

To initiate the BusyBox configuration, the command is the same as that used with the Linux kernel for the `ncurses` library-based configuration utility:

```
$ make menuconfig
```

Figure 11-1 shows the top-level BusyBox configuration.

---

[1] We cover the details of symbolic links shortly.

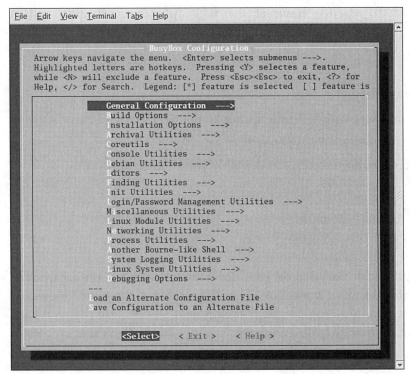

FIGURE 11-1
Top-Level BusyBox Configuration menu

Space does not permit coverage of each configuration option. However, some of the options deserve mention. Some of the more important BusyBox configuration options are found under `Build Options`. Here you will find configuration options necessary to cross-compile the BusyBox application. Listing 11-1 details the options found under `Build Options` in a recent BusyBox snapshot. Select Build Options from the top-level BusyBox configuration utility to navigate to this screen.

Listing 11-1

BusyBox Build Options

```
[ ] Build BusyBox as a static binary (no shared libs)
[ ] Build with Large File Support (for accessing files > 2 GB)
[ ] Do you want to build BusyBox with a Cross Compiler?
() Any extra CFLAGS options for the compiler?
```

The first option is useful for building very minimal embedded systems. It allows BusyBox to be compiled and linked statically so that no dynamically loaded libraries (libc-2.3.3.so, for example) are required at runtime on the target system. Without this option, BusyBox requires some libraries so it can run. We can easily determine what libraries BusyBox (or any other binary) requires on our target system by using the ldd command. Listing 11-2 contains the output as displayed on my desktop Linux workstation.

Listing 11-2

BusyBox Library Dependencies

```
$ ldd busybox
        linux-gate.so.1 =>  (0xffffe000)
        libc.so.6 => /lib/tls/libc.so.6 (0x42c70000)
        /lib/ld-linux.so.2 => /lib/ld-linux.so.2 (0x42c57000)
```

Notice that the BusyBox utility, as compiled using the default configuration, requires the three shared libraries in Listing 11-2. Had we elected to build BusyBox as a static binary, ldd would simply issue a message telling us that the BusyBox binary is not a dynamic executable. In other words, it requires no shared libraries to resolve any unresolved dependencies in the executable. Static linking yields a smaller footprint on a root file system because no shared libraries are required. However, building an embedded application without shared libraries means that you have none of the familiar C library functions available to your applications.

We cover the other options from Listing 11-1 in the next section.

11.2.1 Cross-Compiling BusyBox

As mentioned at the beginning of the chapter, the authors of BusyBox intended the package to be used in a cross-development environment, so building BusyBox in such an environment is quite easy. In most cases, the only requirement is to specify the prefix to the cross-compiler on your development workstation. This is specified in Build Options in the BusyBox configuration utility by selecting the option to build BusyBox with a cross-compiler. You then are presented with an option to enter the cross-compiler prefix. The prefix you enter depends on your cross-development environment. Some examples include xscale_be- or ppc-linux-. We cover this in more detail in the next chapter when we examine the embedded development environment.

The final option in Listing 11-1 is for any extra flags you might want to include on the compiler command line. These might include options for generating debug information (-g), options for setting the optimization level (-O2, for example), and other compiler options that might be unique to your particular installation and target system.

11.3 BusyBox Operation

When you build BusyBox, you end up with a binary called, you guessed it, busybox. BusyBox can be invoked from the binary name itself, but it is more usually launched via a *symlink*. When BusyBox is invoked without command line parameters, it produces a list of the functions that were enabled via the configuration. Listing 11-3 shows such an output (it has been formatted slightly to fit the page width).

Listing 11-3

BusyBox Usage

```
root@coyote # ./busybox
BusyBox v1.01 (2005.12.03-18:00+0000) multi-call binary

Usage: busybox [function] [arguments]...
   or: [function] [arguments]...

  BusyBox is a multi-call binary that combines many common Unix
  utilities into a single executable. Most people will create a
  link to busybox for each function they wish to use and BusyBox
  will act like whatever it was invoked as!

Currently defined functions:
  [, ash, basename, bunzip2, busybox, bzcat, cat, chgrp, chmod,
  chown, chroot, chvt, clear, cmp, cp, cut, date, dd, deallocvt,
  df, dirname, dmesg, du, echo, egrep, env, expr, false, fgrep,
  find, free, grep, gunzip, gzip, halt, head, hexdump, hostname,
  id, ifconfig, init, install, kill, killall, klogd, linuxrc, ln,
  logger, ls, mkdir, mknod, mktemp, more, mount, mv, openvt, pidof,
  ping, pivot_root, poweroff, ps, pwd, readlink, reboot, reset,
  rm, rmdir, route, sed, sh, sleep, sort, strings, swapoff, swapon,
  sync, syslogd, tail, tar, tee, test, time, touch, tr, true, tty,
  umount, uname, uniq, unzip, uptime, usleep, vi, wc, wget, which,
  whoami, xargs, yes, zcat
```

From Listing 11-3, you can see the list of functions that are enabled in this BusyBox build. They are listed in alphabetical order from `ash` (a shell optimized for small memory footprint) to `zcat`, a utility used to decompress the contents of a compressed file. This is the default set of utilities enabled in this particular BusyBox snapshot.

To invoke a particular function, execute `busybox` with one of the defined functions passed on the command line. Thus, to display a listing of files in the current directory, execute this command:

```
[root@coyote]# ./busybox ls
```

Another important message from the BusyBox usage message in Listing 11-3 is the short description of the program. It describes BusyBox as a multicall binary, combining many common utilities into a single executable. This is the purpose of the symlinks mentioned earlier. BusyBox was intended to be invoked by a symlink named for the function it will perform. This removes the burden of having to type a two-word command to invoke a given function, and it presents the user with a set of familiar commands for the similarly named utilities. Listings 11-4 and 11-5 should make this clear.

Listing 11-4

BusyBox Symlink Structure—Top Level

```
[root@coyote]$ ls -l /
total 12
drwxrwxr-x  2 root    root 4096 Dec  3 13:38 bin
lrwxrwxrwx  1 root    root   11 Dec  3 13:38 linuxrc -> bin/busybox
drwxrwxr-x  2 root    root 4096 Dec  3 13:38 sbin
drwxrwxr-x  4 root    root 4096 Dec  3 13:38 usr
```

Listing 11-4 shows the target directory structure as built by the BusyBox package via the `make install` command. The executable `busybox` file is found in the `/bin` directory, and symlinks have been populated throughout the rest of the structure pointing back to `/bin/busybox`. Listing 11-5 expands on the directory structure of Listing 11-4.

Listing 11-5

BusyBox Symlink Structure—Tree Detail

```
[root@coyote]$ tree
.
|-- bin
|   |-- ash -> busybox
|   |-- busybox
|   |-- cat -> busybox
|   |-- cp -> busybox
|   |-- ...
|   '-- zcat -> busybox
|-- linuxrc -> bin/busybox
|-- sbin
|   |-- halt -> ../bin/busybox
|   |-- ifconfig -> ../bin/busybox
|   |-- init -> ../bin/busybox
|   |-- klogd -> ../bin/busybox
|   |-- ...
|   '-- syslogd -> ../bin/busybox
'-- usr
    |-- bin
    |   |-- [ -> ../../bin/busybox
    |   |-- basename -> ../../bin/busybox
    |-- ...
    |   |-- xargs -> ../../bin/busybox
    |   '-- yes -> ../../bin/busybox
    '-- sbin
        '-- chroot -> ../../bin/busybox
```

The output of Listing 11-5 has been significantly truncated for readability and to avoid a three-page listing. Each line containing an ellipsis (. . .) indicates that this listing has been pruned to show only the first few and last few entries of that given directory. In actuality, more than 100 symlinks can be populated in these directories, depending on what functionality you have enabled using the BusyBox configuration utility.

Notice the busybox executable itself, the second entry from the /bin directory. Also in the /bin directory are symlinks pointing back to busybox for ash, cat, cp ... all the way to zcat. Again, the entries between cp and zcat have been omitted from this listing for readability. With this symlink structure, the user simply enters the actual name of the utility to invoke its functionality. For example, to configure a network interface using the busybox ifconfig utility, the user might enter a command similar to this:

```
$ ifconfig eth1 192.168.1.14
```

This would invoke the `busybox` executable through the `ifconfig` symlink. BusyBox examines how it was called—that is, it reads `argv[0]` to determine what functionality is executed.

11.3.1 BusyBox Init

Notice the symlink in Listing 11-5 called `init`. In Chapter 6, "System Initialization," you learned about the `init` program and its role in system initialization. Recall that the kernel attempts to execute a program called `/sbin/init` as the last step in kernel initialization. There is no reason why BusyBox can't emulate the `init` functionality, and that's exactly how the system illustrated by Listing 11-5 is configured. BusyBox handles the `init` functionality.

BusyBox handles system initialization differently from standard System V init. A Linux system using the System V (SysV) initialization as described in Chapter 6 requires an `inittab` file accessible in the `/etc` directory. BusyBox also reads an `inittab` file, but the syntax of the `inittab` file is different. In general, you should not need to use an `inittab` if you are using BusyBox. I agree with the BusyBox man page: If you need runlevels, use System V initialization.[2]

Let's see what this looks like on an embedded system. We have created a small root file system based on BusyBox. We configured BusyBox for static linking, eliminating the need for any shared libraries. Listing 11-6 contains a tree listing of this root file system. We built this small file system using the steps outlined in Chapter 9, "File Systems," Section 9.10, "Building a Simple File System." We do not detail the procedure again here. The files in our simple file system are those shown in Listing 11-6.

---

[2] We covered the details of System V initialization in Chapter 6.

Listing 11-6

Minimal BusyBox Root File System

```
$ tree
.
|-- bin
|   |-- busybox
|   |-- cat -> busybox
|   |-- dmesg -> busybox
|   |-- echo -> busybox
|   |-- hostname -> busybox
|   |-- ls -> busybox
|   |-- ps -> busybox
|   |-- pwd -> busybox
|   '-- sh -> busybox
|-- dev
|   '-- console
|-- etc
'-- proc
4 directories, 10 files
```

This BusyBox-based root file system occupies little more than the size needed for busybox itself. In this configuration, using static linking and supporting nearly 100 utilities, the BusyBox executable came in at less than 1MB:

```
# ls -l /bin/busybox
-rwxr-xr-x    1 root     root       824724 Dec  3  2005 /bin/busybox
```

Now let's see how this system behaves. Listing 11-7 captures the console output on power-up on this BusyBox-based embedded system.

Listing 11-7

BusyBox Default Startup

```
...
Looking up port of RPC 100003/2 on 192.168.1.9
Looking up port of RPC 100005/1 on 192.168.1.9
VFS: Mounted root (nfs filesystem).
Freeing init memory: 96K
Bummer, could not run '/etc/init.d/rcS': No such file or directory

Please press Enter to activate this console.


BusyBox v1.01 (2005.12.03-19:09+0000) Built-in shell (ash)
Enter 'help' for a list of built-in commands.

-sh: can't access tty; job control turned off
/ #
```

The example of Listing 11-7 was run on an embedded board configured for NFS root mount. We export a directory on our workstation that contains the simple file system image detailed in Listing 11-6. As one of the final steps in the boot process, the Linux kernel on our target board mounts a root file system via NFS. When the kernel attempts to execute `/sbin/init`, it fails because there is no `/sbin/init` on our file system. However, as we have seen, the kernel also attempts to execute `/bin/sh`. In our BusyBox-configured target, this succeeds, and `busybox` is launched via the symlink `/bin/sh` on our root file system.

The first thing BusyBox displays is the complaint that it can't find `/etc/init.d/rcS`. This is the default initialization script that BusyBox searches for. Instead of using `inittab`, this is the preferred method to initialize an embedded system based on BusyBox.

When it has completed initialization, BusyBox displays a prompt asking the user to press Enter to activate a console. When it detects the Enter key, it executes an ash shell session waiting for user input. The final message about job control is a result of the fact that we are creating the system console on a serial terminal. The Linux kernel contains code to disable job control if it detects the console on a serial terminal.

This example produced a working system, with nearly 100 Linux utilities available, including core utilities, file utilities, network support, and a reasonably capable shell. You can see that this simple package provides a powerful platform upon which to build your own system applications. Of course, it should be noted that without any support for `libc` and other system libraries, you would face a formidable task implementing your applications. You would have to provide support for all the usual system calls and other library functions that a typical C program relies on. Alternatively, you could statically link your applications against the libraries it depends on, but if you have more than a couple applications using this method, your applications will likely exceed the combined size of linking dynamically and having the shared libraries on your target.

11.3.2 Example rcS Initialization Script

Before BusyBox spawns an interactive shell, it tries to execute commands from a script called `/etc/init.d/rcS`, as shown in Listing 11-7. It is here where your applications come to life in a BusyBox system. A simple `rcS` initialization script is provided in Listing 11-8.

Listing 11-8

Simple rcs BusyBox Startup Script

```
#!/bin/sh

echo "Mounting proc"
mount -t proc /proc /proc

echo "Starting system loggers"
syslogd
klogd

echo "Configuring loopback interface"
ifconfig lo 127.0.0.1

echo "Starting inetd"
xinetd

# start a shell
busybox sh
```

This simple script is mostly self-explanatory. First, it is important to mount the
/proc file system on its reserved mount point, /proc. This is because many utilities get their information from the /proc file system. This is explained more fully
in Chapter 9. Next we launch the system loggers as early as possible, to capture any
startup problems. Following the system log daemons, we configure the local loopback interface for the system. Again, a number of traditional Linux facilities assume
that a loopback interface is present, and if your system has support for sockets
configured, you should enable this pseudo interface. The last thing we do before
starting a shell is launch the Internet superserver xinetd. This program sits in the
background listening for network requests on any configured network interfaces.
For example, to initiate a telnet session to the board, xinetd intercepts the
request for telnet connection and spawns a telnet server to handle the session.

Instead of starting a shell, your own applications can be launched from this rcs
initialization script. Listing 11-8 is a simple example of a Telnet-enabled target
board running basic services such as system and kernel loggers.

11.3.3 BusyBox Target Installation

The discussion of BusyBox installation can proceed only when you understand the
use and purpose of symlinks. The BusyBox makefile contains a target called
install. Executing make install creates a directory structure containing the

busybox executable and a symlink tree. This environment needs to be migrated to your target embedded system's root directory, complete with the symlink tree. The symlink tree eliminates the need to type busybox command for each command. Instead, to see a listing of files in a given directory, the user need only type ls. The symlink executes busybox as described previously and invokes the ls functionality. Review Listing 11-4 and Listing 11-5 to see the symlink tree. Note that the BusyBox build system creates links only for the functionality that you have enabled via the configuration utility.

The easiest way to populate your root file system with the necessary symlink farm is to let the BusyBox build system do it for you. Simply mount your root file system on your development workstation and pass a PREFIX to the BusyBox makefile. Listing 11-9 shows the procedure.

Listing 11-9

Installing BusyBox on Root File System

```
$ mount -o loop bbrootfs.ext2 /mnt/remote
$ make PREFIX=/mnt/remote install
/bin/sh applets/install.sh /mnt/remote
  /mnt/remote/bin/ash -> busybox
  /mnt/remote/bin/cat -> busybox
  /mnt/remote/bin/chgrp -> busybox
  /mnt/remote/bin/chmod -> busybox
  /mnt/remote/bin/chown -> busybox
...
  /mnt/remote/usr/bin/xargs -> ../../bin/busybox
  /mnt/remote/usr/bin/yes -> ../../bin/busybox
  /mnt/remote/usr/sbin/chroot -> ../../bin/busybox


--------------------------------------------------
You will probably need to make your busybox binary
setuid root to ensure all configured applets will
work properly.
--------------------------------------------------

$ chmod +s /mnt/remote/bin/busybox
$ ls -l /mnt/remote/bin/busybox
-rwsr-sr-x  1 root root 863188 Dec  4 15:54 /mnt/remote/bin/busybox
```

First we mount the root file system binary image on our desired mount point— in this case, /mnt/remote, a favorite of mine. Then we invoke the BusyBox make install command, passing it a PREFIX specifying where we want the symlink tree and `busybox` executable file to be placed. As you can see from the listing, the makefile invokes a script called `applets/install.sh` to do the bulk of the work. The script walks through a file containing all the enabled BusyBox applets and creates a symlink for each one on the path we have specified using the `PREFIX`. The script is very chatty; it outputs a line for each symlink created. For brevity, only the first few and last few symlink announcements are displayed. The ellipsis in the listing represents those we have eliminated.

The message about `setuid` is also displayed by the install script, to remind you that it might be necessary to make your `busybox` executable `setuid` root. This is to allow BusyBox functions that require root access to function properly even when invoked by a nonroot user. This is not strictly necessary, especially in an embedded Linux environment, where it is common to have only a root account on a system. If this is necessary for your installation, the required command (`chmod +s`) is shown in Listing 11-9.

The result of this installation step is that the `busybox` binary and symlink tree are installed on our target root file system. The end result looks very similar to Listing 11-4.

It is useful to note that BusyBox also has an option to enable creation of this symlink tree on the target system at runtime. This option is enabled in the BusyBox configuration and is invoked at runtime by executing `busybox` with the `-install` option. You must have the `/proc` file system mounted on your target system for this support to work.

11.3.4 BusyBox Commands

In a recent BusyBox snapshot, 197 commands (also called *applets*) were documented in the man page. There is sufficient support for reasonably complex shell scripts, including support for Bash shell scripting. BusyBox has support for `awk` and `sed`, frequently found in Bash scripts. BusyBox supports network utilities such as `ping`, `ifconfig`, `traceroute`, and `netstat`. Some commands are specifically included for scripting support, including `true`, `false`, and `yes`.

Spend a few moments perusing Appendix C, "BusyBox Commands," where you can find a summary of each BusyBox command. After you have done so, you will have a better appreciation for the capabilities of BusyBox and how it might be applicable to your own embedded Linux project.

As mentioned at the beginning of this chapter, many of the BusyBox commands contain a limited subset of features and options compared to their full-featured counterparts. In general, you can get help on any given BusyBox command at run-time by invoking the command with the `--help` option. This produces a usage message with a brief description of each supported command option. The BusyBox `gzip` applet is a useful example of a BusyBox command that has support for a limited set of options. Listing 11-10 displays the output from `gzip –help` on a BusyBox target.

Listing 11-10

BusyBox `gzip` Applet Usage

```
/ # gzip --help
BusyBox v1.01 (2005.12.01-21:11+0000) multi-call binary

Usage: gzip [OPTION]... [FILE]...

Compress FILE(s) with maximum compression.
When FILE is '-' or unspecified, reads standard input. Implies -c.

Options:
        -c        Write output to standard output instead of FILE.gz
        -d        Decompress
        -f        Force write when destination is a terminal
```

The BusyBox version of `gzip` supports just three command line options. Its full-featured counterpart contains support for more than 15 different command line options. For example, the full-featured `gzip` utility supports a `--list` option that produces compression statistics for each file on the command line. No such support exists for BusyBox `gzip`. This is usually not a significant limitation for embedded systems. We present this information so you can make an informed choice when deciding on BusyBox. When the full capabilities of a utility are needed, the solution is simple: Delete support for that particular utility in the BusyBox configuration and add the standard Linux utility to your target system.

11.4 Chapter Summary

- BusyBox is a powerful tool for embedded systems that replaces many common Linux utilities in a single multicall binary.

- BusyBox can significantly reduce the size of your root file system image.

- BusyBox is easy to use and has many useful features.

- Configuring BusyBox is straightforward, using an interface similar to that used for Linux configuration.

- BusyBox can be configured as a statically or dynamically linked application, depending on your particular requirements.

- System initialization is somewhat different with BusyBox; those differences were covered in this chapter.

- BusyBox has support for many commands. Appendix C itemizes all the available BusyBox commands from a recent release.

11.4.1 Suggestions for Additional Reading

BusyBox Project home
www.busybox.net/

BusyBox man page
www.busybox.net/downloads/BusyBox.html

# Chapter 12

Embedded Development Environment

In this chapter

The configuration and services enabled on your host development system can have a huge impact on your success as an embedded developer. This chapter examines the unique requirements of a cross-development environment and some of the tools and techniques that an embedded developer needs to know to be productive.

We begin by examining a typical cross-development environment. Using the familiar "hello world" example, we detail the important differences between host-based applications and those targeted at embedded systems. We also look at differences in the toolchains for native versus embedded application development. We then present host system requirements and detail the use of some important elements of your host system. We conclude this chapter with an example of a target board being hosted by a network-based host.

12.1 Cross-Development Environment

Developers new to embedded development often struggle with the concepts and differences between native and cross-development environments. Indeed, there are often three compilers and three (or more) versions of standard header files such as `stdlib.h`. Debugging an application on your target embedded system can be difficult without the right tools and host-based utilities. You must manage and separate the files and utilities designed to run on your host system from those you intend to use on your target.

When we use the term *host* in this context, we are referring to the development workstation that is sitting on your desktop and running your favorite Linux desktop distribution.[1] Conversely, when we use the term *target,* we are referring to your embedded hardware platform. Therefore, *native development* denotes the compilation and building of applications on and for your host system. Cross-development denotes the compilation and building of applications on the host system that will be run on the embedded system. Keeping these definitions in mind will help you stay on track through this chapter.

Figure 12-1 shows the layout of a typical cross-development environment. A host PC is connected to a target board via one or more physical connections. It is most

---

[1] Webster's defines *nonsense* as "an idea that is absurd or contrary to good sense." It is my opinion that developing embedded Linux platforms on a non-Linux/UNIX host is nonsensical.

convenient if both serial and Ethernet ports are available on the target. Later when we discuss kernel debugging, you will realize that a second serial port can be a very valuable asset.

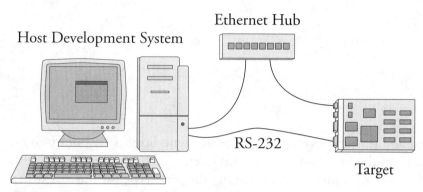

FIGURE 12-1
Cross-development setup

In the most common scenario, the developer has a serial terminal on the host connected to the RS-232 serial port, possibly one or more Telnet terminal sessions to the target board, and potentially one or more debug sessions using Ethernet as the connection medium. This cross-development setup provides a great deal of flexibility. The basic idea is that the host system provides the horsepower to run the compilers, debuggers, editors, and other utilities, while the target executes only the applications designed for it. Yes, you can certainly run compilers and debuggers on the target system, but we assume that your host system contains more resources, including RAM, disk storage, and Internet connectivity. In fact, it is not uncommon for a target embedded board to have no human-input devices or output displays.

12.1.1 "Hello World"—Embedded

A properly configured cross-development system hides a great deal of complexity from the average application developer. Looking at a simple example will help uncover and explain some of the mystery. When we compile a simple "hello world" program, the toolchain (compiler, linker, and associated utilities) makes many assumptions about the host system we are building on and the program we are compiling. Actually, they are not assumptions, but a collection of rules that the compiler references to build a proper binary.

Listing 12-1 reproduces a simple "hello world" program.

Listing 12-1

Hello World Again

```
#include <stdio.h>

int main(int argc, char **argv)
{
    printf("Hello World\n");
    return 0;
}
```

Even the casual application developer will realize some important points about this C source file. First, the function `printf()` is referenced but not defined in this file. If we omit the `#include` directive containing the prototype for the `printf()` function, the compiler emits the familiar message:

```
hello.c:5: warning: implicit declaration of function 'printf'
```

This introduces some interesting questions:

- Where is the file `stdio.h` located, and how is it found?
- Where does the `printf()` function live, and how is this reference resolved in the binary executable?

Somehow it seems that the compiler just *knows* how to put together a proper binary file that is executable from the command line. To further complicate matters, the final executable contains startup and shutdown prologue code that we never see but that the linker automatically includes. This prologue deals with details such as the environment and arguments passed to your program, startup and shutdown housekeeping, exit handling, and more.

To build the "hello world" application, we can use a simple command line invocation of the compiler, similar to this:

```
$ gcc -o hello hello.c
```

This produces the binary executable file called `hello`, which we can execute directly from the command line. Defaults referenced by the compiler provide guidance on where `include` files will be found. In a similar fashion, the linker knows how to resolve the reference to the `printf()` function by including a reference to the library where it is defined. This, of course, is the standard C library.

We can query the toolchain to see some of the defaults that were used. Listing 12-2 is a partial listing of the output from cpp when passed the -v flag. You might already know that cpp is the C preprocessor component of the gcc toolchain. We have added some formatting (whitespace only) to improve the readability.

Listing 12-2

Default Native cpp Search Directories

```
$ cpp -v
Reading specs from /usr/lib/gcc-lib/i386-redhat-linux/3.3.3/specs
Configured with: ../configure --prefix=/usr
└ --mandir=/usr/share/man --infodir=/usr/share/info
└ --enable-shared --enable-threads=posix --disable-checking
└ --disable-libunwind-exceptions --with-system-zlib
└ --enable-__cxa_atexit -host=i386-redhat-linux

Thread model: posix
gcc version 3.3.3 20040412 (Red Hat Linux 3.3.3-7)
 /usr/lib/gcc-lib/i386-redhat-linux/3.3.3/cc1 -E -quiet -v -
ignoring nonexistent directory "/usr/i386-redhat-linux/include"

#include "..." search starts here:
#include <...> search starts here:
 /usr/local/include
 /usr/lib/gcc-lib/i386-redhat-linux/3.3.3/include
 /usr/include
End of search list.
/usr/lib/
```

This simple query produces some very useful information. First, we can see how the compiler was configured using the familiar ./configure utility. The default thread model is posix, which determines the thread library your application gets linked against if you employ threading functions. Finally, you see the default search directories for #include directives.

But what if we want to build hello.c for a different architecture, such as PowerPC? When we compile an application program for a PowerPC target using a cross-compiler on our host machine, we must make sure that the compiler does not use the default *host* include directories or library paths. Using a properly configured cross-compiler is the first step, and having a well designed cross-development environment is the second.

Listing 12-3 is the output from a popular open-source cross-development toolchain known as the Embedded Linux Development Kit (ELDK), assembled and maintained by Denx Software Engineering. This particular installation was configured for the PowerPC 82xx toolchain. Again, we have added some whitespace to the output for readability.

Listing 12-3

Default Cross-Search Directories

```
$ ppc_82xx-cpp -v
Reading specs from /opt/eldk/usr/bin/..
↳ /lib/gcc-lib/ppc-linux/3.3.3/specs

Configured with: ../configure --prefix=/usr
↳ --mandir=/usr/share/man --infodir=/usr/share/info
↳ --enable-shared --enable-threads=posix --disable-checking
↳ --with-system-zlib --enable-__cxa_atexit --with-newlib
↳ --enable-languages=c,c++ --disable-libgcj
↳ --host=i386-redhat-linux -target=ppc-linux

Thread model: posix

gcc version 3.3.3 (DENX ELDK 3.1.1 3.3.3-10)
 /opt/eldk/usr/bin/../lib/gcc-lib/ppc-linux/3.3.3/cc1
↳ -E -quiet -v -iprefix /opt/eldk/usr/bin/..
↳ /lib/gcc-lib/ppc-linux/3.3.3/ -D__unix__ -D__gnu_linux__
↳ -D__linux__ -Dunix -D__unix -Dlinux -D__linux -Asystem=unix
↳ -Asystem=posix - -mcpu=603

ignoring nonexistent directory "/opt/eldk/usr/ppc-linux/sys-include"
ignoring nonexistent directory "/opt/eldk/usr/ppc-linux/include"
#include "..." search starts here:

#include <...> search starts here:
 /opt/eldk/usr/lib/gcc-lib/ppc-linux/3.3.3/include
 /opt/eldk/ppc_82xx/usr/include

End of search list.
```

Here you can see that the default search paths for include directories are now adjusted to point to your cross versions instead of the native include directories. This seemingly obscure detail is critical to being able to develop applications and compile open-source packages for your embedded system. It is one of the most confusing topics to even experienced application developers who are new to embedded systems.

12.2 Host System Requirements

Your development workstation must include several important components and systems. Of course, you need a properly configured cross toolchain. You can download and compile one yourself or obtain one of the many commercial toolchains available. Building one yourself is beyond the scope of this book, although there are several good references available. See Section 12.4.1, "Suggestions for Additional Reading," at the end of this chapter for recommendations.

The next major item you need is a Linux distribution targeted for your embedded system architecture. This includes hundreds to potentially thousands of files that will populate your embedded system's file systems. Again, the choices are to build your own or to obtain one of the commercial ones. One of the more popular embedded system distributions available on the Internet is the aforementioned ELDK. The ELDK is available for some PowerPC and other embedded targets. Building an embedded Linux distribution from scratch would require a book of this size in itself and, therefore, is beyond the scope of our discussions here.

In summary, your development host requires four separate and distinct capabilities:

- Cross toolchain and libraries
- Target system packages, including programs, utilities, and libraries
- Host tools such as editors, debuggers, and utilities
- Servers for hosting your target board, covered in the next section

If you install a ready-built embedded Linux development environment on your workstation, either a commercial variety or one freely available in the open source community, the toolchain and components have already been preconfigured to work together. For example, the toolchain has been configured with default directory search paths that match the location of the target header files and system libraries on your development workstation. The situation becomes much more complex if your requirements include having support for multiple architectures and processors on your development workstation. This is the reason that embedded Linux distributions exist.

12.2.1 Hardware Debug Probe

In addition to the components listed previously, you should consider some type of hardware-assisted debugging. This consists of a hardware probe connected to your host (often via Ethernet) and connected to your target via a debug connector on the board. Many solutions are on the market today. We cover this topic in detail in Chapter 14, "Kernel Debugging Techniques."

12.3 Hosting Target Boards

Referring back to Figure 12-1, you will notice an Ethernet connection from the target-embedded board to the host-development system. This is not strictly necessary, and, indeed, some smaller embedded devices do not have an Ethernet interface. However, this is the exception rather than the rule. Having an Ethernet connection available on your target board is worth its cost in silicon!

While developing the kernel, you will compile and download kernels to your embedded board many times. Many embedded development systems and boot-loaders have support for TFTP and assume that the developer will use it. TFTP is a lightweight protocol for moving files between a TFTP server and TFTP client, similar to FTP.

Using TFTP from your bootloader to load the kernel will save you countless hours waiting for serial downloads even at higher serial baud rates. And loading your ramdisk can take much longer because ramdisk images can grow to many tens of megabytes and more, depending on your requirements. The investment in your time to configure and use TFTP will surely pay off and is highly recommended. There are very few designs that can't afford the real estate to include an Ethernet port during development, even if it is depopulated for production.

12.3.1 TFTP Server

Configuring TFTP on your Linux development host is not difficult. Of course, the details might vary, depending on which Linux distribution you choose for your development workstation. The guidelines presented here are based on Red Hat and Fedora Core Linux distributions.

TFTP is a TCP/IP service that must be enabled on your workstation. To enable TFTP service, you must instruct your server to respond to incoming TFTP packets and spawn your TFTP server. On many Linux distributions, this is done by editing a configuration file used by the xinetd Internet superserver. For example, on the Red Hat and Fedora desktop Linux distributions, this file is /etc/xinetd.d/tftp. Listing 12-4 contains a TFTP configuration from a Fedora Core 2 development workstation to enable the TFTP service. It has been slightly rearranged to fit the page.

Listing 12-4

TFTP Configuration

```
# default: off
# description: The tftp server serves files using the trivial
# file transfer protocol.  The tftp protocol is often used to
# boot diskless workstations, download configuration files to
# network-aware printers, and to start the installation process
# for some operating systems.

service tftp
{
        socket_type             = dgram
        protocol                = udp
        wait                    = yes
        user                    = root
        server                  = /usr/sbin/in.tftpd
        server_args             = -c -s /tftpboot
        disable                 = no
        per_source              = 11
        cps                     = 100 2
        flags                   = IPv4
}
```

In this typical setup, the TFTP service has been enabled (disable = no) and configured to serve files located in this workstation's /tftpboot directory. When the xinetd Internet superserver receives an incoming TFTP request, it consults this configuration and spawns the server specified (/usr/sbin/in.tftpd). The command line arguments specified by server_args are passed to the in.tftpd process. In this case, the -s switch tells in.tftpd to switch to the specified directory (/tftpboot), and the -c flag allows the creation of new files. This is useful to write files to the server from the target.

Consult the documentation that came with your desktop distribution for details specific to your environment.

12.3.2 BOOTP/DHCP Server

Having a DHCP server on your development host simplifies the configuration management for your embedded target. We have already established the reasons why an Ethernet interface on your target hardware is a good idea. When Linux boots on your target board, it needs to configure the Ethernet interface before the interface will be useful. Moreover, if you are using an NFS root mount configuration on your target board, Linux needs to configure your target's Ethernet interface before the boot process can complete. We covered NFS in detail in Chapter 9, "File Systems."

In general, Linux can use two methods to initialize its Ethernet/IP interface during boot:

- Hard-code the Ethernet interface parameters either on the Linux kernel command line or in the default configuration

- Configure the kernel to automatically detect the network settings at boot time

For obvious reasons, the latter choice is the most flexible. DHCP or BOOTP is the protocol your target and server use to accomplish the automatic detection of network settings. For details of the DHCP or BOOTP protocols, see Section 12.4.1 at the end of this chapter.

A DHCP server controls the IP address assignments for IP subnets for which it has been configured, and for DHCP or BOOTP clients that have been configured to participate. A DHCP server listens for requests from a DHCP client (such as your target board), and assigns addresses and other pertinent information to the client as part of the boot process. A typical DHCP exchange (see Listing 12-5) can be examined by starting your DHCP server with the -d debug switch and observing the output when a target machine requests configuration.

Listing 12-5

Typical DHCP Exchange

```
tgt> DHCPDISCOVER from 00:09:5b:65:1d:d5 via eth0
svr> DHCPOFFER on 192.168.0.9 to 00:09:5b:65:1d:d5 via eth0
tgt> DHCPREQUEST for 192.168.0.9 (192.168.0.1) from \
        00:09:5b:65:1d:d5 via eth0
svr> DHCPACK on 192.168.0.9 to 00:09:5b:65:1d:d5 via eth0
```

The sequence starts with the client (target) transmitting a broadcast frame attempting to discover a DHCP server. This is shown by the DHCPDISCOVER message shown. The server responds (if it has been so configured and enabled) by offering an IP address for the client. This is evidenced by the DHCPOFFER message. The client then responds by testing this IP address locally. The testing includes sending the DHCPREQUEST packet to the DHCP server, as shown. Finally, the server responds by acknowledging the IP address assignment to the client, thus completing the automatic target configuration.

It is interesting to note that a properly configured client will remember the last address it was assigned by a DHCP server. The next time it boots, it will skip the DHCPDISCOVER stage and proceed directly to the DHCPREQUEST stage, assuming that it can reuse the same IP address that the server previously assigned. A booting Linux kernel does not have this capability and emits the same sequence every time it boots.

Configuration of your host's DHCP server is not difficult. As usual, our advice is to consult the documentation that came with your desktop Linux distribution. On a Red Hat or Fedora Core distribution, the configuration entry for a single target might look like Listing 12-6.

Listing 12-6

Example DHCP Server Configuration

```
# Example DHCP Server configuration
allow bootp;

subnet 192.168.1.0 netmask 255.255.255.0 {
 default-lease-time 1209600;      # two weeks
  option routers 192.168.1.1;
  option domain-name-servers 1.2.3.4;
  group {
    host pdna1 {
      hardware ethernet 00:30:bd:2a:26:1f;
      fixed-address 192.168.1.68;
      filename "uImage-pdna";
      option root-path "/home/chris/sandbox/pdna-target";
    }
  }
}
```

This is a simple example, meant only to show the kind of information you can pass to your target system. There is a one-to-one mapping of the target MAC address to its assigned IP address. In addition to its fixed IP address, you can pass other information to your target. In this example, the default router and DNS server addresses are passed to your target, along with the filename of a file of your choice, and a root path for your kernel to mount an NFS root mount from. The filename might be used by your bootloader to load a kernel image from your TFTP server. You can also configure your DHCP server to hand out IP addresses from a predefined range, but it is very convenient to use a fixed address such as that shown in Listing 12-6.

You must enable the DHCP server on your Linux development workstation. This is typically done through your main menu or via the command line. Consult the documentation for your own Linux distribution for details suitable for your environment. For example, to enable the DHCP server on a Fedora Core 2 Linux distribution, simply type the following command from a root command prompt:

```
$ /etc/init.d/dhcpd start (or restart)
```

You must do this each time you start your development workstation, unless you configure it to start automatically.

Many nuances are involved with installing a DHCP server, so unless your server is on a private network, it is advisable to check with your system administrator before going live with your own. If you coexist with a corporate LAN, it is very possible that you will interfere with its own DHCP service.

12.3.3 NFS Server

Using an NFS root mount for your target board is a very powerful development tool. Some of the advantages of this configuration for development are:

- Your root file system is not size-restricted by your board's own limited resources, such as Flash memory.

- Changes made to your application files during development are immediately available to your target system.

- You can debug and boot your kernel before developing and debugging your root file system.

Setting up an NFS server varies depending on the desktop Linux distribution you are using. As with the other services described in this chapter, you must consult the documentation for your own Linux distribution for the details appropriate to your configuration. The NFS service must be started from either your startup scripts, a graphical menu, or the command line. For example, the command to start NFS services from a root command prompt for a Fedora Core 2 Linux desktop is as follows:

```
$ /etc/init.d/nfs start (or restart)
```

You must do this each time you start your desktop Linux workstation. (This and other services can be started automatically on booting—consult the documentation for your desktop Linux distribution.) In addition to enabling the service, your kernel must be compiled with support for NFS. Although DHCP and TFTP are both user space utilities, NFS requires kernel support. This is true on both your development workstation and your target board. Figure 12-2 illustrates the configuration options for NFS in the kernel. Notice that there are configuration options for both NFS server and client support. Note also the option for root file system on NFS. Your target kernel must have this option configured for NFS root mount operation.

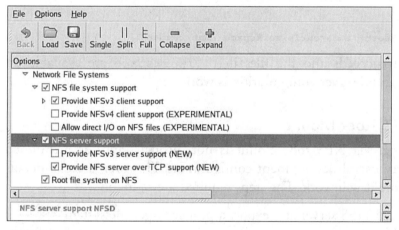

FIGURE 12-2
NFS kernel configuration

The NFS server gets its instructions from an exports file located on your server. It is commonly found in /etc/exports. Listing 12-7 is an example of a simple exports entry.

Listing 12-7

Simple NFS exports File

```
$ cat /etc/exports
# /etc/exports
/home/chris/sandbox/coyote-target *(rw,sync,no_root_squash)
/home/chris/sandbox/pdna-target *(rw,sync,no_root_squash)
/home/chris/workspace *(rw,sync,no_root_squash)
```

These entries on my workstation allow a client to remotely mount any of the three directories shown. The attributes following the directory specification instruct the NFS server to allow connections from any IP address (*) and to mount the respective directories with the given attributes (read/write with `no_root_squash`). The latter attribute enables a client with root privileges to exercise those privileges on the given directory. It is usually required when working with embedded systems because they often have only root accounts.

You can test your NFS configuration right from your workstation. Assuming that you have NFS services enabled (requires both NFS server and client components enabled), you can mount a local NFS export as you would mount any other file system:

```
# mount -t nfs localhost:/home/chris/workspace /mnt/remote
```

If this command succeeds and the files in `.../workspace` are available on `/mnt/remote`, your NFS server configuration is working.

12.3.4 Target NFS Root Mount

Mounting your target via NFS root mount is not difficult, and, as mentioned elsewhere, it is a very useful development configuration. However, a set of details must be correct before it will work. The steps required are as follows:

1. Configure your NFS server and export a proper target file system for your architecture.

2. Configure your target kernel with NFS client services and root file system on NFS.

3. Enable kernel-level autoconfiguration of your target's Ethernet interface.

4. Provide your target Ethernet IP configuration via the kernel command line or static kernel configuration option.

5. Provide a kernel command line enabled for NFS.

We presented the kernel configuration in Figure 12-2 when we explained the NFS server configuration. You must make sure that your target kernel configuration has NFS client services enabled, and, in particular, you must enable the option for Root file system on NFS. Specifically, make sure that your kernel has CONFIG_NFS_FS=y and CONFIG_ROOT_NFS=y. Obviously, you cannot configure NFS as loadable modules if you intend to boot NFS root mount.

Kernel-level autoconfiguration is a TCP/IP configuration option found under the Networking tab in the kernel configuration utility. Enable CONFIG_IP_PNP on your target kernel. When selected, you are presented with several options for automatic configuration. Select either BOOTP or DHCP, as described earlier. Figure 12-3 illustrates the kernel configuration for kernel-level autoconfiguration.

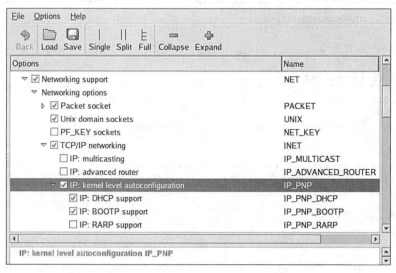

FIGURE 12-3
Kernel-level autoconfiguration

When your server and target kernel are configured, you need to provide your target Ethernet configuration via one of the methods described earlier. If your bootloader supports a kernel command line, that is the easiest method. Here is what a kernel command line might look like to support NFS root mount:

```
console=ttyS0,115200 root=/dev/nfs rw ip=dhcp \
    nfsroot=192.168.1.9:/home/chris/sandbox/pdna-target
```

12.3.5 U-Boot NFS Root Mount Example

U-Boot is a good example of a bootloader that supports a configurable kernel command line. Using U-Boot's nonvolatile environment feature, we can store our kernel command line in a parameter specially named for this purpose. To enable the NFS command line in U-Boot, we do the following (all on one line in our serial terminal):

```
setenv bootargs console=ttyS0,115200 root=/dev/nfs rw \
    ip=dhcp nfsroot=192.168.1.9:/home/chris/sandbox/pdna-target
```

Then we load a kernel via our TFTP server. Listing 12-8 shows what this might look like on a PowerPC embedded target.

Listing 12-8

Loading Kernel via TFTP Server

```
=> tftpboot 200000 uImage-pdna          <<< Entered at U-Boot prompt
Using FEC ETHERNET device
TFTP from server 192.168.1.9; our IP address is 192.168.1.68
Filename 'uImage-pdna'.
Load address: 0x200000
Loading: #################################################
        #################################################
        ######################################
done
Bytes transferred = 911984 (dea70 hex)
=>
```

When we boot the kernel, we see specific evidence of our NFS root mount configuration. Listing 12-9 reproduces selected output from the kernel boot messages to demonstrate this. This output has been formatted (many lines omitted and whitespace added) for readability.

Listing 12-9

Booting with NFS Root Mount

```
Uncompressing Kernel Image ... OK
Linux version 2.6.14 (chris@pluto) (gcc version 3.3.3
└ (DENX ELDK 3.1.1 3.3.3-10)) #1 Mon Jan 2 11:58:48 EST 2006
.
.
Kernel command line: console=ttyS0,115200 root=/dev/nfs rw
└ nfsroot=192.168.1.9:/home/chris/sandbox/pdna-target ip=dhcp
.
.
Sending DHCP requests ... OK
IP-Config: Got DHCP answer from 192.168.1.9, my address is 192.168.1.68
IP-Config: Complete:
     device=eth0, addr=192.168.1.68, mask=255.255.255.0,
     gw=255.255.255.255, host=192.168.1.68, domain=,
     nis-domain=(none), bootserver=192.168.1.9,
     rootserver=192.168.1.9,
     rootpath=/home/chris/sandbox/pdna-target
.
.
Looking up port of RPC 100003/2 on 192.168.1.9
Looking up port of RPC 100005/1 on 192.168.1.9
VFS: Mounted root (nfs filesystem).
.
.
BusyBox v0.60.5 (2005.06.07-07:03+0000) Built-in shell (msh)
Enter 'help' for a list of built-in commands.

#
```

From Listing 12-9, first we see the kernel banner followed by the kernel command line. We specified four items in this kernel command line:

- Console device (/dev/console)

- Root device (/dev/nfs)

- NFS root path (/home/chris/sandbox/pdna-target)

- IP kernel-level autoconfiguration method (dhcp)

Shortly thereafter, we see the kernel attempting kernel-level autoconfiguration via DHCP. When the server responds and the DHCP exchange completes, the kernel displays the detected configuration in the following lines. You can see from this listing that the DHCP server has assigned the target the IP address 192.168.1.68. Compare the detected settings with those specified in Listing 12-6. That was similar to the DHCP server configuration that resulted in this configuration.

When the kernel has completed the IP autoconfiguration, it is capable of mounting the root file system using the supplied parameters. You can see this from the three lines ending with the VFS (virtual file subsystem) message announcing that it has mounted the root NFS file system. After the NFS root file system has been mounted, initialization completes as described in Chapter 5, "Kernel Initialization."

It is also possible to pass target IP settings to the kernel in a static fashion instead of having the kernel obtain IP settings from a DHCP or BOOTP server. IP settings can be passed via the kernel command line directly. In this case, the kernel command line might look similar to this:

```
console=console=ttyS0,115200 \
⌐    ip=192.168.1.68:192.168.1.9::255.255.255.0:pdna:eth0:off \
⌐    root=/dev/nfs rw nfsroot=192.168.1.9:/home/chris/pdna-target
```

12.4 Chapter Summary

- Many features of a development environment greatly facilitate efficiency for embedded cross-development. Most of these fall under the category of tools and utilities. We cover this aspect in detail in the next chapter, where we cover development tools.

- A properly configured development host is a critical asset for the embedded developer.

- Toolchains employed for cross-development must be properly configured to match your host system's target Linux environment.

- Your development host must have target components installed that your toolchain and binary utilities can reference. These components include target header files, libraries, target binaries, and their associated configuration files. In short, you need to assemble or obtain an embedded Linux distribution.

- Configuring target servers such as TFTP, DHCP, and NFS will greatly increase your productivity as an embedded Linux developer. This chapter introduced configuration examples for each.

12.4.1 Suggestions for Additional Reading

GCC online documentation
http://gcc.gnu.org/onlinedocs/

Building and testing gcc/glibc cross toolchains
http://kegel.com/crosstool/

The TFTP Protocol, Version 2
RFC 1350
www.ietf.org/rfc/rfc1350.txt?number=1350

Bootstrap Protocol (BOOTP)
RFC 951
www.ietf.org/rfc/rfc0951.txt?number=951

Dynamic Host Configuration Protocol
RFC 2131
www.ietf.org/rfc/rfc2131.txt?number=2131

Development Tools

In this chapter

A typical embedded Linux distribution includes many useful tools. Some are complex and require a great deal of proficiency to master. Others are simple and have been all but ignored by developers of embedded systems. Some tools might require customization for a particular environment. Many will run "right out of the box" and provide the developer with useful information without much effort. This chapter presents a cross-section of the most important (and frequently neglected) tools available to the embedded Linux engineer.

It is impossible to provide complete details on the tools and utilities presented in this chapter. That would take an entire book by itself! Rather than provide a complete reference, our goal is to provide an introduction on the basic usage of each one. You are encouraged to pursue additional study on these and other important development tools. The man page (or other documentation) for each tool is a great place to start.

The GNU Debugger (GDB) is introduced first, followed by a brief look at the Data Display Debugger, a graphical front end for GDB. Next we introduce a series of utilities designed to give the developer a look at the behavior of programs and the system as a whole. These include `strace`, `ltrace`, `top`, and `ps`, often overlooked by inexperienced Linux developers. We then present some crash dump and memory-analysis tools. The chapter concludes by introducing some of the more useful binary utilities.

13.1 GNU Debugger (GDB)

If you spend much time developing Linux applications, you will undoubtedly spend many hours getting to know the GNU Debugger. GDB is arguably the most important tool in the developer's toolbox. It has a long history, and its capabilities have blossomed to include low-level hardware-specific debugging support for a wide variety of architectures and microprocessors. It should be noted that the user manual for GDB is nearly as large as this book. Our intention here is to introduce GDB to get you started. You are encouraged to study the user manual referenced later under Section 13.7.1, "Suggestions for Additional Reading."

Because this is a book about embedded Linux development, we use a version of GDB that has been compiled as a cross-debugger. That is, the debugger itself runs on your development host, but it understands binary executables in the architecture for which it was configured at compile time. In the next few examples, we use GDB compiled for a Red Hat Linux–compatible development host, and an XScale

(ARM) target processor. Although we use the short name gdb, we are presenting examples based on the XScale-enabled cross-gdb from the Monta Vista embedded Linux distribution for ARM XScale. The binary is called xscale_be-gdb. It is still GDB, simply configured for a cross-development environment.

The GDB debugger is a complex program with many configuration options during the build process. It is not our intention to provide guidance on building gdb—that has been covered in other literature. For the purposes of this chapter, we assume that you have obtained a working GDB configured for the architecture and host development environment you will be using.

13.1.1 Debugging a Core Dump

One of the most common reasons to drag GDB out of the toolbox is to evaluate a *core dump.* It is quick and easy, and often leads to immediate identification of the offending code. A core dump results when an application program generates a fault, such as accessing a memory location that it does not own. Many conditions can trigger a core dump,[1] but SIGSEGV (segmentation fault) is by far the most common. A SIGSEGV is a Linux kernel *signal* that is generated on illegal memory accesses by a user process. When this signal is generated, the kernel terminates the process. The kernel then dumps a core image, if so enabled.

To enable generation of a core dump, your process must have the resource limits to enable a core dump. This is achieved by setting the process's resource limits using the setrlimit() function call, or from a BASH or BusyBox shell command prompt, using ulimit. It is not uncommon to find the following line in the initialization scripts of an embedded system to enable the generation of core dumps on process errors:

```
$ ulimit -c unlimited
```

This BASH built-in command is used to set the size limit of a core dump. In the previous instance, the size is set to unlimited.

When an application program generates a segmentation fault (for example, by writing to a memory address outside its permissible range), Linux terminates the process and generates a core dump, if so enabled. The core dump is a snapshot of the running process at the time the segmentation fault occurred.

---

[1] See SIG_KERNEL_COREDUMP_MASK in .../kernel/signal.c for a definition of which signals generate a core dump.

It helps to have debugging symbols enabled in your binary. GDB produces much more useful output with debugging symbols (gcc -g) enabled during the build. However, it is still possible to determine the sequence of events leading to the segmentation fault, even if the binary was compiled without debugging symbols. You might need to do a bit more investigative work without the aid of debugging symbols. You must manually correlate virtual addresses to locations within your program.

Listing 13-1 shows the results of a core dump analysis session using GDB. The output has been reformatted slightly to fit the page. We have used some demonstration software to intentionally produce a segmentation fault. Here is the output of the process (called webs) that generated the segmentation fault:

```
root@coyote:/workspace/websdemo# ./webs
   Segmentation fault (core dumped)
```

Listing 13-1

Core Dump Analysis Using GDB

```
$ xscale_be-gdb webs core
GNU gdb 6.3 (MontaVista 6.3-20.0.22.0501131 2005-07-23)
Copyright 2004 Free Software Foundation, Inc.
GDB is free software, covered by the GNU General Public
License, and you are welcome to change it and/or distribute cop-
ies of it under certain conditions.
Type "show copying" to see the conditions.
There is absolutely no warranty for GDB.  Type "show warranty"
for details.
This GDB was configured as "--host=i686-pc-linux-gnu -target=armv5teb-
L montavista-linuxeabi"...

Core was generated by './webs'.
Program terminated with signal 11, Segmentation fault.
Reading symbols from /opt/montavista/pro/.../libc.so.6...done.
Loaded symbols for /opt/montavista/pro/.../libc.so.6
Reading symbols from /opt/montavista/pro/.../ld-linux.so.3...done.
Loaded symbols for /opt/montavista/pro/.../ld-linux.so.3
#0  0x00012ac4 in ClearBlock (RealBigBlockPtr=0x0, l=100000000) at led.c:43
43                       *ptr = 0;

(gdb) l
38
39      static int ClearBlock(char * BlockPtr, int l)
40      {
41          char * ptr;
42          for (ptr = BlockPtr; (ptr - BlockPtr) < l; ptr++)
```

```
43                 *ptr = 0;
44          return 0;
45      }
46      static int InitBlock(char * ptr, int n)
47      {
(gdb) p ptr
$1 = 0x0
(gdb)
```

13.1.2 Invoking GDB

The first line of Listing 13-1 shows how GDB was invoked from the command line. Because we are doing cross-debugging, we need the cross-version of GDB that has been compiled for our host and target system. We invoke our version of cross-gdb as shown and pass xscale_be-gdb the name of the binary followed by the name of the core dump file—in this case, simply core. After GDB prints several banner lines describing its configuration and other information, it prints the reason for the termination: signal 11, the indication of a segmentation fault.[2] Several lines follow as GDB loads the binary, the libraries it depends on, and the core file. The last line printed upon GDB startup is the current location of the program when the fault occurred. The line preceded by the #0 string indicates the stack frame (stack frame zero in a function called ClearBlock() at virtual address 0x00012ac4). The following line preceded by 43 is the line number of the offending source line from a file called led.c. From there, GDB displays its command prompt and waits for input.

To provide some context, we enter the gdb list command, using its abbreviated form l. GDB recognizes command abbreviations where there is no ambiguity. Here the program error begins to present itself. The offending line, according to GDB's analysis of the core dump is:

```
43                 *ptr = 0;
```

Next we issue the gdb print command on the ptr variable, again abbreviated as p. As you can see from Listing 13-1, the value of the pointer ptr is 0. So we conclude that the reason for the segmentation fault is the dereference of a null pointer,

---

[2] Signals and their associated numbers are defined in . . . /asm-<arch>/signal.h in your Linux kernel source tree.

a common programming error. From here, we can elect to use the backtrace command to see the call chain leading to this error, which might lead us back to the actual source of the error. Listing 13-2 displays these results.

Listing 13-2

Backtrace Command

```
(gdb) bt
#0   0x00012ac4 in ClearBlock (RealBigBlockPtr=0x0, l=100000000) at led.c:43
#1   0x00012b08 in InitBlock (ptr=0x0, n=100000000) at led.c:48
#2   0x00012b50 in ErrorInHandler (wp=0x325c8, urlPrefix=0x2f648 "/Error",
     webDir=0x2f660 "", arg=0, url=0x34f30 "/Error", path=0x34d68 "/Error",
     query=0x321d8 "") at led.c:61
#3   0x000126cc in websUrlHandlerRequest (wp=0x325c8) at handler.c:273
#4   0x0001f518 in websGetInput (wp=0x325c8, ptext=0xbefffc40,
     pnbytes=0xbefffc38) at webs.c:664
#5   0x0001ede0 in websReadEvent (wp=0x325c8) at webs.c:362
#6   0x0001ed34 in websSocketEvent (sid=1, mask=2, iwp=206280) at webs.c:319
#7   0x00019740 in socketDoEvent (sp=0x34fc8) at sockGen.c:903
#8   0x00019598 in socketProcess (sid=1) at sockGen.c:845
#9   0x00012be8 in main (argc=1, argv=0xbefffe14) at main.c:99
(gdb)
```

The backtrace displays the call chain all the way back to main(), the start of the user's program. A stack frame number precedes each line of the backtrace. You can switch to any given stack frame using the gdb frame command. Listing 13-3 is an example of this. Here we switch to stack frame 2 and display the source code in that frame. As in the previous examples, the lines preceded with (gdb) are the commands we issue to GDB, and the other lines are the GDB output.

Listing 13-3

Moving Around Stack Frames in GDB

```
(gdb) frame 2
#2   0x00012b50 in ErrorInHandler (wp=0x325c8, urlPrefix=0x2f648 "/Error",
     webDir=0x2f660 "", arg=0, url=0x34f30 "/Error", path=0x34d68 "/Error",
     query=0x321d8 "") at led.c:61
61              return InitBlock(p, siz);
(gdb) l
56
57              siz = 10000 * sizeof(BigBlock);
58
59              p = malloc(siz);
60          /*  if (p) */
```

```
61                      return InitBlock(p, siz);
62              /*  else return (0);   */
63      }
64
65
(gdb)
```

As you can see, with a little help from the source code available using the `list` command, it would not be difficult to trace the code back to the source of the errant null pointer. In fact, the astute reader will notice the source of the segmentation fault we have produced for this example. From Listing 13-3, we see that the check of the return value in the call to `malloc()` has been commented out. In this example, the `malloc()` call failed, leading to the operation on a null pointer two frames later in the call chain. Although this example is both contrived and trivial, many crashes of this type are remarkably easy to track down using a similar method with GDB and core dumps. You can also see the null pointer by looking at the parameter values in the function call. This often leads you directly to the frame where the null pointer originated.

13.1.3 Debug Session in GDB

We conclude this introduction to GDB by showing a typical debug session. In the previous demonstration of a program crash, we could have elected to step through the code to narrow down the cause of the failure. Of course, if you get a core dump, you should always start there. However, in other situations, you might want to set breakpoints and step through running code. Listing 13-4 details how we start GDB in preparation for a debug session. Note that the program must have been compiled with the debug flag enabled in the `gcc` command line for GDB to be useful in this context. Refer back to Figure 12-1 in Chapter 12, "Embedded Development Environment"; this is a cross-debug session with GDB running on your development host, debugging a program running on your target. We cover complete details of remote application debugging in Chapter 15, "Debugging Embedded Linux Applications."

Listing 13-4

Initiating a GDB Debug Session

```
$ xscale_be-gdb -silent webs

(gdb) target remote 192.168.1.21:2001
0x40000790 in ?? ()
(gdb) b main
Breakpoint 1 at 0x12b74: file main.c, line 78.
(gdb) c
Continuing.

Breakpoint 1, main (argc=1, argv=0xbefffe04) at main.c:78
78                bopen(NULL, (60 * 1024), B_USE_MALLOC);
(gdb) b ErrorInHandler
Breakpoint 2 at 0x12b30: file led.c, line 57.
(gdb) c
Continuing.

Breakpoint 2, ErrorInHandler (wp=0x311a0, urlPrefix=0x2f648 "/Error",
    webDir=0x2f660 "", arg=0, url=0x31e88 "/Error", path=0x31918 "/Error",
    query=0x318e8 "") at led.c:57
57                siz = 10000 * sizeof(BigBlock);
(gdb) next
59                p = malloc(siz);
(gdb) next
61                return InitBlock(p, siz);
(gdb) p p
$1 =(unsigned char *) 0x0
(gdb) p siz
$2 =  100000000
(gdb)
```

Following through this simple debug session, first we connect to our target board using the gdb target command. We cover remote debugging in more detail in Chapter 15. When we are connected to our target hardware, we set a breakpoint at main() using the gdb break (abbreviated b) command. Then we issue the gdb continue (abbreviated c) command to resume execution of the program. If we had any program arguments, we could have issued them on the command line when we invoked GDB.

We hit the breakpoint set at main(), and set another one at ErrorInHandler(), followed by the continue command, again abbreviated. When this new breakpoint is hit, we begin to step through the code using the next command. There we encounter the call to malloc(). Following the malloc() call, we examine the return value and discover the failure as indicated by the null return value. Finally, we print the value of the parameter in the `malloc()` call and see that a very large memory region (100 million bytes) is being requested, which fails.

Although trivial, the GDB examples in this section should enable the newcomer to become immediately productive with GDB. Few of us have really mastered GDB—it is very complex and has many capabilities. Later in Section 13.2, "Data Display Debugger," we introduce a graphical front end to GDB that can ease the transition for those unfamiliar with GDB.

One final note about GDB: No doubt you have noticed the many banner lines GDB displays on the console when it is first invoked, as in Listing 13-1. In these examples, as stated earlier, we used a cross-gdb from the Monta Vista embedded Linux distribution. The banner lines contain a vital piece of information that the embedded developer must be aware of: GDB's host and target specifications. From Listing 13-1, we saw the following output when GDB was invoked:

```
This GDB was configured as "--host=i686-pc-linux-gnu -
↳ target=armv5teb-montavista-linuxeabi"
```

In this instance, we were invoking a version of GDB that was compiled to execute from a Linux PC—specifically, an i686 running the GNU/Linux operating system. Equally critical, this instance of GDB was compiled to debug ARM binary code generated from the `armv5teb` big endian toolchain.

One of the most common mistakes made by newcomers to embedded development is to use the wrong GDB while trying to debug target executables. If something isn't working right, you should immediately check your GDB configuration to make sure that it makes sense for your environment. You cannot use your native GDB to debug target code!

13.2 Data Display Debugger

The Data Display Debugger (DDD) is a graphical front end to GDB and other command line debuggers. DDD has many advanced features beyond simply viewing source code and stepping through a debug session. Figure 13-1 is a screen shot of the DDD's main screen.

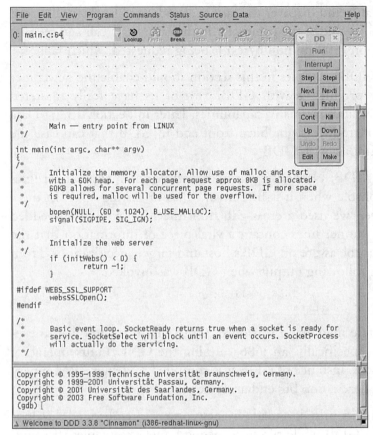

FIGURE 13-1
Data Display Debugger

DDD is invoked as follows:

```
$ ddd --debugger xscale_be-gdb webs
```

Without the --debugger flag, DDD would attempt to invoke the native GDB on your development host, which is not what you want if you are planning to debug an application on your target system. The second argument on the DDD command line is the program you will be debugging. See the man page for DDD for additional details.

Using the command tool as shown in Figure 13-1, you can step through your program. You can set breakpoints either graphically or via the GDB console window at the bottom of the DDD screen. For target debugging, you must first connect your debugger to the target system as we did in Listing 13-4, using the target command. This command is issued in the GDB window of the ddd main screen.

When you are connected to the target, you can execute similar commands to the sequence described in the previous example to isolate the program failure. Figure 13-2 shows the DDD display during the later phase of this debugging session.

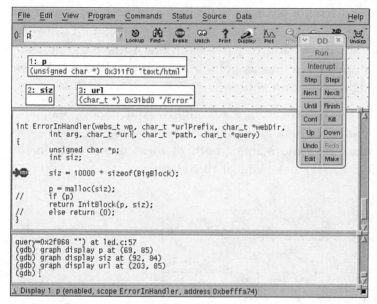

FIGURE 13-2
Debug session in DDD

Notice that in Figure 13-2 we have initiated the display of some important program variables that can help us narrow the cause of the segmentation fault. We can watch these variables as we step through the program using the command tool shown in the figure.

DDD is a powerful graphical front end for GDB. It is relatively easy to use and widely supported for many development hosts. Consult Section 13.7.1 at the end of this chapter for a link to the GNU DDD documentation.

13.3 cbrowser/cscope

We mention cbrowser here because support for this handy tool has found its way into the Linux kernel source tree.[3] cbrowser is a simple source-code browsing tool that makes it easy to bounce around a large source tree following symbols.

---

[3] Actually, support for the underlying engine that cbrowser uses is in the Linux build system.

The Linux kernel makefile supports building the database that `cbrowser` uses. Here is an example invocation from a recent Linux kernel snapshot:

```
$ make ARCH=ppc CROSS_COMPILE=ppc_82xx- cscope
```

This produces the `cscope` symbol database that `cbrowser` uses. `cscope` is the engine; `cbrowser` is the graphical user interface. You can use `cscope` on its own if you want. It is command line driven and very powerful, but not quite as quick or easy for navigating a large source tree in this point-and-click era. If vi is still your favorite editor, `cscope` might be just for you!

To invoke `cbrowser`, enter the directory that contains your `cscope` database, and simply type the `cbrowser` command without arguments. Figure 13-3 shows an example session. You can read more about both of these useful tools in the references listed in Section 13.7.1 at the end of this chapter.

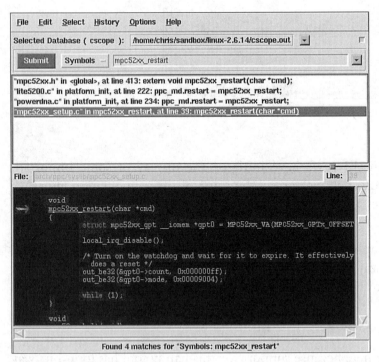

FIGURE 13-3
`cbrowser` in action

13.4 Tracing and Profiling Tools

Many useful tools can provide you with various views of the system. Some tools offer a high-level perspective, such as what processes are running on your system and which processes are consuming the most CPU bandwidth. Other tools can provide detailed analysis, such as where memory is being allocated or, even more useful, where it is being leaked. The next few sections introduce the most important tools and utilities in this category. We have space for only a cursory introduction to these tools; references are provided where appropriate if you want more details.

13.4.1 strace

This useful system trace utility is found in virtually all Linux distributions. strace captures and displays useful information for every kernel system call executed by a Linux application program. strace is especially handy because it can be run on programs for which no source code is available. It is not necessary to compile the program with debug symbols as it is with GDB. Furthermore, strace can be a very insightful educational tool. As the man page states, "Students, hackers and the overly-curious will find that a great deal can be learned about a system and its system calls by tracing even ordinary programs."

While preparing the example software for the GDB section earlier in this chapter, I decided to use a software project unfamiliar to me, an early version of the GoAhead web server. The first attempt at compiling and linking the project led to an interesting example for strace. Starting the application from the command line silently returned control back to the console. No error messages were produced, and a look into the system logs also produced no clues! It simply would not run.

strace quickly identified the problem. The output from invoking strace on this software package is produced in Listing 13-5. Many lines from this output have been deleted due to space considerations. The unedited output is over one hundred lines long.

Listing 13-5

strace Output: GoAhead Web Demo

```
01 root@coyote:/home/websdemo$ strace ./websdemo
02 execve("./websdemo", ["./websdemo"], [/* 14 vars */]) = 0
03 uname({sys="Linux", node="coyote", ...}) = 0
04 brk(0)                                   = 0x10031050
```

(continues)

Listing 13-5 (continued)

```
05 open("/etc/ld.so.preload", O_RDONLY)     = -1 ENOENT (No such file or
↳ directory)
06 open("/etc/ld.so.cache", O_RDONLY)       = -1 ENOENT (No such file or
↳ directory)
07 open("/lib/libc.so.6", O_RDONLY)         = 3
08 read(3, "\177ELF\1\2\1\0\0\0\0\0\0\0\0\0\0\3\0\24\0\0\0\1\0\1\322"..., 1024)
↳ = 1024
09 fstat64(0x3, 0x7fffefc8)                 = 0
10 mmap(0xfe9f000, 1379388, PROT_READ|PROT_EXEC, MAP_PRIVATE, 3, 0) = 0xfe9f000
11 mprotect(0xffd8000, 97340, PROT_NONE)    = 0
12 mmap(0xffdf000, 61440, PROT_READ|PROT_WRITE|PROT_EXEC,MAP_PRIVATE|MAP_FIXED,
↳ 3, 0x130000) = 0xffdf000
13 mmap(0xffee000, 7228, PROT_READ|PROT_WRITE|PROT_EXEC, MAP_PRIVATE|MAP_FIXED|
↳ MAP_ANONYMOUS, -1, 0) = 0xffee000
14 close(3)                                 = 0
15 brk(0)                                   = 0x10031050
16 brk(0x10032050)                          = 0x10032050
17 brk(0x10033000)                          = 0x10033000
18 brk(0x10041000)                          = 0x10041000
19 rt_sigaction(SIGPIPE, {SIG_IGN}, {SIG_DFL}, 8) = 0
20 stat("./umconfig.txt", 0x7ffff9b8)       = -1 ENOENT (No such file or
↳ directory)
21 uname({sys="Linux", node="coyote", ...}) = 0
22 gettimeofday({3301, 178955}, NULL)       = 0
23 getpid()                                 = 156
24 open("/etc/resolv.conf", O_RDONLY)       = 3
25 fstat64(0x3, 0x7fffd7f8)                 = 0
26 mmap(NULL, 4096, PROT_READ|PROT_WRITE, MAP_PRIVATE|MAP_ANONYMOUS, -1, 0) =
↳ 0x30017000
27 read(3, "#\n# resolv.conf  This file is th"..., 4096) = 83
28 read(3, "", 4096)                        = 0
29 close(3)                                 = 0
...     <<< Lines 30-81 removed for brevity
82 socket(PF_INET, SOCK_DGRAM, IPPROTO_IP) = 3
83 connect(3, {sa_family=AF_INET, sin_port=htons(53), sin_addr=inet_addr
↳ ("0.0.0.0")}, 28) = 0
84 send(3, "\267s\1\0\0\1\0\0\0\0\0\0\6coyotea\0\0\1\0\1", 24, 0) = 24
85 gettimeofday({3301, 549664}, NULL)       = 0
86 poll([{fd=3, events=POLLIN, revents=POLLERR}], 1, 5000) = 1
87 ioctl(3, 0x4004667f, 0x7fffe6a8)         = 0
88 recvfrom(3, 0x7ffff1f0, 1024, 0, 0x7fffe668, 0x7fffe6ac) = -1 ECONNREFUSED
↳ (Connection refused)
89 close(3)                                 = 0
90 socket(PF_INET, SOCK_DGRAM, IPPROTO_IP) = 3
91 connect(3, {sa_family=AF_INET, sin_port=htons(53), sin_addr=inet_addr
↳ ("0.0.0.0")}, 28) = 0
92 send(3, "\267s\1\0\0\1\0\0\0\0\0\0\6coyote\0\0\1\0\1", 24, 0) = 24
93 gettimeofday({3301, 552839}, NULL)       = 0
```

```
⁴94 poll([{fd=3, events=POLLIN, revents=POLLERR}], 1, 5000) = 1
95 ioctl(3, 0x4004667f, 0x7fffe6a8)           = 0
96 recvfrom(3, 0x7ffff1f0, 1024, 0, 0x7fffe668, 0x7fffe6ac) = -1 ECONNREFUSED
└ (Connection refused)
97 close(3)                                   = 0
98 exit(-1)                                   = ?
99 root@coyote:/home/websdemo#
```

Line numbers have been added to the output produced by strace to make this listing more readable. Invocation of the command is found on line number 01. In its simplest form, simply add the strace command directly in front of the program you want to examine. This is how the output in Listing 13-5 was produced.

Each line of this trace represents the websdemo process making a system call into the kernel. We don't need to analyze and understand each line of the trace, although it is quite instructive to do so. We are looking for any anomalies that might help pinpoint why the program won't run. In the first several lines, Linux is setting up the environment in which the program will execute. We see several open() system calls to /etc/ld.so.*, which are the Linux dynamic linker-loader (ld.so) doing its job. In fact, line 06 was my clue that this example embedded board had not been properly configured. There should be a linker cache produced by running ldconfig. (The linker cache substantially speeds up searching for shared library references.) This was subsequently resolved by running ldconfig on the target.

Down through line 19 is more basic housekeeping, mostly by the loader and libc initializing. Notice in line 20 that the program is looking for a configuration file but did not find one. That could be an important issue when we get the software running. Starting with line 24, the program begins to set up and configure the appropriate networking resources that it needs. Lines 24 through 29 open and read a Linux system file containing instructions for the DNS service to resolve hostnames. Local network configuration activity continues through line 81. Most of this activity consists of network setup and configuration necessary to build the networking infrastructure for the program itself. This portion of the listing has been removed for brevity and clarity.

Notice especially the network activity starting with line 82. Here we have the program trying to establish a TCP/IP connection to an IP address of all zeros. Line 82 is reproduced here for convenience:

```
socket(PF_INET, SOCK_DGRAM, IPPROTO_IP) = 3
```

---

[4] See man ldconfig for details on creating a linker cache for your target system.

A couple points about Listing 13-5 are worth noting. We might not know all the details of every system call, but we can get a general idea of what is happening. The socket() system call is similar to a file system open() call. The return value, indicated by the = sign, in this case, represents a Linux file descriptor. Knowing this, we can associate the activity from line 82 through the close() system call in line 89 with file descriptor 3.

We are interested in this group of related system calls because we see an error message in line 88: "Connection refused." At this point, we still don't know why the program won't run, but this appears abnormal. Let's investigate. Line 82, the system call to socket(), establishes an endpoint for IP communication. Line 83 is quite curious because it tries to establish a connection to a remote endpoint (socket) containing an IP address of all zeros. We don't have to be network experts to suspect that this might be causing trouble.[5] Line 83 provides another important clue: The port parameter is set to 53. A quick Google search for TCP/IP port numbers reveals that port 53 is the Domain Name Service, or DNS.

Line 84 provides yet another clue. Our board has a hostname of coyote. This can be seen as part of the command prompt in line 01 of Listing 13-5. It appears that this activity is a DNS lookup for our board's hostname, which is failing. As an experiment, we add an entry in our target system's /etc/hosts[6] file to associate our locally defined hostname with the board's IP locally assigned IP address, as follows:

```
Coyote  192.168.1.21          #The IP address we assigned
```

Voilà: Our program begins to function normally. Although we might not know exactly why this would lead to a program failure (TCP/IP networking experts might), our strace output led us to the fact that a DNS lookup for our board name was failing. When we corrected that, the program started up happily and began serving web pages. To recap, this was a program for which we had no source code to reference, and it had no symbols compiled into its binary image. Using strace, we were able to determine the cause of the program failure, and implement a solution.

---

[5] Sometimes an all-zeros address is appropriate in this context. However, we are investigating why the program bailed abnormally, so we should consider this suspect.

[6] See man hosts for details of this system administration file.

13.4.2 strace Variations

The `strace` utility has many command line options. One of the more useful includes the capability to select a subset of system calls for tracing. For example, if you want to see only the network-related activity of a given process, issue the command as follows:

```
$ strace -e trace=network process_name
```

This produces a trace of all the network-related system calls, such as `socket()`, `connect()`, `recvfrom()`, and `send()`. This is a powerful way to view the network activity of a given program. Several other subsets are available. For example, you can view only the file-related activities of a program, with `open()`, `close()`, `read()`, `write()`, and so on. Additional subsets include process-related system calls, signal-related system calls, and IPC-related system calls.

It is worth noting that `strace` is capable of dealing with tracing programs that spawn additional processes. Invoking `strace` with the `-f` option instructs `strace` to follow child processes that are created using the `fork()` system call. Numerous possibilities exist with the `strace` command. The best way to become proficient with this powerful utility is to use it. Make it a point with this and all the tools we present to seek out and read the latest open-source documentation. In this case, `man strace` on most Linux hosts will produce enough material to keep you experimenting for an afternoon!

One very useful way to employ `strace` is using the `-c` option. This option produces a high-level profiling of your application. Using the `-c` option, `strace` accumulates statistics on each system call, how many times it was encountered, how many times errors were returned, and the time spent in each system call. Listing 13-6 is an example of running `strace -c` on the webs demo from the previous example.

Listing 13-6

Profiling Using `strace`

```
root@coyote$ strace -c ./webs
% time     seconds  usecs/call     calls    errors syscall
------ ----------- ----------- --------- --------- --------
 29.80    0.034262         189       181           send
 18.46    0.021226        1011        21        10 open
 14.11    0.016221         130       125           read
 11.87    0.013651         506        27         8 stat64
  5.88    0.006762         193        35           select
  5.28    0.006072          76        80           fcntl64
  3.47    0.003994          65        61           time
  2.79    0.003205        3205         1           execve
  1.71    0.001970          90        22         3 recv
  1.62    0.001868          85        22           close
  1.61    0.001856         169        11           shutdown
  1.38    0.001586         144        11           accept
  0.41    0.000470          94         5           mmap2
  0.26    0.000301         100         3           mprotect
  0.24    0.000281          94         3           brk
  0.17    0.000194         194         1         1 access
  0.13    0.000150         150         1           lseek
  0.12    0.000141          47         3           uname
  0.11    0.000132         132         1           listen
  0.11    0.000128         128         1           socket
  0.09    0.000105          53         2           fstat64
  0.08    0.000097          97         1           munmap
  0.06    0.000064          64         1           getcwd
  0.05    0.000063          63         1           bind
  0.05    0.000054          54         1           setsockopt
  0.04    0.000048          48         1           rt_sigaction
  0.04    0.000046          46         1           gettimeofday
  0.03    0.000038          38         1           getpid
------ ----------- ----------- --------- --------- --------
100.00    0.114985                   624        22 total
```

This is a very useful way to get a high-level view of where your application is consuming time and where errors are occurring. Some errors might be a normal part of your application's operation, but others might be consuming time that you hadn't intended. From Listing 13-6, we can see that the syscall with the longest duration was the `execve()`, which is the call that the shell used to spawn the application. As you can see, it was called only once. Another interesting observation is that the `send()` system call was the most frequently used syscall. This makes sense—the application is a small web server.

Bear in mind that, like the other tools we have been discussing here, `strace` must be compiled for your target architecture. `strace` is executed on your target board, not your development host. You must use a version that is compatible with your architecture. If you purchase a commercial embedded Linux distribution, you should make sure that this utility is included for your chosen architecture.

13.4.3 ltrace

The `ltrace` and `strace` utilities are closely related. The `ltrace` utility does for library calls what `strace` does for system calls. It is invoked in a similar fashion: Precede the program to be traced by the tracer utility, as follows:

```
$ ltrace ./example
```

Listing 13-7 reproduces the output of `ltrace` on a small example program that executes a handful of standard C library calls.

Listing 13-7

Example `ltrace` Output

```
$ ltrace ./example
__libc_start_main(0x8048594, 1, 0xbffff944, 0x80486b4, 0x80486fc
└ <unfinished ...>
malloc(256)                                     = 0x804a008
getenv("HOME")                                  = "/home/chris"
strncpy(0x804a008, "/home", 5)                  = 0x804a008
fopen("foo.txt", "w")                           = 0x804a110
printf("$HOME = %s\n", "/home/chris"$HOME = /home/chris
)                    = 20
fprintf(0x804a110, "$HOME = %s\n", "/home/chris") = 20
fclose(0x804a110)                               = 0
remove("foo.txt")                               = 0
free(0x804a008)                                 = <void>
+++ exited (status 0) +++
$
```

For each library call, the name of the call is displayed, along with varying portions of the parameters to the call. Similar to `strace`, the return value of the library call is then displayed. As with `strace`, this tool can be used on programs for which source code is not available.

As with `strace`, a variety of switches affect the behavior of `ltrace`. You can display the value of the program counter at each library call, which can be helpful in understanding your application's program flow. As with `strace`, you can use -c to accumulate and report count, error, and time statistics, making a useful simple profiling tool. Listing 13-8 displays the results of our simple example program using the -c option.

Listing 13-8

Profiling Using `ltrace`

```
$ ltrace -c ./example
$HOME = /home/chris
% time     seconds     usecs/call    calls     function
------  -----------  -----------  ---------  ----------------
 24.16    0.000231         231        1 printf
 16.53    0.000158         158        1 fclose
 16.00    0.000153         153        1 fopen
 13.70    0.000131         131        1 malloc
 10.67    0.000102         102        1 remove
  9.31    0.000089          89        1 fprintf
  3.35    0.000032          32        1 getenv
  3.14    0.000030          30        1 free
  3.14    0.000030          30        1 strncpy
------  -----------  -----------  ---------  ----------------
100.00    0.000956                      9 total
```

The `ltrace` tool is available only for programs that have been compiled to use dynamically linked shared library objects. This is the usual default, so unless you explicitly specify `-static` when compiling, you can use `ltrace` on the resulting binary. Again similar to `strace`, you must use an `ltrace` binary that has been compiled for your target architecture. These utilities are run on the target, not the host development system.

13.4.4 ps

With the possible exception of `strace` and `ltrace`, no tools are more often neglected by the embedded systems developer than `top` and `ps`. Given the myriad options available for each utility, we could easily devote an entire chapter to these useful system-profiling tools. They are almost universally available in embedded Linux distributions.

Both of these utilities make use of the `/proc` file system, as described in Chapter 9, "File Systems." Much of the information they convey can be learned from the `/proc` file system if you know what to look for and how to parse the resulting information. These tools present that information in a convenient human-readable form.

The `ps` utility lists all the running processes on a machine. However, it is very flexible and can be tailored to provide much useful data on the state of a running machine and the processes running on it. For example, `ps` can display the scheduling policy of each process. This is particularly useful for systems that employ real-time processes.

Without any options, ps displays all processes with the same user ID as the user who invoked the command, and only those processes associated with the terminal on which the command was issued. This is useful when many jobs have been spawned by that user and terminal.

Passing options to ps can be confusing because ps supports a wide variety of standards (as in POSIX versus UNIX) and three distinct options styles: BSD, UNIX, and GNU. In general, BSD options are single or multiple letters, with no dash. UNIX options are the familiar dash-letter combinations, and GNU uses long argument formats preceded by double dashes. Refer to the man page for details of your ps implementation.

Everyone who uses ps likely has a favorite invocation. One particularly useful general-purpose invocation is ps aux. This displays every process on the system. Listing 13-9 is an example from a running embedded target board.

Listing 13-9

Process Listing

```
$ ps aux
USER       PID %CPU %MEM    VSZ   RSS TTY     STAT START   TIME COMMAND
root         1  0.0  0.8   1416   508 ?       S    00:00   0:00 init [3]
root         2  0.0  0.0      0     0 ?       S<   00:00   0:00 [ksoftirqd/0]
root         3  0.0  0.0      0     0 ?       S<   00:00   0:00 [desched/0]
root         4  0.0  0.0      0     0 ?       S<   00:00   0:00 [events/0]
root         5  0.0  0.0      0     0 ?       S<   00:00   0:00 [khelper]
root        10  0.0  0.0      0     0 ?       S<   00:00   0:00 [kthread]
root        21  0.0  0.0      0     0 ?       S<   00:00   0:00 [kblockd/0]
root        62  0.0  0.0      0     0 ?       S    00:00   0:00 [pdflush]
root        63  0.0  0.0      0     0 ?       S    00:00   0:00 [pdflush]
root        65  0.0  0.0      0     0 ?       S<   00:00   0:00 [aio/0]
root        36  0.0  0.0      0     0 ?       S    00:00   0:00 [kapmd]
root        64  0.0  0.0      0     0 ?       S    00:00   0:00 [kswapd0]
root       617  0.0  0.0      0     0 ?       S    00:00   0:00 [mtdblockd]
root       638  0.0  0.0      0     0 ?       S    00:00   0:00 [rpciod]
bin        834  0.0  0.7   1568   444 ?       Ss   00:00   0:00 /sbin/portmap
root       861  0.0  0.0      0     0 ?       S    00:00   0:00 [lockd]
root       868  0.0  0.9   1488   596 ?       Ss   00:00   0:00 /sbin/syslogd -r
root       876  0.0  0.7   1416   456 ?       Ss   00:00   0:00 /sbin/klogd -x
root       884  0.0  1.1   1660   700 ?       Ss   00:00   0:00 /usr/sbin/rpc.statd
root       896  0.0  0.9   1668   584 ?       Ss   00:00   0:00 /usr/sbin/inetd
root       909  0.0  2.2   2412  1372 ?       Ss+  00:00   0:00 -bash
telnetd    953  0.3  1.1   1736   732 ?       S    05:58   0:00 in.telnetd
root       954  0.2  2.1   2384  1348 pts/0   Ss   05:58   0:00 -bash
root       960  0.0  1.2   2312   772 pts/0   R+   05:59   0:00 ps aux
```

This is but one of the many ways to view output data using ps. The columns are explained in the following text.

- The USER and process ID (PID) fields should be self-explanatory.

- The %CPU field expresses the percent of CPU utilization since the beginning of the process's lifetime; thus, CPU usage will virtually never add up to 100 percent.

- The %MEM field indicates the ratio of the process's resident memory footprint to the total available physical memory.

- The VSZ field is the virtual memory size of the process in kilobytes.

- RSS is resident set size and indicates the nonswapped physical memory that a process has used, also in kilobytes.

- TTY is the controlling terminal of the process.

Most of the processes in this example are not associated with a controlling terminal. The ps command that generated Listing 13-9 was issued from a Telnet session, which is indicated by the pts/0 terminal device.

The STAT field describes the state of the process at the time this snapshot was produced. Here, S means that the process is sleeping, waiting on an event of some type, often I/O. R means that the process is in a runnable state (that is, the scheduler is free to give it control of the CPU if nothing of a higher priority is waiting). The left bracket next to the state letter is an indication that this process has a higher priority.

The final column is the command name. Those listed in brackets are kernel threads. Many more symbols and options are available; refer to the man page for ps for complete details.

13.4.5 top

Whereas ps is a one-time snapshot of the current system, top takes periodic snapshots of the state of the system and its processes. Similar to ps, top has numerous command line and configuration options. It is interactive and can be reconfigured while operating to customize the display to your particular needs.

Entered without options, `top` displays all running processes in a fashion very similar to the `ps aux` command presented in Listing 13-9, updated every 3 seconds. Of course, this and many other aspects of `top` are user configurable. The first few lines of the `top` screen display system information, also updated every 3 seconds. This includes the system uptime, the number of users, information on the number of processes and their state, and much more.

Listing 13-10 shows `top` in its default configuration, resulting from executing `top` from the command line without parameters.

Listing 13-10

top

```
top - 06:23:14 up  6:23,   2 users,  load average: 0.00, 0.00, 0.00
Tasks:  24 total,   1 running,  23 sleeping,   0 stopped,   0 zombie
Cpu(s):   0.0% us,   0.3% sy,   0.0% ni, 99.7% id,   0.0% wa,   0.0% hi,   0.0% si
Mem:      62060k total,   17292k used,    44768k free,        0k buffers
Swap:         0k total,       0k used,        0k free,    11840k cached

  PID USER      PR  NI  VIRT  RES  SHR S %CPU %MEM    TIME+  COMMAND
  978 root      16   0  1924  952  780 R  0.3  1.5   0:01.22 top
    1 root      16   0  1416  508  452 S  0.0  0.8   0:00.47 init
    2 root       5 -10     0    0    0 S  0.0  0.0   0:00.00 ksoftirqd/0
    3 root       5 -10     0    0    0 S  0.0  0.0   0:00.00 desched/0
    4 root      -2  -5     0    0    0 S  0.0  0.0   0:00.00 events/0
    5 root      10  -5     0    0    0 S  0.0  0.0   0:00.09 khelper
   10 root      18  -5     0    0    0 S  0.0  0.0   0:00.00 kthread
   21 root      20  -5     0    0    0 S  0.0  0.0   0:00.00 kblockd/0
   62 root      20   0     0    0    0 S  0.0  0.0   0:00.00 pdflush
   63 root      15   0     0    0    0 S  0.0  0.0   0:00.00 pdflush
   65 root      19  -5     0    0    0 S  0.0  0.0   0:00.00 aio/0
   36 root      25   0     0    0    0 S  0.0  0.0   0:00.00 kapmd
   64 root      25   0     0    0    0 S  0.0  0.0   0:00.00 kswapd0
  617 root      25   0     0    0    0 S  0.0  0.0   0:00.00 mtdblockd
  638 root      15   0     0    0    0 S  0.0  0.0   0:00.34 rpciod
  834 bin       15   0  1568  444  364 S  0.0  0.7   0:00.00 portmap
  861 root      20   0     0    0    0 S  0.0  0.0   0:00.00 lockd
  868 root      16   0  1488  596  504 S  0.0  1.0   0:00.11 syslogd
  876 root      19   0  1416  456  396 S  0.0  0.7   0:00.00 klogd
  884 root      18   0  1660  700  612 S  0.0  1.1   0:00.02 rpc.statd
  896 root      16   0  1668  584  504 S  0.0  0.9   0:00.00 inetd
  909 root      15   0  2412 1372 1092 S  0.0  2.2   0:00.34 bash
  953 telnetd   16   0  1736  736  616 S  0.0  1.2   0:00.27 in.telnetd
  954 root      15   0  2384 1348 1096 S  0.0  2.2   0:00.16 bash
```

The default columns from Listing 13-10 are the PID, the user, the process priority, the process *nice* value, the virtual memory used by the process, the resident memory footprint, the amount of shared memory used by the task, and other fields that are identical to those described in the previous ps example.

Space permits only a cursory introduction to these useful utilities. You are encouraged to spend an afternoon with the man pages for top and ps to explore the richness of their capabilities.

13.4.6 mtrace

The mtrace package is a simple utility that analyzes and reports on calls to malloc(), realloc(), and free() in your application. It is easy to use and can potentially help spot trouble in your application. As with other userland tools we have been describing in this chapter, you must have the mtrace package configured and compiled for your architecture. mtrace is a malloc replacement library that is installed on your target. Your application enables it with a special function call. Your embedded Linux distribution should contain the mtrace package.

To demonstrate this utility, we created a simple program that creates dynamic data on a simple linked list. Each list item was dynamically generated, as was each data item we placed on the list. Listing 13-11 reproduces the simple list structure.

Listing 13-11

Simple Linear Linked List

```
struct blist_s {
  struct blist_s *next;
  char *data_item;
  int item_size;
  int index;
};
```

Each list item was dynamically created using malloc() as follows and subsequently placed at the end of the linked list:

```
struct blist_s *p = malloc( sizeof(struct blist_s) );
```

Each variable-sized data item in the list was also dynamically generated and added to the list item before being placed at the end of the list. This way, every list item was created using two calls to `malloc()`, one for the list item itself, represented by `struct blist_s` just shown, and one for the variable data item. We then generated 10,000 records on the list containing variable string data, resulting in 20,000 calls to `malloc()`.

To use `mtrace`, three conditions must be satisfied:

- A header file, `mcheck.h`, must be included in the source file.

- The application must call `mtrace()` to install the handlers.

- The environment variable `MALLOC_TRACE` must specify the name of a writeable file to which the trace data is written.

When these conditions are satisfied, each call to one of the traced functions generates a line in the raw trace file defined by `MALLOC_TRACE`. The trace data looks like this:

```
@ ./mt_ex:[0x80486ec] + 0x804a5f8 0x10
```

The `@` sign signals that the trace line contains an address or function name. In the previous example, the program was executing at the address in square brackets, `0x80486ec`. Using binary utilities or a debugger, we could easily associate this address with a function. The plus sign (+) indicates that this is a call to allocate memory. A call to `free()` would be indicated by a minus sign. The next field indicates the virtual address of the memory location being allocated or freed. The last field is the size, which is included in every call to allocate memory.

This data format is not very user friendly. For this reason, the `mtrace` package includes a utility[7] that analyzes the raw trace data and reports on any inconsistencies. In the simplest case, the Perl script simply prints a single line with the message "No memory leaks". Listing 13-12 contains the output when memory leaks are detected.

---

[7] The analysis utility is a Perl script supplied with the `mtrace` package.

Listing 13-12

mtrace Error Report

```
$ mtrace ./mt_ex mtrace.log

Memory not freed:
-----------------
   Address      Size     Caller
0x0804aa70     0x0a   at /home/chris/temp/mt_ex.c:64
0x0804abc0     0x10   at /home/chris/temp/mt_ex.c:26
0x0804ac60     0x10   at /home/chris/temp/mt_ex.c:26
0x0804acc8     0x0a   at /home/chris/temp/mt_ex.c:64
```

As you can see, this simple tool can help you spot trouble before it happens, as well as find it when it does. Notice that the Perl script has displayed the filename and line number of each call to malloc() that does not have a corresponding call to free() for the given memory location . This requires debugging information in the executable file generated by passing the -g flag to the compiler. If no debugging information is found, the script simply reports the address of the function calling malloc().

13.4.7 dmalloc

dmalloc picks up where mtrace leaves off. The mtrace package is a simple, relatively nonintrusive package most useful for simple detection of malloc/free unbalance conditions. The dmalloc package enables the detection of a much wider range of dynamic memory-management errors. Compared to mtrace, dmalloc is highly intrusive. Depending on the configuration, dmalloc can slow your application to a crawl. It is definitely not the right tool if you suspect memory errors due to race conditions or other timing issues. dmalloc (and mtrace, to a lesser extent) will definitely change the timing of your application.

dmalloc is a very powerful dynamic memory-analysis tool. It is highly configurable and, therefore, somewhat complex. It takes some time to learn and master this tool. However, from QA testing to bug squashing, it could become one of your favorite development tools.

dmalloc is a debug malloc library replacement. These conditions must be satisfied to use dmalloc:

- Application code must include the dmalloc.h header file.
- The application must be linked against the dmalloc library.

- The `dmalloc` library and utility must be installed on your embedded target.

- Certain environment variables that the `dmalloc` library references must be defined before running your application on the target.

Although it is not strictly necessary, you should include `dmalloc.h` in your application program. This allows `dmalloc` to include file and line number information in the output.

Link your application against the `dmalloc` library of your choice. The `dmalloc` package can be configured to generate several different libraries, depending on your selections during package configuration. In the examples to follow, we have chosen to use the `libdmalloc.so` shared library object. Place the library (or a symlink to it) in a path where your compiler can find it. The command to compile your application might look something like this:

```
$ ppc_82xx-gcc -g -Wall -o mtest_ex -L../dmalloc-5.4.2/ \
    -ldmalloc mtest_ex.c
```

This command line assumes that you've placed the `dmalloc` library (`libdmalloc.so`) in a location searched by the `-L` switch on the command line—namely, the `../dmalloc-5.4.2` directly just above the current directory.

To install the `dmalloc` library on your target, place it in your favorite location (perhaps `/usr/local/lib`). You might need to configure your system to find this library. On our example PowerPC system, we added the path `/usr/local/lib` to the `/etc/ld.so.conf` file and invoked the ldconfig utility to update the library search cache.

The last step in preparation is to set an environment variable that the `dmalloc` library uses to determine the level of debugging that will be enabled. The environment variable contains a debug bit mask that concatenates a number of features into a single convenient variable. Yours might look something like this:

```
DMALLOC_OPTIONS=debug=0x4f4ed03,inter=100,log=dmalloc.log
```

Here, `debug` is the debug-level bit mask, and `inter` sets an interval count at which the `dmalloc` library performs extensive checks on itself and the heap. The `dmalloc` library writes its log output to the file indicated by the `log` variable.

The `dmalloc` package comes with a utility to generate the DMALLOC_OPTIONS environment variable based on flags passed to it. The previous example was

generated with the following `dmalloc` invocation. The documentation in the
`dmalloc` package details this quite thoroughly, so we shall not reproduce that here.

```
$ dmalloc -p check-fence -l dmalloc.log -i 100 high
```

When these steps are complete, you should be able to run your application
against the `dmalloc` debug library.

`dmalloc` produces a quite detailed output log. Listing 13-13 reproduces a sample `dmalloc` log output for an example program that intentionally generates some memory leaks.

Listing 13-13

`dmalloc` Log Output

```
2592: 4002: Dmalloc version '5.4.2' from 'http://dmalloc.com/'
2592: 4002: flags = 0x4f4e503, logfile 'dmalloc.log'
2592: 4002: interval = 100, addr = 0, seen # = 0, limit = 0
2592: 4002: starting time = 2592
2592: 4002: process pid = 442
2592: 4002: Dumping Chunk Statistics:
2592: 4002: basic-block 4096 bytes, alignment 8 bytes
2592: 4002: heap address range: 0x30015000 to 0x3004f000, 237568 bytes
2592: 4002:    user blocks: 18 blocks, 73652  bytes (38%)
2592: 4002:    admin blocks: 29 blocks, 118784 bytes (61%)
2592: 4002:    total blocks: 47 blocks, 192512 bytes
2592: 4002: heap checked 41
2592: 4002: alloc calls: malloc 2003, calloc 0, realloc 0, free 1999
2592: 4002: alloc calls: recalloc 0, memalign 0, valloc 0
2592: 4002: alloc calls: new 0, delete 0
2592: 4002:   current memory in use: 52 bytes (4 pnts)
2592: 4002:   total memory allocated: 27546 bytes (2003 pnts)
2592: 4002:   max in use at one time: 27546 bytes (2003 pnts)
2592: 4002: max alloced with 1 call: 376 bytes
2592: 4002: max unused memory space: 37542 bytes (57%)
2592: 4002: top 10 allocations:
2592: 4002:   total-size   count in-use-size   count   source
2592: 4002:        16000    1000           32       2   mtest_ex.c:36
2592: 4002:        10890    1000           20       2   mtest_ex.c:74
2592: 4002:          256       1            0       0   mtest_ex.c:154
2592: 4002:        27146    2001           52       4   Total of 3
2592: 4002: Dumping Not-Freed Pointers Changed Since Start:
2592: 4002:   not freed: '0x300204e8|s1' (10 bytes) from 'mtest_ex.c:74'
2592: 4002:   not freed: '0x30020588|s1' (16 bytes) from 'mtest_ex.c:36'
2592: 4002:   not freed: '0x30020688|s1' (16 bytes) from 'mtest_ex.c:36'
2592: 4002:   not freed: '0x300208a8|s1' (10 bytes) from 'mtest_ex.c:74'
2592: 4002:   total-size   count   source
```

```
2592: 4002:             32       2   mtest_ex.c:36
2592: 4002:             20       2   mtest_ex.c:74
2592: 4002:             52       4   Total of 2
2592: 4002: ending time = 2592, elapsed since start = 0:00:00
```

It is important to note that this log is generated upon program exit. (dmalloc has many options and modes of operation; it is possible to configure dmalloc to print output lines when errors are detected.)

The first half of the output log reports high-level statistics about the heap and the overall memory usage of the application. Totals are produced for each of the malloc library calls, such as malloc(), free(), and realloc(). Interestingly, this default log reports on the top 10 allocations and the source location where they occurred. This can be very useful for overall system-level profiling.

Toward the end of the log, we see evidence of memory leaks in our application. You can see that the dmalloc library detected four instances of memory that was allocated that was apparently never freed. Because we included dmalloc.h and compiled with debug symbols, the source location where the memory was allocated is indicated in the log.

As with the other tools we've covered in this chapter, space permits only a brief introduction of this very powerful debug tool. dmalloc can detect many other conditions and limits. For example, dmalloc can detect when a freed pointer has been written. It can tell whether a pointer was used to access data outside its bounds but within the application's permissible address range. In fact, dmalloc can be configured to log almost any memory transaction through the malloc family of calls. dmalloc is a tool that is sure to pay back many times the effort taken to become proficient with it.

13.4.8 Kernel Oops

Although not strictly a tool, a *kernel oops* contains much useful information to help you troubleshoot the cause. A kernel oops results from a variety of kernel errors from simple memory errors produced by a process (fully recoverable, in most cases) to a hard kernel panic. Recent Linux kernels support display of symbolic information in addition to the raw hexadecimal address values. Listing 13-14 reproduces a kernel oops from a PowerPC target.

Listing 13-14

Kernel Oops

```
$ modprobe loop
Oops: kernel access of bad area, sig: 11 [#1]
NIP: C000D058 LR: C0085650 SP: C7787E80 REGS: c7787dd0 TRAP: 0300   Not tainted
MSR: 00009032 EE: 1 PR: 0 FP: 0 ME: 1 IR/DR: 11
DAR: 00000000, DSISR: 22000000
TASK = c7d187b0[323] 'modprobe' THREAD: c7786000
Last syscall: 128
GPR00: 0000006C C7787E80 C7D187B0 00000000 C7CD25CC FFFFFFFF 00000000 80808081
GPR08: 00000001 C034AD80 C036D41C C034AD80 C0335AB0 1001E3C0 00000000 00000000
GPR16: 00000000 00000000 00000000 100170D8 100013E0 C9040000 C903DFD8 C9040000
GPR24: 00000000 C9040000 C9040000 00000940 C778A000 C7CD25C0 C7CD25C0 C7CD25CC
NIP [c000d058] strcpy+0x10/0x1c
LR [c0085650] register_disk+0xec/0xf0
Call trace:
 [c00e170c] add_disk+0x58/0x74
 [c90061e0] loop_init+0x1e0/0x430 [loop]
 [c002fc90] sys_init_module+0x1f4/0x2e0
 [c00040a0] ret_from_syscall+0x0/0x44
Segmentation fault
```

Notice that the register dump includes symbolic information, where appropriate. Your kernel must have KALLSYSMS enabled for this symbolic information to be available. Figure 13-4 shows the configuration options under the General Setup main menu.

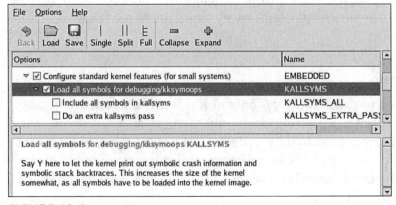

FIGURE 13-4
Symbol support for oops

Much of the information in a kernel oops message is directly related to the processor. Having some knowledge of the underlying architecture is necessary to fully understand the oops message.

Analyzing the oops in Listing 13-14, we see right away that the oops was generated due to a "kernel access of bad area, sig: 11". We already know from previous examples in this chapter that signal 11 is a segmentation fault.

The first section is a summary showing the reason for the oops, a few important pointers, and the offending task. In Listing 13-14, NIP is the next instruction pointer, which is decoded later in the oops message. This points to the offending code that led to the oops. LR is a PowerPC register and usually indicates the return address for the currently executing subroutine. SP is the stack pointer. REGS indicates the kernel address for the data structure containing the register dump data, and TRAP indicates the type of exception that this oops message relates to. Referring to the PowerPC architecture reference manual referenced at the end of Chapter 7, "Bootloaders," we see that a TRAP 0300 is the PowerPC Data Storage Interrupt, which is triggered by a data memory access error.

On the third line of the oops message, we see additional PowerPC machine registers, such as MSR (machine state register) and a decode of some of its bits. On the next line, we see the DAR (data access register), which often contains the offending memory address. The DSISR register contents can be used in conjunction with the PowerPC architecture reference to discover much detail about the specific reason for the exception.

An oops message also contains the task pointer and the decoded task name to quickly determine what task or thread was running at the time of the oops. We also see a detailed processor register dump, which can be used for additional clues. Again, we need knowledge of the architecture and compiler register usage to make sense of the clues from the register values. For example, the PowerPC architecture uses the r3 register for return values from C functions.

The last part of the oops message provides a stack backtrace with symbol decode if symbols are enabled in the kernel. Using this information, we can construct a sequence of events that led to the offending condition.

In this simple example, we have learned a great deal of information from this oops message. We know that it was a PowerPC Data Storage Exception, caused by an error in a data memory access (as opposed to an instruction fetch memory access). The DAR register tells us that the data address that generated this exception was 0x0000_0000. We know that the `modprobe` process produced the error. From the backtrace and NIP (next instruction pointer), we know that it was in a call to `strcpy()` that can be traced directly back to the `loop_init()` function in the `loop.ko` module, which `modprobe` was trying to insert at the time of the exception. Given this information, tracking down the source of this errant null pointer dereference should be quite trivial.

13.5 Binary Utilities

Binary utilities, or `binutils`, are a critical component of any toolchain. Indeed, to build a compiler, you must first have successfully built `binutils`. In this section, we briefly introduce the more useful tools that the embedded developer needs to know about. As with most of the other tools in this chapter, these are cross-utilities and must be built to execute on your development host while operating on binary files targeted to your chosen architecture. Alternatively, you could compile or obtain versions of these to run on your target, but we assume a cross-development environment for these examples.

13.5.1 readelf

The `readelf` utility examines the composition of your target ELF binary file. This is particularly useful for building images targeted for ROM or Flash memory where explicit control of the image layout is required. It is also a great tool for learning how your toolchain builds images and for understanding the ELF file format.

For example, to display the symbol table in an ELF image, use this command:

```
$ readelf -s <elf-image>
```

To discover and display all the sections in your ELF image, use this command:

```
$ readelf -e <elf-image>
```

Use the `-S` flag to list the section headers in your ELF image. You might be surprised to learn that even a simple seven-line "hello world" program contains 38 separate sections. Some of them will be familiar to you, such as the `.text` and `.data` sections. Listing 13-15 contains a partial listing of sections from our "hello world" example. For simplicity, we have listed only those sections that are likely to be familiar or relevant to the embedded developer.

Listing 13-15

`readelf` Section Headers

```
$ ppc_82xx-readelf -S  hello-ex
There are 38 section headers, starting at offset 0x32f4:

Section Headers:
[ Nr] Name           Type         Addr      Off    Size   ES Flg Lk Inf Al
...
 [11] .text          PROGBITS     100002f0 0002f0 000568 00  AX  0   0  4
...
 [13] .rodata        PROGBITS     10000878 000878 000068 00   A  0   0  4
...
 [15] .data          PROGBITS     100108e0 0008e0 00000c 00  WA  0   0  4
...
 [22] .sdata         PROGBITS     100109e0 0009e0 00001c 00  WA  0   0  4
 [23] .sbss          NOBITS       100109fc 0009fc 000000 00  WA  0   0  1
...
 [25] .bss           NOBITS       10010a74 0009fc 00001c 00  WA  0   0  4
...
```

The .text section contains the executable program code. The .rodata section contains constant data in your program. The .data section generally contains initialized global data used by the C library prologue code and can contain large initialized data items from your application. The .sdata section is used for smaller initialized global data items and exists only on some architectures. Some processor architectures can make use of optimized data access when the attributes of the memory area are known. The .sdata and .sbss sections enable these optimizations. The .bss and .sbss sections contain uninitialized data in your program. These sections occupy no space in the program image—their memory space is allocated and initialized to zero on program startup by C library prologue code.

We can dump any of these sections and display the contents. Given this line in your C program declared outside of any function, we can examine how it is placed in the .rodata section:

```
char *hello_rodata = "This is a read-only data string\n";
```

Issue the `readelf` command specifying the section number we want to dump from Listing 13-15:

```
$ ppc_82xx-readelf -x 13 hello-ex
Hex dump of section '.rodata':
  0x10000878 100189e0 10000488 1000050c 1000058c ................
  0x10000888 00020001 54686973 20697320 61207265 ....This is a read-
  0x10000898 61642d6f 6e6c7920 64617461 20737472 only data string
  0x100008a8 696e670a 00000000 54686973 20697320 .....This is
  0x100008b8 73746174 69632064 6174610a 00000000 static data.....
  0x100008c8 48656c6c 6f20456d 62656464 65640a00 Hello Embedded..
  0x100008d8 25730a00 25780a00                    %s..%x..
```

We see that the initialized global variable that we declared is represented in the `.rodata` section, together with all the constant strings defined in the program.

13.5.2 Examining Debug Info Using readelf

One of the more useful features of `readelf` is to display the debug information contained in an ELF file. When the `-g` compiler flag is issued during a compilation, the compiler generates debug information in a series of sections within the resulting ELF file. We can use `readelf` to display these ELF section headers within the ELF file:

```
$ ppc-linux-readelf -S ex_sync | grep debug
  [28] .debug_aranges     PROGBITS    00000000 000c38 0000b8 00    0   0  8
  [29] .debug_pubnames    PROGBITS    00000000 000cf0 00007a 00    0   0  1
  [30] .debug_info        PROGBITS    00000000 000d6a 00079b 00    0   0  1
  [31] .debug_abbrev      PROGBITS    00000000 001505 000207 00    0   0  1
  [32] .debug_line        PROGBITS    00000000 00170c 000354 00    0   0  1
  [33] .debug_frame       PROGBITS    00000000 001a60 000080 00    0   0  4
  [34] .debug_str         PROGBITS    00000000 001ae0 00014d 00    0   0  1
```

Using `readelf` with the `--debug-dump` option, we can display the contents of any one of these `.debug_*` sections. You will see how this information can be useful in Chapter 14, "Kernel Debugging Techniques," when we discuss the challenge of debugging optimized kernel code.

Debug information can be very large. Displaying all the debug information in the Linux kernel ELF file `vmlinux` produces more than six million lines of output. However daunting it might appear, having at least a familiarity with debug information will make you a better embedded engineer.

Listing 13-16 is a partial listing of the contents of the .debug_info section from a small example application. For space considerations, we have shown only a few records.

Listing 13-16

Partial Debug Info Dump

```
$ ppc-linux-readelf -debug-dump=info ex_sync
1 The section .debug_info contains:
2
3   Compilation Unit @ 0:
4   Length:        109
5   Version:       2
6   Abbrev Offset: 0
7   Pointer Size:  4
8 <0><b>: Abbrev Number: 1 (DW_TAG_compile_unit)
9       DW_AT_stmt_list   : 0
10      DW_AT_low_pc      : 0x10000368
11      DW_AT_high_pc     : 0x1000038c
12      DW_AT_name        :
../sysdeps/powerpc/powerpc32/elf/start.S
13      DW_AT_comp_dir    : /var/tmp/BUILD/glibc-2.3.3/csu
14      DW_AT_producer    : GNU AS 2.15.94
15      DW_AT_language    : 32769   (MIPS assembler)
...
394 <1><5a1>: Abbrev Number: 14 (DW_TAG_subprogram)
395      DW_AT_sibling    : <5fa>
396      DW_AT_external   : 1
397      DW_AT_name       : main
398      DW_AT_decl_file  : 1
399      DW_AT_decl_line  : 9
400      DW_AT_prototyped : 1
401      DW_AT_type       : <248>
402      DW_AT_low_pc     : 0x100004b8
403      DW_AT_high_pc    : 0x10000570
404      DW_AT_frame_base : 1 byte block: 6f       (DW_OP_reg31)
...
423 <2><5e9>: Abbrev Number: 16 (DW_TAG_variable)
424      DW_AT_name       : mybuf
425      DW_AT_decl_file  : 1
426      DW_AT_decl_line  : 11
427      DW_AT_type       : <600>
428      DW_AT_location   : 2 byte block: 91 20    (DW_OP_fbreg: 32)
...
```

The first record identified by the *Dwarf2*[8] tag `DW_TAG_compile_unit` identifies the first compilation unit of this PowerPC executable. It is a file called `start.S`, which provides startup prologue for a C program. The next record identified by `DW_TAG_subprogram` identifies the start of the user program, the familiar function `main()`. This Dwarf2 debug record contains a reference to the file and line number where `main()` is found. The final record in Listing 13-16 identifies a local variable in the `main()` routine called `mybuf`. Again, the line number and file are provided by this record. You can deduce from this information that `main()` is at line 9, and `mybuf` is at line 11 of the source file. Other debug records in the ELF file correlate the filename via the Dwarf2 `DW_AT_decl_file` attribute.

You can discover all the details of the Dwarf2 debug information format via the reference given in Section 13.7.1 at the end of this chapter.

13.5.3 objdump

The `objdump` utility has considerable overlap with the `readelf` tool. However, one of the more useful features of `objdump` is its capability to display disassembled object code. Listing 13-17 provides an example of disassembly of the `.text` section of the simple "hello world" PowerPC version. We include only the `main()` routine, to save space. The entire dump, including C library prologue and epilogue, would consume many pages.

Listing 13-17

Disassembly Using objdump

```
$ ppc_82xx-objdump -S -m powerpc:common -j .text hello
...
10000488 <main>:
10000488:       94 21 ff e0     stwu    r1,-32(r1)
1000048c:       7c 08 02 a6     mflr    r0
10000490:       93 e1 00 1c     stw     r31,28(r1)
10000494:       90 01 00 24     stw     r0,36(r1)
10000498:       7c 3f 0b 78     mr      r31,r1
1000049c:       90 7f 00 08     stw     r3,8(r31)
100004a0:       90 9f 00 0c     stw     r4,12(r31)
100004a4:       3d 20 10 00     lis     r9,4096
100004a8:       38 69 08 54     addi    r3,r9,2132
100004ac:       4c c6 31 82     crclr   4*cr1+eq
100004b0:       48 01 05 11     bl      100109c0
```

---

[8] A reference for the Dwarf2 Debug Information Specification is provided at the end of this chapter.

```
<__bss_start+0x60>
100004b4:        38 00 00 00       li       r0,0
100004b8:        7c 03 03 78       mr       r3,r0
100004bc:        81 61 00 00       lwz      r11,0(r1)
100004c0:        80 0b 00 04       lwz      r0,4(r11)
100004c4:        7c 08 03 a6       mtlr     r0
100004c8:        83 eb ff fc       lwz      r31,-4(r11)
100004cc:        7d 61 5b 78       mr       r1,r11
100004d0:        4e 80 00 20       blr
...
```

Much of the code from the simple main() routine is stack frame creation and destruction. The actual call to printf() is represented by the branch link (bl) instruction near the center of the listing at address 0x100004b0. This is a PowerPC function call. Because this program was compiled as a dynamically linked object, we will not have an address for the printf() function until runtime, when it is linked with the shared library printf() routine. Had we compiled this as a statically linked object, we would see the symbol and corresponding address for the call to printf().

13.5.4 objcopy

objcopy formats and, optionally, converts the format of a binary object file. This utility is quite useful for generating code for ROM or Flash resident images. The U-Boot bootloader introduced in Chapter 7 makes use of objcopy to produce binary and s-record[9] output formats from the final ELF file. This example usage illustrates the capabilities of objcopy and its use to build Flash images.

```
$ ppc_82xx-objcopy --gap-fill=0xff -O binary u-boot u-boot.bin
```

This objcopy invocation shows how an image might be prepared for Flash memory. The input file—u-boot, in this example—is the complete ELF U-Boot image, including symbols and relocation information. The objcopy utility takes only the relevant sections containing program code and data and places the image in the output file, specified here as u-boot.bin.

Flash memory contains all ones in its erased state. Therefore, filling gaps in a binary image with all ones improves programming efficiency and prolongs the life of the Flash memory, which today has limited write cycles. This is done with the --gap-fill parameter to objcopy.

---

[9] S-record files are an ASCII representation of a binary file, used by many device programmers and software binary utilities.

This is but one simple example usage of objcopy. This utility can be used to generate s-records and convert from one format to another. See the man page for complete details.

13.6 Miscellaneous Binary Utilities

Your toolchain contains several additional useful utilities. Learning to use these utilities is straightforward. You will find many uses for these helpful tools.

13.6.1 strip

The strip utility can be used to remove symbols and debug information from a binary. This is frequently used to save space on an embedded device. In the cross-development model, it is convenient to place stripped binaries on the target system and leave the unstripped version on your development host. Using this method, symbols are available for cross-debugging on your development host while saving space on the target. strip has many options, which are described in the man page.

13.6.2 addr2line

When we highlighted mtrace in Listing 13-12, you saw that the output from the mtrace analysis script contained file and line number information. The mtrace Perl script used the addr2line utility to read the debug information contained in the executable ELF file and display a line number corresponding to the address. Using the same mtrace example executable, we can find a filename and line number for a virtual address:

```
$ addr2line -f -e mt_ex 0x80487c6
    put_data
    /home/chris/examples/mt_ex.c:64
```

Notice that the function put_data() is also listed together with the file and line number. This says that the address 0x80487c6 is on line 64 of the mt_ex.c file, in the put_data() function. This is even more useful in larger binaries consisting of multiple filenames, such as the Linux kernel:

```
$ ppc_82xx-addr2line -f -e vmlinux c000d95c
    mpc52xx_restart
    arch/ppc/syslib/mpc52xx_setup.c:41
```

This particular example highlights one of the points repeated throughout this chapter: This is an architecture-specific tool. You must use a tool configured and compiled to match the architecture of the target binary that you are using. As with the cross-compiler, addr2line is a cross-tool and part of the binary utilities package.

13.6.3 strings

The strings utility examines ASCII string data in binary files. This is especially useful for examining memory dumps when source code or debug symbols might not be available. You might often discover that you can narrow the cause of a crash by tracing the strings back to the offending binary. Although strings does have a few command line options, it is easy to learn and use. See the man page for further details.

13.6.4 ldd

Although not strictly a binary utility, the ldd script is another useful tool for the embedded developer. It is part of the C library package and exists on virtually every Linux distribution. ldd lists the shared object library dependencies for a given object file or files. We introduced ldd in Chapter 11, "BusyBox." See Listing 11-2 for an example usage. The ldd script is particularly useful during development of ramdisk images. One of the most common failures asked about on the various embedded Linux mailing lists is a kernel panic after mounting root:

```
VFS: Mounted root (nfs filesystem).
Freeing unused kernel memory: 96k init
Kernel panic - not syncing: No init found.  Try passing init=option to kernel.
```

One of the most common causes is that the root file system image (be it ramdisk, Flash, or NFS root file system) does not have the supporting libraries for the binaries that the kernel is trying to execute. Using ldd, you can determine which libraries each of your binaries requires and make sure that you include them in your ramdisk or other root file system image. In the previous example kernel panic, init was indeed on the file system, but the Linux dynamic loader, ld.so.1, was missing. Using ldd is quite straightforward:

```
$ xscale_be-ldd init
    libc.so.6 => /opt/mvl/.../lib/libc.so.6 (0xdead1000)
    ld-linux.so.3 => /opt/mvl/.../lib/ld-linux.so.3 (0xdead2000)
```

This simple example demonstrates that the init binary requires two dynamic library objects: `libc` and `ld-linux`. Both must be on your target and must be accessible to your `init` binary—that is, they must be readable and executable.

13.6.5 nm

The `nm` utility displays symbols from an object file. This can be useful for a variety of tasks. For example, when cross-compiling a large application, you encounter unresolved symbols. You can use `nm` to find which object module contains those symbols and then modify your build environment to include it.

The `nm` utility provides attributes for each symbol. For example, you can discover whether this symbol is local or global, or whether it is defined or referenced only in a particular object module. Listing 13-18 reproduces several lines from the output of `nm` run on the U-Boot ELF image `u-boot`.

Listing 13-18

Displaying Symbols Using nm

```
$ ppc_85xx-nm u-boot
...
fff23140 b base_address
fff24c98 B BootFile
fff06d64 T BootpRequest
fff00118 t boot_warm
fff21010 d border
fff23000 A __bss_start
...
```

Notice the link addresses of these U-Boot symbols. They were linked for a Flash device that lives in the highest portion of the memory map on this particular board. This listing contains only a few example symbols, for discussion purposes. The middle column is the symbol type. A capitalized letter indicates a global symbol, and lower case indicates a local symbol. B indicates that the symbol is located in the .bss section. T indicates that the symbol is located in the .text section. D indicates that the symbol is located in the .data section. A indicates that this address is absolute and is not subject to modification by an additional link stage. This absolute symbol indicates the start of the .bss section and is used by the code that clears the .bss on startup, as required for a C execution environment.

13.6.6 prelink

The `prelink` utility is often used in systems in which startup time is important. A dynamically linked ELF executable must be linked at runtime when the program is first loaded. This can take significant time in a large application. `prelink` prepares the shared libraries and the object files that depend on them to provide a-priori knowledge of the unresolved library references. In effect, this can reduce the start-up time of a given application. The man page has complete details on the use of this handy utility.

13.7 Chapter Summary

- The GNU Debugger (GDB) is a complex and powerful debugger with many capabilities. We presented the basics to get you started.

- The DDD graphical front end for GDB integrates source code and data display with the power of GDB command line interface capabilities.

- `cbrowser` is a useful aid for understanding large projects. It uses the `cscope` database to rapidly find and display symbols and other elements of C source code.

- Linux is supported by many profiling and trace tools. We presented several, including `strace`, `ltrace`, `top`, and `ps`, and the memory profilers `mtrace` and `dmalloc`.

- Embedded developers often need to build custom images such as those required for bootloaders and firmware images. For these tasks, knowledge of `binutils` is indispensable. We presented many of the utilities found in `binutils`, including `readelf`, `objdump`, `objcopy`, and several others.

13.7.1 Suggestions for Additional Reading

GDB: The GNU Project Debugger:
www.gnu.org/software/gdb/gdb.html

GDB *Pocket Reference*
Arnold Robbins
O'Reilly Media, 2005

Data Display Debugger:
www.gnu.org/software/ddd/

cbrowser home page:
http://cbrowser.sourceforge.net/

cscope home page:
http://cscope.sourceforge.net/index.html

dmalloc—Debug Malloc Library:
http://dmalloc.com/

Tool Interface Standard (TIS) Executable and Linking Format (ELF)
Specification
Version 1.2
TIS Committee, May 1995

Tool interface standards:
DWARF Debugging Information Format Specification
Version 2.0
TIS Committee, May 1995

14

Kernel Debugging Techniques

In this chapter

Often the pivotal factor in achieving development timetables comes down to one's efficiency in finding and fixing bugs. Debugging inside the Linux kernel can be quite challenging. No matter how you approach it, kernel debugging will always be complex. This chapter examines some of the complexities and presents ideas and methods to improve your debugging skills inside the kernel and device drivers.

14.1 Challenges to Kernel Debugging

Debugging a modern operating system involves many challenges. Virtual memory operating systems present their own unique challenges. Gone are the days when we could replace a processor with an in-circuit emulator. Processors have become far too fast and complex. Moreover, pipeline architectures hide important code-execution details, partly because memory accesses on the bus can be ordered differently from code execution, and particularly because of internal caching of instruction streams. It is not always possible to correlate external bus activity to internal processor instruction execution, except at a rather coarse level.

Some of the challenges you will encounter while debugging Linux kernel code are:

- Linux kernel code is highly optimized for speed of execution in many areas.

- Compilers use optimization techniques that complicate the correlation of C source to actual machine instruction flow. Inline functions are a good example of this.

- Single-stepping through compiler optimized code often produces unusual and unexpected results.

- Virtual memory isolates user space memory from kernel memory and can make various debugging scenarios especially difficult.

- Some code cannot be stepped through with traditional debuggers.

- Startup code can be especially difficult because of its proximity to the hardware and the limited resources available (for example, no console, limited memory mapping, and so on).

The Linux kernel has matured into a very high-performance operating system capable of competing with the best commercial operating systems. Many areas within the kernel do not lend themselves to easy analysis by simply reading the source code. Knowledge of the architecture and detailed design are often necessary to understand the code flow in a particular area. Several good books are available that describe the kernel design in detail. Refer to Section 14.6.1, "Suggestions for Additional Reading," for recommendations.

GCC is an optimizing compiler. By default, the Linux kernel is compiled with the -O2 compiler flag. This enables many optimization algorithms that can change the fundamental structure and order of your code.[1] For example, the Linux kernel makes heavy use of *inline* functions. Inline functions are small functions declared with the `inline` keyword, which results in the function being included directly in the execution thread instead of generating a function call and the associated overhead.[2] `Inline` functions require a minimum of -O1 optimization level. Therefore, you cannot turn off optimization, which would be desirable for easier debugging.

In many areas within the Linux kernel, single-stepping through code is difficult or impossible. The most obvious examples are code paths that modify the virtual memory settings. When your application makes a system call that results in entry into the kernel, this results in a change in address space as seen by the process. In fact, any transition that involves a processor exception changes the operational context and can be difficult or impossible to single-step through.

14.2 Using KGDB for Kernel Debugging

Two popular methods enable symbolic source-level debugging within the Linux kernel:

- Using KGDB as a remote `gdb` agent
- Using a hardware JTAG probe to control the processor

We cover JTAG debugging in Section 14.4, "Hardware-Assisted Debugging."

KGDB (Kernel GDB) is a set of Linux kernel patches that provide an interface to `gdb` via its remote serial protocol. KGDB implements a `gdb` stub that communicates to a `cross-gdb` running on your host development workstation. Until very

---

[1] See the GCC manual referenced at the end of this chapter in Section 14.6.1, "Suggestions for Additional Reading" for details on the optimization levels.

[2] Inline functions are like macros, but with the advantage of compile-time type checking.

recently, KGDB on the target required a serial connection to the development host. Some targets support KGDB connection via Ethernet, although this is relatively new. Complete support for KGDB is still not in the mainline `kernel.org` kernel. You need to port KGDB to your chosen target or obtain an embedded Linux distribution for your chosen architecture and platform that contains KGDB support. Most embedded Linux distributions available today support KGDB.

Figure 14-1 describes the KGDB debug setup. Up to three connections to the target board are used. Ethernet is used to enable NFS root mount and telnet sessions from the host. If your board has a ramdisk image in Flash that it mounts as a root file system, you can eliminate the Ethernet connection.

A serial port is dedicated for the connection between KGBD and `gdb` running on the development host system, and an optional second serial port serves as a console. Systems that have only one serial port make KGDB somewhat more cumbersome to use.

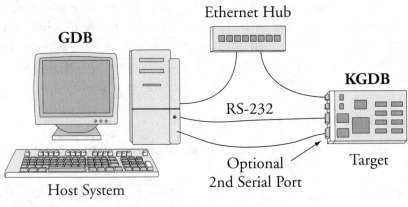

FIGURE 14-1
KGDB debug setup

As you can see in Figure 14-1, the debugger (your cross-version of `gdb`) runs on your development host system. KGDB is part of the kernel running on your target system. KGDB implements the hooks required to interface `gdb` with your target board to enable features such as setting breakpoints, examining memory, and enabling single-step program execution.

14.2.1 KGDB Kernel Configuration

KGDB is a kernel feature and must be enabled in your kernel. KGDB is selected from the Kernel Hacking menu, as shown in Figure 14-2. As part of the configuration, you must select the serial port for KGDB to use. Notice also from Figure 14-2 that we enabled the option to compile the kernel with debug information. This adds the -g compiler flag to the build process to enable symbolic debugging.

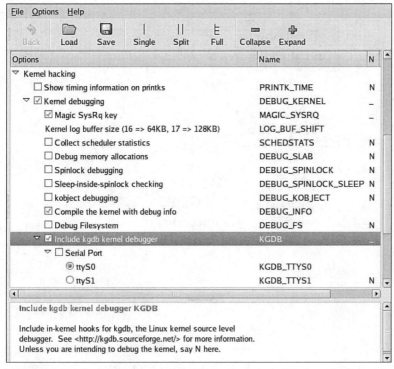

FIGURE 14-2
Kernel configuration for KGDB

14.2.2 Target Boot with KGDB Support

After your kernel is built with KGDB support, it must be enabled. Unfortunately, the method to enable it is not yet uniform across all architectures and implementations. In general, KGDB is enabled by passing a command line switch to the kernel via the kernel command line. If KGDB support is compiled into the kernel but not enabled via a command line switch, it does nothing. When KGDB is enabled, the kernel stops at a KGDB-enabled breakpoint very early in the boot cycle to allow you to connect to the target using gdb. Figure 14-3 shows the logic for generating an initial breakpoint when KGDB is enabled.

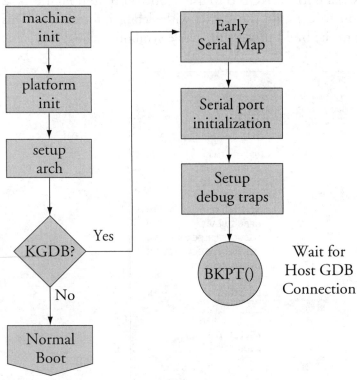

FIGURE 14-3
KGDB logic

KGDB requires a serial port for connection to the host.[3] The first step in setting up KGDB is to enable a serial port very early in the boot process. In many architectures, the hardware UART must be mapped into kernel memory before access. After the address range is mapped, the serial port is initialized. Debug trap handlers are installed to allow processor exceptions to trap into the debugger.

Listing 14-1 displays the terminal output when booting with KGDB enabled. This example is based on the AMCC 440EP Evaluation Kit (Yosemite board), which ships with the U-Boot bootloader.

---

[3] Notwithstanding the comments made earlier about KGDB over Ethernet.

Listing 14-1

Booting with KGDB Enabled Using U-Boot

```
=> sete bootargs console=ttyS1,115200 root=/dev/nfs rw ip=dhcp gdb
=> bootm 200000
## Booting image at 00200000 ...
   Image Name:    Linux-2.6.13
   Image Type:    PowerPC Linux Kernel Image (gzip compressed)
   Data Size:     1064790 Bytes =  1 MB
   Load Address:  00000000
   Entry Point:   00000000
   Verifying Checksum ... OK
   Uncompressing Kernel Image ... OK
$T0440:c000ae5c;01:c0205fa0;#d9      <<< See text
```

Most of the boot sequence is familiar from our coverage of U-Boot in Chapter 7, "Bootloaders." This kernel boot sequence has two unique features: the command-line parameter to enable KGDB and the odd-looking text string after the kernel is uncompressed.

Recall from Chapter 7 that the kernel command line is defined by the U-Boot bootargs environment variable. Notice that we have added the gdb parameter, which instructs the kernel to force an early breakpoint and wait for the host debugger (your cross-gdb) to connect.

As diagrammed in Figure 14-3, the kernel detects the presence of the gdb parameter and attempts to pass control to the remote (host-based) debugger. This is evidenced by the sequence of ASCII characters dumped to the serial port in Listing 14-1. If you are curious about this gdb remote serial protocol, it is documented in the gdb manual cited at the end of this chapter. In this example, KGDB is sending a *Stop Reply* packet reporting the breakpoint trap to the remote gdb session on the host. The two 32-bit parameters indicate the location of the program and the stack frame.

Now that the kernel is set up and waiting for the host debugger, we can begin our debugging session. We invoke cross-gdb from our host development workstation and connect to the target via gdb's remote protocol. In this example, we are sharing the serial port, so we must disconnect the terminal emulator from the target before trying to connect with gdb. Listing 14-2 highlights the gdb connection process. This assumes that we have already exited our terminal emulator and freed the serial port for gdb to use.

Listing 14-2

Connecting to KGDB

```
$ ppc_4xx-gdb --silent vmlinux
(gdb) target remote /dev/ttyS0
Remote debugging using /dev/ttyS0
breakinst () at arch/ppc/kernel/ppc-stub.c:825
825        }
(gdb) l
820                        return;
821              }
822
823              asm("    .globl breakinst        \n\
824                   breakinst: .long 0x7d821008");
825        }
826
827     #ifdef CONFIG_KGDB_CONSOLE
828     /* Output string in GDB O-packet format if GDB has connected.
If nothing
829          output, returns 0 (caller must then handle output). */
(gdb)
```

Here we have performed three actions:

- Invoked gdb, passing it the kernel ELF file vmlinux

- Connected to the target using the target remote command within gdb

- Issued the list command, using its abbreviated form to display our location in the source code

At the risk of pointing out the obvious, the vmlinux image that we pass to gdb must be from the same kernel build that produced the target kernel binary. It also must have been compiled with the -g compiler flag to contain debug information.

When we issued the target remote command, gdb responded by displaying the location of the program counter (PC). In this example, the kernel is stopped at the breakpoint defined by the inline assembler statement at line 823 in file .../arch/ppc/kernel/ppc-stub.c. When we issue the continue (c) command, execution resumes starting at line 825, as indicated.

14.2.3 Useful Kernel Breakpoints

We have now established a debug connection with the kernel on our target board. When we issue the gdb continue (c) command, the kernel proceeds to boot, and if there are no problems, the boot process completes. There is one minor limitation of using KGDB on many architectures and processors. An engineering trade-off was made between the need to support very early kernel debugging (for example, before a full-blown interrupt-driven serial port driver is installed) and the desire to keep the complexity of the KGDB debug engine itself very simple and, therefore, robust and portable. KGDB uses a simple polled serial driver that has zero overhead when the kernel is running. As a drawback to this implementation, the traditional Ctl-C or Break sequence on the serial port will have no effect. Therefore, it will be impossible to stop execution of the running kernel unless a breakpoint or other fault is encountered.

For this reason, it has become common practice to define some system-wide breakpoints, which provide the capability to halt the current thread of execution. Two of the most common are highlighted in Listing 14-3.

Listing 14-3

Common Kernel Breakpoints

```
(gdb) b panic
Breakpoint 1 at 0xc0016b18: file kernel/panic.c, line 74.
(gdb) b sys_sync
Breakpoint 2 at 0xc005a8c8: file fs/buffer.c, line 296.
(gdb)
```

Using the gdb breakpoint command, again using its abbreviated version, we enter two breakpoints. One is at panic() and the other is at the sync system call entry sys_sync(). The former allows the debugger to be invoked if a later event generates a panic. This enables examination of the system state at the time of the panic. The second is a useful way to halt the kernel and trap into the debugger from user space by entering the sync command from a terminal running on your target hardware.

We are now ready to proceed with our debugging session. We have a KGDB-enabled kernel running on our target, paused at a KGDB-defined early breakpoint. We established a connection to the target with our host-based cross debugger—in this case, invoked as ppc_4xx-gdb—and we have entered a pair of useful system breakpoints. Now we can direct our debugging activities to the task at hand.

One caveat: By definition, we cannot use KGDB for stepping through code before the breakpoint() function in .../arch/ppc/setup.c used to establish the connection between a KGDB-enabled kernel and cross-gdb on our host.

Figure 14-3 is a rough guide to the code that executes before KGDB gains control. Debugging this early code requires the use of a hardware-assisted debug probe. We cover this topic shortly in Section 14.4, "Hardware-Assisted Debugging."

14.3 Debugging the Linux Kernel

One of the more common reasons you might find yourself stepping through kernel code is to modify or customize the platform-specific code for your custom board. Let's see how this might be done using the AMCC Yosemite board. We place a breakpoint at the platform-specific architecture setup function and then continue until that breakpoint is encountered. Listing 14-4 shows the sequence.

Listing 14-4

Debugging Architecture-Setup Code

```
(gdb) b yosemite_setup_arch
    Breakpoint 3 at 0xc021a488:
        file arch/ppc/platforms/4xx/yosemite.c, line 308.
(gdb) c
Continuing.
Can't send signals to this remote system.  SIGILL not sent.

Breakpoint 3, yosemite_setup_arch () at arch/ppc/platforms/4xx/yosemite.c:308
308             yosemite_set_emacdata();
(gdb) l
303     }
304
305     static void __init
306     yosemite_setup_arch(void)
307     {
308             yosemite_set_emacdata();
309
310             ibm440gx_get_clocks(&clocks, YOSEMITE_SYSCLK, 6 * 1843200);
311             ocp_sys_info.opb_bus_freq = clocks.opb;
312
(gdb)
```

When the breakpoint at `yosemite_setup_arch()` is encountered, control passes to `gdb` at line 308 of `yosemite.c`. The `list` (`l`) command displays the source listing centered on the breakpoint at line 308. The warning message displayed by `gdb` after the `continue` (`c`) command can be safely ignored. It is part of `gdb`'s way of testing the capabilities of the remote system. It first sends a remote `continue_with_signal` command to the target. The KGDB implementation for this target board does not support this command; therefore, it is NAK'd by the target.

gdb responds by displaying this informational message and issuing the standard remote `continue` command instead.

14.3.1 gdb Remote Serial Protocol

gdb includes a debug switch that enables us to observe the remote protocol being used between gdb on your development host and the target. This can be very useful for understanding the underlying protocol, as well as troubleshooting targets that exhibit unusual or errant behavior. To enable this debug mode, issue the following command:

(gdb) **set debug remote 1**

With remote debugging enabled, it is instructive to observe the `continue` command in action and the steps taken by gdb. Listing 14-5 illustrates the use of the `continue` command with remote debugging enabled.

Listing 14-5

continue Remote Protocol Example

```
(gdb) c
Continuing.
Sending packet: $mc0000000,4#80...Ack
Packet received: c022d200
Sending packet: $Mc0000000,4:7d821008#68...Ack
Packet received: OK
Sending packet: $mc0016de8,4#f8...Ack
Packet received: 38600001
Sending packet: $Mc0016de8,4:7d821008#e0...Ack
Packet received: OK
Sending packet: $mc005bd5c,4#23...Ack
Packet received: 38600001
Sending packet: $Mc005bd5c,4:7d821008#0b...Ack
Packet received: OK
Sending packet: $mc021a488,4#c8...Ack
Packet received: 4bfffbad
Sending packet: $Mc021a488,4:7d821008#b0...Ack
Packet received: OK
Sending packet: $c#63...Ack
     <<< program running, gdb waiting for event
```

Although it might look daunting at first, what is happening here is easily understood. In summary, gdb is restoring all its breakpoints on the target. Recall from Listing 14-3 that we entered two breakpoints, one at `panic()` and one at `sys_sync()`. Later in Listing 14-4, we added a third breakpoint at `yosemite_setup_arch()`. Thus, there are three active user-specified breakpoints.

These can be displayed by issuing the `gdb info breakpoints` command. As usual, we use the abbreviated version.

```
(gdb) i b
Num Type           Disp Enb Address     What
1   breakpoint     keep y   0xc0016de8 in panic at kernel/panic.c:74
2   breakpoint     keep y   0xc005bd5c in sys_sync at fs/buffer.c:296
3   breakpoint     keep y   0xc021a488 in yosemite_setup_arch at
arch/ppc/platforms/4xx/yosemite.c:308
        breakpoint already hit 1 time
(gdb)
```

Now compare the previous breakpoint addresses with the addresses in the `gdb` remote `$m` packet in Listing 14-5. The `$m` packet is a "read target memory" command, and the `$M` packet is a "write target memory" command. Once for each breakpoint, the address of the breakpoint is read from target memory, stored away locally on the host by `gdb` (so it can be restored later), and replaced with the PowerPC `trap` instruction `twge r2, r2 (0x7d821008)`, which results in control passing back to the debugger. Figure 14-4 illustrates this action.

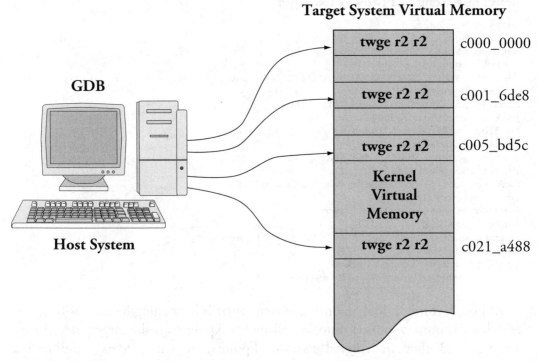

FIGURE 14-4
gdb inserting target memory breakpoints

You might have noticed that gdb is updating four breakpoints, whereas we entered only three. The first one at target memory location 0xc000_0000 is put there by gdb automatically upon startup. This location is the base address of the linked kernel image from the ELF file—essentially, _start. It is equivalent to a breakpoint at main() for user space debugging and is done by gdb automatically. The other three breakpoints are the ones we entered earlier.

The same thing happens in reverse when an event occurs that returns control to gdb. Listing 14-6 details the action when our breakpoint at yosemite_setup_arch() is encountered.

Listing 14-6

Remote Protocol: Breakpoint Hit

```
Packet received: T0440:c021a488;01:c020ff90;
Sending packet: $mc0000000,4#80...Ack  <<< Read memory @c0000000
Packet received: 7d821008
Sending packet: $Mc0000000,4:c022d200#87...Ack  <<< Write memory
Packet received: OK
Sending packet: $mc0016de8,4#f8...Ack
Packet received: 7d821008
Sending packet: $Mc0016de8,4:38600001#a4...Ack
Packet received: OK
Sending packet: $mc005bd5c,4#23...Ack
Packet received: 7d821008
Sending packet: $Mc005bd5c,4:38600001#cf...Ack
Packet received: OK
Sending packet: $mc021a488,4#c8...Ack
Packet received: 7d821008
Sending packet: $Mc021a488,4:4bfffbad#d1...Ack
Packet received: OK

Sending packet: $mc021a484,c#f3...Ack
Packet received: 900100244bfffbad3fa0c022
Breakpoint 3, yosemite_setup_arch () at arch/ppc/platforms/4xx/yosemite.c:308
308             yosemite_set_emacdata();
(gdb)
```

The $T packet is a gdb Stop Reply packet. It is sent by the target to gdb when a breakpoint is encountered. In our example, the $T packet returned the value of the program counter and register r1.[4] The rest of the activity is the reverse of that

---

[4] As pointed out earlier, the gdb remote protocol is detailed in the gdb manual cited at the end of this chapter in Section 14.6.1, "Suggestions for Additional Reading."

in Listing 14-5. The PowerPC trap breakpoint instructions are removed, and gdb restores the original instructions to their respective memory locations.

14.3.2 Debugging Optimized Kernel Code

At the start of this chapter, we said that one of the challenges identified in debugging kernel code results from compiler optimization. We noted that the Linux kernel is compiled by default with optimization level -O2. In the examples up to this point, we used -O1 optimization to simplify the debugging task. Here we illustrate one of the many ways optimization can complicate debugging.

The related Internet mail lists are strewn with questions related to what appear to be broken tools. Sometimes the poster reports that his debugger is single-stepping backward or that his line numbers do not line up with his source code. Here we present an example to illustrate the complexities that optimizing compilers bring to source-level debugging. In this example, the line numbers that gdb reports when a breakpoint is hit do not match up with the line numbers in our source file due to *function inlining*.

For this demonstration, we use the same debug code snippet as shown in Listing 14-4. However, for this example, we have compiled the kernel with the compiler optimization flag -O2. This is the default for the Linux kernel. Listing 14-7 shows the results of this debugging session.

Listing 14-7

Optimized Architecture-Setup Code

```
$ ppc_44x-gdb --silent vmlinux
(gdb) target remote /dev/ttyS0
Remote debugging using /dev/ttyS0
breakinst () at arch/ppc/kernel/ppc-stub.c:825
825        }
(gdb) b panic
Breakpoint 1 at 0xc0016b18: file kernel/panic.c, line 74.
(gdb) b sys_sync
Breakpoint 2 at 0xc005a8c8: file fs/buffer.c, line 296.
(gdb) b yosemite_setup_arch
Breakpoint 3 at 0xc020f438: file arch/ppc/platforms/4xx/yosemite.c, line 116.
(gdb) c
Continuing.

Breakpoint 3, yosemite_setup_arch ()
    at arch/ppc/platforms/4xx/yosemite.c:116
```

```
116                     def = ocp_get_one_device(OCP_VENDOR_IBM, OCP_FUNC_EMAC, 0);
(gdb) l
111                     struct ocp_def *def;
112                     struct ocp_func_emac_data *emacdata;
113
114                     /* Set mac_addr and phy mode for each EMAC */
115
116                     def = ocp_get_one_device(OCP_VENDOR_IBM, OCP_FUNC_EMAC, 0);
117                     emacdata = def->additions;
118                     memcpy(emacdata->mac_addr, __res.bi_enetaddr, 6);
119                     emacdata->phy_mode = PHY_MODE_RMII;
120
(gdb) p yosemite_setup_arch
$1 = {void (void)} 0xc020f41c <yosemite_setup_arch>
```

Referring back to Listing 14-4, notice that the function yosemite_setup_arch() actually falls on line 306 of the file yosemite.c. Compare that with Listing 14-7. We hit the breakpoint, but gdb reports the breakpoint at file yosemite.c line 116. It appears at first glance to be a mismatch of line numbers between the debugger and the corresponding source code. Is this a gdb bug? First let's confirm what the compiler produced for debug information. Using the readelf[5] tool described in Chapter 13, "Development Tools," we can examine the debug information for this function produced by the compiler.

```
$ ppc_44x-readelf --debug-dump=info vmlinux | grep -u6 \
  yosemite_setup_arch | tail -n 7
    DW_AT_name          : (indirect string, offset: 0x9c04): yosemite_setup_arch
    DW_AT_decl_file     : 1
    DW_AT_decl_line     : 307
    DW_AT_prototyped    : 1
    DW_AT_low_pc        : 0xc020f41c
    DW_AT_high_pc       : 0xc020f794
    DW_AT_frame_base    : 1 byte block: 51       (DW_OP_reg1)
```

We don't have to be experts at reading DWARF2 debug records[6] to recognize that the function in question is reported at line 307 in our source file. We can confirm this using the addr2line utility, also introduced in Chapter 13. Using the address derived from gdb in Listing 14-7:

```
$ ppc_44x-addr2line  -e vmlinux 0xc020f41c
  arch/ppc/platforms/4xx/yosemite.c:307
```

---

[5] Remember to use your cross-version of readelf—for example, ppc_44x-readelf for the PowerPC 44x architecture.

[6] A reference for the Dwarf debug specification appears at the end of this chapter in Section 14.6.1, "Suggestions for Additional Reading."

At this point, gdb is reporting our breakpoint at line 116 of the yosemite.c file. To understand what is happening, we need to look at the assembler output of the function as reported by gdb. Listing 14-8 is the output from gdb after issuing the disassemble command on the yosemite_setup_arch() function.

Listing 14-8

Disassemble Function `yosemite_setup_arch`

```
(gdb) disassemble yosemite_setup_arch
0xc020f41c <yosemite_setup_arch+0>:        mflr     r0
0xc020f420 <yosemite_setup_arch+4>:        stwu     r1,-48(r1)
0xc020f424 <yosemite_setup_arch+8>:        li       r4,512
0xc020f428 <yosemite_setup_arch+12>:       li       r5,0
0xc020f42c <yosemite_setup_arch+16>:       li       r3,4116
0xc020f430 <yosemite_setup_arch+20>:       stmw     r25,20(r1)
0xc020f434 <yosemite_setup_arch+24>:       stw      r0,52(r1)
0xc020f438 <yosemite_setup_arch+28>:       bl       0xc000d344
<ocp_get_one_device>
0xc020f43c <yosemite_setup_arch+32>:       lwz      r31,32(r3)
0xc020f440 <yosemite_setup_arch+36>:       lis      r4,-16350
0xc020f444 <yosemite_setup_arch+40>:       li       r28,2
0xc020f448 <yosemite_setup_arch+44>:       addi     r4,r4,21460
0xc020f44c <yosemite_setup_arch+48>:       li       r5,6
0xc020f450 <yosemite_setup_arch+52>:       lis      r29,-16350
0xc020f454 <yosemite_setup_arch+56>:       addi     r3,r31,48
0xc020f458 <yosemite_setup_arch+60>:       lis      r25,-16350
0xc020f45c <yosemite_setup_arch+64>:       bl       0xc000c708
<memcpy>
0xc020f460 <yosemite_setup_arch+68>:       stw      r28,44(r31)
0xc020f464 <yosemite_setup_arch+72>:       li       r4,512
0xc020f468 <yosemite_setup_arch+76>:       li       r5,1
0xc020f46c <yosemite_setup_arch+80>:       li       r3,4116
0xc020f470 <yosemite_setup_arch+84>:       addi     r26,r25,15104
0xc020f474 <yosemite_setup_arch+88>:       bl       0xc000d344
<ocp_get_one_device>
0xc020f478 <yosemite_setup_arch+92>:       lis      r4,-16350
0xc020f47c <yosemite_setup_arch+96>:       lwz      r31,32(r3)
0xc020f480 <yosemite_setup_arch+100>:      addi     r4,r4,21534
0xc020f484 <yosemite_setup_arch+104>:      li       r5,6
0xc020f488 <yosemite_setup_arch+108>:      addi     r3,r31,48
0xc020f48c <yosemite_setup_arch+112>:      bl       0xc000c708
<memcpy>
0xc020f490 <yosemite_setup_arch+116>:      lis      r4,1017
0xc020f494 <yosemite_setup_arch+120>:      lis      r5,168
0xc020f498 <yosemite_setup_arch+124>:      stw      r28,44(r31)
0xc020f49c <yosemite_setup_arch+128>:      ori      r4,r4,16554
0xc020f4a0 <yosemite_setup_arch+132>:      ori      r5,r5,49152
0xc020f4a4 <yosemite_setup_arch+136>:      addi     r3,r29,-15380
0xc020f4a8 <yosemite_setup_arch+140>:      addi     r29,r29,-15380
0xc020f4ac <yosemite_setup_arch+144>:      bl       0xc020e338
```

```
<ibm440gx_get_clocks>
0xc020f4b0 <yosemite_setup_arch+148>:    li      r0,0
0xc020f4b4 <yosemite_setup_arch+152>:    lis     r11,-16352
0xc020f4b8 <yosemite_setup_arch+156>:    ori     r0,r0,50000
0xc020f4bc <yosemite_setup_arch+160>:    lwz     r10,12(r29)
0xc020f4c0 <yosemite_setup_arch+164>:    lis     r9,-16352
0xc020f4c4 <yosemite_setup_arch+168>:    stw     r0,8068(r11)
0xc020f4c8 <yosemite_setup_arch+172>:    lwz     r0,84(r26)
0xc020f4cc <yosemite_setup_arch+176>:    stw     r10,8136(r9)
0xc020f4d0 <yosemite_setup_arch+180>:    mtctr   r0
0xc020f4d4 <yosemite_setup_arch+184>:    bctrl
0xc020f4d8 <yosemite_setup_arch+188>:    li      r5,64
0xc020f4dc <yosemite_setup_arch+192>:    mr      r31,r3
0xc020f4e0 <yosemite_setup_arch+196>:    lis     r4,-4288
0xc020f4e4 <yosemite_setup_arch+200>:    li      r3,0
0xc020f4e8 <yosemite_setup_arch+204>:    bl      0xc000c0f8
<ioremap64>
End of assembler dump.
(gdb)
```

Once again, we need not be PowerPC assembly language experts to understand what is happening here. Notice the labels associated with the PowerPC bl instruction. This is a function call in PowerPC mnemonics. The symbolic function labels are the important data points. After a cursory analysis, we see several function calls near the start of this assembler listing:

Address	Function
0xc020f438	ocp_get_one_device()
0xc020f45c	memcpy()
0xc020f474	ocp_get_one_device()
0xc020f48c	memcpy()
0xc020f4ac	ibm440gx_get_clocks()

Listing 14-9 reproduces portions of the source file yosemite.c. Correlating the functions we found in the gdb disassemble output, we see those labels occurring in the function yosemite_set_emacdata(), around the line numbers reported by gdb when the breakpoint at yosemite_setup_arch() was encountered. The key to understanding the anomaly is to notice the subroutine call at the very start of yosemite_setup_arch(). The compiler has inlined the call to yosemite_set_emacdata() instead of generating a function call, as would be expected by simple inspection of the source code. This inlining produced the mismatch in the line numbers when gdb hit the breakpoint. Even though the `yosemite_set_emacdata()` function was not declared using the inline keyword, GCC inlined the function as a performance optimization.

Listing 14-9

Portions of Source File `yosemite.c`

```
109 static void __init yosemite_set_emacdata(void)
110 {
111         struct ocp_def *def;
112         struct ocp_func_emac_data *emacdata;
113
114         /* Set mac_addr and phy mode for each EMAC */
115
116         def = ocp_get_one_device(OCP_VENDOR_IBM, OCP_FUNC_EMAC, 0);
117         emacdata = def->additions;
118         memcpy(emacdata->mac_addr, __res.bi_enetaddr, 6);
119         emacdata->phy_mode = PHY_MODE_RMII;
120
121         def = ocp_get_one_device(OCP_VENDOR_IBM, OCP_FUNC_EMAC, 1);
122         emacdata = def->additions;
123         memcpy(emacdata->mac_addr, __res.bi_enet1addr, 6);
124         emacdata->phy_mode = PHY_MODE_RMII;
125 }
126
...
304
305 static void __init
306 yosemite_setup_arch(void)
307 {
308         yosemite_set_emacdata();
309
310         ibm440gx_get_clocks(&clocks, YOSEMITE_SYSCLK, 6 * 1843200);
311         ocp_sys_info.opb_bus_freq = clocks.opb;
312
313         /* init to some ~sane value until calibrate_delay() runs */
314         loops_per_jiffy = 50000000/HZ;
315
316         /* Setup PCI host bridge */
317         yosemite_setup_hose();
318
319 #ifdef CONFIG_BLK_DEV_INITRD
320         if (initrd_start)
321                 ROOT_DEV = Root_RAM0;
322         else
323 #endif
324 #ifdef CONFIG_ROOT_NFS
325                 ROOT_DEV = Root_NFS;
326 #else
327                 ROOT_DEV = Root_HDA1;
328 #endif
```

```
329
330             yosemite_early_serial_map();
331
332             /* Identify the system */
333             printk( "AMCC PowerPC " BOARDNAME " Platform\n" );
334 }
335
```

To summarize the previous discussion:

- We entered a breakpoint in gdb at yosemite_setup_arch().

- When the breakpoint was hit, we found ourselves at line 116 of the source file, which was far removed from the function where we defined the breakpoint.

- We produced a disassembly listing of the code at yosemite_setup_arch() and discovered the labels to which this sequence of code was branching.

- Comparing the labels back to our source code, we discovered that the compiler had placed the yosemite_set_emacdata() subroutine inline with the function where we entered a breakpoint, causing potential confusion.

This explains the line numbers reported by gdb when the original breakpoint in yosemite_setup_arch() was hit.

Compilers employ many different kinds of optimization algorithms. This example presented but one: function inlining. Each can confuse a debugger (the human and the machine) in a different way. The challenge is to understand what is happening at the machine level and translate that into what we as developers had intended. You can see now the benefits of using the minimum possible optimization level for debugging.

14.3.3 gdb User-Defined Commands

You might already realize that gdb looks for an initialization file on startup, called .gdbinit. When first invoked, gdb loads this initialization file (usually found in the user's home directory) and acts on the commands within it. One of my favorite combinations is to connect to the target system and set initial breakpoints. In this case, the contents of .gdbinit would look like Listing 14-10.

Listing 14-10

Simple gdb Initialization File

```
$ cat ~/.gdbinit
set history save on
set history filename ~/.gdb_history
set output-radix 16

define connect
#     target remote bdi:2001
      target remote /dev/ttyS0
      b panic
      b sys_sync
end
```

This simple .gdbinit file enables the storing of command history in a user-specified file and sets the default output radix for printing of values. Then it defines a gdb *user-defined command* called connect. (User-defined commands are also often called macros.) When issued at the gdb command prompt, gdb connects to the target system via the desired method and sets the system breakpoints at panic() and sys_sync(). One method is commented out; we discuss this method shortly in Section 14.4.

There is no end to the creative use of gdb user-defined commands. When debugging in the kernel, it is often useful to examine global data structures such as task lists and memory maps. Here we present several useful gdb user-defined commands capable of displaying specific kernel data that you might need to access during your kernel debugging.

14.3.4 Useful Kernel gdb Macros

During kernel debugging, it is often useful to view the processes that are running on the system, as well as some common attributes of those processes. The kernel maintains a linked list of tasks described by struct task_struct. The address of the first task in the list is contained in the kernel global variable init_task, which represents the initial task spawned by the kernel during startup. Each task contains a struct list_head, which links the tasks in a circular linked list. These two ubiquitous kernel structures are described in the following header files:

struct task_struct	.../include/linux/sched.h
struct list_head	.../include/linux/list.h

Using gdb macros, we can traverse the task list and display useful information about the tasks. It is easy to modify the macros to extract the data you might be interested in. It is also a very useful tool for learning the details of kernel internals.

The first macro we examine (in Listing 14-11) is a simple one that searches the kernel's linked list of task_struct structures until it finds the given task. If it is found, it displays the name of the task.

Listing 14-11

gdb find_task Macro

```
 1 # Helper function to find a task given a PID or the
 2 # address of a task_struct.
 3 # The result is set into $t
 4 define find_task
 5   # Addresses greater than _end: kernel data...
 6   # ...user passed in an address
 7   if ((unsigned)$arg0 > (unsigned)&_end)
 8     set $t=(struct task_struct *)$arg0
 9   else
10     # User entered a numeric PID
11     # Walk the task list to find it
12     set $t=&init_task
13     if (init_task.pid != (unsigned)$arg0)
14       find_next_task $t
15       while (&init_task!=$t && $t->pid != (unsigned)$arg0)
16         find_next_task $t
17       end
18       if ($t == &init_task)
19         printf "Couldn't find task; using init_task\n"
20       end
21     end
22   end
23   printf "Task \"%s\":\n", $t->comm
24 end
```

Place this text into your .gdbinit file and restart gdb, or source[7] it using gdb's source command. (We explain the find_next_task macro later in Listing 14-15.) Invoke it as follows:

```
(gdb) find_task 910
  Task "syslogd":
```

or

```
(gdb) find_task 0xCFFDE470
  Task "bash":
```

---

[7] A helpful shortcut for macro development is the gdb source command. This command opens and reads a source file containing macro definitions.

Line 4 defines the macro name. Line 7 decides whether the input argument is a PID (numeric entry starting at zero and limited to a few million) or a task_struct address that must be greater than the end of the Linux kernel image itself, defined by the symbol _end.[8] If it's an address, the only action required is to cast it to the proper type to enable dereferencing the associated task_struct. This is done at line 8. As the comment in line 3 states, this macro returns a gdb convenience variable typecasted to a pointer to a struct task_struct.

If the input argument is a numeric PID, the list is traversed to find the matching task_struct. Lines 12 and 13 initialize the loop variables (gdb does not have a for statement in its macro command language), and lines 15 through 17 define the search loop. The find_next_task macro is used to extract the pointer to the next task_struct in the linked list. Finally, if the search fails, a sane return value is set (the address of init_task) so that it can be safely used in other macros.

Building on the find_task macro in Listing 14-11, we can easily create a simple ps command that displays useful information about each process running on the system.

Listing 14-12 defines a gdb macro that displays interesting information from a running process, extracted from the struct task_struct for the given process. It is invoked like any other gdb command, by typing its name followed by any required input parameters. Notice that this user-defined command requires a single argument, either a PID or the address of a task_struct.

Listing 14-12

gdb Macro: Print Process Information

```
1 define ps
2    # Print column headers
3    task_struct_header
4    set $t=&init_task
5    task_struct_show $t
6    find_next_task $t
7    # Walk the list
8    while &init_task!=$t
9       # Display useful info about each task
10      task_struct_show $t
11      find_next_task $t
12   end
```

---

[8] The symbol _end is defined in the linker script file during the final link.

```
13 end
14
15 document ps
16 Print points of interest for all tasks
17 end
```

This `ps` macro is similar to the `find_task` macro, except that it requires no input arguments and it adds a macro (`task_struct_show`) to display the useful information from each `task_struct`. Line 3 prints a banner line with column headings. Lines 4 through 6 set up the loop and display the first task. Lines 8 through 11 loop through each task, calling the `task_struct_show` macro for each.

Notice also the inclusion of the `gdb` `document` command. This allows the `gdb` user to get help by issuing the `help ps` command from the `gdb` command prompt as follows:

```
(gdb) help ps
    Print points of interest for all tasks
```

Listing 14-13 displays the output of this macro on a target board running only minimal services.

Listing 14-13

gdb ps Macro Output

```
(gdb) ps
Address         PID State          User_NIP    Kernel-SP   device  comm
0xC01D3750        0 Running                    0xC0205E90  (none)  swapper
0xC04ACB10        1 Sleeping       0x0FF6E85C  0xC04FFCE0  (none)  init
0xC04AC770        2 Sleeping                   0xC0501E90  (none)  ksoftirqd/0
0xC04AC3D0        3 Sleeping                   0xC0531E30  (none)  events/0
0xC04AC030        4 Sleeping                   0xC0533E30  (none)  khelper
0xC04CDB30        5 Sleeping                   0xC0535E30  (none)  kthread
0xC04CD790       23 Sleeping                   0xC06FBE30  (none)  kblockd/0
0xC04CD3F0       45 Sleeping                   0xC06FDE50  (none)  pdflush
0xC04CD050       46 Sleeping                   0xC06FFE50  (none)  pdflush
0xC0054B7B0      48 Sleeping                   0xC0703E30  (none)  aio/0
0xC0054BB50      47 Sleeping                   0xC0701E20  (none)  kswapd0
0xC0054B410     629 Sleeping                   0xC0781E60  (none)  kseriod
0xC0054B070     663 Sleeping                   0xCFC59E30  (none)  rpciod/0
0xCFFDE0D0      675 Sleeping       0x0FF6E85C  0xCF86DCE0  (none)  udevd
0xCF95B110      879 Sleeping       0x0FF0BE58  0xCF517D80  (none)  portmap
0xCFC24090      910 Sleeping       0x0FF6E85C  0xCF61BCE0  (none)  syslogd
0xCF804490      918 Sleeping       0x0FF66C7C  0xCF65DD70  (none)  klogd
0xCFE350B0      948 Sleeping       0x0FF0E85C  0xCF67DCE0  (none)  rpc.statd
0xCFFDE810      960 Sleeping       0x0FF6E85C  0xCF5C7CE0  (none)  inetd
```

```
0xCFC24B70   964 Sleeping   0x0FEEBEAC 0xCF64FD80 (none)  mvltd
0xCFE35B90   973 Sleeping   0x0FF66C7C 0xCFEF7CE0 ttyS1   getty
0xCFE357F0   974 Sleeping   0x0FF4B85C 0xCF6EBCE0 (none)  in.telnetd
0xCFFDE470   979 Sleeping   0x0FEB6950 0xCF675DB0 ttyp0   bash
0xCFFDEBB0   982<Running    0x0FF6EB6C 0xCF7C3870 ttyp0   sync
(gdb)
```

The bulk of the work done by this `ps` macro is performed by the `task_struct_show` macro. As shown in Listing 14-13, the `task_struct_show` macro displays the following fields from each `task_struct`:

- `Address`—Address of the `task_struct` for the process
- `PID`—Process ID
- `State`—Current state of the process
- `User_NIP`—Userspace Next Instruction Pointer
- `Kernel_SP`—Kernel Stack Pointer
- `device`—Device associated with this process
- `comm`—Name of the process (or command)

It is relatively easy to modify the macro to show the items of interest for your particular kernel debugging task. The only complexity is in the simplicity of the macro language. Because function equivalents such as `strlen` do not exist in `gdb`'s user-defined command language, screen formatting must be done by hand.

Listing 14-14 reproduces the `task_struct_show` macro that produced the previous listing.

Listing 14-14

gdb `task_struct_show` Macro

```
1 define task_struct_show
2   # task_struct addr and PID
3   printf "0x%08X %5d", $arg0, $arg0->pid
4
5   # Place a '<' marker on the current task
6   #  if ($arg0 == current)
7   # For PowerPC, register r2 points to the "current" task
8   if ($arg0 == $r2)
9     printf "<"
10  else
11    printf " "
```

```
12    end
13
14    # State
15    if ($arg0->state == 0)
16      printf "Running    "
17    else
18      if ($arg0->state == 1)
19        printf "Sleeping   "
20      else
21        if ($arg0->state == 2)
22          printf "Disksleep "
23        else
24          if ($arg0->state == 4)
25            printf "Zombie     "
26          else
27            if ($arg0->state == 8)
28              printf "sTopped    "
29            else
30              if ($arg0->state == 16)
31                printf "Wpaging    "
32              else
33                printf "%2d         ", $arg0->state
34              end
35            end
36          end
37        end
38      end
39    end
40
41    # User NIP
42    if ($arg0->thread.regs)
43      printf "0x%08X ", $arg0->thread.regs->nip
44    else
45      printf "           "
46    end
47
48    # Display the kernel stack pointer
49    printf "0x%08X ", $arg0->thread.ksp
50
51    # device
52    if ($arg0->signal->tty)
53      printf "%s    ", $arg0->signal->tty->name
54    else
55      printf "(none) "
56    end
57
58    # comm
59    printf "%s\n", $arg0->comm
60 end
```

Line 3 displays the address of the `task_struct`. Lines 8 through 12 display the process ID. If this is the current process (the process that was currently running on this CPU at the time the breakpoint was hit), it is marked with a < character.

Lines 14 through 39 decode and display the state of the process. This is followed by displaying the user process next instruction pointer (NIP) and the kernel stack pointer (SP). Finally, the device associated with the process is displayed, followed by the name of the process (stored in the `->comm` element of the `task_struct`.)

It is important to note that this macro is architecture dependent, as shown in lines 7 and 8. In general, macros such as these are highly architecture- and version-dependent. Any time a change in the underlying structure is made, macros such as these must be updated. However, if you spend a lot of time debugging the kernel using `gdb`, the payback is often worth the effort.

For completeness, we present the `find_next_task` macro. Its implementation is less than obvious and deserves explanation. (It is assumed that you can easily deduce the `task_struct_header` that completes the series necessary for the `ps` macro presented in this section. It is nothing more than a single line arranging the column headers with the correct amount of whitespace.) Listing 14-15 presents the `find_next_task` macro used in our `ps` and `find_task` macros.

Listing 14-15

gdb `find_next_task` Macro

```
define find_next_task
  # Given a task address, find the next task in the linked list
  set $t = (struct task_struct *)$arg0
  set $offset=( (char *)&$t->tasks - (char *)$t)
  set $t=(struct task_struct *)( (char *)$t->tasks.next- (char *)$offset)
end
```

The function performed by this macro is simple. The implementation is slightly less than straightforward. The goal is to return the `->next` pointer, which points to the next `task_struct` on the linked list. However, the `task_struct` structures are linked by the address of the `struct list_head` member called `tasks`, as opposed to the common practice of being linked by the starting address of the `task_struct` itself. Because the `->next` pointer points to the address of the `task` structure element in the next `task_struct` on the list, we must subtract to get the address of the top of the `task_struct` itself. The value we subtract from the `->next` pointer is the offset from that pointer's address to the top of `task_struct`. First we calculate the offset and then we use that offset to adjust the `->next` pointer to point to the top of `task_struct`. Figure 14-5 should make this clear.

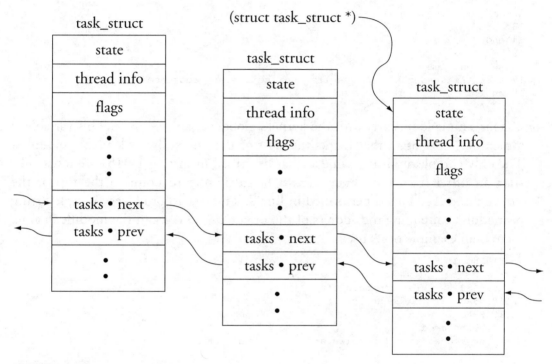

FIGURE 14-5
Task structure list linking

Now we present one final macro that will be useful in the next section when we discuss debugging loadable modules. Listing 14-16 is a simple macro that displays the kernel's list of currently installed loadable modules.

Listing 14-16

gdb List Modules Macro

```
1 define lsmod
2    printf "Address\t\tModule\n"
3    set $m=(struct list_head *)&modules
4    set $done=0
5    while ( !$done )
```

```
 6       # list_head is 4-bytes into struct module
 7       set $mp=(struct module *)((char *)$m->next - (char *)4)
 8       printf "0x%08X\t%s\n", $mp, $mp->name
 9       if ( $mp->list->next == &modules)
10         set $done=1
11       end
12       set $m=$m->next
13     end
14 end
15
16 document lsmod
17 List the loaded kernel modules and their start addresses
18 end
```

This simple loop starts with the kernel's global variable `module`. This variable is a `struct list_head` that marks the start of the linked list of loadable modules. The only complexity is the same as that described in Listing 14-15. We must subtract an offset from the `struct list_head` pointer to point to the top of the `struct module`. This is performed in line 7. This macro produces a simple listing of modules containing the address of the `struct module` and the module's name. Here is an example of its use:

```
(gdb) lsmod
Address         Module
0xD1012A80      ip_conntrack_tftp
0xD10105A0      ip_conntrack
0xD102F9A0      loop
(gdb) help lsmod
List the loaded kernel modules and their start addresses
(gdb)
```

Macros such as the ones presented here are very powerful debugging aids. You can create macros in a similar fashion to display anything in the kernel that lends itself to easy access, especially the major data structures maintained as linked lists. Examples include process memory map information, module information, file system information, and timer lists and so on. The information presented here should get you started.

14.3.5 Debugging Loadable Modules

The most common reason for using KGDB is to debug loadable kernel modules, that is, device drivers. One of the more convenient features of loadable modules is that, under most circumstances, it is not necessary to reboot the kernel for each new debugging session. You can start a debugging session, make some changes, recompile, and reload the module without the hassle and delay of a complete kernel reboot.

The complication associated with debugging loadable modules is in gaining access to the symbolic debug information contained in the module's object file. Because loadable modules are dynamically linked when they are loaded into the kernel, the symbolic information contained in the object file is useless until the symbol table is adjusted.

Recall from our earlier examples how we invoke gdb for a kernel debugging session:

```
$ ppc_4xx-gdb vmlinux
```

This launches a gdb debugging session on your host, and reads the symbol information from the Linux kernel ELF file vmlinux. Of course, you will not find symbols for any loadable modules in this file. Loadable modules are separate compilation units and are linked as individual standalone ELF objects. Therefore, if we intend to perform any source-level debugging on a loadable module, we need to load its debug symbols from the ELF file. gdb provides this capability in its add-symbol-file command.

The add-symbol-file command loads symbols from the specified object file, assuming that the module itself has already been loaded. However, we are faced with the chicken-and-egg syndrome. We don't have any symbol information until the loadable module has been loaded into the kernel and the add-symbol-file command is issued to read in the module's symbol information. However, after the module has been loaded, it is too late to set breakpoints and debug the module's *_init and related functions because they have already executed.

The solution to this dilemma is to place a breakpoint in the kernel code that is responsible for loading the module, after it has been linked but before its initialization function has been called. This work is done by .../kernel/module.c. Listing 14-17 reproduces the relevant portions of module.c.

Listing 14-17

module.c: Module Initialization

```
. . .
1901            down(&notify_mutex);
1902            notifier_call_chain(&module_notify_list, MODULE_STATE_COMING, mod);
1903            up(&notify_mutex);
```

```
1904
1905            /* Start the module */
1906            if (mod->init != NULL)
1907                    ret = mod->init();
1908            if (ret < 0) {
1909                    /* Init routine failed: abort.  Try to protect us from
1910                            buggy refcounters. */
1911                    mod->state = MODULE_STATE_GOING;
...
```

We load the module using the `modprobe` utility, which was demonstrated in Listing 8-5 in Chapter 8, "Device Driver Basics," and looks like this:

$ **modprobe loop**

This command issues a special system call that directs the kernel to load the module. The module loading begins at `sys_init_module()` in `module.c`. After the module has been loaded into kernel memory and dynamically linked, control is passed to the module's _init function. This is shown in lines 1906 and 1907 of Listing 14-17. We place our breakpoint here. This enables us to add the symbol file to `gdb` and subsequently set breakpoints in the module. We demonstrate this process using the Linux kernel's loopback driver called `loop.ko`. This module has no dependencies on other modules and is reasonably easy to demonstrate.

Listing 14-18 shows the `gdb` commands to initiate this debugging session on `loop.ko`.

Listing 14-18

Initiate Module Debug Session: `loop.ko`

```
 1 $ ppc-linux-gdb --silent vmlinux
 2 (gdb) connect
 3 breakinst () at arch/ppc/kernel/ppc-stub.c:825
 4 825      }
 5 Breakpoint 1 at 0xc0016b18: file kernel/panic.c, line 74.
 6 Breakpoint 2 at 0xc005a8c8: file fs/buffer.c, line 296.
 7 (gdb) b module.c:1907
 8 Breakpoint 3 at 0xc003430c: file kernel/module.c, line 1907.
 9 (gdb) c
10 Continuing.
11 >>>> Here we let the kernel finish booting
12      and then load the loop.ko module on the target
13
14 Breakpoint 3, sys_init_module (umod=0x30029000, len=0x2473e,
15     uargs=0x10016338 "") at kernel/module.c:1907
```

```
16 1907                          ret = mod->init();
17 (gdb) lsmod
18 Address           Module
19 0xD102F9A0        loop
20 (gdb) set $m=(struct module *)0xD102F9A0.
21 (gdb) p $m->module_core
22 $1 = (void *) 0xd102c000
23 (gdb) add-symbol-file ./drivers/block/loop.ko 0xd102c000
24 add symbol table from file "./drivers/block/loop.ko" at
25          .text_addr = 0xd102c000
26 (y or n) y
27 Reading symbols from /home/chris/sandbox/linux-2.6.13-amcc/
drivers/block       /loop.ko...done.
```

Starting with line 2, we use the gdb user-defined macro connect created earlier in Listing 14-10 to connect to the target board and set our initial breakpoints. We then add the breakpoint in module.c, as shown in line 7, and we issue the continue command (c). Now the kernel completes the boot process and we establish a telnet session into the target and load the loop.ko module (not shown). When the loopback module is loaded, we immediately hit breakpoint #3. gdb then displays the information shown in lines 14 through 16.

At this point, we need to discover the address where the Linux kernel linked our module's .text section. Linux stores this address in the module information structure struct module in the module_core element. Using the lsmod macro we defined in Listing 14-16, we obtain the address of the struct module associated with our loop.ko module. This is shown in lines 17 through 19. Now we use this structure address to obtain the module's .text address from the module_core structure member. We pass this address to the gdb add-symbol-file command, and gdb uses this address to adjust its internal symbol table to match the actual addresses where the module was linked into the kernel. From there, we can proceed in the usual manner to set breakpoints in the module, step through code, examine data, and so on.

We conclude this section with a demonstration of placing a breakpoint in the loopback module's initialization function so that we can step through the module's initialization code. The complication here is that the kernel loads the module's initialization code into a separately allocated portion of memory so that it can be freed after use. Recall from Chapter 5, "Kernel Initialization," our discussion of the __init macro. This macro expands into a compiler attribute that directs the linker to place the marked portion of code into a specially named ELF section. In essence, any function defined with this attribute is placed in a separate ELF section named `.init.text`. Its use is similar to the following:

```
static int __init loop_init(void){...}
```

This invocation would place the compiled `loop_init()` function into the `.init.text` section of the `loop.ko` object module. When the module is loaded, the kernel allocates a chunk of memory for the main body of the module, which is pointed to by the `struct module` member named `module_core`. It then allocates a separate chunk of memory to hold the `.init.text` section. After the initialization function is called, the kernel frees the memory that contained the initialization function. Because the object module is split like this, we need to inform `gdb` of this addressing scheme to be able to use symbolic data for debugging the initialization function.[9] Listing 14-19 demonstrates these steps.

Listing 14-19

Debugging Module `init` Code

```
$ ppc_4xx-gdb -slient vmlinux
(gdb) target remote /dev/ttyS0
Remote debugging using /dev/ttyS0
breakinst () at arch/ppc/kernel/ppc-stub.c:825
825            }

<< Place a breakpoint before calling module init >>
(gdb) b module.c:1907
Breakpoint 1 at 0xc0036418: file kernel/module.c, line 1907.
(gdb) c
Continuing.

Breakpoint 1, sys_init_module (umod=0xd102ef40, len=0x23cb3, uargs=0x10016338 "")
    at kernel/module.c:1907
1907                      ret = mod->init();

<< Discover init addressing from struct module >>
(gdb) lsmod
Address         Module
0xD102EF40      loop
(gdb) set $m=(struct module *)0xD102EF40
(gdb) p $m->module_core
$1 = (void *) 0xd102b000
(gdb) p $m->module_init
$2 = (void *) 0xd1031000
```

---

[9] As of this writing, there is a bug in `gdb` that prevents this technique from working properly. Hopefully, by the time you read this, it will be fixed.

```
<< Now load a symbol file using the core and init addrs >>
(gdb) add-symbol-file ./drivers/block/loop.ko 0xd102b000 -s .init.text
0xd1031000
add symbol table from file "./drivers/block/loop.ko" at
        .text_addr = 0xd102b000
        .init.text_addr = 0xd1031000
(y or n) y
Reading symbols from /home/chris/sandbox/linux-2.6.13-
amcc/drivers/block/loop.ko...done.
(gdb) b loop_init
Breakpoint 3 at 0xd1031000: file drivers/block/loop.c, line 1244.
(gdb) c
Continuing.

<< Breakpoint hit, proceed to debug module init function >>
Breakpoint 3, 0xd1031000 in loop_init () file drivers/block/loop.c, line 1244
1244            if (max_loop < 1 || max_loop > 256) {
(gdb)
```

14.3.6 printk Debugging

Debugging kernel and device driver code using `printk` is a popular technique, mostly because `printk` has evolved into a very robust method. You can call `printk` from almost any context, including from interrupt handlers. `printk` is the kernel's version of the familiar `printf()` C library function. `printk` is defined in `.../kernel/printk.c`.

It is important to understand the limitations of using `printk` for debugging. First, `printk` requires a console device. Moreover, although the console device is configured as early as possible during kernel initialization, there are many calls to `printk` before the console device has been initialized. We present a method to cope with this limitation later, in Section 14.5, "When It Doesn't Boot."

The `printk` function allows the addition of a string marker that identifies the level of severity of a given message. The header file `.../include/linux/kernel.h` defines eight levels:

```
#define     KERN_EMERG      "<0>" /* system is unusable */
#define     KERN_ALERT      "<1>" /* action must be taken immediately */
#define     KERN_CRIT       "<2>" /* critical conditions */
#define     KERN_ERR        "<3>" /* error conditions */
#define     KERN_WARNING    "<4>" /* warning conditions */
#define     KERN_NOTICE     "<5>" /* normal but significant condition */
#define     KERN_INFO       "<6>" /* informational */
#define     KERN_DEBUG      "<7>" /* debug-level messages */
```

A simple `printk` message might look like this:

```
printk("foo() entered w/ %s\n", arg);
```

If the severity string is omitted, the kernel assigns a default severity level, which is defined in `printk.c`. In recent kernels, this is set at severity level 4, `KERN_WARNING`. Specifying `printk` with a severity level might look something like this:

```
printk(KERN_CRIT "vmalloc failed in foo()\n");
```

By default, all `printk` messages below a predefined *loglevel* are displayed on the system console device. The default loglevel is defined in `printk.c`. In recent Linux kernels, it has the value 7. This means that any `printk` message that is greater in importance than `KERN_DEBUG` will be displayed on the console.

You can set the default kernel loglevel in a variety of ways. At boot time, you can specify the default loglevel on your target board by passing the appropriate kernel command line parameters to the kernel at boot time. Three kernel command line options defined in `main.c` affect the default loglevel:

- `debug`—Sets the console loglevel to 10

- `quiet`—Sets the console loglevel to 4

- `loglevel=`—Sets the console loglevel to your choice of value

Using `debug` effectively displays every `printk` message. Using `quiet` displays all `printk` messages of severity `KERN_ERR` or higher.

`printk` messages can be logged to files on your target or via the network. Use `klogd` (kernel log daemon) and `syslogd` (system log daemon) to control the logging behavior of `printk` messages. These popular utilities are described in man pages and many Linux references, and are not described here.

14.3.7 Magic SysReq Key

This useful debugging aid is invoked through a series of special predefined key sequences that send messages directly to the kernel. For many target architectures and boards, you use a simple terminal emulator on a serial port as a system console. For these architectures, the Magic SysReq key is defined as a break character followed by a command character. Consult the documentation on the terminal emulator you use for how to send a break character. Many Linux developers use the `minicom` terminal emulator. For `minicom`, the break character is sent by typing

Ctl-A F. After sending the break in this manner, you have 5 seconds to enter the command character before the command times out.

This useful kernel tool can be very helpful for development and debugging, but it can also cause data loss and system corruption. Indeed, the b command immediately reboots your system without any notification or preparation. Open files are not closed, disks are not synced, and file systems are not unmounted. When the reboot (b) command is issued, control is immediately passed to the reset vector of your architecture in a most abrupt and stunning manner. Use this powerful tool at your own peril!

This feature is well documented in the Linux kernel documentation subdirectory in a file called sysrq.txt. There you find the details for many architectures and the description of available commands.

For example, another way to set the kernel loglevel just discussed is to use the Magic SysReq key. The command is a number from 0 through 9, which results in the default loglevel being set to the number of the command. From minicom, press Ctl-A F followed by a number, such as 9. Here is how it looks on the terminal:

```
$ SysRq : Changing Loglevel
  Loglevel set to 9
```

Commands can be used to dump registers, shut down your system, reboot your system, dump a list of processes, dump current memory information to your console, and more. See the documentation file in any recent Linux kernel for the details.

This feature is most commonly used when something causes your system to lock up. Often the Magic SysReq key provides a way to learn something from an otherwise dead system.

14.4 Hardware-Assisted Debugging

By now you've probably realized that you cannot debug very early kernel-startup code with KGDB. This is because KGDB is not initialized until after most of the low-level hardware-initialization code has executed. Furthermore, if you are assigned the task of bringing up a brand-new board design and porting a bootloader and the Linux kernel, having a hardware-debug probe is without a doubt the most efficient means of debugging problems in these early stages of board porting.

You can choose from a wide variety of hardware-debug probes. For the examples in this section, we use a unit manufactured by Abatron called the BDI-2000 (see www.abatron.ch). These units are often called JTAG probes because they use a low-level communications method that was first employed for boundary scan testing of integrated circuits defined by the Joint Test Action Group (JTAG).

A JTAG probe contains a small connector designed for connection to your target board. It is often a simple square-pin header and ribbon cable arrangement. Most modern high-performance CPUs contain a JTAG interface that is designed to provide this software debugging capability. The JTAG probe connects to this CPU JTAG interface. The other side of the JTAG probe connects to your host development system usually via Ethernet, USB, or a parallel port. Figure 14-6 details the setup for the Abatron unit.

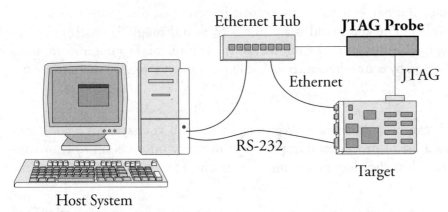

FIGURE 14-6
Hardware JTAG probe debugging

JTAG probes can be complicated to set up. This is a direct result of the complexity of the CPU to which it is connected. When power is applied to a target board and its CPU comes out of reset, almost nothing is initialized. In fact, many processors need at least a small amount of initialization before they can do anything. Many methods are available for getting this initial configuration into the CPU. Some CPUs read a hardware-configuration word or initial values of specific pins to learn their power-on configuration. Others rely on reading a default location in a simple nonvolatile storage device such as Flash. When using a JTAG probe, especially for bringing up a new board design, a minimum level of CPU and board initialization must be performed before anything else can be done. Many JTAG probes rely on a configuration file for this initialization.

The Abatron unit uses a configuration file to initialize the target hardware it is connected to, as well as to define other operational parameters of the debugger. This configuration file contains directives that initialize the CPU, memory system, and other necessary board-level hardware. It is the developer's responsibility to customize this configuration file with the proper directives for his own board. The details on the configuration command syntax can be found in the JTAG probe's documentation. However, only the embedded developer can create the unique configuration file required for a given board design. This requires detailed knowledge of the CPU and board-level design features. Much like creating a custom Linux port for a new board, there is no shortcut or substitute for this task.

Appendix F, "Sample BDI-2000 Configuration File," contains a sample Abatron configuration file for a custom board based on the Freescale Semiconductor MPC5200 embedded controller. In that appendix, you can see the necessary setup for a custom board. Notice the liberal use of comments describing various registers and initialization details. This makes it easier to update and maintain over time, and it can help you to get it right the first time.

Hardware probes are generally used in two ways. Most have a user interface of some type that enables the developer to use features of the probe. Examples of this are to program Flash or download binary images. The second usage is as a front end to gdb or other source-level debuggers. We demonstrate both usage scenarios.

14.4.1 Programming Flash Using a JTAG Probe

Many hardware probes include the capability to program a wide variety of Flash memory chips. The Abatron BDI-2000 is no exception. The BDI-2000 configuration file includes a [FLASH] section to define the characteristics of the target Flash. Refer to Appendix F for a sample. The [FLASH] section defines attributes of the Flash chip as used in a particular design, such as the chip type, the size of the device, and its data bus width. Also defined are the location in memory and some way to describe the chip's storage organization.

When updating one portion of the Flash, you often want to preserve the contents of other portions of the same Flash. In this case, your hardware probe must have some way to limit the sectors that are erased. In the case of the Abatron unit, this is done by adding a line starting with the keyword ERASE for each sector to be erased. When the `erase` command is issued to the Abatron unit via its `telnet` user interface, all sectors defined with an ERASE specification are erased. Listing 14-20 demonstrates erasing a portion of Flash on a target board and subsequently programming a new U-Boot bootloader image.

Listing 14-20

Erase and Program Flash

```
$ telnet bdi
Trying 192.168.1.129...
Connected to bdi (192.168.1.129).
Escape character is '^]'.
BDI Debugger for Embedded PowerPC
==================================
...  (large volume of help text)

uei> erase
Erasing flash at 0xfff00000
Erasing flash at 0xfff10000
Erasing flash at 0xfff20000
Erasing flash at 0xfff30000
Erasing flash at 0xfff40000
Erasing flash passed
uei> prog 0xfff00000 u-boot.bin BIN
Programming u-boot.bin , please wait ....
Programming flash passed
uei>
```

First we establish a `telnet` session to the Abatron BDI-2000. After some initialization, we are presented with a command prompt. When the `erase` command is issued, the Abatron displays a line of output for each section defined in the configuration file. With the configuration shown in Appendix F, we defined five erase sectors. This reserves up to 256KB of space for the U-Boot bootloader binary.

The `prog` command is shown with all three of its optional parameters. These specify the location in memory where the new image is to be loaded, the name of the image file, and the format of the file—in this case, a binary file. You can specify these parameters in the BDI-2000 configuration file. In this case, the command reduces to simply `prog` without parameters.

This example only scratches the surface of these two BDI-2000 commands. Many more combinations of usage and capabilities are supported. Each hardware JTAG probe has its own way to specify Flash erasure and programming capabilities. Consult the documentation for your particular device for the specifics.

14.4.2 Debugging with a JTAG Probe

Instead of interfacing directly with a JTAG probe via its user interface, many JTAG probes can interface with your source-level debugger. By far the most popular debugger supported by hardware probes is the gdb debugger. In this usage scenario, gdb is instructed to begin a debug session with the target via an external connection, usually an Ethernet connection. Rather than communicate directly with the JTAG probe via a user interface, the debugger passes commands back and forth between itself and the JTAG probe. In this model, the JTAG probe uses the gdb remote protocol to control the hardware on behalf of the debugger. Refer again to Figure 14-6 for connection details.

JTAG probes are especially useful for source-level debugging of bootloader and early startup code. In this example, we demonstrate the use of gdb and an Abatron BDI-2000 for debugging portions of the U-Boot bootloader on a PowerPC target board.

Many processors contain debugging registers that include the capability to set traditional address breakpoints (stop when the program reaches a specific address) as well as data breakpoints (stop on conditional access of a specified memory address). When debugging code resident in read-only memory such as Flash, this is the only way to set a breakpoint. However, these registers are typically limited. Many processors contain only one or two such registers. This limitation must be understood before using hardware breakpoints. The following example demonstrates this.

Using a setup such as that shown in Figure 14-6, assume that our target board has U-Boot stored in Flash. When we presented bootloaders in Chapter 7, you learned that U-Boot and other bootloaders typically copy themselves into RAM as soon as possible after startup. This is because hardware read (and write) cycles from RAM are orders of magnitude faster than typical read-only memory devices such as Flash. This presents two specific debugging challenges. First, we cannot modify the contents of read-only memory (to insert a software breakpoint), so we must rely on processor-supported breakpoint registers for this purpose.

The second challenge comes from the fact that only one of the execution contexts (Flash or RAM) can be represented by the ELF executable file from which gdb reads its symbolic debugging information. In the case of U-Boot, it is linked for the Flash environment where it is initially stored. The early code relocates itself and performs any necessary address adjustments. This means that we need to work with gdb within both of these execution contexts. Listing 14-21 shows an example of such a debug session.

Listing 14-21

U-Boot Debugging Using JTAG Probe

```
$ ppc-linux-gdb --silent u-boot
(gdb) target remote bdi:2001
Remote debugging using bdi:2001
_start () at /home/chris/sandbox/u-boot-1.1.4/cpu/mpc5xxx/start.S:91
91              li        r21, BOOTFLAG_COLD    /* Normal Power-On */
Current language:  auto; currently asm

<< Debug a flash resident code snippet >>
(gdb) mon break hard
(gdb) b board_init_f
Breakpoint 1 at 0xfff0457c: file board.c, line 366.
(gdb) c
Continuing.

Breakpoint 1, board_init_f (bootflag=0x7fc3afc) at board.c:366
366               gd = (gd_t *) (CFG_INIT_RAM_ADDR + CFG_GBL_DATA_OFFSET);
Current language:  auto; currently c
(gdb) bt
#0  board_init_f (bootflag=0x1) at board.c:366
#1  0xfff0456c in board_init_f (bootflag=0x1) at board.c:353
(gdb) i frame
Stack level 0, frame at 0xf000bf50:
 pc = 0xfff0457c in board_init_f (board.c:366); saved pc 0xfff0456c
 called by frame at 0xf000bf78
 source language c.
 Arglist at 0xf000bf50, args: bootflag=0x1
 Locals at 0xf000bf50, Previous frame's sp is 0x0

<< Now debug a memory resident code snippet after relocation >>
(gdb) del 1
(gdb) symbol-file
Discard symbol table from '/home/chris/sandbox/u-boot-1.1.4-powerdna/u-boot'?
(y or n) y
No symbol file now.
(gdb) add-symbol-file u-boot 0x7fa8000
add symbol table from file "u-boot" at
         .text_addr = 0x7fa8000
(y or n) y
Reading symbols from u-boot...done.
(gdb) b board_init_r
Breakpoint 2 at 0x7fac6c0: file board.c, line 608.
(gdb) c
Continuing.
```

```
Breakpoint 2, board_init_r (id=0x7f85f84, dest_addr=0x7f85f84) at board.c:608
608               gd = id;        /* initialize RAM version of global data */
(gdb) i frame
Stack level 0, frame at 0x7f85f38:
 pc = 0x7fac6c0 in board_init_r (board.c:608); saved pc 0x7fac6b0
 called by frame at 0x7f85f68
 source language c.
 Arglist at 0x7f85f38, args: id=0x7f85f84, dest_addr=0x7f85f84
 Locals at 0x7f85f38, Previous frame's sp is 0x0
(gdb) mon break soft
(gdb)
```

Study this example carefully. Some subtleties are definitely worth taking the time to understand. First, we connect to the Abatron BDI-2000 using the target remote command. The IP address in this case is that of the Abatron unit, represented by the symbolic name bdi.[10] The Abatron BDI-2000 uses port 2001 for its remote gdb protocol connection.

Next we issue a command to the BDI-2000 using the gdb mon command. The mon command tells gdb to pass the rest of the command directly to the remote hardware device. Therefore, mon break hard sets the BDI-2000 into hardware breakpoint mode.

We then set a hardware breakpoint at board_init_f. This is a routine that executes while still running out of Flash memory at address 0xfff0457c. After the breakpoint is defined, we issue the continue c command to resume execution. Immediately, the breakpoint at board_init_f is encountered, and we are free to do the usual debugging activities, including stepping through code and examining data. You can see that we have issued the bt command to examine the stack backtrace and the i frame command to examine the details of the current stack frame.

Now we continue execution again, but this time we know that U-Boot copies itself to RAM and resumes execution from its copy in RAM. So we need to change the debugging context while keeping the debugging session alive. To accomplish this, we discard the current symbol table (symbol-file command with no arguments) and load in the same symbol file again using the add-symbol-file command. This time, we instruct gdb to offset the symbol table to match where U-Boot has relocated itself to memory. This ensures that our source code and symbolic debugging information match the actual memory resident image.

---

[10] An entry in the host system's /etc/hosts file enables the symbolic IP address reference.

After the new symbol table is loaded, we can add a breakpoint to a location that we know will reside in RAM when it is executed. This is where one of the subtle complications is exposed. Because we know that U-Boot is currently running in Flash but is about to move itself to RAM and jump to its RAM-based copy, we must still use a hardware breakpoint. Consider what happens at this point if we use a software breakpoint. gdb dutifully writes the breakpoint opcode into the specified memory location, but U-Boot overwrites it when it copies itself to RAM. The net result is that the breakpoint is never hit, and we begin to suspect that our tools are broken. After U-Boot has entered the RAM copy and our symbol table has been updated to reflect the RAM-based addresses, we are free to use RAM-based breakpoints. This is reflected by the last command in Listing 14-21 setting the Abatron unit back to soft breakpoint mode.

Why do we care about using hardware versus software breakpoints? If we had unlimited hardware breakpoint registers, we wouldn't. But this is never the case. Here is what it looks like when you run out of processor-supported hardware breakpoint registers during a debug session:

```
(gdb) b flash_init
Breakpoint 3 at 0x7fbebe0: file flash.c, line 70.
(gdb) c
Continuing.
warning: Cannot insert breakpoint 3:
Error accessing memory address 0x7fbebe0: Unknown error 4294967295.
```

Because we are debugging remotely, we aren't told about the resource constraint until we try to resume after entering additional breakpoints. This is because of the way gdb handles breakpoints. When a breakpoint is hit, gdb restores all the breakpoints with the original opcodes for that particular memory location. When it resumes execution, it restores the breakpoint opcodes at the specified locations. You can observe this behavior by enabling gdb's remote debug mode:

```
(gdb) set debug remote 1
```

14.5 When It Doesn't Boot

One of the most frequently asked questions on the various mailing lists that serve embedded Linux goes something like this:

I am trying to boot Linux on my board, and I get stuck after this message prints to my console:

"Uncompressing Kernel Image . . . OK."

Thus starts the long and sometimes frustrating learning curve of embedded Linux! Many things that can go wrong could lead to this common failure. With some knowledge and a JTAG debugger, there are ways to determine what went awry.

14.5.1 Early Serial Debug Output

The first tool you might have available is CONFIG_SERIAL_TEXT_DEBUG. This Linux kernel-configuration option adds support for debug messages very early in the boot process. At the present time, this feature is limited to the PowerPC architecture, but nothing prevents you from duplicating the functionality in other architectures. Listing 14-22 provides an example of this feature in use on a PowerPC target using the U-Boot bootloader.

Listing 14-22

Early Serial Text Debug

```
## Booting image at 00200000 ...
   Image Name:    Linux-2.6.14
   Created:       2005-12-19  22:24:03 UTC
   Image Type:    PowerPC Linux Kernel Image (gzip compressed)
   Data Size:     607149 Bytes = 592.9 kB
   Load Address: 00000000
   Entry Point:  00000000
   Verifying Checksum ... OK
   Uncompressing Kernel Image ... OK
id mach(): done      <== Start of messages enabled by
MMU:enter            <== CONFIG_SERIAL_TEXT_DEBUG
MMU:hw init
MMU:mapin
MMU:setio
MMU:exit
setup_arch: enter
setup_arch: bootmem
arch: exit
arch: real exit
```

Using this feature, you can often tell where your board is getting stuck during the boot process. Of course, you can add your own early debug messages in other places in the kernel. Here is an example of its usage found in .../arch/ppc/mm/init.c:

```
    /* Map in all of RAM starting at KERNELBASE */
    if (ppc_md.progress)
          ppc_md.progress("MMU:mapin", 0x301);
    mapin_ram();
```

The AMCC Yosemite platform is an excellent example of this infrastructure. Consult the following files in the Linux source tree[11] for details of how this debugging system is implemented:

File	Function	Purpose
`gen550_dbg.c`	`gen550_init`	Serial port setup, called by `yosemite.c` platform-initialization file
`gen550_dbg.c`	`gen550_progress`	Low-level serial output routine
`ibm44x_common.c`	`ibm44x_platform_init`	Binds platform-specific progress routine to generic ppc machine-dependent infrastructure

14.5.2 Dumping the printk Log Buffer

When we discussed `printk` debugging in Section 14.3.6, we pointed out some of the limitations of this method. `printk` itself is a very robust implementation. One of its shortcomings is that you can't see any `printk` messages until later in the boot sequence when the console device has been initialized. Very often, when your board hangs on boot, quite a few messages are stuck in the `printk` buffer. If you know where to find them, you can often pinpoint the exact problem that is causing the boot to hang. Indeed, many times you will discover that the kernel has encountered an error that led to a call to `panic()`. The output from `panic()` has likely been dumped into the `printk` buffer, and you can often pinpoint the exact line of offending code.

This is best accomplished with a JTAG debugger, but it is still possible to use a bootloader and its memory dump capability to display the contents of the `printk` buffer after a reset. Some corruption of memory contents might occur as a result of the reset, but log buffer text is usually very readable.

The actual buffer where `printk` stores its message text is declared in the `printk` source file `.../kernel/printk.c`.

```
static char __log_buf[__LOG_BUF_LEN];
```

---

[11] All these filenames are unique, so they can be found without full pathname references.

We can easily determine the linked location of this buffer from the Linux kernel map file System.map.

```
$ grep __log_buf System.map
  c022e5a4 b __log_buf
```

Now if the system happens to hang upon booting, right after displaying the "Uncompressing Kernel Image . . . OK" message, reboot and use the bootloader to examine the buffer. Because the relationship between kernel virtual memory and physical memory is fixed and constant on a given architecture, we can do a simple conversion. The address of __log_buf shown earlier is a kernel virtual address; we must convert it to a physical address. On this particular PowerPC architecture, that conversion is a simple subtraction of the constant KERNELBASE address, 0xc0000000. This is where we probe in memory to read the contents, if any, of the printk log buffer.

Listing 14-23 is an example of the listing as displayed by the U-Boot memory dump command.

Listing 14-23

Dump of Raw printk Log Buffer

```
=> md 22e5a4
0022e5a4: 3c353e4c 696e7578 20766572 73696f6e    <5>Linux version
0022e5b4: 20322e36 2e313320 28636872 6973406a     2.6.13 (chris@
0022e5c4: 756e696f 72292028 67636320 76657273    junior) (gcc
0022e5d4: 696f6e20 332e342e 3320284d 6f6e7461    version 3.4.3 (Monta
0022e5e4: 56697374 6120332e 342e332d 32352e30    Vista 3.4.3-25.0
0022e5f4: 2e37302e 30353031 39363120 32303035    .70.0501961 2005
0022e604: 2d31322d 31382929 20233131 20547565    -12-18)) #11 Tue
0022e614: 20466562 20313420 32313a30 353a3036     Feb 14 21:05:06
0022e624: 20455354 20323030 360a3c34 3e414d43     EST 2006.<4>AMC
0022e634: 4320506f 77657250 43203434 30455020    C PowerPC 440EP
0022e644: 596f7365 6d697465 20506c61 74666f72    Yosemite Platform.
0022e654: 6d0a3c37 3e4f6e20 6e6f6465 20302074    <7>On node 0 t
0022e664: 6f74616c 70616765 733a2036 35353336    otalpages: 65536
0022e674: 0a3c373e 2020444d 41207a6f 6e653a20    .<7>   DMA zone:
0022e684: 36353533 36207061 6765732c 204c4946    65536 pages, LIF
0022e694: 4f206261 7463683a 33310a3c 373e2020    O batch:31.<7>
=>
0022e6a4: 4e6f726d 616c207a 6f6e653a 20302070    Normal zone: 0 p
0022e6b4: 61676573 2c204c49 464f2062 61746368    ages, LIFO batch
0022e6c4: 3a310a3c 373e2020 48696768 4d656d20    :1.<7>   HighMem
0022e6d4: 7a6f6e65 3a203020 70616765 732c204c    zone: 0 pages, L
0022e6e4: 49464f20 62617463 683a310a 3c343e42    IFO batch:1.<4>B
0022e6f4: 75696c74 2031207a 6f6e656c 69737473    uilt 1 zonelists
```

```
0022e704:  0a3c353e  4b65726e  656c2063  6f6d6d61      .<5>Kernel command
0022e714:  6e64206c  696e653a  20636f6e  736f6c65      line: console
0022e724:  3d747479  53302c31  31353230  3020726f      =ttyS0,115200
0022e734:  6f743d2f  6465762f  6e667320  72772069      root=/dev/nfs rw
0022e744:  703d6468  63700a3c  343e5049  44206861      ip=dhcp.<4>PID ha
0022e754:  73682074  61626c65  20656e74  72696573      sh table entries
0022e764:  3a203230  34382028  6f726465  723a2031      : 2048 (order: 1
0022e774:  312c2033  32373638  20627974  6573290a      1, 32768 bytes).
0022e784:  00000000  00000000  00000000  00000000      ................
0022e794:  00000000  00000000  00000000  00000000      ................
=>
```

It's not very pretty to read, but the data is there. We can see in this particular example that the kernel crashed someplace after initializing the PID hash table entries. With some additional use of printk messages, we can begin to close in on the actual source of the crash.

As shown in this example, this is a technique that can be used with no additional tools. You can see the importance of some kind of early serial port output during boot if you are working on a new board port.

14.5.3 KGDB on Panic

If KGDB is enabled, the kernel attempts to pass control back to KGDB upon error exceptions. In some cases, the error itself will be readily apparent. To use this feature, a connection must already be established between KGDB and gdb. When the exception condition occurs, KGDB emits a Stop Reply packet to gdb, indicating the reason for the trap into the debug handler, as well as the address where the trap condition occurred. Listing 14-24 illustrates the sequence.

Listing 14-24

Trapping Crash on Panic Using KGDB

```
$ ppc-_4xx-gdb --silent vmlinux
(gdb) target remote /dev/ttyS0
Remote debugging using /dev/ttyS0
Malformed response to offset query, qOffsets
(gdb) target remote /dev/ttyS0
Remote debugging using /dev/ttyS0
breakinst () at arch/ppc/kernel/ppc-stub.c:825
825        }
(gdb) c
Continuing.
```

```
<< KGDB gains control from panic() on crash >>
Program received signal SIGSEGV, Segmentation fault.
0xc0215d6c in pcibios_init () at arch/ppc/kernel/pci.c:1263
1263              *(int *)-1 = 0;
(gdb) bt
#0  0xc0215d6c in pcibios_init () at arch/ppc/kernel/pci.c:1263
#1  0xc020e728 in do_initcalls () at init/main.c:563
#2  0xc020e7c4 in do_basic_setup () at init/main.c:605
#3  0xc0001374 in init (unused=0x20) at init/main.c:677
#4  0xc00049d0 in kernel_thread ()
Previous frame inner to this frame (corrupt stack?)
(gdb)
```

The crash in this example was contrived by a simple write to an invalid memory location (all ones). We first establish a connection from gdb to KGDB and allow the kernel to continue to boot. Notice that we didn't even bother to set breakpoints. When the crash occurs, we see the line of offending code and get a nice backtrace to help us determine its cause.

14.6 Chapter Summary

- Linux kernel debugging presents many complexities, especially in a cross-development environment. Understanding how to navigate these complexities is the key to successful kernel debugging.

- KGDB is a very useful kernel-level gdb stub that enables direct symbolic source-level debugging inside the Linux kernel and device drivers. It uses the gdb remote protocol to communicate to your host-based cross-gdb.

- Understanding (and minimizing) compiler optimizations helps make sense of seemingly strange debugger behavior when stepping through compiler-optimized code.

- gdb supports user-defined commands, which can be very useful for automating tedious debugging tasks such as iterating kernel linked lists and accessing complex variables.

- Kernel-loadable modules present their own challenges to source-level debugging. The module's initialization routine can be debugged by placing a breakpoint in module.c at the call to module->init().

- printk and the Magic SysReq key provide additional tools to help isolate problems during kernel development and debugging.

- Hardware-assisted debugging via a JTAG probe enables debugging Flash or ROM resident code where other debugging methods can be cumbersome or otherwise impossible.

- Enabling `CONFIG_SERIAL_TEXT_DEBUG` on architectures where this feature is supported is a powerful tool for debugging a new kernel port.

- Examining the `printk log_buf` often leads to the cause of a silent kernel crash on boot.

- `KGDB` passes control to `gdb` on a kernel panic, enabling you to examine a backtrace and isolate the cause of the kernel panic.

14.6.1 Suggestions for Additional Reading

Linux Kernel Development, 2nd Edition
Robert Love
Novell Press, 2005

The Linux Kernel Primer
Claudia Salzberg Rodriguez et al.
Prentice Hall, 2005

"Using the GNU Compiler Collection"
Richard M. Stallman and the GCC Developer Community
GNU Press, a division of Free Software Foundation
http://gcc.gnu.org/onlinedocs/

KGDB Sourceforge home page
http://sourceforge.net/projects/KGDB

Debugging with GDB
Richard Stallman, Roland Pesch, Stan Shebs, et al.
Free Software Foundation
www.gnu.org/software/gdb/documentation/

Tool Interface Standards
DWARF Debugging Information Format Specification
Version 2.0
TIS Committee, May 1995

Chapter 15

Debugging Embedded Linux Applications

In this chapter

n the previous chapter, we explored the use of GDB for debugging kernel code
and code resident in Flash, such as bootloader code. In this chapter, we continue our coverage of GDB for debugging application code in user space. We
extend our coverage of remote debugging and the tools and techniques used for
this peculiar debugging environment.

15.1 Target Debugging

We already explored several important debugging tools in Chapter 13,
"Development Tools." strace and ltrace can be used to observe and character-
ize a process's behavior and often isolate problems. dmalloc can help isolate memory leaks and profile memory usage. ps and top are both useful for examining the
state of processes. These relatively small tools are designed to run directly on the target hardware.

Debugging Linux application code on an embedded system has its own unique
challenges. Resources on your embedded target are often limited. RAM and nonvolatile storage limitations might prevent you from running target-based development tools. You might not have an Ethernet port or other high-speed connection.
Your target embedded system might not have a graphical display, keyboard, or mouse.

This is where your cross-development tools and an NFS root mount environment can yield large dividends. Many tools, especially GDB, have been architected
to execute on your development host while actually debugging code on a remote
target. GDB can be used to interactively debug your target code or to perform a
postmortem analysis of a core file generated by an application crash. We covered the
details of application core dump analysis in Chapter 13.

15.2 Remote (Cross) Debugging

Cross-development tools were developed primarily to overcome the resource limitations of embedded platforms. A modest-size application compiled with symbolic
debug information can easily exceed several megabytes. With cross-debugging, the
heavy lifting can be done on your development host. When you invoke your cross-
version of GDB on your development host, you pass it an ELF file compiled with
symbolic debug information. On your target, there is no reason you can't strip[1] the

---

[1] Remember to use your cross-version of strip, for example ppc_82xx-strip.

ELF file of all unnecessary debugging info to keep the resulting image to its minimum size.

We introduced the `readelf` utility in Chapter 13. In Chapter 14, "Kernel Debugging Techniques," we used it to examine the debug information in an ELF file compiled with symbolic debugging information. Listing 15-1 contains the output of `readelf` for a relatively small web server application compiled for the ARM architecture.

Listing 15-1

ELF File Debug Info for Example Program

```
$ xscale_be-readelf -S websdemo
There are 39 section headers, starting at offset 0x3dfd0:

Section Headers:
[Nr] Name              Type        Addr     Off    Size   ES Flg Lk Inf Al
[ 0]                   NULL        00000000 000000 000000 00      0   0  0
[ 1] .interp           PROGBITS    00008154 000154 000013 00   A  0   0  1
[ 2] .note.ABI-tag     NOTE        00008168 000168 000020 00   A  0   0  4
[ 3] .note.numapolicy  NOTE        00008188 000188 000074 00   A  0   0  4
[ 4] .hash             HASH        000081fc 0001fc 00022c 04   A  5   0  4
[ 5] .dynsym           DYNSYM      00008428 000428 000460 10   A  6   1  4
[ 6] .dynstr           STRTAB      00008888 000888 000211 00   A  0   0  1
[ 7] .gnu.version      VERSYM      00008a9a 000a9a 00008c 02   A  5   0  2
[ 8] .gnu.version_r    VERNEED     00008b28 000b28 000020 00   A  6   1  4
[ 9] .rel.plt          REL         00008b48 000b48 000218 08   A  5  11  4
[10] .init             PROGBITS    00008d60 000d60 000018 00  AX  0   0  4
[11] .plt              PROGBITS    00008d78 000d78 000338 04  AX  0   0  4
[12] .text             PROGBITS    000090b0 0010b0 019fe4 00  AX  0   0  4
[13] .fini             PROGBITS    00023094 01b094 000018 00  AX  0   0  4
[14] .rodata           PROGBITS    000230b0 01b0b0 0023d0 00   A  0   0  8
[15] .ARM.extab        PROGBITS    00025480 01d480 000000 00   A  0   0  1
[16] .ARM.exidx        ARM_EXIDX   00025480 01d480 000008 00  AL 12   0  4
[17] .eh_frame_hdr     PROGBITS    00025488 01d488 00002c 00   A  0   0  4
[18] .eh_frame         PROGBITS    000254b4 01d4b4 00007c 00   A  0   0  4
[19] .init_array       INIT_ARRAY  0002d530 01d530 000004 00  WA  0   0  4
[20] .fini_array       FINI_ARRAY  0002d534 01d534 000004 00  WA  0   0  4
[21] .jcr              PROGBITS    0002d538 01d538 000004 00  WA  0   0  4
[22] .dynamic          DYNAMIC     0002d53c 01d53c 0000d0 08  WA  6   0  4
[23] .got              PROGBITS    0002d60c 01d60c 000118 04  WA  0   0  4
[24] .data             PROGBITS    0002d728 01d728 0003c0 00  WA  0   0  8
[25] .bss              NOBITS      0002dae8 01dae8 0001c8 00  WA  0   0  4
[26] .comment          PROGBITS    00000000 01dae8 000940 00      0   0  1
[27] .debug_aranges    PROGBITS    00000000 01e428 0004a0 00      0   0  8
[28] .debug_pubnames   PROGBITS    00000000 01e8c8 001aae 00      0   0  1
```

```
[29] .debug_info       PROGBITS      00000000 020376 013d27 00      0   0  1
[30] .debug_abbrev     PROGBITS      00000000 03409d 002ede 00      0   0  1
[31] .debug_line       PROGBITS      00000000 036f7b 0034a2 00      0   0  1
[32] .debug_frame      PROGBITS      00000000 03a420 003380 00      0   0  4
[33] .debug_str        PROGBITS      00000000 03d7a0 000679 00      0   0  1
[34] .note.gnu.arm.ide NOTE          00000000 03de19 00001c 00      0   0  1
[35] .debug_ranges     PROGBITS      00000000 03de35 000018 00      0   0  1
[36] .shstrtab         STRTAB        00000000 03de4d 000183 00      0   0  1
[37] .symtab           SYMTAB        00000000 03e5e8 004bd0 10     38 773  4
[38] .strtab           STRTAB        00000000 0431b8 0021bf 00      0   0  1
Key to Flags:
W (write), A (alloc), X (execute), M (merge), S (strings)
I (info), L (link order), G (group), x (unknown)
O (extra OS processing required) o (OS specific), p (processor specific)
$
```

You can see from Listing 15-1 that there are many sections containing debug information. There is also a `.comment` section that contains more than 2KB (0x940) of information that is not necessary for the application to function. The size of this example file, including debug information, is more than 275KB.

```
$ ls -l websdemo
-rwxrwxr-x  1 chris chris 283511 Nov 8 18:48 websdemo
```

If we strip this file using the `strip` utility, we can minimize its size to preserve resources on our target system. Listing 15-2 shows the results.

Listing 15-2

Strip Target Application

```
$ xscale_be-strip -s -R .comment -o websdemo-stripped websdemo
$ ls -l websdemo*
-rwxrwxr-x  1 chris chris 283491 Apr  9 09:19 websdemo
-rwxrwxr-x  1 chris chris 123156 Apr  9 09:21 websdemo-stripped
$
```

Here we strip both the symbolic debug information and the `.comment` section from the executable file. We specify the name of the stripped binary using the `-o` command line switch. You can see that the resulting size of the stripped binary is less than half of its original size. Of course, for larger applications, this space savings can be even more significant. A recent Linux kernel compiled with debug information was larger than 18MB. After stripping as in Listing 15-2, the resulting binary was slightly larger than 2MB!

For debugging in this fashion, you place the stripped version of the binary on your target system and keep a local unstripped copy on your development workstation containing symbolic information needed for debugging. You use `gdbserver` on your target board to provide an interface back to your development host where you run the full-blown version of GDB on your nonstripped binary.

15.2.1 gdbserver

Using `gdbserver` allows you to run GDB from a development workstation rather than on the target embedded Linux platform. This configuration has obvious benefits. For starters, it is common that your development workstation has far more CPU power, memory, and hard-drive storage than the embedded platform. In addition, it is common for the source code for your application under debug to exist on the development workstation and not on the embedded platform.

`gdbserver` is a small program that runs on the target board and allows remote debugging of a process on the board. It is invoked on the target board specifying the program to be debugged, as well as an IP address and port number on which it will listen for connection requests from GDB. Listing 15-3 shows the startup sequence on the target board.

Listing 15-3

Starting gdbserver on Target Board

```
$ gdbserver localhost:2001 websdemo-stripped
Process websdemo-stripped created; pid = 197
Listening on port 2001
```

This particular example starts `gdbserver` configured to listen for an Ethernet TCP/IP connection on port 2001, ready to debug our stripped binary program called `websdemo-stripped`.

From our development workstation, we launch GDB, passing it the name of the binary executable containing symbolic debug information that we want to debug as an argument. After GDB starts up, we issue a command to connect to the remote target board. Listing 15-4 shows this sequence.

Listing 15-4

Starting Remote GDB Session

```
$ xscale_be-gdb -q websdemo
(gdb) target remote 192.168.1.141:2001
Remote debugging using 192.168.1.141:2001
0x40000790 in ?? ()
(gdb) p main        <<<< display address of main function
$1 = {int (int, char **)} 0x12b68 <main>
(gdb) b main        <<<< Place breakpoint at main()
Breakpoint 1 at 0x12b80: file main.c, line 72.
(gdb)
```

The sequence in Listing 15-4 invokes `cross-gdb` on your development host. When GDB is running, we issue the `gdb target remote` command. This command causes GDB to initiate a TCP/IP connection from your development workstation to your target board, with the indicated IP address on port 2001. When gdbserver accepts the connection request, it prints a line similar to this:

```
Remote debugging from host 192.168.0.10
```

Now GDB is connected to the target board's `gdbserver` process, ready to accept commands from GDB. The rest of the session is exactly the same as if you were debugging an application locally. This is a powerful tool, allowing you to use the power of your development workstation for the debug session, leaving only a small, relatively unobtrusive GDB stub and your program being debugged on the target board. In case you were wondering, `gdbserver` for this particular ARM target is only 54KB.

```
root@coyote:~# ls -l /usr/bin/gdbserver
-rwxr-xr-x  1 root root 54344 Jul 23  2005 /usr/bin/gdbserver
```

There is one caveat, and it is the subject of a frequently asked question (FAQ) on many mailing lists. You must be using a GDB on your development host that was configured as a *cross-debugger*. It is a binary program that runs on your development workstation but understands binary executable images compiled for another architecture. This is an important and frequently overlooked fact. You cannot debug a PowerPC target with a native GDB such as that found in a typical Red Hat Linux installation. You must have a GDB configured for your host and target combination.

When GDB is invoked, it displays a banner consisting of several lines of information and then displays its compiled configuration. Listing 15-5 is an example of the GDB used for some examples in this book, which is part of an embedded Linux distribution provided by MontaVista Software configured for PowerPC cross-development.

Listing 15-5

Invocation of cross-gdb

```
$ ppc_82xx-gdb
GNU gdb 6.0 (MontaVista 6.0-8.0.4.0300532 2003-12-24)
Copyright 2003 Free Software Foundation, Inc.
GDB is free software, covered by the GNU General Public License, and
you are welcome to change it and/or distribute copies of it under
certain conditions.  Type "show copying" to see the conditions.
There is absolutely no warranty for GDB. Type "show warranty" for
details.
This GDB was configured as "--host=i686-pc-linux-gnu
--target=powerpc-hardhat-linux".
(gdb)
```

Notice the last lines of this GDB startup message. This is the configuration compiled into this version of GDB. It was compiled to execute on a Pentium (i686) PC host running GNU/Linux and to debug binary programs compiled for a PowerPC processor running GNU/Linux. This is specified by the `--host` and `--target` variables displayed by the banner text, and is also a part of the configuration string passed to `./configure` when building GDB.

15.3 Debugging with Shared Libraries

Now that you understand how to invoke a remote debug session using GDB on the host and `gdbserver` on the target, we turn our attention to the complexities of shared libraries and debug symbols. Unless your application is a statically linked executable (linked with the `-static` linker command line switch), many symbols in your application will reference code outside your application. Obvious examples include the use of standard C library routines such as `fopen`, `printf`, `malloc`, and `memcpy`. Less obvious examples might include calls to application-specific functions, such as `jack_transport_locate()` (a routine from the JACK low-latency audio server), which calls a library function outside the standard C libraries.

To have symbols from these routines available, you must satisfy two requirements for GDB:

- You must have debug versions of the libraries available.

- GDB must know where to find them.

If you don't have debug versions of the libraries available, you can still debug your application; you just won't have any debug information available for library routines called by your application. Often this is perfectly acceptable, unless, of course, you are developing a shared library object as part of your embedded project.

Look back at Listing 15-4, where we invoked GDB on a remote target. After GDB connected via the `target remote` command, GDB issued a two-line response:

```
Remote debugging using 192.168.1.141:2001
0x40000790 in ?? ()
```

This confirms that GDB connected to our target at the indicated IP address and port. GDB then reports the location of the program counter as 0x40000790. Why do we get question marks instead of a symbolic location? Because this is the Linux dynamic loader (`ld-x.y.z.so`), and on this particular platform, we do not have debug symbols available for this shared library. How do we know this?

Recall our introduction of the `/proc` file system from Chapter 9, "File Systems." One of the more useful entries was the `maps` entry (see Listing 9-16, in Chapter 9) in the per-process directory structure. We know the process ID (PID) of our target application from the `gdbserver` output in Listing 15-3. Our process was assigned PID 197. Given that, we can see the memory segments in use right after process startup, as shown in Listing 15-6.

Listing 15-6

Initial Target Memory Segment Mapping

```
root@coyote:~# cat /proc/197/maps
00008000-00026000 r-xp 00000000 00:0e 4852444      ./websdemo-stripped
0002d000-0002e000 rw-p 0001d000 00:0e 4852444      ./websdemo-stripped
40000000-40017000 r-xp 00000000 00:0a 4982583      /lib/ld-2.3.3.so
4001e000-40020000 rw-p 00016000 00:0a 4982583      /lib/ld-2.3.3.so
bedf9000-bee0e000 rwxp bedf9000 00:00 0            [stack]
root@coyote:~#
```

Here we see the target `websdemo-stripped` application occupying two memory segments. The first is the read-only executable segment at 0x8000, and the second is a read-write data segment at 0x2d000. The third memory segment is the one of interest. It is the Linux dynamic linker's executable code segment. Notice that it starts at address 0x40000000. If we investigate further, we can confirm that GDB is actually sitting at the first line of code for the dynamic linker, before any code from our own application has been executed. Using our cross version of `readelf`, we can confirm the starting address of the linker as follows:

```
# xscale_be-readelf -S ld-2.3.3.so | grep \.text
[ 9] .text    PROGBITS    00000790 000790 012c6c 00  AX  0   0 16
```

From this data, we conclude that the address GDB reports on startup is the first instruction from `ld-2.3.3.so`, the Linux dynamic linker/loader. You can use this technique to get rough ideas of where your code is if you don't have symbolic debug information for a process or shared library.

Remember that we are executing this cross `readelf` command on our development host. Therefore, the `ld-2.3.3.so` file, itself an XScale binary object, must be accessible to your development host. Most typically, this file resides on your development host, and is a component of your embedded Linux distribution installed on your host.

15.3.1 Shared Library Events in GDB

GDB can alert you to shared library events. This can be useful for understanding your application's behavior or the behavior of the Linux loader, or for setting breakpoints in shared library routines you want to debug or step through. Listing 15-7 illustrates this technique. Normally, the complete path to the library is displayed. This listing has been edited for better readability.

Listing 15-7

Stopping GDB on Shared Library Events

```
$ xscale_be-gdb -q websdemo
(gdb) target remote 192.168.1.141:2001
Remote debugging using 192.168.1.141:2001
0x40000790 in ?? ()
(gdb) i shared          <<< Display loaded shared libs
No shared libraries loaded at this time.
(gdb) b main            <<< Break at main
Breakpoint 1 at 0x12b80: file main.c, line 72.
```

```
(gdb) c
Continuing.

Breakpoint 1, main (argc=0x1, argv=0xbec7fdc4) at main.c:72
72              int localvar = 9;
(gdb) i shared
From        To          Syms Read    Shared Object Library
0x40033300  0x4010260c  Yes          /opt/mvl/.../lib/tls/libc.so.6
0x40000790  0x400133fc  Yes          /opt/mvl/.../lib/ld-linux.so.3
(gdb) set stop-on-solib-events 1
(gdb) c
Continuing.
Stopped due to shared library event
(gdb) i shared
From        To          Syms Read    Shared Object Library
0x40033300  0x4010260c  Yes          /opt/mvl/.../lib/tls/libc.so.6
0x40000790  0x400133fc  Yes          /opt/mvl/.../lib/ld-linux.so.3
0x4012bad8  0x40132104  Yes          /opt/mvl/.../libnss_files.so.2
(gdb)
```

When the debug session is first started, of course, no shared libraries are loaded. You can see this with the first i shared command. This command displays the shared libraries that are currently loaded. Setting a breakpoint at our application's main() function, we see that two shared libraries are now loaded. These are the Linux dynamic linker/loader and the standard C library component libc.

From here, we issue the set stop-on-solib-event command and continue program execution. When the application tries to execute a function from another shared library, that library is loaded. In case you are wondering, the gethostbyname() function is encountered and causes the next shared object load.

This example illustrates an important cross-development concept. The binary application (ELF image) running on the target contains information on the libraries it needs to resolve its external references. We can view this information easily using the ldd command introduced in Chapter 11, "BusyBox," and detailed in Chapter 13. Listing 15-8 shows the output of ldd invoked from the target board.

Listing 15-8

ldd Executed on Target Board

```
root@coyote:/workspace# ldd websdemo
        libc.so.6 => /lib/tls/libc.so.6 (0x40020000)
        /lib/ld-linux.so.3 (0x40000000)
root@coyote:/workspace#
```

Notice that the paths to the shared libraries on the target are absolute paths starting at `/lib` on the root file system. But GDB running on your host development workstation cannot use these paths to find the libraries. You should realize that to do so would result in your host GDB loading libraries from the wrong architecture. Your host is likely x86, whereas, in this example, the target is ARM XScale.

If you invoke your cross version of `ldd`, you will see the paths that were preconfigured into your toolchain. Your toolchain must have knowledge of where these files exist on your host development system.[2] Listing 15-9 illustrates this. Again, we have edited the listing for readability; long paths have been abbreviated.

Listing 15-9

`ldd` Executed on Development Host

```
$ xscale_be-ldd websdemo
    libc.so.6 => /opt/mvl/.../xscale_be/target/lib/libc.so.6 (0xdead1000)
    ld-linux.so.3 => /opt/mvl/.../xscale_be/target/lib/ld-linux.so.3 (0xdead2000)
$
```

Your cross toolchain should be preconfigured with these library locations. Not only does your host GDB need to know where they are located, but, of course, your compiler and linker also need this knowledge.[3] GDB can tell you where it is configured to look for these libraries using the show `solib-absolute-prefix` command:

```
(gdb) show solib-absolute-prefix
Prefix for loading absolute shared library symbol files is
"/opt/mvl/pro/devkit/arm/xscale_be/target".
(gdb)
```

You can set or change where GDB searches for shared libraries using the GDB commands `set solib-absolute-prefix` and `set solib-search-path`. If you are developing your own shared library modules or have custom library locations on your system, you can use `solib-search-path` to instruct GDB where to look for

---

[2] It is certainly possible to pass these locations to your compiler, linker, and debugger for every invocation, but any good embedded Linux distribution will configure these defaults into the toolchain as a convenience to the developer.

[3] Of course, your compiler also needs to know the location of target files such as architecture-specific system and library header files.

your libraries. For more details about these and other GDB commands, consult the online GDB manual referenced at the end of this chapter in Section 15.6.1, "Suggestions for Additional Reading."

One final note about `ldd`. You might have noticed the addresses from Listing 15-8 and 15-9 associated with the libraries. `ldd` displays the load address for the start of these code segments as they would be if the program were loaded by the Linux dynamic linker/loader. Executed on the target, the addresses in Listing 15-5 make perfect sense, and we can correlate these with the `/proc/<pid>/maps` listing of the running process on the target. Listing 15-10 displays the memory segments for this target process after it is completely loaded and running.

Listing 15-10

Memory Segments from `/proc/<pid>/maps` on Target

```
root@coyote:~# cat /proc/197/maps
00008000-00026000 r-xp 00000000 00:0e 4852444    /workspace/websdemo-stripped
0002d000-0002e000 rw-p 0001d000 00:0e 4852444    /workspace/websdemo-stripped
0002e000-0005e000 rwxp 0002e000 00:00 0          [heap]
40000000-40017000 r-xp 00000000 00:0a 4982583    /lib/ld-2.3.3.so
40017000-40019000 rw-p 40017000 00:00 0
4001e000-4001f000 r--p 00016000 00:0a 4982583    /lib/ld-2.3.3.so
4001f000-40020000 rw-p 00017000 00:0a 4982583    /lib/ld-2.3.3.so
40020000-4011d000 r-xp 00000000 00:0a 4982651    /lib/tls/libc-2.3.3.so
4011d000-40120000 ---p 000fd000 00:0a 4982651    /lib/tls/libc-2.3.3.so
40120000-40124000 rw-p 000f8000 00:0a 4982651    /lib/tls/libc-2.3.3.so
40124000-40126000 r--p 000fc000 00:0a 4982651    /lib/tls/libc-2.3.3.so
40126000-40128000 rw-p 000fe000 00:0a 4982651    /lib/tls/libc-2.3.3.so
40128000-4012a000 rw-p 40128000 00:00 0
4012a000-40133000 r-xp 00000000 00:0a 4982652    /lib/tls/libnss_files-2.3.3.so
40133000-4013a000 ---p 00009000 00:0a 4982652    /lib/tls/libnss_files-2.3.3.so
4013a000-4013b000 r--p 00008000 00:0a 4982652    /lib/tls/libnss_files-2.3.3.so
4013b000-4013c000 rw-p 00009000 00:0a 4982652    /lib/tls/libnss_files-2.3.3.so
becaa000-becbf000 rwxp becaa000 00:00 0          [stack]
root@coyote:~#
```

Notice the correlation of the target `ldd` output from Listing 15-8 to the memory segments displayed in the `/proc` file system for this process. The start (beginning of `.text` segment) of the Linux loader is `0x40000000` and the start of `libc` is at `0x40020000`. These are the virtual addresses where these portions of the application have been loaded, and are reported by the target invocation of `ldd`. However, the load addresses reported by the cross version of `ldd` in Listing 15-9 (`0xdead1000` and `0xdead2000`) are there to remind you that these libraries cannot be loaded on your host system (they are ARM architecture binaries), and the load addresses are simply placeholders.

15.4 Debugging Multiple Tasks

Generally the developer is presented with two different debugging scenarios when dealing with multiple threads of execution. Processes can exist in their own address space or can share an address space (and other system resources) with other threads of execution. The former (independent processes not sharing common address space) must be debugged using separate independent debug sessions. Nothing prevents you from using gdbserver on multiple processes on your target system, and using a separate invocation of GDB on your development host to coordinate a debug session for multiple cooperating but independent processes.

15.4.1 Debugging Multiple Processes

When a process being debugged under GDB uses the fork() system call[4] to spawn a new process, GDB can take two courses of action. It can continue to control and debug the parent process, or it can stop debugging the parent process and attach to the newly formed child process. You can control this behavior using the set follow-fork-mode command. The two modes are follow parent and follow child. The default behavior is for GDB to follow the parent. In this case, the child process executes immediately upon a successful fork.

Listing 15-11 reproduces a snippet of a simple program that forks multiple processes from its main() routine.

Listing 15-11

Using fork() to Spawn a Child Process

```
...
  for( i=0; i<MAX_PROCESSES; i++ ) {
    /* Creating child process */
    pid[i] = fork();                /* Parent gets non-zero PID */
    if ( pid[i] == -1 ) {
      perror("fork failed");
      exit(1);
    }
```

---

[4] We will use the term system call, but fork() in this context is actually the C library function which in turn calls the Linux sys_fork() system call.

```
    if ( pid[i] == 0 ) {       /* Indicates child's code path */
      worker_process();        /* The forked process calls this */
    }
  }

  /* Parent's main control loop */
  while ( 1 ) {
...
  }
```

This simple loop creates `MAX_THREADS` new processes using the `fork()` system call. Each newly spawned process executes a body of code defined by the function `worker_process()`. When run under GDB in the default mode, GDB detects the creation of the new threads of execution (processes) but remains *attached* to the parent's thread of execution. Listing 15-12 illustrates this GDB session.

Listing 15-12

GDB in `follow-fork-mode = parent`

```
(gdb) target remote 192.168.1.141:2001
0x40000790 in ?? ()
(gdb) b main
Breakpoint 1 at 0x8888: file forker.c, line 104.
(gdb) c
Continuing.
[New Thread 356]
[Switching to Thread 356]

Breakpoint 1, main (argc=0x1, argv=0xbe807dd4) at forker.c:104
104           time(&start_time);
(gdb) b worker_process
Breakpoint 2 at 0x8784: file forker.c, line 45.
(gdb) c
Continuing.
Detaching after fork from child process 357.
Detaching after fork from child process 358.
Detaching after fork from child process 359.
Detaching after fork from child process 360.
Detaching after fork from child process 361.
Detaching after fork from child process 362.
Detaching after fork from child process 363.
Detaching after fork from child process 364.
```

Notice that eight child processes were spawned, with PID values from 357 to 364. The parent process was instantiated with PID 356. When the breakpoint in `main()` was hit, we entered a breakpoint at the `worker_process()` routine, which each child process executes upon fork(). Letting the program continue from main, we see each of the new processes spawned and detached by the debugger. They never hit the breakpoint because GDB is attached to the main process, which never executes the worker_process() routine.

If you need to debug each process, you must execute a separate independent GDB session and attach to the child process after it is forked(). The GDB documentation referenced at the end of this chapter outlines a useful technique to place a call to sleep() in the child process, giving you time to attach a debugger to the new process. Attaching to a new process is explained in Section 15.5.2, "Attaching to a Running Process."

If you simply need to follow the child process, set the follow-fork-mode to follow child before your parent reaches the fork() system call. Listing 15-13 shows this.

Listing 15-13

GDB in follow-fork-mode = child

```
(gdb) target remote 192.168.1.141:2001
0x40000790 in ?? ()
(gdb) set follow-fork-mode child
(gdb) b worker_process
Breakpoint 1 at 0x8784: file forker.c, line 45.
(gdb) c
Continuing.
[New Thread 401]
Attaching after fork to child process 402.
[New Thread 402]
[Switching to Thread 402]

Breakpoint 1, worker_process () at forker.c:45
45          int my_pid = getpid();
(gdb) c
Continuing.
```

Here we see the parent process being instantiated as PID 401. When the first child is spawned by the fork() system call, GDB detaches silently from the parent thread of execution and attaches to the newly spawned child process having PID 402. GDB is now in control of the first child process and honors the breakpoint set at worker_process(). Notice, however, that the other child processes spawned by the code snippet from Listing 15-11 are not debugged and continue to run to their own completion.

In summary, using GDB in this fashion, you are limited to debugging a single process at a time. You can debug through the `fork()` system call, but you have to decide which thread of execution to follow through the `fork()` call, either the parent or the child. As mentioned in the introduction to this section, you can use multiple independent GDB sessions if you must debug more than one cooperating process at a time.

15.4.2 Debugging Multithreaded Applications

If your application uses the POSIX thread library for its threading functions, GDB has additional capabilities to handle concurrent debugging of a multithreaded application. The Native Posix Thread Library (NPTL) has become the de facto standard thread library in use on Linux systems, including embedded Linux systems. The rest of this discussion assumes that you are using this thread library.

For this section, we use a demonstration program that spawns a number of threads using the `pthread_create()` library function in a simple loop. After the threads are spawned, the `main()` routine simply waits for keyboard input to terminate the application. Each thread displays a short message on the screen and sleeps for a predetermined time. Listing 15-14 shows the startup sequence on the target board.

Listing 15-14

Target Threads Demo Startup

```
root@coyote:/workspace # gdbserver localhost:2001 ./tdemo
Process ./tdemo created; pid = 671
Listening on port 2001
Remote debugging from host 192.168.1.10
    ^^^^^  Previous three lines displayed by gdbserver

tdemo main() entered: My pid is 671
Starting worker thread 0
Starting worker thread 1
Starting worker thread 2
Starting worker thread 3
```

As in our previous examples, `gdbserver` prepares the application for running and waits for a connection from our host-based cross-gdb. When GDB connects, `gdbserver` reports the connection with the `Remote debugging...` message. Now we start GDB on the host and connect. Listing 15-15 reproduces this half of the session.

Listing 15-15

Host GDB Connecting to Target Threads Demo

```
$ xscale_be-gdb -q tdemo
(gdb) target remote 192.168.1.141:2001
0x40000790 in ?? ()
(gdb) b tdemo.c:97
Breakpoint 1 at 0x88ec: file tdemo.c, line 97.
(gdb) c
Continuing.
[New Thread 1059]
[New Thread 1060]
[New Thread 1061]
[New Thread 1062]
[New Thread 1063]
[Switching to Thread 1059]

Breakpoint 1, main (argc=0x1, argv=0xbefffdd4) at tdemo.c:98
98              int c = getchar();
(gdb)
```

Here we connect to the target (resulting in the "Remote debugging..." message in Listing 15-14), set a breakpoint just past the loop where we spawned the new threads, and continue. When the new thread is created, GDB displays a notice along with the thread ID. Thread 1059 is the tdemo application, doing its work directly from the main() function. Threads 1060 through 1063 are the new threads created from the call to pthread_create().

When GDB hits the breakpoint, it displays the message [Switching to Thread 1059], indicating that this was the thread of execution that encountered the breakpoint. It is the active thread for the debugging session, referred to as the *current thread* in the GDB documentation.

GDB enables us to switch between threads and perform the usual debugging operations such as setting additional breakpoints, examining data, displaying a backtrace, and working with the individual stack frames within the current thread. Listing 15-16 provides examples of these operations, continuing directly with our debugging session started in Listing 15-15.

Listing 15-16

GDB Operations on Threads

```
...
(gdb) c
Continuing.
                    <<< Ctl-C to interrupt program execution
Program received signal SIGINT, Interrupt.
0x400db9c0 in read () from /opt/mvl/.../lib/tls/libc.so.6
(gdb) i threads
  5 Thread 1063  0x400bc714 in nanosleep ()
   from /opt/mvl/.../lib/tls/libc.so.6
  4 Thread 1062  0x400bc714 in nanosleep ()
   from /opt/mvl/.../lib/tls/libc.so.6
  3 Thread 1061  0x400bc714 in nanosleep ()
   from /opt/mvl/.../lib/tls/libc.so.6
  2 Thread 1060  0x400bc714 in nanosleep ()
   from /opt/mvl/.../lib/tls/libc.so.6
* 1 Thread 1059  0x400db9c0 in read ()
   from /opt/mvl/.../lib/tls/libc.so.6
(gdb) thread 4              <<< Make Thread 4 the current thread
[Switching to thread 4 (Thread 1062)]
#0  0x400bc714 in nanosleep ()
   from /opt/mvl/.../lib/tls/libc.so.6
(gdb) bt
#0  0x400bc714 in nanosleep ()
   from /opt/mvl/.../lib/tls/libc.so.6
#1  0x400bc4a4 in __sleep (seconds=0x0) at sleep.c:137
#2  0x00008678 in go_to_sleep (duration=0x5) at tdemo.c:18
#3  0x00008710 in worker_2_job (random=0x5) at tdemo.c:36
#4  0x00008814 in worker_thread (threadargs=0x2) at tdemo.c:67
#5  0x40025244 in start_thread (arg=0xffffffdfc) at pthread_create.c:261
#6  0x400e8fa0 in clone () at../sysdeps/unix/sysv/linux/arm/clone.S:82
#7  0x400e8fa0 in clone () at../sysdeps/unix/sysv/linux/arm/clone.S:82
(gdb) frame 3
#3  0x00008710 in worker_2_job (random=0x5) at tdemo.c:36
36           go_to_sleep(random);
(gdb) l                    <<< Generate listing of where we are
31       }
32
33       static void worker_2_job(int random)
34       {
35           printf("t2 sleeping for %d\n", random);
36           go_to_sleep(random);
37       }
38
39       static void worker_3_job(int random)
40       {
(gdb)
```

A few points are worth mentioning. GDB assigns its own integer value to each thread and uses these values to reference the individual threads. When a breakpoint is hit in a thread, all threads within the process are halted for examination. GDB marks the current thread with an asterisk (*). You can set unique breakpoints within each thread—assuming, of course, that they exist in a unique context. If you set a breakpoint in a common portion of code where all threads execute, the thread that hits the breakpoint first is arbitrary.

The GDB user documentation referenced at the end of this chapter contains more useful information related to debugging in a multithreaded environment.

15.4.3 Debugging Bootloader/Flash Code

Debugging Flash resident code presents its own unique challenges. The most obvious limitation is the way in which GDB and `gdbserver` cooperate in setting target breakpoints. When we discussed the GDB remote serial protocol in Chapter 14, you learned how breakpoints are inserted into an application.[5] GDB replaces the opcode at the breakpoint location with an architecture-specific opcode that passes control to the debugger. However, in ROM or Flash, GDB cannot overwrite the opcode, so this method of setting breakpoints is useless.

Most modern processors contain some number of debug registers that can be used to get around this limitation. These capabilities must be supported by architecture- and processor-specific hardware probes or stubs. The most common technique for debugging Flash and ROM resident code is to use JTAG hardware probes. These probes support the setting of processor-specific hardware breakpoints. This topic was covered in detail in Chapter 14. Refer back to Section 14.4.2, "Debugging with a JTAG Probe," for details.

15.5 Additional Remote Debug Options

Sometimes you might want to use a serial port for remote debugging. For other tasks, you might find it useful to attach the debugger to a process that is already running. These simple but useful operations are detailed here.

---

[5] Refer back to Listing 14-5 in Chapter 14.

15.5.1 Debugging via Serial Port

Debugging via serial port is quite straightforward. Of course, you must have a serial port available on your target that is not being used by another process, such as a serial console. The same limitation applies to your host. A serial port must be available. If both of these conditions can be met, simply replace the `IP:Port` specification passed to `gdbserver` with a serial port specification. Use the same technique when connecting to your target from your host-based GDB.

On your target:

```
root@coyote:/workspace # gdbserver /dev/ttyS0 ./tdemo
Process ./tdemo created; pid = 698
Remote debugging using /dev/ttyS0
```

From your host:

```
$ xscale_be-gdb -q tdemo
(gdb) target remote /dev/ttyS1
Remote debugging using /dev/ttyS1
0x40000790 in ?? ()
```

15.5.2 Attaching to a Running Process

It is often advantageous to connect to a process to examine its state while it is running instead of killing the process and starting it again. With `gdbserver`, it is trivial:

```
root@coyote:/workspace # ps ax | grep tdemo
 1030 pts/0    S1+    0:00 ./tdemo
root@coyote:/workspace # gdbserver localhost:2001 --attach 1030
Attached; pid = 1030
Listening on port 2001
```

When you are finished examining the process under debug, you can issue the `gdb` `detach` command. This detaches the `gdbserver` from the application on the target and terminates the debug session. The application continues where it left off. This is a very useful technique for examining a running program. Be aware, though, that when you attach to the process, it halts, waiting for instructions from you. It will not resume execution until instructed to do so, using either the `continue` command or the `detach` command. Also note that you can use the `detach` command at almost any time to end the debug session and leave the application running on the target.

15.6 Chapter Summary

- Remote (cross) debugging enables symbolic debugging using host development workstation resources for the heavy lifting, preserving often scarce target resources.

- `gdbserver` runs on the target system and acts as the glue between the cross-gdb running on a development host and the process being debugged on the target.

- GDB on the host typically uses IP connections via Ethernet to send and receive commands to `gdbserver` running on the target. The GDB remote serial protocol is used between GDB and `gdbserver`.

- GDB can halt on shared library events and can automatically load shared library symbols when available. Your toolchain should be configured for the default paths on your cross-development system. Alternatively, you can use GDB commands to set the search paths for shared library objects.

- GDB can be used to debug multiple independent processes via multiple concurrent GDB sessions.

- GDB can be configured to follow a forked process on a `fork()` system call. Its default mode is to continue to debug the parent—that is, the caller of `fork()`.

- GDB has features to facilitate debugging multithreaded applications written to POSIX thread APIs. The current default Linux thread library is the Native Posix Threads Library (NPTL).

- GDB supports attaching to and detaching from an already running process.

15.6.1 Suggestions for Additional Reading

GDB: The GNU Project Debugger
Online Documentation
http://sourceware.org/gdb/onlinedocs/

GDB Pocket Reference
Arnold Robbins
O'Reilly Media, 2005

Chapter 16

Porting Linux

In this chapter

I t is not difficult to port Linux to a new hardware platform. The Linux source tree contains ports for numerous boards spanning more than 20 architectures and many more individual processors. Knowing where to start is often the hardest part.

This chapter covers the basics of porting Linux to a custom board providing support for basic Ethernet and serial console operation. We examine the organization of the Linux source code from an architectural and platform perspective. We then delve into the early kernel initialization code to understand the mechanisms provided for platform initialization. Finally, we look at a typical porting effort to a custom PowerPC hardware platform.

16.1 Linux Source Organization

Not too long ago, there were numerous homes[1] for the various versions of Linux. There was a dedicated place for the PowerPC version of Linux, one for the ARM version, and so on. This wasn't necessarily by design, but by necessity. It took time to merge the various architecture infrastructure and features into the mainline kernel, and having a separate source tree meant quicker access to the latest features in a given architecture.

The kernel developers have gone to great lengths to unify the Linux kernel source code to bring together the disparate architectures under one common source tree. With few exceptions, this is the case today with the Linux 2.6 source. It is possible to download and compile working kernels for a variety of processors and industry-standard reference boards directly from www.kernel.org.

16.1.1 The Architecture Branch

In Chapter 4, "The Linux Kernel: A Different Perspective," we introduced the overall structure of the Linux kernel source tree. We spend the majority of this chapter examining the architecture-specific branch of the Linux kernel sources. Listing 16-1 shows the contents of .../arch from a recent kernel snapshot. As we pointed out in Chapter 4, the .../arch subdirectory is the second largest in terms of size, and in a recent Linux release, the largest in terms of file count (excluding the .../include directory). Only the .../drivers subdirectory is larger in size.

---

[1] By "homes," we mean a public source code repository, such as a web server on the Internet.

Listing 16-1

Linux Kernel ... /arch Directory Listing

```
[chris@pluto linux]$ ls ./arch
alpha   cris    i386    m68k       parisc  s390    sparc     v850
arm     frv     ia64    m68knommu  ppc     sh      sparc64   x86_64
arm26   h8300   m32r    mips       ppc64   sh64    um        xtensa
```

From this listing, you can see support for 24 separate architectures within the Linux kernel. We refer to each as an *architecture branch* to facilitate our discussions.

Each architecture branch has some common components. For example, each top-level architecture branch contains a Kconfig file. You will recall from Chapter 4 that Kconfig drives the kernel configuration utility. Of course, each top-level architecture branch also has a corresponding makefile. All the top-level architectures contain a kernel subdirectory because a number of kernel features are architecture dependent. All but two contain an mm subdirectory. This is where the architecture-dependent memory management code is found.

Many top-level architecture branches contain a boot subdirectory, which is used to build (through its own makefile) a specific bootable target for that architecture. Many also contain mach-* subdirectories. These are used to hold code for specific machines or hardware platforms. Another subdirectory that appears frequently in the architecture branch is configs. This subdirectory exists for many of the more popular architectures and contains default configurations for each supported hardware platform.

Throughout the rest of this chapter, we focus our discussion and examples on the PowerPC architecture. It is one of the most popular, with support for many processors and boards. Listing 16-2 shows the contents of the configs directory for the ... /arch/ppc PowerPC branch of a recent Linux kernel release.

Listing 16-2

PowerPC configs Directory Contents

```
[chris@pluto linux]$ ls ./arch/ppc/configs/
ads8272_defconfig   IVMS8_defconfig     prpmc750_defconfig
apus_defconfig      katana_defconfig    prpmc800_defconfig
bamboo_defconfig    lite5200_defconfig  radstone_defconfig
bseip_defconfig     lopec_defconfig     redwood5_defconfig
bubinga_defconfig   luan_defconfig      redwood6_defconfig
chestnut_defconfig  mbx_defconfig       rpx8260_defconfig
```

```
common_defconfig       mpc834x_sys_defconfig   rpxcllf_defconfig
cpci405_defconfig      mpc8540_ads_defconfig   rpxlite_defconfig
cpci690_defconfig      mpc8548_cds_defconfig   sandpoint_defconfig
ebony_defconfig        mpc8555_cds_defconfig   spruce_defconfig
ep405_defconfig        mpc8560_ads_defconfig   stx_gp3_defconfig
est8260_defconfig      mpc86x_ads_defconfig    sycamore_defconfig
ev64260_defconfig      mpc885ads_defconfig     TQM823L_defconfig
ev64360_defconfig      mvme5100_defconfig      TQM8260_defconfig
FADS_defconfig         ocotea_defconfig        TQM850L_defconfig
gemini_defconfig       pmac_defconfig          TQM860L_defconfig
hdpu_defconfig         power3_defconfig        walnut_defconfig
ibmchrp_defconfig      pplus_defconfig
```

Each one of these entries in the `configs` directory of the PowerPC architecture branch represents a specific port to a hardware platform. For example, `walnut_defconfig` defines the default configuration for the AMCC Walnut PPC405 evaluation platform. The `mpc8540_ads_defconfig` file represents the default configuration for the Freescale MPC8540 ADS evaluation board. As described in Chapter 4, to build a kernel for these reference platforms you first configure your kernel source tree with these configuration defaults, as follows:

```
$ make ARCH=ppc CROSS_COMPILE=ppc_85xx- mpc8540_ads_defconfig
```

This invocation of `make` (from the top-level Linux directory) configures the kernel source tree with a default configuration for the Freescale MPC8540 ADS evaluation board.

One aspect of the Linux kernel source tree that has not achieved significant unification is the way in which each architecture handles platform-specific files. In the PowerPC branch, you find a `platforms` directory that contains platform-specific code. Looking through this directory, you will see many source files named after the respective hardware platform. There are also a few subdirectories under `.../arch/ppc/platforms` for specific PowerPC variants.

In contrast, the ARM branch contains a series of `mach-*` directories, each representing a specific hardware platform, while the MIPS branch has a set of subdirectories named for a specific platform.

16.2 Custom Linux for Your Board

When we ported U-Boot to a new hardware platform in Chapter 7, "Bootloaders," we found the configuration that most closely matched our new board and borrowed from that port. We use a similar technique to port Linux to our new board. We assume that the chosen CPU is already supported in the kernel. Porting to a new CPU is significantly more challenging and beyond the scope of this book.

We have chosen to port Linux to a custom controller board based on the Freescale MPC5200 32-bit embedded PowerPC processor. Looking through the default configurations from a recent Linux release (as depicted in Listing 16-2), we find one that contains the MPC5200 CPU. Because it appears that this is the only configuration that supports this processor, we use it as our baseline.

The hardware platform that we use for this exercise was supplied courtesy of United Electronic Industries. The board is called the PowerDNA Controller. It has a simple block diagram, containing onboard Flash memory, dynamic RAM, a serial port, and a variety of I/O devices, mostly integrated into the MPC5200 processor. Figure 16-1 is the block diagram of the PowerDNA Controller.

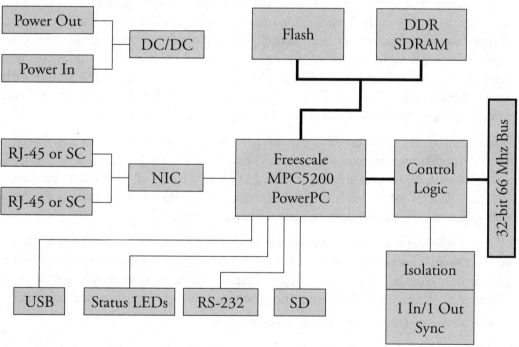

FIGURE 16-1
UEI PowerDNA Controller board

16.2.1 Prerequisites and Assumptions

The Linux kernel makes some fundamental assumptions when it is passed control from a bootloader. Most important among them is that the bootloader must have initialized the DRAM controller. Linux does not participate in chip-level SDRAM controller setup. Linux assumes that system RAM is present and fully functional. The PowerDNA Controller we are targeting contains the U-Boot bootloader, which has initialized the CPU, DRAM, and other related hardware required for minimal system operation.

The bootloader should also initialize the system memory map. This is usually done via a set of processor registers that define what chip select signals are active within a given memory address range. Chapter 3 in the Freescale MPC5200 User's Guide describes the registers used for this task.

The bootloader might have additional hardware-related initialization tasks. On some boards, the kernel assumes that the serial port is configured. This makes it possible to display early kernel boot messages to the serial port, long before the kernel's own serial driver has been installed. Some architectures and hardware platforms contain functions such as `*_serial_putc()`, which can send strings to a serial port that has been preconfigured by the bootloader or by some simple early kernel setup code. You can find examples of this in the PowerPC architecture branch using grep and searching for `CONFIG_SERIAL_TEXT_DEBUG`.

In summary, the fundamental prerequisite for porting Linux to our new board is that a bootloader has been ported and installed on our board, and any board-specific low-level hardware initialization has been completed. It is not necessary to initialize devices for which Linux has direct device driver support, such as Ethernet controllers or I2C controllers; the kernel handles these.

It is a good idea to configure and build your Linux kernel for the board closest to your own. This provides you with a known good starting point—a Linux kernel source tree configured for your board that compiles without error. Recall from Chapter 5, "Kernel Initialization," the command to compile a Linux 2.6 kernel:

```
$ make ARCH=ppc CROSS_COMPILE=ppc_82xx- uImage
```

This command line results in a Linux bootable image compatible with the U-Boot bootloader. The `uImage` target specifies this.

16.2.2 Customizing Kernel Initialization

Now that we have a baseline kernel source tree from which to start, let's determine where to begin customizing for our particular board. We discovered that for the PowerPC architecture, the board-specific files reside in a directory called `.../arch/ppc/platforms`. Of course, this is not strictly necessary, but if you ever intend to submit your patches to the Linux kernel development community for consideration, proper form and consistency matter!

We find in the `platforms` directory a file called `lite5200.c`. It's a fairly simple file, containing two data structures and five functions. Listing 16-3 presents the functions from this file.

Listing 16-3

Functions from 5200 Platform File

```
lite5200_show_cpuinfo()   /* Prints user specified text string */
lite5200_map_irq()        /* Sets h/w specific INT logic routing */
lite5200_setup_cpu()      /* CPU specific initialization */
lite5200_setup_arch()     /* Arch. specific initialization */
platform_init()           /* Machine or board specific init */
```

Let's look at how these functions are used. We briefly examined the low-level kernel initialization in Chapter 5. Here we look at the details for a particular architecture. Details differ between architectures, but when you can navigate one, the others will be easier to learn.

From Chapter 5, we saw the early flow of control on power-up. The bootloader passed control to the kernel's bootstrap loader, which then passed control to the Linux kernel via the kernel's `head.o` module. Here the platform-specific initialization begins. Listing 16-4 reproduces the pertinent lines from `.../arch/ppc/kernel/head.S`.

Listing 16-4

Calling Early Machine Initialization

```
        ...
/*
 * Do early bootinfo parsing, platform-specific initialization,
 * and set up the MMU.
 */
    mr      r3,r31
    mr      r4,r30
```

```
mr     r5,r29
mr     r6,r28
mr     r7,r27
bl     machine_init
bl     MMU_init
...
```

Here you can see the assembly language call to `machine_init`. Of particular significance is the setup of the registers `r3` through `r7`. These registers are expected to contain well-known values, which you will see momentarily. They were stored away very early in the boot sequence to the PowerPC general-purpose registers `r27` through `r31`. Here they are reloaded from these stored values.

The `machine_init()` function is defined in a C file called `setup.c`, in the same architecture-specific kernel directory: `.../arch/ppc/kernel/setup.c`. The start of this routine is reproduced here in Listing 16-5.

Listing 16-5

Function `machine_init()` in `setup.c`

```
void __init
machine_init(unsigned long r3, unsigned long r4, unsigned long r5,
             unsigned long r6, unsigned long r7)
{
#ifdef CONFIG_CMDLINE
      strlcpy(cmd_line, CONFIG_CMDLINE, sizeof(cmd_line));
#endif /* CONFIG_CMDLINE */

#ifdef CONFIG_6xx
      ppc_md.power_save = ppc6xx_idle;
#endif
#ifdef CONFIG_POWER4
      ppc_md.power_save = power4_idle;
#endif

      platform_init(r3, r4, r5, r6, r7);

      if (ppc_md.progress)
            ppc_md.progress("id mach(): done", 0x200);
}
```

There is some very useful knowledge in this simple function. First, notice that the parameters to `machine_init()` represent the PowerPC general-purpose registers `r3` through `r7`.[2] You saw that they were initialized just before the machine

---

[2] By convention, parameters in C are passed in these PowerPC registers.

language call to `machine_init`. As you can see from Listing 16-5, these register values are passed unmodified to `platform_init()`. We need to modify this function for our platform. (We have more to say about that in a moment.)

Listing 16-5 also contains some machine-specific calls for power-management functions. If your kernel is configured for PowerPC 6xx support (`CONFIG_6xx` defined in your `.config` file), a pointer to a machine-specific power-management function (`ppc6xx_idle`) is stored in a structure. Similarly, if your kernel is configured for a PowerPC G5 core (`CONFIG_POWER4`), a pointer to its machine-specific power-management routine is stored in the same structure member. This structure is described in Section 16.3.3, "Machine-Dependent Calls."

16.2.3 Static Kernel Command Line

One of the more interesting operations in the `machine_init()` function reproduced in Listing 16-5 is to store the *default* kernel command line. This operation is enabled if `CONFIG_CMDLINE` is enabled in your kernel configuration. On some platforms, the bootloader does not supply the kernel command line. In these cases, the kernel command line can be statically compiled into the kernel. Figure 16-2 illustrates the configuration options for this.

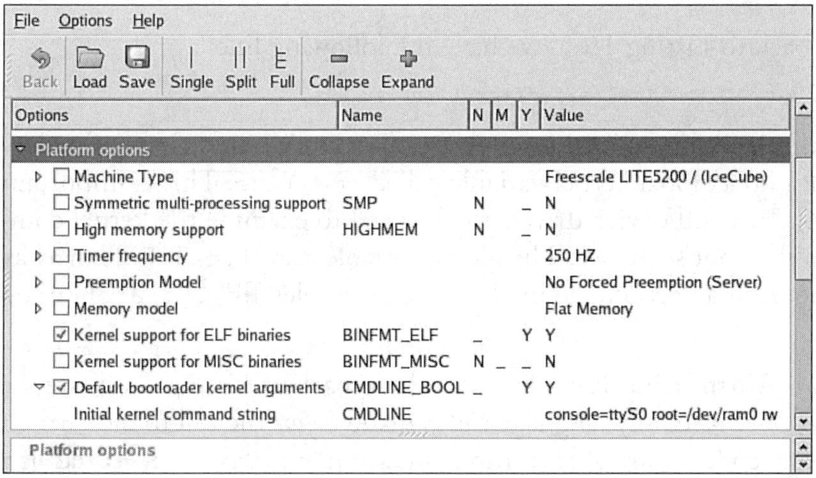

FIGURE 16-2
Default kernel command line

Enable "Default bootloader kernel arguments" in the configuration in Figure 16-2 and edit the "Initial kernel command string" as shown. This results in a set of entries in the `.config` file, as shown in Listing 16-6.

Listing 16-6

Configuration for Default Kernel Command Line

```
...
CONFIG_CMDLINE_BOOL=y
CONFIG_CMDLINE="console=ttyS0 root=/dev/ram0 rw"
...
```

The ellipses in Listing 16-6 indicate that we have taken only a small snippet of the `.config` file. When these configuration symbols are processed by the kernel build system, they become entries in the `.../include/linux/autoconf.h` file, as detailed in Listing 16-7.

Listing 16-7

File `autoconf.h` Entries for Default Kernel Command Line

```
...
  #define CONFIG_CMDLINE_BOOL 1
  #define CONFIG_CMDLINE "console=ttyS0 root=/dev/ram0 rw"
...
```

Now referring back to Listing 16-5, we have the following line:

```
strlcpy(cmd_line, CONFIG_CMDLINE, sizeof(cmd_line));
```

You can see that this kernel-based string-copy function copies the string defined by `CONFIG_CMDLINE` into a global kernel variable called `cmd_line`. This is important because many functions and device drivers might need to examine the kernel command line early in the boot sequence. The global variable `cmd_line` is hidden away at the start of the `.data` section, defined in the assembler file `.../arch/ppc/kernel/head.S`.

A subtle detail is worth mentioning here. Looking back at Listing 16-4, we see that the `machine_init` assembly language call is made *before* the call to `MMU_init`. That means that any code we are able to run from `machine_init` is executed in a context with limited support for accessing memory. Many of today's processors that contain an MMU cannot access any memory without some initial mapping via hardware registers in the processor.[3] Typically, a small amount of memory is made available at boot time to accommodate loading and decompressing the kernel and a ramdisk image. Trying to access code or data beyond these early limits will fail. Each architecture and platform might have different early limits for accessing memory. Values on the order of 8 to 16MB are not untypical. We must remember that any code we execute from machine_init, including our platform initialization, takes place in this context. If you encounter data access errors (PowerPC DSI exception[4]) while debugging your new kernel port, you should immediately suspect that you have not properly mapped the memory region your code is trying to access.

16.3 Platform Initialization

Following is a quick review of the code flow during early initialization. Figure 16-3 shows the flow of execution from the bootloader or bootstrap loader to your platform-initialization code.

From bootloader

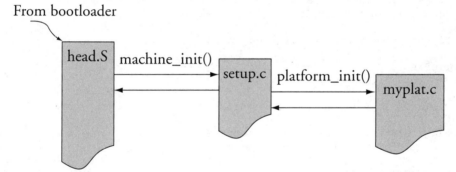

FIGURE 16-3
Platform initialization flow of control

The files head.S and setup.c are both found in the .../arch/ppc/kernel directory for the PowerPC architecture. Our custom platform-initialization file will be placed in the .../arch/ppc/platforms directory. In Figure 16-3, it is represented by the file myplat.c. We are now in a position to examine the platform-specific initialization file in detail.

---

[3] The AMCC PPC405 is a perfect example of this. The interested reader is encouraged to examine the BAT registers in this processor.

[4] Refer to the Programming Environments Manual referenced at the end of this chapter for details of the PowerPC DSI exception.

In Listing 16-3, we listed the functions in the `lite5200.c` platform-
initialization file. Every function except `platform_init()` is declared as static.
Therefore, as shown in Figure 16-3, this is the entry point for the platform-
initialization file. The rest of the functions in the file are referenced only from
within the file itself.

Let's examine the entry function `platform_init()`. Listing 16-8 reproduces the
`platform_init()` function from the `lite5200.c` file.

Listing 16-8

Lite5200 `platform_init` Function

```
void __init
platform_init(unsigned long r3, unsigned long r4,
              unsigned long r5, unsigned long r6,
              unsigned long r7)
{
    /* Generic MPC52xx platform initialization */
    /* TODO Create one and move a max of stuff in it.
       Put this init in the syslib */

    struct bi_record *bootinfo = find_bootinfo();

    if (bootinfo)
        parse_bootinfo(bootinfo);
    else {
        /* Load the bd_t board info structure */
    if (r3)
        memcpy((void*)&__res,(void*)(r3+KERNELBASE),
               sizeof(bd_t));

#ifdef CONFIG_BLK_DEV_INITRD
    /* Load the initrd */
        if (r4) {
            initrd_start = r4 + KERNELBASE;
            initrd_end = r5 + KERNELBASE;
        }
#endif

    /* Load the command line */
    if (r6) {
            *(char *)(r7+KERNELBASE) = 0;
            strcpy(cmd_line, (char *)(r6+KERNELBASE));
        }
    }

    /* PPC Sys identification */
    identify_ppc_sys_by_id(mfspr(SPRN_SVR));
```

```
    /* BAT setup */
    mpc52xx_set_bat();

    /* No ISA bus by default */
    isa_io_base         = 0;
    isa_mem_base        = 0;

    /* Powersave */
    /* This is provided as an example on how to do it. But you
        need to be aware that NAP disable bus snoop and that may
        be required for some devices to work properly, like USB
        ... */
    /* powersave_nap = 1; */


    /* Setup the ppc_md struct */
    ppc_md.setup_arch   = lite5200_setup_arch;
    ppc_md.show_cpuinfo = lite5200_show_cpuinfo;
    ppc_md.show_percpuinfo      = NULL;
    ppc_md.init_IRQ             = mpc52xx_init_irq;
    ppc_md.get_irq              = mpc52xx_get_irq;
#ifdef CONFIG_PCI
    ppc_md.pci_map_irq  = lite5200_map_irq;
#endif

    ppc_md.find_end_of_memory = mpc52xx_find_end_of_memory;
    ppc_md.setup_io_mappings  = mpc52xx_map_io;

    ppc_md.restart          = mpc52xx_restart;
    ppc_md.power_off        = mpc52xx_power_off;
    ppc_md.halt             = mpc52xx_halt;

    /* No time keeper on the LITE5200 */
    ppc_md.time_init        = NULL;
    ppc_md.get_rtc_time     = NULL;
    ppc_md.set_rtc_time     = NULL;

    ppc_md.calibrate_decr       = mpc52xx_calibrate_decr;
#ifdef CONFIG_SERIAL_TEXT_DEBUG
    ppc_md.progress             = mpc52xx_progress;
#endif
}
```

This function contains much of the customizing that is required for this particular platform. It starts by searching for board-specific data supplied by the bootloader. We defer discussion of the details of this until Section 16.3.2, "Board Information Structure."

Following this, if your kernel is configured for an initial ramdisk (initrd),[5] the start and end addresses of the ramdisk image are saved. Notice that they are passed in the PowerPC general-purpose registers r4 and r5 by convention. It is the boot-loader's responsibility to pass the initrd addresses in these registers. Later, the kernel will use these addresses to load the initrd image from raw memory (where the bootloader placed it, or a nonvolatile Flash image) into an internal kernel ramdisk structure.

Next we see code to store the kernel command line, whose address is passed into platform_init() via registers r6 and r7, marking the start and end addresses, respectively. This differs from the method described earlier for storing a static kernel command line in one specific detail: this kernel command line was passed to platform_init() from the bootloader, as opposed to being compiled into the kernel.

Copying the initrd and kernel command line is very straightforward. Basically, the registers passed in from the bootloader contain the memory addresses where these data structures reside. There is one minor subtlety, however. You may have already wondered about the purpose of the constant KERNELBASE. Understanding this is key to grasping one of the more complex parts of the boot sequence.

The addresses the bootloader provides are *physical* addresses. This means they are the real hardware addresses where the data resides in the memory chips. The boot-loader typically operates without support for virtual memory. However, the kernel itself is statically linked to a well-known, user-configured base address. This address is KERNELBASE. (The value itself is not relevant to the discussion—it is user con-figurable but virtually never changed from its default value of 0xC0000000.)

This sets up an interesting situation in head.s. When the kernel is decompressed and relocated to RAM (usually to location 0), all of its code and data symbols are linked at the kernel's virtual address, KERNELBASE. This can be seen by examining the kernel symbol map file, produced during the kernel build process, System.map.[6] However, the execution context prior to enabling the MMU is such that physical addresses are real hardware addresses. This means that all the code prior to enabling the MMU and virtual memory mapping must be relocatable, and access to symbols must be *fixed up*. This involves adding an offset to the symbol's address to access it. An example will make this clear.

---

[5] The initial ramdisk, or initrd, was introduced in Chapter 6.

[6] We introduced the System.map file in Chapter 4.

16.3.1 Early Variable Access

Let's assume that a code segment very early in the boot process needs to access the variable cmd_line—so early that we're executing in 1:1 real to physical mapping. As pointed out earlier, this variable is defined in head.s and will end up in the .data section when the kernel is linked. From the Linux kernel's System.map file, you can find the linked addresses for cmd_line:

```
$ cat System.map | grep cmd_line
  c0115000 D cmd_line
```

If we were running in real = physical mode (MMU disabled) and accessed this variable using its symbol, we would be trying to read or write to an address greater than 3GB. Most smaller embedded systems don't have any RAM in this region, and the results would be undefined or would result in a crash. Even if we had physical RAM at that address, it is unlikely that it would be mapped and accessible this early in the boot process. So we have to adjust our reference to this variable to access it.

Listing 16-9 reproduces a code snippet from head.s that does just that.

Listing 16-9

Variable Reference Fixup

```
relocate_kernel:
      addis r9,r26,klimit@ha /* fetch klimit */
      lwz    r25,klimit@l(r9)
      addis r25,r25,-KERNELBASE@h
```

This code snippet from the PowerPC head.s is a good example of the issue we are describing. The variable klimit represents the end of the kernel image. It is defined elsewhere as char *klimit. Therefore, it is a pointer—it is an address that contains an address. In Listing 16-9, we fetch the address of klimit, sum it with a previously calculated offset that is passed in r26, and deposit the resulting value in register r9. Register r9 now contains the high-order 16 bits of the adjusted address of klimit, with the low-order bits zeroed.[7] It was adjusted by the offset value previously calculated and passed in register r26.

In the next line, the lwz instruction uses register r9 together with the offset of klimit (the lower 16 bits of the klimit address) as an effective address from which

---

[7] For details of PPC assembly language syntax, see Section 16.5.1, "Suggestions for Additional Reading" at the end of this chapter.

to load register r25. (Remember, `klimit` is a pointer, and we are interested in the value that `klimit` points to.) Register r25 now holds the pointer that was stored in the variable `klimit`. In the final line of Listing 16-9, we subtract the kernel's linked base address (`KERNELBASE`) from r25 to adjust the pointer to our actual physical address. In C, it would look like this:

```
unsigned int *tmp;           /* represents r25 */
tmp = *klimit;
tmp -= KERNELBASE;
```

In summary, we referenced a pointer stored in `klimit` and adjusted its value to our real (physical) address so we can use its contents. When the kernel enables the MMU and virtual addressing, we no longer have to worry about this—the kernel will be running at the address where it was linked, regardless of where in physical memory it is actually located.

16.3.2 Board Information Structure

Many bootloaders are used for PowerPC platforms, but there is still no unified way to pass in board-specific data such as serial port baud rate, memory size, and other low-level hardware parameters that the bootloader has configured. The platform-initialization file from Listing 16-8 supports two different methods, data stored as `struct bi_record` and data stored as `struct bd_info`.[8] Both methods provide similar results: hardware-specific data is passed from the bootloader to the kernel in these structures.

From Listing 16-8, here is the code snippet that saves the bootloader-supplied hardware configuration:

```
struct bi_record *bootinfo = find_bootinfo();

if (bootinfo)
    parse_bootinfo(bootinfo);
else {
    /* Load the bd_t board info structure */
    if (r3)
        memcpy((void*)&__res,(void*)(r3+KERNELBASE),
               sizeof(bd_t));
```

---

[8] Each method has its own roots. The `struct bd_info` originated in U-Boot, and `struct bi_record` was an attempt to unify across all platforms. Both are supported by many platforms.

First, we search for a special tag that identifies the data structure as a `struct bi_record`. If that is found, the `bootinfo` pointer is set to the address of the start of the `bootinfo` records. From there, the records are parsed and the hardware related data is gathered. This can be seen by inspecting .../arch/ppc/kernel/setup.c. Currently, `bi_records` can contain the kernel command line, the start and end address of the `initrd` image, the machine type, and the size of the memory. Of course, you can extend this for your own requirements.

If no `bi_record` data is found, the PowerPC architecture expects this data in the form of U-Boot board information structure, or `bd_info`. It is the bootloader's responsibility to construct this data structure and pass the address in register `r3`. Currently, many bits of hardware information are available in the `bd_info` structure, including information on DRAM, FLASH, SRAM, processor clock rates, bus frequencies, serial port baud rate setting, and more.

The `bi_record` structure can be examined in .../include/asm-ppc/bootinfo.h, and the `bd_info` structure can be found in .../include/asm-ppc/ppcboot.h.

It is the responsibility of the platform-initialization routines to make use of any of the data that might be necessary to complete the hardware setup, or to communicate it to the kernel. For example, `platform_init()` sets up a pointer to a function whose name reveals its purpose. The code from Listing 16-8 is reproduced here:

```
ppc_md.find_end_of_memory = mpc52xx_find_end_of_memory;
```

Looking at the function `mpc52xx_find_end_of_memory()`, which is found in .../arch/ppc/syslib/mpc52xx_setup.c, we find the following:

```
u32 ramsize = __res.bi_memsize;

if (ramsize == 0) {
        ...    /* Find it another way */
}

return ramsize;
```

The `__res` data structure above is the board information structure, whose address was passed to us from the bootloader in register `r3` above. As you can see, the generic setup code stored the *residual* data (as it is often called) passed in by the bootloader, but it's up to the machine or platform-specific code to make use of it.

16.3.3 Machine-Dependent Calls

Many common routines that the kernel needs either for initialization or for operation are architecture and machine (CPU) dependent. From the `platform_init()` function reproduced in Listing 16-8, we saw the following:

```
...
    /* Setup the ppc_md struct */
    ppc_md.setup_arch   = lite5200_setup_arch;
    ppc_md.show_cpuinfo = lite5200_show_cpuinfo;
    ppc_md.show_percpuinfo   = NULL;
    ppc_md.init_IRQ          = mpc52xx_init_irq;
    ppc_md.get_irq           = mpc52xx_get_irq;

#ifdef CONFIG_PCI
    ppc_md.pci_map_irq       = lite5200_map_irq;
#endif

    ppc_md.find_end_of_memory = mpc52xx_find_end_of_memory;
    ppc_md.setup_io_mappings  = mpc52xx_map_io;

    ppc_md.restart    = mpc52xx_restart;
    ppc_md.power_off  = mpc52xx_power_off;
    ppc_md.halt       = mpc52xx_halt;
...
```

Lines similar to these make up the rest of the `platform_init()` function. Here the bulk of the platform-specific needs are communicated to the Linux kernel. The global variable `ppc_md`, of type `struct machdep_calls`, provides the hooks to easily customize the Linux kernel for a PowerPC platform. This variable is declared in `.../arch/ppc/kernel/setup.c`. Many places in the PowerPC-specific kernel branch call functions indirectly through this structure. For example, Listing 16-10 reproduces a portion of `.../arch/ppc/kernel/setup.c`, which contains support for the restart, power-off, and halt functions:

Listing 16-10

Generic PowerPC Machine Functions

```
void machine_restart(char *cmd)
{
#ifdef CONFIG_NVRAM
        nvram_sync();
#endif
        ppc_md.restart(cmd);
}
```

```
void machine_power_off(void)
{
#ifdef CONFIG_NVRAM
        nvram_sync();
#endif
        ppc_md.power_off();
}

void machine_halt(void)
{
#ifdef CONFIG_NVRAM
        nvram_sync();
#endif
        ppc_md.halt();
}
```

These functions are called via the ppc_md structure and contain the machine- or platform-specific variants of these functions. You can see that some of these functions are machine specific and come from mpc52xx_* variants of the functions. Examples of these include mpc52xx_restart and mpc52xx_map_io. Others are specific to the hardware platform. Examples of platform-specific routines include lite5200_map_irq and lite5200_setup_arch.

16.4 Putting It All Together

Now that we have a reference from which to proceed, we can create the necessary files and functions for our own custom board. We copy the Lite5200 platform files for our baseline and modify them for our custom PowerPC platform. We'll call our new platform *PowerDNA*. The steps we will perform for this custom port are as follows:

1. Add a new configuration option to ...arch/ppc/Kconfig.

2. Copy lite5200.* to powerdna.* as a baseline.

3. Edit new powerdna.* files as appropriate for our platform.

4. Edit .../arch/ppc/Makefile to conditionally include powerdna.o.

5. Compile, load, and debug!

You learned how to add a configuration option to Kconfig in Chapter 4. The configuration option for our new PowerDNA port is detailed in Listing 16-11.

Listing 16-11

Configuration Option for PowerDNA

```
config POWERDNA
        bool "United Electronics Industries PowerDNA"
        select PPC_MPC52xx
        help
           Support for the UEI PowerDNA board
```

This Kconfig entry is added just below the entry for LITE5200 because they are related.[9] Figure 16-4 illustrates the results when the configuration utility is invoked.

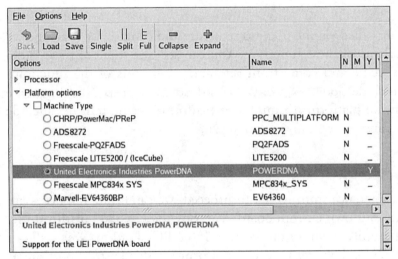

FIGURE 16-4
Machine type option for PowerDNA

Notice that when the user selects POWERDNA, two important actions are performed:

1. The CONFIG_PPC_MPC52xx configuration option is automatically selected. This is accomplished by the select keyword in Listing 16-11.

2. A new configuration option, CONFIG_POWERDNA, is defined that will drive the configuration for our build.

---

[9] To preserve space, we temporarily removed many machine types in Figure 16-4 prior to LITE5200.

The next step is to copy the files closest to our platform as the basis of our new platform-initialization files. We have already decided that the Lite5200 platform fits the bill. Copy `lite5200.c` to `powerdna.c`, and `lite5200.h` to `powerdna.h`. The difficult part comes next. Using the hardware specifications, schematics, and any other data you have on the hardware platform, edit the new `powerdna.*` files as appropriate for your hardware. Get the code to compile, and then proceed to boot and debug your new kernel. There is no shortcut here, nor any substitute for experience. It is the hard work of porting, but now at least you know where to start. Many tips and techniques for kernel debugging are presented in Chapter 14, "Kernel Debugging Techniques."

To summarize our porting effort, Listing 16-12 details the files that have been added or modified to get Linux running on the PowerDNA board.

Listing 16-12

PowerDNA New or Modified Kernel Files

```
linux-2.6.14/arch/ppc/configs/powerdna_defconfig
linux-2.6.14/arch/ppc/Kconfig
linux-2.6.14/arch/ppc/platforms/Makefile
linux-2.6.14/arch/ppc/platforms/powerdna.c
linux-2.6.14/arch/ppc/platforms/powerdna.h
linux-2.6.14/drivers/net/fec_mpc52xx/fec.c
linux-2.6.14/drivers/net/fec_mpc52xx/fec.h
linux-2.6.14/drivers/net/fec_mpc52xx/fec_phy.h
linux-2.6.14/include/asm-ppc/mpc52xx.h
```

The first file is the default configuration, which enables a quick kernel configuration based on defaults. It is enabled by invoking `make` as follows:

```
$ make ARCH=ppc CROSS_COMPILE=<cross-prefix> powerdna_defconfig
```

We've already discussed the changes to the `Kconfig` file. Modification to the makefile is trivial—the purpose is to add support for the new kernel configuration based on `CONFIG_POWERDNA`. The change consists of adding a single line:

```
obj-$(CONFIG_POWERDNA)        += powerdna.o
```

The heart of the changes come in the `powerdna.[c|h]` files and changes to the FEC (Fast Ethernet Controller) layer. There were minor differences between `powerdna.c` and `lite5200.c`, the file from which it was derived. Two primary issues required changes. First, PCI was disabled because it is not used in the PowerDNA design. This required some minor tweaking. Second, the PowerDNA design incorporates an unmanaged Ethernet physical-layer chip that required slight changes in the hardware setup and the FEC layer. This work constituted the majority of the porting effort. The patch file consists of 1120 lines, but the bulk of those lines are the default configuration, which is only a convenience for the developer and is not strictly necessary. Removing that, the patch reduces to 411 lines.

16.4.1 Other Architectures

We examined the details of how a given platform fits into the kernel, and the facilities that exist for porting to a new board. Our reference for this chapter and the discussions within came from the PowerPC architecture branch of the kernel. The other architectures differ in many detailed aspects of how various hardware platforms are incorporated, but the concepts are similar. When you have learned how to navigate a single architecture, you have the knowledge and tools to learn the details of the other architectures.

16.5 Chapter Summary

- Porting Linux to a custom board based on a Linux-supported CPU can be relatively straightforward. There is no substitute for experience and knowledge of the Linux code base and your hardware platform.

- Starting from a working reference configuration based on a hardware platform already supported provides an excellent basis for your own modifications.

- Understanding the flow of initialization code is the key to an easy porting effort. We made every effort to leave all generic kernel code untouched and to modify only those files necessary for the platform itself. A significant part of this chapter is devoted to this early flow of control related to platform initialization.

- Make doubly certain that your low-level hardware platform initialization is correct before proceeding. If you find yourself debugging in some obscure part of the Linux slab allocator, for example, it's a good bet you've messed something up with your hardware memory initialization.

- This chapter focused primarily on the PowerPC architecture branch of the Linux kernel. Learning the details of one architecture paves the way for understanding the rest.

16.5.1 Suggestions for Additional Reading

Programming Environments Manual for 32-Bit Implementations of the PowerPC Architecture
MPCFPE32B/AD 12/2001 REV 2
Freescale Semiconductor, Inc.

MPC5200 User's Guide
MPC5200UG Rev 3 01/22005
Freescale Semiconductor, Inc.

Chapter 17

Linux and Real Time

In this chapter

When Linux began life on an Intel i386 processor, no one ever expected the success Linux would enjoy in server applications. That success has led to Linux being ported to many different architectures and used by developers for embedded systems from cellular handsets to telecommunications switches. Not long ago, if your application had real-time requirements, you might not have included Linux among the choices for your operating system. That has all changed with the developments in real-time Linux driven, in large part, by audio and multimedia applications.

In this chapter, we start with a brief look at the historical development of real-time Linux features. Then we look at the facilities available to the real-time programmer and how these facilities are used.

17.1 What Is Real Time?

Ask five people what "real time" means, and, chances are, you will get five different answers. Some might even cite some numbers. For the purposes of the discussion to follow, we discuss some scenarios and then propose a definition. Many requirements might be said to be soft real time, while others are called hard real time.

17.1.1 Soft Real Time

Most agree that soft real time means that the operation has a deadline, but if the deadline is missed, the quality of the experience could be diminished (but not fatal). Your desktop workstation is a perfect example of soft real-time requirements. When you are editing a document, you expect to see the results of your keystrokes immediately on the screen. When playing your favorite .mp3 file, you expect to have high-quality audio without any clicks, pops, or gaps in the music.

In general terms, humans cannot see or hear delays below a few tens of milliseconds. Of course, the musicians in the crowd will tell you that music can be *colored* by delays smaller than that. If a deadline is missed by these so-called soft real-time events, the results may be undesirable, leading to a lower level of "quality" of the experience, but not catastrophic.

17.1.2 Hard Real Time

Hard real time is characterized by the results of a missed deadline. In a hard real-time system, if a deadline is missed, the results are often catastrophic. Of course, *catastrophic* is a relative term. If your embedded device is controlling the fuel flow to a jet aircraft engine, missing a deadline to respond to pilot input or a change in operational characteristics can lead to disastrous results.

Note that the duration of the deadline has no bearing on the real-time characteristic. Servicing the tick on an atomic clock is such an example. As long as the tick is processed within the 1-second window before the next tick, the data remains valid. Missing the processing on a tick might throw off our global positioning systems by feet or even miles!

With this in mind, we draw on a commonly used set of definitions for soft and hard real time. For soft real-time systems, the value of a computation or result is diminished if a deadline is missed. For hard real-time systems, if a single deadline is missed, the system is considered to have failed, and might have catastrophic consequences.

17.1.3 Linux Scheduling

UNIX and Linux were both designed for fairness in their process scheduling. That is, the scheduler tries its best to allocate available resources across all processes that need the CPU and guarantee each process that they can make progress. This very design objective is counter to the requirement for a real-time process. A real-time process must run as soon as possible after it is ready to run. Real time means having predictable and repeatable latency.

17.1.4 Latency

Real-time processes are often associated with a physical event, such as an interrupt arriving from a peripheral device. Figure 17-1 illustrates the latency components in a Linux system. Latency measurement begins upon receipt of the interrupt we want to process. This is indicated by time t0 in Figure 17-1. Sometime later, the interrupt is taken and control is passed to the Interrupt Service Routine (ISR). This is indicated by time t1. This interrupt latency is almost entirely dictated by the maximum interrupt off time[1]—the time spent in a thread of execution that has hardware interrupts disabled.

---

[1] We neglect the context switching time for interrupt processing because it is often negligible compared to interrupt off time.

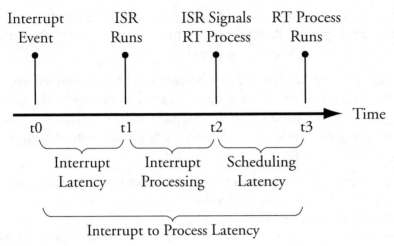

FIGURE 17-1
Latency components

It is considered good design practice to minimize the processing done in the actual interrupt service routine. Indeed, this execution context is limited in capability (for example, an ISR cannot call a blocking function, one that might sleep), so it is desirable to simply service the hardware device and leave the data processing to a Linux *bottom half*,[2] also called softIRQs.

When the ISR/bottom half has finished its processing, the usual case is to wake up a user space process that is waiting for the data. This is indicated by time t2 in Figure 17-1. At some point in time later, the real-time process is selected by the scheduler to run and is given the CPU. This is indicated by time t3 in Figure 17-1. Scheduling latency is affected primarily by the number of processes waiting for the CPU and the priorities among them. Setting the Real Time attribute on a process gives it higher priority over normal Linux processes and allows it to be the next process selected to run, assuming that it is the highest priority real-time process waiting for the CPU. The highest-priority real-time process that is ready to run (not blocked on I/O) will always run. You'll see how to set this attribute shortly.

---

[2] Robert Love explains bottom-half processing in great detail in his book *Linux Kernel Development*. See Section 17.5.1, "Suggestions for Additional Reading," at the end of this chapter for the reference.

17.2 Kernel Preemption

In the early Linux days of Linux 1.*x*, there was no kernel preemption. This meant that when a user space process requested kernel services, no other task could be scheduled to run until that process either blocked (goes to sleep) waiting on something (usually I/O), or until the kernel request is completed. Making the kernel preemptable[3] means that while one process is running in the kernel, another process can preempt the first and be allowed to run even though the first process had not completed its in-kernel processing. Figure 17-2 illustrates this.

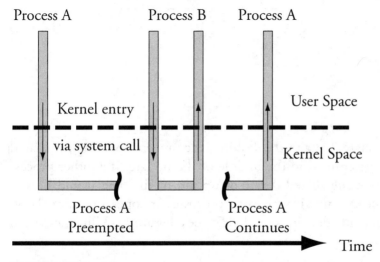

FIGURE 17-2
Kernel preemption

In this figure, Process A has entered the kernel via a system call. Perhaps it was a call to `write()` to a device such as the console or a file. While executing in the kernel on behalf of Process A, Process B with higher priority is woken up by an interrupt. The kernel *preempts* Process A and assigns the CPU to Process B, even though Process A had neither blocked nor completed its kernel processing.

17.2.1 Impediments to Preemption

The challenge in making the kernel fully preemptable is to identify all the places in the kernel that must be protected from preemption. These are the *critical sections*

---

[3] Interestingly, there is much debate on the correct spelling of *preemptable*. I defer to the survey done by Rick Lehrbaum on www.linuxdevices.com/articles/AT5136316996.html.

within the kernel where preemption cannot be allowed to occur. For example, assume that Process A in Figure 17-2 is executing in the kernel performing a file system operation. At some point, the code might need to write to an in-kernel data structure representing a file on the file system. To protect that data structure from corruption, the process must lock out all other processes from accessing the shared data structure. Listing 17-1 illustrates this concept using C syntax.

Listing 17-1

Locking Critical Sections

```
...
  preempt_disable();
  ...
  /* Critical section */
  update_shared_data();
  ...
  preempt_enable();
...
```

If we did not protect shared data in this fashion, the process updating the shared data structure could be preempted in the middle of the update. If another process attempted to update the same shared data, corruption of the data would be virtually certain. The classic example is when two processes are operating directly on common variables and making decisions on their values. Figure 17-3 illustrates such a case.

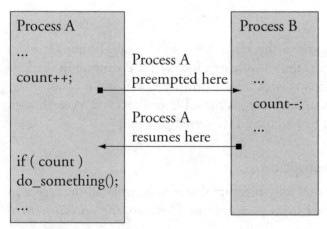

FIGURE 17-3
Shared data concurrency error

In Figure 17-3, Process A is interrupted after updating the shared data but before it makes a decision based on it. By design, Process A cannot detect that it has been preempted. Process B changes the value of the shared data before Process A gets to run again. As you can see, Process A will be making a decision based on a value determined by Process B. If this is not the behavior you seek, you must disable preemption in Process A around the shared data—in this case, the operation and decision on the variable count.

17.2.2 Preemption Models

The first solution to kernel preemption was to place checks at strategic locations within the kernel code where it was known to be safe to preempt the current thread of execution. These locations included entry and exit to system calls, release of certain kernel locks, and return from interrupt processing. At each of these points, code similar to Listing 17-2 was used to perform preemption.

Listing 17-2

Check for Preemption a la Linux 2.4 + Preempt Patch

```
...
  /*
   * This code is executed at strategic locations within
   * the Linux kernel where it is known to be safe to
   * preempt the current thread of execution
   */
  if (kernel_is_preemptable() && current->need_resched)
    preempt_schedule();
...

  /*
   * This code is in .../kernel/sched.c and is invoked from
   * those strategic locations as above
   */
  #ifdef CONFIG_PREEMPT
  asmlinkage void preempt_schedule(void)
  {
        while (current->need_resched) {
                ctx_sw_off();
                current->state |= TASK_PREEMPTED;
                schedule();
                current->state &= ~TASK_PREEMPTED;
                ctx_sw_on_no_preempt();
        }
  }
  #endif
...
```

The first snippet of code in Listing 17-2 (simplified from the actual code) is invoked at those strategic locations described earlier, where it is known that the kernel is safe to preempt. The second snippet of code in Listing 17-2 is the actual code from an early Linux 2.4 kernel with the preempt patch applied. This interesting `while` loop causes a context switch via the call to `schedule()` until all requests for preemption have been satisfied.

Although this approach led to reduced latencies in the Linux system, it was not ideal. The developers working on low-latency soon realized the need to "flip the logic." With earlier preemption models, we had this:

- The Linux kernel was fundamentally nonpreemptable.

- Preemption checks were sprinkled around the kernel at strategic locations known to be safe for preemption.

- Preemption was enabled only at these known-safe points.

To achieve a further significant reduction in latency, we want this in a preemptable kernel:

- The Linux kernel is fully preemptable everywhere.

- Preemption is disabled only around critical sections.

This is where the kernel developers have been heading since the original preemptable kernel patch series. However, this is no easy task. It involves poring over the entire kernel source code base, analyzing exactly what data must be protected from concurrency, and disabling preemption at only those locations. The method used for this has been to instrument the kernel for latency measurements, find the longest latency code paths, and fix them. The more recent Linux 2.6 kernels can be configured for very low-latency applications because of the effort that has gone into this "lock-breaking" methodology.

17.2.3 SMP Kernel

It is interesting to note that much of the work involved in creating an efficient multiprocessor architecture also benefits real time. The SMP challenge is more complex than the uniprocessor challenge because there is an additional element of concurrency to protect against. In the uniprocessor model, only a single task can be executing in the kernel at a time. Protection from concurrency involves only protection from interrupt or exception processing. In the SMP model, multiple threads of execution in the kernel are possible in addition to the threat from interrupt and exception processing.

SMP has been supported from early Linux 2.*x* kernels. A *Big Kernel Lock* (BKL) was used to protect against concurrency in the transition from uniprocessor to SMP operation. The BKL is a global spinlock, which prevents any other tasks from executing in the kernel. In his excellent book *Linux Kernel Development* (Novell Press, 2005), Robert Love characterized the BKL as the "redheaded stepchild of the kernel." In describing the characteristics of the BKL, Robert jokingly added "evil" to its list of attributes!

Early implementations of the SMP kernel based on the BKL led to significant inefficiencies in scheduling. It was found that one of the CPUs could be kept idle for long periods of time. Much of the work that led to an efficient SMP kernel also directly benefited real-time applications—primarily lowered latency. Replacing the BKL with smaller-grained locking surrounding only the actual shared data to be protected led to significantly reduced preemption latency.

17.2.4 Sources of Preemption Latency

A real-time system must be capable of servicing its real-time tasks within a specified upper boundary of time. Achieving consistently low preemption latency is critical to a real-time system. The two single largest contributors to preemption latency are interrupt-context processing and critical section processing where interrupts are disabled. You have already learned that a great deal of effort has been targeted at reducing the size (and thus, duration) of the critical sections. This leaves interrupt-context processing as the next challenge. This was answered with the Linux 2.6 real-time patch.

17.3 Real-Time Kernel Patch

Support for hard real time is not in the mainline `kernel.org` source tree. To enable hard real time, a patch must be applied. The real-time kernel patch is the cumulative result of several initiatives to reduce Linux kernel latency. The patch had many contributors, and it is currently maintained by Ingo Molnar; you can find it at http://people.redhat.com/~mingo/realtime-preempt. The soft real-time performance of the 2.6 Linux kernel has improved significantly since the early 2.6 kernel releases. When 2.6 was first released, the 2.4 Linux kernel was substantially better in soft real-time performance. Since about Linux 2.6.12, soft real-time performance in the single-digit milliseconds on a reasonably fast x86 processor is readily achieved. To get repeatable performance beyond this requires the real-time patch.

The real-time patch adds several important features to the Linux kernel. Figure 17-4 displays the configuration options for Preemption mode when the real-time patch has been applied.

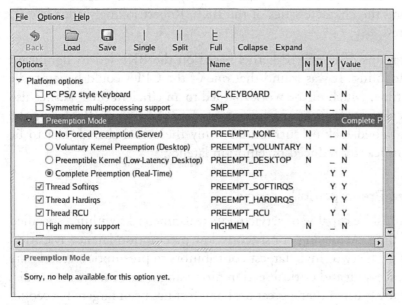

FIGURE 17-4
Preemption modes with real-time patch

The real-time patch adds a fourth preemption mode called PREEMPT_RT, or Preempt Real Time. The four preemption modes are as follows:

- PREEMPT_NONE: No forced preemption. Overall latency is, on average, good, but there can be some occasional long delays. Best suited for applications for which overall throughput is the top design criteria.

- PREEMPT_VOLUNTARY: First stage of latency reduction. Additional explicit preemption points are placed at strategic locations in the kernel to reduce latency. Some loss of overall throughput is traded for lower latency.

- `PREEMPT_DESKTOP`: This mode enables preemption everywhere in the kernel except when processing within critical sections. This mode is useful for soft real-time applications such as audio and multimedia. Overall throughput is traded for further reductions in latency.

- `PREEMPT_RT`: Features from the real-time patch are added, including replacing spinlocks with preemptable mutexes. This enables involuntary preemption everywhere within the kernel except for those areas protected by `preempt_disable()`. This mode significantly smoothes out the variation in latency (jitter) and allows a low and predictable latency for time-critical real-time applications.

If kernel preemption is enabled in your kernel configuration, it can be disabled at boot time by adding the following kernel parameter to the kernel command line:

```
preempt=0
```

17.3.1 Real-Time Features

Several new Linux kernel features are enabled with `CONFIG_PREEMPT_RT`. From Figure 17-4, we see several new configuration settings. These and other features of the real-time Linux kernel patch are described here.

17.3.1.1 Spinlock Converted to Mutex

The real-time patch converts most spinlocks in the system to mutexes. This reduces overall latency at the cost of slightly reduced throughput. The benefit of converting spinlocks to mutexes is that they can be preempted. If Process A is holding a lock, and Process B at a higher priority needs the same lock, Process A can preempt Process B in the case where it is holding a mutex.

17.3.1.2 ISRs as Kernel Tasks

With `CONFIG_PREEMPT_HARDIRQ` selected, interrupt service routines[4] (ISRs) are forced to run in process context. This gives the developer control over the priority of ISRs because they become schedulable entities. As such, they also become preemptable to allow higher-priority hardware interrupts to be handled first.

---

[4] Also called HARDIRQs.

This is a powerful feature. Some hardware architectures do not enforce interrupt priorities. Those that do might not enforce the priorities consistent with your specified real-time design goals. Using CONFIG_PREEMPT_HARDIRQ, you are free to define the priorities at which each IRQ will run.

Conversion of ISRs to threads can be disabled at runtime through the /proc file system or at boot time by entering a parameter on the kernel command line. When enabled in the configuration, unless you specify otherwise, ISR threading is enabled by default.

To disable ISR threading at runtime, issue the following command as root:

```
# echo '0' >/proc/sys/kernel/hardirq_preemption
```

To verify the setting, display it as follows:

```
# cat /proc/sys/kernel/hardirq_preemption
1
```

To disable ISR threading at boot time, add the following parameter to the kernel command line:

```
hardirq-preempt=0
```

17.3.1.3 Preemptable Softirqs

CONFIG_PREEMPT_SOFTIRQ reduces latency by running softirqs within the context of the kernel's softirq daemon (ksoftirqd). ksoftirqd is a proper Linux task (process). As such, it can be prioritized and scheduled along with other tasks. If your kernel is configured for real time, and CONFIG_PREEMPT_SOFTIRQ is enabled, the ksoftirqd kernel task is elevated to real-time priority to handle the softirq processing.[5] Listing 17-3 shows the code responsible for this from a recent Linux kernel, found in .../kernel/softirq.c.

---

[5] See *Linux Kernel Development,* referenced at the end of this chapter, to learn more about softirqs.

Listing 17-3

Promoting `ksoftirq` to Real-Time Status

```
static int ksoftirqd(void * __bind_cpu)
{
        struct sched_param param = { .sched_priority = 24 };

        printk("ksoftirqd started up.\n");

#ifdef CONFIG_PREEMPT_SOFTIRQS
        printk("softirq RT prio: %d.\n", param.sched_priority);
        sys_sched_setscheduler(current->pid, SCHED_FIFO, &param);
#else
        set_user_nice(current, -10);
#endif
...
```

Here we see that if `CONFIG_PREEMPT_SOFTIRQS` is enabled in the kernel configuration, the `ksoftirqd` kernel task is promoted to a real-time task (`SCHED_FIFO`) at a real-time priority of 24 using the `sys_sched_setscheduler()` kernel function.

SoftIRQ threading can be disabled at runtime through the `/proc` file system, as well as through the kernel command line at boot time. When enabled in the configuration, unless you specify otherwise, SoftIRQ threading is enabled by default. To disable SoftIRQ threading at runtime, issue the following command as root:

```
# echo '0' >/proc/sys/kernel/softirq_preemption
```

To verify the setting, display it as follows:

```
# cat /proc/sys/kernel/softirq_preemption
1
```

To disable SoftIRQ threading at boot time, add the following parameter to the kernel command line:

```
softirq-preempt=0
```

17.3.1.4 Preempt RCU

RCU (Read-Copy-Update)[6] is a special form of synchronization primitive in the Linux kernel designed for data that is read frequently but updated infrequently. You can think of RCU as an optimized reader lock. The real-time patch adds `CONFIG_PREEMPT_RCU`, which improves latency by making certain RCU sections preemptable.

---

[6] See www.rdrop.com/users/paulmck/RCU/ for an in-depth discussion of RCU.

17.3.2 O(1) Scheduler

The O(1) scheduler has been around since the days of Linux 2.5. It is mentioned here because it is a critical component of a real-time solution. The O(1) scheduler is a significant improvement over the previous Linux scheduler. It scales better for systems with many processes and helps produce lower overall latency.

In case you are wondering, O(1) is a mathematical designation for a system of the first order. In this context, it means that the time it takes to make a scheduling decision is not dependent on the number of processes on a given runqueue. The old Linux scheduler did not have this characteristic, and its performance degraded with the number of processes.[7]

17.3.3 Creating a Real-Time Process

You can designate a process as real time by setting a process attribute that the scheduler uses as part of its scheduling algorithm. Listing 17-4 shows the general method.

Listing 17-4

Creating a Real-Time Process

```
#include <sched.h>

#define MY_RT_PRIORITY MAX_USER_RT_PRIO /* Highest possible */

int main(int argc, char **argv)
{
        ...
        int rc, old_scheduler_policy;
        struct sched_param my_params;
        ...

        /* Passing zero specifies caller's (our) policy */
        old_scheduler_policy = sched_getscheduler(0);

        my_params.sched_priority = MY_RT_PRIORITY;
        /* Passing zero specifies callers (our) pid */
        rc = sched_setscheduler(0, SCHED_RR, &my_params);
        if ( rc == -1 )
                handle_error();
        ...
}
```

---

[7] We refer you again to Robert Love's book for an excellent discussion of the O(1) scheduler, and a delightful diatribe on algorithmic complexity, from which the notation O(1) derives.

This code snippet does two things in the call to `sched_setscheduler()`. It changes the scheduling policy to `SCHED_RR` and raises its priority to the maximum possible on the system. Linux supports three scheduling policies:

- `SCHED_OTHER`: Normal Linux process, fairness scheduling

- `SCHED_RR`: Real-time process with a time slice—that is, if it does not block, it is allowed to run for a given period of time determined by the scheduler

- `SCHED_FIFO`: Real-time process that runs until it either blocks or explicitly yields the processor, or until another higher-priority `SCHED_FIFO` process becomes runnable

The man page for `sched_setscheduler` provides more detail on the three different scheduling policies.

17.3.4 Critical Section Management

When writing kernel code, such as a custom device driver, you will encounter data structures that you must protect from concurrent access. The easiest way to protect critical data is to disable preemption around the critical section. Keep the critical path as short as possible to maintain a low maximum latency for your system. Listing 17-5 shows an example.

Listing 17-5

Protecting Critical Section in Kernel Code

```
...
/*
 * Declare and initialize a global lock for your
 * critical data
 */
DEFINE_SPINLOCK(my_lock);
...

int operate_on_critical_data()
{
    ...
    spin_lock(&my_lock);
    ...
    /* Update critical/shared data */
    ...
    spin_unlock(&my_lock);
    ...
}
```

When a task successfully acquires a spinlock, preemption is disabled and the task that acquired the spinlock is allowed into the critical section. No task switches can occur until a `spin_unlock` operation takes place. The `spin_lock()` function is actually a macro that has several forms, depending on the kernel configuration. They are defined at the top level (architecture-independent definitions) in `.../include/linux/spinlock.h`. When the kernel is patched with the real-time patch, these spinlocks are promoted to mutexes to allow preemption of higher-priority processes when a spinlock is held.

Because the real-time patch is largely transparent to the device driver and kernel developer, the familiar constructs can be used to protect critical sections, as described in Listing 17-5. This is a major advantage of the real-time patch for real-time applications; it preserves the well-known semantics for locking and interrupt service routines.

Using the macro `DEFINE_SPINLOCK` as in Listing 17-5 preserves future compatibility. These macros are defined in `.../include/linux/spinlock_types.h`.

17.4 Debugging the Real-Time Kernel

Several configuration options facilitate debugging and performance analysis of the real-time patched kernel. They are detailed in the following subsections.

17.4.1 Soft Lockup Detection

To enable soft lockup detection, enable `CONFIG_DETECT_SOFTLOCKUP` in the kernel configuration. This feature enables the detection of long periods of running in kernel mode without a context switch. This feature exists in non-real-time kernels but is useful for detecting very high latency paths or soft deadlock conditions. To use it, simply enable the feature and watch for any reports on the console or system log. Reports will be emitted similar to this:

```
BUG: soft lockup detected on CPU0
```

When this message is emitted by the kernel, it is usually accompanied by a back-trace and other information such as the process name and PID. It will look similar to a kernel oops message complete with processor registers. See `.../kernel/softlockup.c` for details. This information can be used to help track down the source of the lockup condition.

17.4.2 Preemption Debugging

To enable preemption debugging, enable CONFIG_DEBUG_PREEMPT in the kernel configuration. This debug feature enables the detection of unsafe use of preemption semantics such as preemption count underflows and attempts to sleep while in an invalid context. To use it, simply enable the feature and watch for any reports on the console or system log. Here is just a small sample of reports possible when preemption debugging is enabled:

```
BUG: <me> <mypid>, possible wake_up race on <proc> <pid>
   BUG: lock recursion deadlock detected!  <more info>
   BUG: nonzero lock count <n> at exit time?
```

Many more messages are possible—these are just a few examples of the kinds of problems that can be detected. These messages will help you avoid deadlocks and other erroneous or dangerous programming semantics when using real-time kernel features. For more details on the messages and conditions under which they are emitted, browse the Linux kernel source file .../kernel/rt-debug.c.

17.4.3 Debug Wakeup Timing

To enable wakeup timing, enable CONFIG_WAKEUP_TIMING in the kernel configuration. This debug option enables measurement of the time taken from waking up a high-priority process to when it is scheduled on a CPU. Using it is simple. When configured, measurement is disabled. To enable the measurement, do the following as root:

```
# echo '0' >/proc/sys/kernel/preempt_max_latency
```

When this /proc file is set to zero, each successive maximum wakeup timing result is written to this file. To read the current maximum, simply display the value:

```
# cat /proc/sys/kernel/preempt_max_latency
84
```

As long as any of the latency-measurement modes are enabled in the kernel configuration, preempt_max_latency will always be updated with the maximum latency value. It cannot be disabled. Writing 0 to this /proc variable simply resets the maximum to zero to restart the cumulative measurement.

17.4.4 Wakeup Latency History

To enable wakeup latency history, enable CONFIG_WAKEUP_LATENCY_HIST while CONFIG_WAKEUP_TIMING is also enabled. This option dumps all the wakeup timing measurements enabled by CONFIG_WAKEUP_TIMING into a file for later analysis. An example of this file and its contents is presented shortly when we examine interrupt off history.

- CRITICAL_PREEMPT_TIMING: Measures the time spent in critical sections with preempt disabled.

- PREEMPT_OFF_HIST: Similar to WAKEUP_LATENCY_HIST. Gathers preempt off timing measurements into a bin for later analysis.

17.4.5 Interrupt Off Timing

To enable measurement of maximum interrupt off timing, configure your kernel with CRITICAL_IRQSOFF_TIMING enabled. This option measures time spent in critical sections with irqs disabled. This feature works in the same way as wakeup latency timing. To enable the measurement, do the following as root:

```
# echo '0' >/proc/sys/kernel/preempt_max_latency
```

When this /proc file is set to zero, each successive maximum interrupt off timing result is written to this file. To read the current maximum, simply display the value:

```
# cat /proc/sys/kernel/preempt_max_latency
97
```

You will notice that the latency measurements for both wakeup latency and interrupt off latency are enabled and displayed using the same /proc file. This means, of course, that only one measurement can be configured at a time, or the results might not be valid. Because these measurements add significant runtime overhead, it isn't wise to enable them all at once anyway.

17.4.6 Interrupt Off History

Enabling INTERRUPT_OFF_HIST provides functionality similar to that with WAKEUP_LATENCY_HIST. This option gathers interrupt off timing measurements into a file for later analysis. This data is formatted as a histogram, with bins ranging from 0 microseconds to just over 10,000 microseconds. In the example just given, we saw that the maximum latency was 97 microseconds from that particular sample. Therefore, we can conclude that the latency data in histogram form will not contain any useful information beyond the 97-microsecond bin.

History data is obtained by reading a special /proc file. This output is redirected to a regular file for analysis or plotting as follows:

```
# cat /proc/latency_hist/interrupt_off_latency/CPU0 > hist_data.txt
```

Listing 17-6 displays the first 10 lines of the history data.

Listing 17-6

Interrupt Off Latency History (Head)

```
$ cat /proc/latency_hist/interrupt_off_latency/CPU0 | head
#Minimum latency: 0 microseconds.
#Average latency: 1 microseconds.
#Maximum latency: 97 microseconds.
#Total samples: 60097595
#There are 0 samples greater or equal than 10240 microseconds
#usecs          samples
     0         13475417
     1         38914907
     2          2714349
     3           442308
...
```

From Listing 17-6 we can see the minimum and maximum values, the average of all the values, and the total number of samples. In this case, we accumulated slightly more than 60 million samples. The histogram data follows the summary and contains up to around 10,000 bins. We can easily plot this data using gnuplot as shown in Figure 17-5.

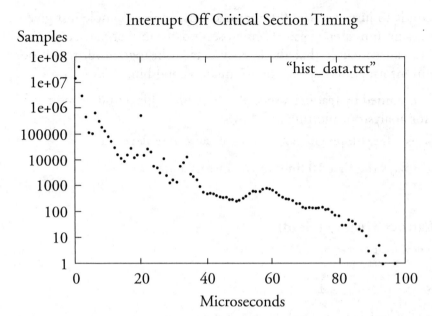

FIGURE 17-5
Interrupt off latency data

17.4.7 Latency Tracing

The LATENCY_TRACE configuration option enables generation of kernel trace data associated with the last maximum latency measurement. It is also made available through the /proc file system. A latency trace can help you isolate the longest-latency code path. For each new maximum latency measurement, an associated trace is generated that facilitates tracing the code path of the associated maximum latency.

Listing 17-7 reproduces an example trace for a 78-microsecond maximum. As with the other measurement tools, enable the measurement by writing a 0 to /proc/sys/kernel/preempt_max_latency.

Listing 17-7

Interrupt Off Maximum Latency Trace

```
$ cat /proc/latency_trace
preemption latency trace v1.1.5 on 2.6.14-rt-intoff-tim_trace
--------------------------------------------------------------
 latency: 78 us, #50/50, CPU#0 | (M:rt VP:0, KP:0, SP:1 HP:1)
    ----------------
    | task: softirq-timer/0-3 (uid:0 nice:0 policy:1 rt_prio:1)
    ----------------

                    _------=> CPU#
                   / _-----=> irqs-off
                  | / _----=> need-resched
                  || / _---=> hardirq/softirq
                  ||| / _--=> preempt-depth
                  |||| /
                  |||||      delay
  cmd      pid |||||  time  |  caller
     \    /   |||||   \    |    /
    cat-6637  0D...    1us : common_interrupt ((0))
    cat-6637  0D.h.    2us : do_IRQ (c013d91c 0 0)
    cat-6637  0D.h1    3us+: mask_and_ack_8259A (__do_IRQ)
    cat-6637  0D.h1   10us : redirect_hardirq (__do_IRQ)
    cat-6637  0D.h.   12us : handle_IRQ_event (__do_IRQ)
    cat-6637  0D.h.   13us : timer_interrupt (handle_IRQ_event)
    cat-6637  0D.h.   15us : handle_tick_update (timer_interrupt)
    cat-6637  0D.h1   16us : do_timer (handle_tick_update)
    ...    <we're in the timer interrupt function>
    cat-6637  0D.h.   22us : run_local_timers (update_process_times)
    cat-6637  0D.h.   22us : raise_softirq (run_local_timers)
    cat-6637  0D.h.   23us : wakeup_softirqd (raise_softirq)
    ...    <softirq work pending - need to preempt is signaled>
    cat-6637  0Dnh.   34us : wake_up_process (wakeup_softirqd)
    cat-6637  0Dnh.   35us+: rcu_pending (update_process_times)
    cat-6637  0Dnh.   39us : scheduler_tick (update_process_times)
    cat-6637  0Dnh.   39us : sched_clock (scheduler_tick)
    cat-6637  0Dnh1   41us : task_timeslice (scheduler_tick)
    cat-6637  0Dnh.   42us+: preempt_schedule (scheduler_tick)
    cat-6637  0Dnh1   45us : note_interrupt (__do_IRQ)
    cat-6637  0Dnh1   45us : enable_8259A_irq (__do_IRQ)
    cat-6637  0Dnh1   47us : preempt_schedule (enable_8259A_irq)
    cat-6637  0Dnh.   48us : preempt_schedule (__do_IRQ)
    cat-6637  0Dnh.   48us : irq_exit (do_IRQ)
    cat-6637  0Dn..   49us : preempt_schedule_irq (need_resched)
    cat-6637  0Dn..   50us : __schedule (preempt_schedule_irq)
    ...    <here is the context switch to softirqd-timer thread>
  <...>-3    0D..2   74us+: __switch_to (__schedule)
  <...>-3    0D..2   76us : __schedule <cat-6637> (74 62)
  <...>-3    0D..2   77us : __schedule (schedule)
  <...>-3    0D..2   78us : trace_irqs_on (__schedule)
    ...    <output truncated here for brevity>
```

We have trimmed this listing significantly for clarity, but the key elements of this trace are obvious. This trace resulted from a timer interrupt. In the `hardirq` thread, little is done beyond queuing up some work for later in a `softirq` context. This is seen by the `wakeup_softirqd()` function at 23 microseconds and is typical for interrupt processing. This triggers the `need_resched` flag, as shown in the trace by the n in the third column of the second field. At 49 microseconds, after some processing in the timer `softirq`, the scheduler is invoked for preemption. At 74 microseconds, control is passed to the actual `softirqd-timer/0` thread running in this particular kernel as PID 3. (The process name was truncated to fit the field width and is shown as `<...>`.)

Most of the fields of Listing 17-7 have obvious meanings. The `irqs-off` field contains a D for sections of code where interrupts are off. Because this latency trace is an interrupts off trace, we see this indicated throughout the trace. The `need_resched` field mirrors the state of the kernel's `need_resched` flag. An n indicates that the scheduler should be run at the soonest opportunity, and a period (.) means that this flag is not active. The `hardirq/softirq` field indicates a thread of execution in `hardirq` context with h, and `softirq` context with s. The preempt-depth field indicates the value of the kernel's `preempt_count` variable, an indicator of nesting level of locks within the kernel. Preemption can occur only when this variable is at zero.

17.4.8 Debugging Deadlock Conditions

The `DEBUG_DEADLOCKS` kernel configuration option enables detection and reporting of deadlock conditions associated with the semaphores and spinlocks in the kernel. When enabled, potential deadlock conditions are reported in a fashion similar to this:

```
==========================================
  [ BUG: lock recursion deadlock detected! |
  ----------------------------------------
  ...
```

Much information is displayed after the banner line announcing the deadlock detection, including the lock descriptor, lock name (if available), lock file and name (if available), lock owner, who is currently holding the lock, and so on. Using this debug tool, it is possible to immediately determine the offending processes. Of course, fixing it might not be so easy!

17.4.9 Runtime Control of Locking Mode

The `DEBUG_RT_LOCKING_MODE` option enables a runtime control to switch the real-time mutex back into a nonpreemptable mode, effectively changing the behavior of the real-time (spinlocks as mutexes) kernel back to a spinlock-based kernel. As with the other configuration options we have covered here, this tool should be considered a development aid to be used only in a development environment.

It does not make sense to enable all of these debug modes at once. As you might imagine, most of these debug modes add size and significant processing overhead to the kernel. They are meant to be used as development aids and should be disabled for production code.

17.5 Chapter Summary

- Linux is increasingly being used in systems where real-time performance is required. Examples include multimedia applications and robot, industrial, and automotive controllers.

- Real-time systems are characterized by deadlines. When a missed deadline results in inconvenience or a diminished customer experience, we refer to this as soft real time. In contrast, hard real-time systems are considered failed when a deadline is missed.

- Kernel preemption was the first significant feature in the Linux kernel that addressed system-wide latency.

- Recent Linux kernels support several preemption modes, ranging from no preemption to full real-time preemption.

- The real-time patch adds several key features to the Linux kernel, resulting in reliable low latencies.

- The real-time patch includes several important measurement tools to aid in debugging and characterizing a real-time Linux implementation.

17.5.1 Suggestions for Additional Reading

Linux Kernel Development, 2nd Edition
Robert Love
Novell Press, 2005

Appendix A

GNU Public License

This is an exact reproduction of the GLP license as authored and published by the Free Software Foundation. An electronic copy can be obtained at www.fsf.org.

Version 2, June 1991

Copyright © 1989, 1991 Free Software Foundation, Inc.

51 Franklin Street, Fifth Floor, Boston, MA 02110-1301, USA

Everyone is permitted to copy and distribute verbatim copies of this license document, but changing it is not allowed.

Preamble

The licenses for most software are designed to take away your freedom to share and change it. By contrast, the GNU General Public License is intended to guarantee your freedom to share and change free software—to make sure the software is free for all its users. This General Public License applies to most of the Free Software Foundation's software and to any other program whose authors commit to using it. (Some other Free Software Foundation software is covered by the GNU Lesser General Public License instead.) You can apply it to your programs, too.

When we speak of free software, we are referring to freedom, not price. Our General Public Licenses are designed to make sure that you have the freedom to distribute copies of free software (and charge for this service if you wish), that you receive source code or can get it if you want it, that you can change the software or use pieces of it in new free programs; and that you know you can do these things.

To protect your rights, we need to make restrictions that forbid anyone to deny you these rights or to ask you to surrender the rights. These restrictions translate to certain responsibilities for you if you distribute copies of the software, or if you modify it.

For example, if you distribute copies of such a program, whether gratis or for a fee, you must give the recipients all the rights that you have. You must make sure that they, too, receive or can get the source code. And you must show them these terms so they know their rights.

We protect your rights with two steps: (1) copyright the software, and (2) offer you this license which gives you legal permission to copy, distribute and/or modify the software.

Also, for each author's protection and ours, we want to make certain that everyone understands that there is no warranty for this free software. If the software is modified by someone else and passed on, we want its recipients to know that what they have is not the original, so that any problems introduced by others will not reflect on the original authors' reputations.

Finally, any free program is threatened constantly by software patents. We wish to avoid the danger that redistributors of a free program will individually obtain patent licenses, in effect making the program proprietary. To prevent this, we have made it clear that any patent must be licensed for everyone's free use or not licensed at all.

The precise terms and conditions for copying, distribution and modification follow.

Terms and Conditions for Copying, Distribution and Modification

0. This License applies to any program or other work which contains a notice placed by the copyright holder saying it may be distributed under the terms of this General Public License. The "Program", below, refers to any such program or work, and a "work based on the Program" means either the Program or any derivative work under copyright law: that is to say, a work containing the Program or a portion of it, either verbatim or with modifications and/or translated into another language. (Hereinafter, translation is included without limitation in the term "modification".) Each licensee is addressed as "you".

    Activities other than copying, distribution and modification are not covered by this License; they are outside its scope. The act of running the Program is not restricted, and the output from the Program is covered only if its contents constitute a work based on the Program (independent of having been made by running the Program). Whether that is true depends on what the Program does.

1. You may copy and distribute verbatim copies of the Program's source code as you receive it, in any medium, provided that you

conspicuously and appropriately publish on each copy an appropriate copyright notice and disclaimer of warranty; keep intact all the notices that refer to this License and to the absence of any warranty; and give any other recipients of the Program a copy of this License along with the Program.

You may charge a fee for the physical act of transferring a copy, and you may at your option offer warranty protection in exchange for a fee.

2. You may modify your copy or copies of the Program or any portion of it, thus forming a work based on the Program, and copy and distribute such modifications or work under the terms of Section 1 above, provided that you also meet all of these conditions:

   a. You must cause the modified files to carry prominent notices stating that you changed the files and the date of any change.

   b. You must cause any work that you distribute or publish, that in whole or in part contains or is derived from the Program or any part thereof, to be licensed as a whole at no charge to all third parties under the terms of this License.

   c. If the modified program normally reads commands interactively when run, you must cause it, when started running for such interactive use in the most ordinary way, to print or display an announcement including an appropriate copyright notice and a notice that there is no warranty (or else, saying that you provide a warranty) and that users may redistribute the program under these conditions, and telling the user how to view a copy of this License. (Exception: if the Program itself is interactive but does not normally print such an announcement, your work based on the Program is not required to print an announcement.)

These requirements apply to the modified work as a whole. If identifiable sections of that work are not derived from the Program, and can be reasonably considered independent and separate works in themselves, then this License, and its terms, do not apply to those sections when you distribute them as separate works. But when you distribute the same sections as part of a whole which is a work based on the Program, the distribution of the whole must be on the terms of this License, whose permissions for other licensees extend to the entire whole, and thus to each and every part regardless of who wrote it.

Thus, it is not the intent of this section to claim rights or contest your rights to work written entirely by you; rather, the intent is to exercise the right to control the distribution of derivative or collective works based on the Program.

In addition, mere aggregation of another work not based on the Program with the Program (or with a work based on the Program) on a volume of a storage or distribution medium does not bring the other work under the scope of this License.

3. You may copy and distribute the Program (or a work based on it, under Section 2) in object code or executable form under the terms of Sections 1 and 2 above provided that you also do one of the following:

a. Accompany it with the complete corresponding machine-readable source code, which must be distributed under the terms of Sections 1 and 2 above on a medium customarily used for software interchange; or,

b. Accompany it with a written offer, valid for at least three years, to give any third party, for a charge no more than your cost of physically performing source distribution, a complete machine-readable copy of the corresponding source code, to be distributed under the terms of Sections 1 and 2 above on a medium customarily used for software interchange; or,

c. Accompany it with the information you received as to the offer to distribute corresponding source code. (This alternative is allowed only for noncommercial distribution and only if you received the program in object code or executable form with such an offer, in accord with Subsection b above.)

The source code for a work means the preferred form of the work for making modifications to it. For an executable work, complete source code means all the source code for all modules it contains, plus any associated interface definition files, plus the scripts used to control compilation and installation of the executable. However, as a special exception, the source code distributed need not include anything that is normally distributed (in either source or binary form) with the major components (compiler, kernel, and so on) of the operating system on which the executable runs, unless that component itself accompanies the executable.

If distribution of executable or object code is made by offering access to copy from a designated place, then offering equivalent access to copy the source code from the same place counts as distribution of the source code, even though third parties are not compelled to copy the source along with the object code.

4. You may not copy, modify, sublicense, or distribute the Program except as expressly provided under this License. Any attempt otherwise to copy, modify, sublicense or distribute the Program is void, and will automatically terminate your rights under this License. However, parties who have received copies, or rights, from you under this License will not have their licenses terminated so long as such parties remain in full compliance.

5. You are not required to accept this License, since you have not signed it. However, nothing else grants you permission to modify or distribute the Program or its derivative works. These actions are prohibited by law if you do not accept this License. Therefore, by modifying or distributing the Program (or any work based on the Program), you indicate your acceptance of this License to do so, and all its terms and conditions for copying, distributing or modifying the Program or works based on it.

6. Each time you redistribute the Program (or any work based on the Program), the recipient automatically receives a license from the original licensor to copy, distribute or modify the Program subject to these terms and conditions. You may not impose any further restrictions on the recipients' exercise of the rights granted herein. You are not responsible for enforcing compliance by third parties to this License.

7. If, as a consequence of a court judgment or allegation of patent infringement or for any other reason (not limited to patent issues), conditions are imposed on you (whether by court order, agreement or otherwise) that contradict the conditions of this License, they do not excuse you from the conditions of this License. If you cannot distribute so as to satisfy simultaneously your obligations under this License and any other pertinent obligations, then as a consequence you may not distribute the Program at all. For example, if a patent license would not permit royalty-free redistribution of the Program by all those who receive copies directly or indirectly through you, then the only way you could satisfy both it and this License would be to refrain entirely from distribution of the Program.

    If any portion of this section is held invalid or unenforceable under any particular circumstance, the balance of the section is intended to apply and the section as a whole is intended to apply in other circumstances.

    It is not the purpose of this section to induce you to infringe any patents or other property right claims or to contest validity of any such claims; this section has the sole purpose of protecting the integrity of the free software distribution system, which is implemented by public license practices. Many people have made generous contributions to the wide range of software distributed through that system in reliance on consistent application of that system; it is up to the author/donor to decide if he or she is willing to distribute software through any other system and a licensee cannot impose that choice.

    This section is intended to make thoroughly clear what is believed to be a consequence of the rest of this License.

8. If the distribution and/or use of the Program is restricted in certain countries either by patents or by copyrighted interfaces, the original copyright holder who places the Program under this License may add an explicit geographical distribution limitation excluding those countries, so that distribution is permitted only in or among countries not thus excluded. In such case, this License

incorporates the limitation as if written in the body of this License.

9.   The Free Software Foundation may publish revised and/or new versions of the General Public License from time to time. Such new versions will be similar in spirit to the present version, but may differ in detail to address new problems or concerns.

Each version is given a distinguishing version number. If the Program specifies a version number of this License which applies to it and "any later version", you have the option of following the terms and conditions either of that version or of any later version published by the Free Software Foundation. If the Program does not specify a version number of this License, you may choose any version ever published by the Free Software Foundation.

10.   If you wish to incorporate parts of the Program into other free programs whose distribution conditions are different, write to the author to ask for permission. For software which is copyrighted by the Free Software Foundation, write to the Free Software Foundation; we sometimes make exceptions for this. Our decision will be guided by the two goals of preserving the free status of all derivatives of our free software and of promoting the sharing and reuse of software generally.

No Warranty

11.   BECAUSE THE PROGRAM IS LICENSED FREE OF CHARGE, THERE IS NO WARRANTY FOR THE PROGRAM, TO THE EXTENT PERMITTED BY APPLICABLE LAW. EXCEPT WHEN OTHERWISE STATED IN WRITING THE COPYRIGHT HOLDERS AND/OR OTHER PARTIES PROVIDE THE PROGRAM "AS IS" WITHOUT WARRANTY OF ANY KIND, EITHER EXPRESSED OR IMPLIED, INCLUDING, BUT NOT LIMITED TO, THE IMPLIED WARRANTIES OF MERCHANTABILITY AND FITNESS FOR A PARTICULAR PURPOSE. THE ENTIRE RISK AS TO THE QUALITY AND

PERFORMANCE OF THE PROGRAM IS WITH YOU. SHOULD THE PROGRAM PROVE DEFECTIVE, YOU ASSUME THE COST OF ALL NECESSARY SERVICING, REPAIR OR CORRECTION.

12. IN NO EVENT UNLESS REQUIRED BY APPLICABLE LAW OR AGREED TO IN WRITING WILL ANY COPYRIGHT HOLDER, OR ANY OTHER PARTY WHO MAY MODIFY AND/OR REDISTRIBUTE THE PROGRAM AS PERMITTED ABOVE, BE LIABLE TO YOU FOR DAMAGES, INCLUDING ANY GENERAL, SPECIAL, INCIDENTAL OR CONSEQUENTIAL DAMAGES ARISING OUT OF THE USE OR INABILITY TO USE THE PROGRAM (INCLUDING BUT NOT LIMITED TO LOSS OF DATA OR DATA BEING RENDERED INACCURATE OR LOSSES SUSTAINED BY YOU OR THIRD PARTIES OR A FAILURE OF THE PROGRAM TO OPERATE WITH ANY OTHER PROGRAMS), EVEN IF SUCH HOLDER OR OTHER PARTY HAS BEEN ADVISED OF THE POSSIBILITY OF SUCH DAMAGES

Appendix B

U-Boot Configurable Commands

U-Boot has more than 60 configurable commands. These are summarized here in Table B-1 from a recent U-Boot snapshot. In addition to these are a large number of nonstandard commands, some of which depend on specific hardware or are experimental. For the complete and up-to-date listing, consult the source code. The commands are defined in the `.../include/cmd_confdefs.h` header file from the top-level U-Boot source directory.

TABLE B-1
U-Boot Configurable Commands

Command Set	Commands
CFG_CMD_BDI	bdinfo
CFG_CMD_LOADS	loads
CFG_CMD_LOADB	loadb
CFG_CMD_IMI	iminfo
CFG_CMD_CACHE	icache, dcache
CFG_CMD_FLASH	flinfo, erase, protect
CFG_CMD_MEMORY	md, mm, nm, mw, cp, cmp, crc, base, loop, mtest
CFG_CMD_NET	bootp, tftpboot, rarpboot
CFG_CMD_ENV	saveenv
CFG_CMD_KGDB	kgdb
CFG_CMD_PCMCIA	PCMCIA support
CFG_CMD_IDE	IDE hard disk support
CFG_CMD_PCI	pciinfo
CFG_CMD_IRQ	irqinfo
CFG_CMD_BOOTD	bootd
CFG_CMD_CONSOLE	coninfo
CFG_CMD_EEPROM	EEPROM read/write support
CFG_CMD_ASKENV	ask for environment variable
CFG_CMD_RUN	run command in environment variable
CFG_CMD_ECHO	echo arguments

Command Set	Commands
CFG_CMD_I2C	I2C serial bus support
CFG_CMD_REGINFO	Register dump
CFG_CMD_IMMAP	IMMR dump support
CFG_CMD_DATE	Support for RTC, date/time, and so on.
CFG_CMD_DHCP	DHCP support
CFG_CMD_BEDBUG	Includes BedBug debugger
CFG_CMD_FDC	Floppy disk support
CFG_CMD_SCSI	SCSI support
CFG_CMD_AUTOSCRIPT	Autoscript support
CFG_CMD_MII	MII support
CFG_CMD_SETGETDCR	DCR support on 4xx
CFG_CMD_BSP	Board-specific functions
CFG_CMD_ELF	ELF (VxWorks) load/boot command
CFG_CMD_MISC	Miscellaneous functions, such as sleep
CFG_CMD_USB	USB support
CFG_CMD_DOC	Disk-on-chip support
CFG_CMD_JFFS2	JFFS2 support
CFG_CMD_DTT	Digital therm and thermostat
CFG_CMD_SDRAM	SDRAM DIMM SPD info printout
CFG_CMD_DIAG	Diagnostics
CFG_CMD_FPGA	FPGA configuration support
CFG_CMD_HWFLOW	RTS/CTS hardware flow control
CFG_CMD_SAVES	Saves S record dump
CFG_CMD_SPI	SPI utility
CFG_CMD_FDOS	Floppy DOS support
CFG_CMD_VFD	VFD support (TRAB)

(continues)

TABLE B-1 (Continued)

Command Set	Commands
CFG_CMD_NAND	NAND support
CFG_CMD_BMP	BMP support
CFG_CMD_PORTIO	Port I/O
CFG_CMD_PING	Ping support
CFG_CMD_MMC	MMC support
CFG_CMD_FAT	FAT support
CFG_CMD_IMLS	Lists all found images
CFG_CMD_ITEST	Integer (and string) test
CFG_CMD_NFS	NFS support
CFG_CMD_REISER	Reiserfs support
CFG_CMD_CDP	Cisco Discovery Protocol
CFG_CMD_XIMG	Loads part of multi-image
CFG_CMD_UNIVERSE	Tundra Universe support
CFG_CMD_EXT2	EXT2 support
CFG_CMD_SNTP	SNTP support
CFG_CMD_DISPLAY	Display support

Appendix C

BusyBox Commands

BusyBox has many useful commands. Here is a list of the commands documented in a recent BusyBox snapshot.

addgroup	Adds a group to the system
adduser	Adds a user to the system
adjtimex	Reads and optionally sets system timebase parameters
ar	Extracts or lists files from an `ar` archive
arping	Pings hosts by ARP requests/replies
ash	The ash shell (command interpreter)
awk	Pattern-scanning and -processing language
basename	Strips directory path and suffixes from files
bunzip2	Uncompresses a file (or standard input if no input file specified)
bzcat	Uncompresses to `stdout`
cal	Displays a calendar
cat	Concatenates file(s) and prints them to `stdout`
chgrp	Changes the group membership of each file
chmod	Changes file access permissions
chown	Changes the owner and/or group of file(s)
chroot	Runs the command with root directory set to new root
chvt	Changes the foreground virtual terminal to `/dev/ttyN`
clear	Clears screen
cmp	Compares files
cp	Copies files
cpio	Extracts or lists files from a `cpio` archive
crond	BusyBox's version of `cron` daemon
crontab	Manages `crontab` control file
cut	Prints selected fields from each input file to standard output
date	Displays or sets the system time
dc	Tiny RPN calculator
dd	Copies a file, converting and formatting according to options

`deallocvt`	Deallocates unused virtual terminal `/dev/ttyN`
`delgroup`	Deletes a group from the system
`deluser`	Deletes a user from the system
`devfsd`	Obsolete daemon for managing `devfs` permissions and old device name symlinks
`df`	Prints the file system space used and space available
`dirname`	Strips a nondirectory suffix from a filename
`dmesg`	Prints or controls the kernel ring buffer
`dos2unix`	Converts a file from DOS format to UNIX format
`dpkg`	Utility to install, remove, and manage Debian packages
`dpkg-deb`	Performs actions on Debian packages (debs)
`du`	Summarizes disk space used for each file and/or directory
`dumpkmap`	Prints a binary keyboard-translation table to standard output
`dumpleases`	Displays the DHCP leases granted by `udhcpd`
`echo`	Prints the specified ARGs to `stdout`
`env`	Prints the current environment or runs a program after setting
`expr`	Prints the value of an expression to standard output
`false`	Returns an exit code of `FALSE` (1)
`fbset`	Shows and modifies frame buffer settings
`fdflush`	Forces floppy disk drive to detect disk change
`fdformat`	Low-level-formats a floppy disk
`fdisk`	Changes partition table
`find`	Searches for files in a directory hierarchy
`fold`	Wraps input lines in each file
`free`	Displays the amount of free and used system memory
`freeramdisk`	Frees all memory used by the specified ramdisk
`fsckminix`	Performs a consistency check for MINIX file systems
`ftpget`	Retrieves a remote file via FTP
`ftpput`	Stores a local file on a remote machine via FTP

getopt	Parses command options
getty	Opens a tty, prompts for a login name, and then invokes `/bin/login`
grep	Searches for PATTERN in each file or standard input
gunzip	Uncompresses file (or standard input)
gzip	Compresses file(s) with maximum compression
halt	Halts the system
hdparm	Gets/sets hard disk parameters
head	Prints first 10 lines of each file to standard output
hexdump	Dumps files in user-specified binary, octal, hex, character, or decimal format
hostid	Prints a unique 32-bit identifier for the machine
hostname	Gets or sets the hostname
httpd	Listens for incoming http server requests
hwclock	Queries and sets the hardware clock (RTC)
id	Prints information for USERNAME or the current user
ifconfig	Configures a network interface
ifdown	Deconfigures an interface
ifup	Configure an interface
inetd	Listenss for network connections and launches programs
init	BusyBox version of `init`
insmod	Loads the specified kernel modules into the kernel
install	Copies files and sets attributes
ip	TCP/IP configuration utility
ipaddr	Manipulates interface addresses
ipcalc	Calculates IP network settings from an IP address
iplink	Manipulates interface settings
iproute	Displays/sets routing table entries
iptunnel	BusyBox `iptunnel` utility

kill	Sends a signal (default is SIGTERM) to the specified process(es)
killall	Sends a signal (default is SIGTERM) to the specified process(es)
klogd	Kernel logger
lash	The BusyBox LAme SHell (command interpreter)
last	Shows a listing of the last users who logged into the system
length	Prints the length of the specified STRING
ln	Creates a link named LINK_NAME or DIRECTORY to the specified TARGET
loadfont	Loads a console font from standard input
loadkmap	Loads a binary keyboard-translation table from standard input
logger	Writes MESSAGE to the system log
login	Begins a new session on the system
logname	Prints the name of the current user
logread	Shows the messages from syslogd
losetup	Associates LOOPDEVICE with file
ls	Lists directory contents
lsmod	Lists the currently loaded kernel modules
makedevs	Creates a range of block or character special files
md5sum	Prints or checks MD5 checksums
mesg	mesg controls write access to your terminal
mkdir	Creates directory entries
mkfifo	Creates a named pipe (identical to mknod name p)
mkfsminix	Makes a MINIX file system
mknod	Creates a special file (block, character, or pipe)
mkswap	Prepares a disk partition to be used as a swap partition
mktemp	Creates a temporary file with its name based on TEMPLATE
modprobe	Used for high-level module loading and unloading
more	Filter for viewing files one screenful at a time
mount	Mounts a file system

mt	Controls magnetic tape drive operation
mv	Renames and/or moves files
nameif	Renames a network interface while in the down state
nc	`Netcat` opens a pipe to `IP:port`
netstat	`Netstat` displays Linux networking information
nslookup	Queries the nameserver for the IP address of the given host
od	Dumps files in octal and other formats
openvt	Starts a command on a new virtual terminal
passwd	Changes a user password
patch	BusyBox implementation of `patch`
pidof	Gets PID of named process
ping	Sends `ICMP ECHO_REQUEST` packets to network hosts
ping6	Sends `ICMP ECHO_REQUEST` packets to network hosts
pivot_root	Changes the root file system
poweroff	Halts the system and requests that the kernel shut off the power
printf	Formats and prints arguments according to user format
ps	Reports process status
pwd	Prints the full filename of the current working directory
rdate	Gets and possibly sets the system date and time from a remote `HOST`
readlink	Displays the value of a symbolic link
realpath	Returns the absolute pathnames of a given argument
reboot	Reboots the system
renice	Changes priority of running processes in allowed priorities range
reset	Resets the screen
rm	Removes (unlink) file(s)
rmdir	Removes directory(ies), if they are empty
rmmod	Unloads the specified kernel modules from the kernel
route	Edits the kernel's routing tables
rpm	Manipulates RPM packages

rpm2cpio	Outputs a `cpio` archive of the `rpm` file
run-parts	Runs a bunch of scripts in a directory
rx	Receives a file using the xmodem protocol
sed	Busybox Stream Editor implementation
seq	Prints a range of numbers to standard output
setkeycodes	Sets entries into the kernel's scancode-to-keycode map
sha1sum	Prints or checks SHA1 checksums
sleep	Delay for specified amount of time
sort	Sorts lines of text in the specified files
start-stop-daemon	Program to start and stop services
strings	Displays printable strings in a binary file
stty	Displays and modifies terminal settings
su	Changes user ID or become root
sulogin	Single user login
swapoff	Disables virtual memory page swapping
swapon	Enables virtual memory page swapping
sync	Writes all buffered file system blocks to disk
sysctl	Configures kernel parameters at runtime
syslogd	Linux system and kernel-logging utility
tail	Prints last 10 lines of each file to standard output
tar	Creates, extracts, or lists files from a tar file
tee	Copies standard input to each file and also to standard output
telnet	BusyBox Telnet client implementation
telnetd	BusyBox Telnet server implementation
test	Checks file types and compares values, returning an exit
tftp	Transfers a file using TFTP protocol
time	Measures time used by a program
top	Provides a view of processor activity in real time
touch	Updates the last-modified date on the given FILE[s]

tr	Translates, squeezes, and/or deletes characters
traceroute	Traces the route IP packets follow
true	Returns an exit code of TRUE (0)
tty	Prints the filename of the terminal connected to standard input
udhcpc	BusyBox DHCP client implementation
udhcpd	BusyBox DHCP server implementation
umount	Unmount file systems
uname	Prints certain system information
uncompress	Uncompresses Z file(s)
uniq	Discards all but one of successive identical lines from INPUT
unix2dos	Converts file from UNIX format to DOS format
unzip	Extracts files from ZIP archives
uptime	Displays the time since the last boot
usleep	Pauses for _n_ microseconds
uudecode	Uudecodes a file that is uuencoded
uuencode	Uuencodes a file
vconfig	Lets you create and remove virtual Ethernet devices
vi	BusyBox vi editor
vlock	Locks a virtual terminal and requires a password to unlock it
watch	Executes a program periodically
watchdog	Periodically writes to a specified watchdog device
wc	Prints line, word, and byte counts for each file
wget	Retrieves files via HTTP or FTP
which	Locates a command on the current path
who	Prints the current usernames and related information
whoami	Prints the username associated with the current effective user ID
xargs	Executes a command on every item given by standard input
yes	Repeatedly outputs a line with all specified STRING(s), or y
zcat	Uncompresses to stdout

Appendix D

SDRAM Interface
Considerations

In this appendix

At first glance, programming an SDRAM controller can seem like a formidable task. Indeed, numerous Synchronous Dynamic Random Access Memory (DRAM) technologies have been developed. In a never-ending quest for performance and density, many different architectures and modes of operation have been developed.

We examine the AMCC PowerPC 405GP processor for this discussion of SDRAM interface considerations. You might want to have a copy of the user manual to reference while we explore the issues related to SDRAM interfacing. This document is referenced in Section D.4.1, "Suggestions for Additional Reading."

D.1 SDRAM Basics

To understand SDRAM setup, it is necessary to understand the basics of how an SDRAM device operates. Without going into the details of the hardware design, an SDRAM device is organized as a matrix of cells, with a number of address bits dedicated to row addressing and a number dedicated to column addressing. Figure D-1 illustrates this.

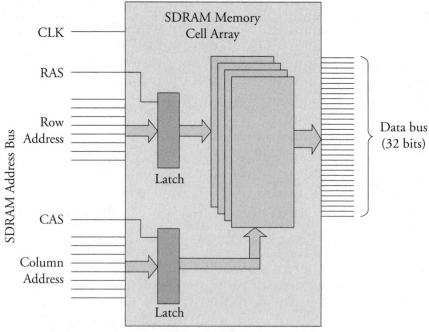

FIGURE D-1
Simplified SDRAM block diagram

Inside the memory matrix, the circuitry is quite complex. A simplified example of a read operation is as follows: A given memory location is referenced by placing a row address on the row address lines and then placing a column address on the column address lines. After some time has passed, the data stored at the location addressed by the row and column inputs are made available to the processor on the data bus.

The processor outputs a row address on the SDRAM address bus and asserts its Row Address Select (RAS) signal. After a short preprogrammed delay to allow the SDRAM circuitry to capture the row address, the processor outputs a column address and asserts its Column Address Select (CAS) signal. The SDRAM controller translates the actual physical memory address into row and column addresses. Many SDRAM controllers can be configured with the row and column width sizes; the PPC405GP is one of those examples. Later you will see that this must be configured as part of the SDRAM controller setup.

This example is much simplified, but the concepts are the same. A burst read, for example, which reads four memory locations at once, outputs a single RAS and CAS cycle, and the internal SDRAM circuitry automatically increments the column address for the subsequent three locations of the burst read, eliminating the need for the processor to issue four separate CAS cycles. This is but one example of performance optimization. The best way to understand this is to absorb the details of an actual memory chip. An example of a well-written data sheet is included in Section D.4.1, "Suggestions for Additional Reading."

D.1.1 SDRAM Refresh

An SDRAM is composed of a single transistor and a capacitor. The transistor supplies the charge, and the capacitor's job is to retain (store) the value of the individual cell. For reasons beyond the scope of this discussion, the capacitor can hold the value for only a small duration. One of the fundamental concepts of dynamic memory is that the capacitors representing each cell must be periodically recharged to maintain their value. This is referred to as SDRAM refresh.

A refresh cycle is a special memory cycle that neither reads nor writes data to the memory. It simply performs the required refresh cycle. One of the primary responsibilities of an SDRAM controller is to guarantee that refresh cycles are issued in time to meet the chip's requirements.

The chip manufacturers specify minimum refresh intervals, and it is the designer's job to guarantee it. Usually the SDRAM controller can be configured directly to select the refresh interval. The PowerPC 405GP presented here has a register specifically for this purpose. We will see this shortly.

D.2 Clocking

The term *synchronous* implies that the data read and write cycles of an SDRAM device coincide with the clock signal from the CPU. SDR SDRAM is read and written on each SDRAM clock cycle. DDR SDRAM is read and written twice on each clock cycle, once on the rising edge of the clock and once on the falling edge.

Modern processors have complex clocking subsystems. Many have multiple clock rates that are used for different parts of the system. A typical processor uses a relatively low-frequency crystal-generated clock source for its primary clock signal. A phase locked loop internal to the processor generates the CPU's primary clock (the clock rate we speak of when comparing processor speeds). Because the CPU typically runs much faster than the memory subsystem, the processor generates a submultiple of the main CPU clock to feed to the SDRAM subsystem. You need to configure this clocking ratio for your particular CPU and SDRAM combination.

The processor and memory subsystem clocks must be correctly configured for your SDRAM to work properly. Your processor manual contains a section on clock setup and management, and you must consult this to properly set up your particular board design.

The AMCC 405GP is typical of processors of its feature set. It takes a single crystal-generated clock input source and generates several internal and external clocks required of its subsystems. It generates clocks for the CPU, PCI interface, Onboard Peripheral Bus (OPB), Processor Local Bus (PLB), Memory Clock (MemClk), and several internal clocks for peripherals such as timer and UART blocks. A typical configuration might look like those in Table D-1.

TABLE D-1
Typical PPC405GP Clock Configuration

Clock	Rate	Comments
Crystal reference	33MHz	Fundamental reference supplied to processor
CPU clock	133MHz	Derived from processor's internal PLL, controlled by hardware pin strapping and register settings.
PLB clock	66MHz	Derived from CPU clock and configured via hardware pin strapping and register settings. Used for internal processor local bus data interchange among its high-speed modules.
OPB clock	66MHz	Derived from PLB clock and configured via register settings. Used for internal connection of peripherals that do not need high-speed connection.
PCI clock	33MHz	Derived from PLB clock and configured via register settings.
MemClk	100MHz	Drives the SDRAM chips directly. Derived from CPU clock and configured via register settings.

Decisions about clock setup normally must be made at hardware design time. Pin strapping options determine initial clock configurations upon application of power to the processor. Some control over derived clocks is often available by setting divider bits accessible through processor internal registers dedicated to clock and subsystem control. In the example we present here based on the 405GP, final clock configuration is determined by pin strapping and firmware configuration. It is the bootloader's responsibility to set the initial dividers and any other clock options configurable via processor register bits very early after power is applied.

D.3 SDRAM Setup

After the clocks have been configured, the next step is to configure the SDRAM controller. Controllers vary widely from processor to processor, but the end result is always the same: You must provide the correct clocking and timing values to enable and optimize the performance of the SDRAM subsystem.

As with other material in this book, there is no substitute for detailed knowledge of the hardware you are trying to configure. This is especially so for SDRAM. It is beyond the scope of this appendix to explore the design of SDRAM, but some basics must be understood. Many manufacturers' data sheets on SDRAM devices contain helpful technical descriptions. You are urged to familiarize yourself with the content of these data sheets. You don't need a degree in hardware engineering to understand what must be done to properly configure your SDRAM subsystem, but you need to invest in some level of understanding.

Here we examine how the SDRAM controller is configured on the 405GP processor as configured by the U-Boot bootloader we covered in Chapter 7, "Bootloaders." Recall from Chapter 7 that U-Boot provides a hook for SDRAM initialization from the assembly language startup code found in start.S in the 4xx-specific cpu directory. Refer back to Section 7.4.4 "Board-Specific Initialization" in Chapter 7. Listing D-1 reproduces the sdram_init() function from U-Boot's .../cpu/ppc4xx/sdram.c file.

Listing D-1

ppc4xx sdram_init() from U-Boot

```
01 void sdram_init(void)
02 {
03          ulong sdtr1;
04          ulong rtr;
05          int i;
06
07          /*
08           * Support for 100MHz and 133MHz SDRAM
09           */
10          if (get_bus_freq(0) > 100000000) {
11                  /*
12                   * 133 MHz SDRAM
13                   */
14                  sdtr1 = 0x01074015;
15                  rtr = 0x07f00000;
16          } else {
17                  /*
18                   * default: 100 MHz SDRAM
19                   */
20                  sdtr1 = 0x0086400d;
21                  rtr = 0x05f00000;
22          }
23
24          for (i=0; i<N_MB0CF; i++) {
25                  /*
26                   * Disable memory controller.
27                   */
28                  mtsdram0(mem_mcopt1, 0x00000000);
29
30                  /*
31                   * Set MB0CF for bank 0.
32                   */
33                  mtsdram0(mem_mb0cf, mb0cf[i].reg);
```

```
34                    mtsdram0(mem_sdtr1, sdtr1);
35                    mtsdram0(mem_rtr, rtr);
36
37                    udelay(200);
38
39                    /*
40                     * Set memory controller options reg, MCOPT1.
41                     * Set DC_EN to '1' and BRD_PRF to '01' for 16 byte PLB
Burst
42                     * read/prefetch.
43                     */
44                    mtsdram0(mem_mcopt1, 0x80800000);
45
46                    udelay(10000);
47
48                    if (get_ram_size(0, mb0cf[i].size) == mb0cf[i].size) {
49                            /*
50                             * OK, size detected -> all done
51                             */
52                            return;
53                    }
54            }
55 }
```

The first action reads the pin strapping on the 405GP processor to determine the design value for the SDRAM clock. In this case, we can see that two possible values are accommodated: 100MHz and 133MHz. Based on this choice, constants are chosen that will be used later in the function to set the appropriate register bits in the SDRAM controller.

Starting on line 24, a loop is used to set the parameters for each of up to five predefined memory sizes. Currently, U-Boot has logic to support a single bank of memory sized at 4MB, 16MB, 32MB, 64MB, or 128MB. These sizes are defined in a table called mb0cf in .../cpu/ppc4xx/sdram.c. The table associates a constant with each of these memory sizes, based on the value required in the 405GP memory bank configuration register. The loop does this:

```
for (i = each possible memory bank size, largest first) {
    select timing constant based on SDRAM clock speed;
    disable SDRAM memory controller;
    configure bank 0 with size[i], timing constants[i]
    re-enable SDRAM memory controller;

    run simple memory test to dynamically determine size;
      /* This is done using get_ram_size() */
    if ( tested size == configured size )
        done;
}
```

This simple logic simply plugs in the correct timing constants in the SDRAM controller based on SDRAM clock speed and configured memory bank size from the hard-coded table in U-Boot. Using this explanation, you can easily correlate the bank configuration values using the 405GP reference manual. For a 64MB DRAM size, the memory bank control register is set as follows:

```
Memory Bank 0 Control Register = 0x000a4001
```

The PowerPC 405GP User's Manual describes the fields in Table D-2 for the memory bank 0 control register.

TABLE D-2
405GP Memory Bank 0-3 Configuration Register Fields

Field	Value	Comments
Bank Address (BA)	0x00	Starting memory address of this bank.
Size (SZ)	0x4	Size of this memory bank—in this case, 64MB.
Addressing Mode (AM)	0x2	Determines the organization of memory, including the number of row and column bits. In this case, Mode 2 = 12 row address bits, and either 9 or 10 column address bits, and up to four internal SDRAM banks. This data is provided in a table in the 405GP user's manual.
Bank Enable (BE)	0x1	Enable bit for the bank configured by this register. There are four of these memory bank configuration registers in the 405GP.

The values in this table must be determined by the designer, based on the choice of memory module in use on the board.

Let's look at a timing example for more detail on the timing requirements of a typical SDRAM controller. Assuming a 100MHz SDRAM clock speed and 64MB memory size, the timing constants selected by the `sdram_init()` function in Listing D-1 are selected as follows:

```
SDRAM Timing Register          = 0x0086400d
Refresh Timing Register        = 0x05f00000
```

The PowerPC 405GP User's Manual describes the fields in Table D-3 for the SDRAM Timing Register.

TABLE D-3
405GP SDRAM Timing Register Fields

Field	Value	Comments
CAS Latency (CASL)	0x1	SDRAM CAS Latency. This value comes directly from the SDRAM chip specifications. It is the delay in clock cycles required by the chip between issuance of the read command (CAS signal) until the data is available on the data bus. In this case, the 0x1 represents two clock cycles, as seen from the 405GP user's manual.
Precharge Command to Next Activate (PTA)	0x1	The SDRAM Precharge command deactivates a given row. In contrast, the Activate command enables a given row for subsequent access, such as during a burst cycle. This timing parameter enforces the minimum time between Precharge to a subsequent Activate cycle and is dictated by the SDRAM chip. The correct value must be obtained from the SDRAM chip specification. In this case, 0x1 represents two clock cycles, as determined from the 405GP user's manual.
Read/Write to Precharge Command Minimum (CTP)	0x2	This timing parameter enforces the minimum time delay between a given SDRAM read or write command to a subsequent Precharge command. The correct value must be obtained from the SDRAM chip specification. In this case, 0x2 represents three clock cycles, as determined from the 405GP user's manual.
SDRAM Command Leadoff (LDF)	0x1	This timing parameter enforces the minimum time delay between assertion of address or command cycle to bank select cycle. The correct value must be obtained from the SDRAM chip specification. In this case, 0x1 represents two clock cycles, as determined from the 405GP user's manual.

The final timing parameter configured by the U-Boot example in Listing D-1 is the refresh timing register value. This register requires a single field that determines the refresh interval enforced by the SDRAM controller. The field representing the interval is treated as a simple counter running at the SDRAM clock frequency. In the example here, we assumed 100MHz as the SDRAM clock frequency. The value programmed into this register in our example is 0x05f0_0000. From the PowerPC

405GP User's Manual, we determine that this will produce a refresh request every 15.2 microseconds. As with the other timing parameters, this value is dictated by the SDRAM chip specifications.

A typical SDRAM chip requires one refresh cycle for each row. Each row must be refreshed in the minimum time specified by the manufacturer. In the chip referenced in Section D.4.1, "Suggestions for Additional Reading," the manufacturer specifies that 8,192 rows must be refreshed every 64 milliseconds. This requires generating a refresh cycle every 7.8 microseconds to meet the specifications for this particular device.

D.4 Summary

SDRAM devices are quite complex. This appendix presented a very simple example to help you navigate the complexities of SDRAM controller setup. The SDRAM controllers perform a critical function and must be properly set up. There is no substitute to diving into a specification and digesting the information presented. The two example documents referenced in this appendix are excellent starting points.

D.4.1 Suggestions for Additional Reading

AMCC 405GP Embedded Processor User's Manual
AMCC Corporation
www.amcc.com/Embedded/

Micron Technology, Inc.
Synchronous DRAM MT48LC64M4A2 Data Sheet
http://download.micron.com/pdf/datasheets/dram/sdram/256MSDRAM.pdf

Appendix E

Open Source Resources

Source Repositories and Developer Information

Several locations on the Web focus on Linux development. Here is a list of the most important websites for the various architectures and projects:

> Primary kernel source tree
> www.kernel.org
>
> Primary kernel GIT repository
> www.kernel.org/git
>
> PowerPC-related development and mailing lists
> http://ozlabs.org/
>
> MIPS-related developments
> www.linux-mips.org
>
> ARM-related Linux development
> www.arm.linux.org.uk
>
> Primary home for a huge collection of open-source projects
> http://sourceforge.net

Mailing Lists

Hundreds, if not thousands, of mailing lists cater to every aspect of Linux and open-source development. Here are a few to consider. Make sure you familiarize yourself with mailing list etiquette before posting to these lists.

Most of these lists maintain archives that are searchable. This is the first place that you should consult. In a great majority of the cases, your question has already been asked and answered. Start your reading here, for advice on how to best use the public mail lists:

> The Linux Kernel Mailing List FAQ
> www.tux.org/lkml
>
> List server serving various Linux kernel–related mail lists
> http://vger.kernel.org
>
> Linux Kernel Mailing—very high volume, kernel development only
> http://vger.kernel.org/vger-lists.html#linux-kernel

Linux News and Developments

Many news sites are worth browsing occasionally. Some of the more popular are listed here.

> LinuxDevices.com
> www.linuxdevices.com

> PowerPC News and other information
> http://penguinppc.org

> General Linux News and Developments
> www.lwn.net

Open Source Insight and Discussion

The following public website contains useful information and education focusing on legal issues around open source.

> www.open-bar.org

Appendix F

Sample BDI-2000
Configuration File

```
; bdiGDB configuration file for the UEI PPC 5200 Board
; Revision 1.0
; Revision 1.1  (Added serial port setup)
; -------------------------------------------------------
; 4 MB Flash (Am29DL323)
; 128 MB Micron DDR DRAM
;
[INIT]
; init core register
WREG    MSR          0x00003002   ;MSR  : FP,ME,RI
WM32    0x80000000  0x00008000   ;MBAR : internal registers at 0x80000000
                ; Default after RESET, MBAR sits at 0x80000000
                ; because it's POR value is 0x0000_8000 (!)


WSPR    311          0x80000000   ; MBAR : save internal register offset
                                 ; SPR311 is the MBAR in G2_LE


WSPR    279          0x80000000   ;SPRG7: save internal memory offsetReg: 279

; Init CDM (Clock Distribution Module)
;   Hardware Reset config {
;        ppc_pll_cfg[0..4] = 01000b
:        XLB:Core -> 1:3
:        Core:f(VCO) -> 1:2
:        XLB:f(VCO) -> 1:6
;
;        xlb_clk_sel = 0 -> XLB_CLK=f(sys) / 4 = 132 MHz
;
;        sys_pll_cfg_1 = 0 -> NOP
;        sys_pll_cfg_0 = 0 -> f(sys) = 16x SYS_XTAL_IN = 528 MHz
;   }
;
;   CDM Configuration Register
WM32    0x8000020c  0x01000101
            ; enable DDR Mode
            ; ipb_clk_sel = 1 -> XLB_CLK / 2 (ipb_clk = 66 MHz)
            ; pci_clk_sel = 01 -> IPB_CLK/2

; CS0 Flash
WM32    0x80000004  0x0000ff00   ;CS0 start = 0xff000000 - Flash memory is on
CS0
WM32    0x80000008  0x0000ffff   ;CS0 stop  = 0xffffffff

; IPBI Register and Wait State Enable
WM32    0x80000054  0x00050001   ;CSE: enable CS0, disable CSBOOT,
                                 ;Wait state enable\
                                 ; CS2 also enabled

WM32    0x80000300  0x00045d30   ;BOOT ctrl
            ; bits 0-7: WaitP  (try 0xff)
            ; bits 8-15: WaitX  (try 0xff)
```

```
                   ; bit 16: Multiplex or non-mux'ed (0x0 = non-muxed)
                   ; bit 17: reserved (Reset value = 0x1, keep it)
                   ; bit 18: Ack Active (0x0)
                   ; bit 19: CE (Enable) 0x1
                   ; bits 20-21: Address Size (0x11 = 25/6 bits)
                   ; bits 22:23: Data size field (0x01 = 16-bits)
                   ; bits 24:25: Bank bits (0x00)
                   ; bits 26-27: WaitType (0x11)
                   ; bits 28: Write Swap (0x0 = no swap)
                   ; bits 29: Read Swap (0x0 = no swap)
                   ; bit 30: Write Only (0x0 = read enable)
                   ; bit 31: Read Only (0x0 = write enable)

; CS2 Logic Registers
WM32     0x80000014  0x0000e00e
WM32     0x80000018  0x0000efff

; LEDS:
;   LED1 - bits 0-7
;   LED2 - bits 8-15
;   LED3 - bits 16-23
;   LED4 - bits 24-31
;   off = 0x01
;   on  = 0x02
; mm 0xe00e2030 0x02020202 1 (all on)
; mm 0xe00e2030 0x01020102 1 (2 on, 2 off)

WM32     0x80000308  0x00045b30  ; CS2 Configuration Register
                                 ; bits 0-7: WaitP  (try 0xff)
                                 ; bits 8-15: WaitX  (try 0xff)
                                 ; bit 16: Multiplex or non-mux'ed (0x0 =
non-muxed)
                                 ; bit 17: reserved (Reset value = 0x1, keep it)
                                 ; bit 18: Ack Active (0x0)
                                 ; bit 19: CE (Enable) 0x1
                                 ; bits 20-21: Address Size (0x10 = 24 bits)
                                 ; bits 22:23: Data size field (0x11 = 32-bits)
                                 ; bits 24:25: Bank bits (0x00)
                                 ; bits 26-27: WaitType (0x11)
                                 ; bits 28: Write Swap (0x0 = no swap)
                                 ; bits 29: Read Swap (0x0 = no swap)
                                 ; bit 30: Write Only (0x0 = read enable)
                                 ; bit 31: Read Only (0x0 = write enable)

WM32   0x80000318  0x01000000    ; Master LPC Enable

;
; init SDRAM controller
;
; For the UEI PPC 5200 Board,
;   Micron 46V32M16-75E (8 MEG x 16 x 4 banks)
```

```
;    64 MB per Chip, for a total of 128 MB
;    arranged as a single "space" (i.e 1 CS)
;    with the following configuration:
;        8 Mb x 16 x 4 banks
;        Refresh count 8K
;        Row addressing: 8K (A0..12) 13 bits
;        Column addressing: 1K (A0..9) 10 bits
;        Bank Addressing: 4 (BA0..1) 2 bits
;    Key Timing Parameters: (-75E)
;            Clockrate (CL=2) 133 MHz
;            DO Window 2.5 ns
;            Access Window: +/- 75 ns
;            DQS - DQ Skew: +0.5 ns
;            t(REFI): 7.8 us MAX
;
; Initialization Requirements (General Notes)
;  The memory Mode/Extended Mode registers must be
;  initialized during the system boot sequence. But before
;  writing to the controller Mode register, the mode_en and
;  cke bits in the Control register must be set to 1. After
;  memory initialization is complete, the Control register
;  mode_en bit should be cleared to prevent subsequent access
;  to the controller Mode register.

; SDRAM init sequence
;  1) Setup and enable chip selects
;  2) Setup config registers
;  3) Setup TAP Delay

; Setup and enable SDRAM CS
WM32    0x80000034  0x0000001a  ;SDRAM CS0, 128MB @ 0x00000000
WM32    0x80000038  0x08000000  ;SDRAM CS1, disabled @ 0x08000000

WM32    0x80000108  0x73722930  ;SDRAM Config 1 Samsung
                    ; Assume CL=2
                    ; bits 0-3: srd2rwp: in clocks (0x6)
                    ; bits 507: swt2rwp: in clocks -> Data sheet suggests
                    ;    0x3 for DDR (0x3)
                    ; bits 8-11: rd_latency -> for DDR 0x7
                    ; bits 13-15: act2rw -> 0x2
                    ; bit 16: reserved
                    ; bits 17-19: pre2act -> 0x02
                    ; bits 20-23: ref2act -> 0x09
                    ; bits 25-27: wr_latency -> for DDR 0x03
                    ; bits 28-31: Reserved

WM32    0x8000010c  0x46770000  ;SDRAM Config 2 Samsung
                    ; bits 0-3: brd2rp -> for DDR 0x4
                        ; bits 4-7: bwt2rwp -> for DDR 0x6
                        ; bits 8-11: brd2wt -> 0x6
                        ; bits 12-15: burst_length -> 0x07 (bl - 1)
                        ; bits 16-13: Reserved
```

```
; Setup initial Tap delay
WM32  0x80000204  0x18000000   ; Start in the end of the range (24 = 0x18)
Samsung

WM32    0x80000104  0xf10f0f00 ;SDRAM Control (was 0xd14f0000)
                               ; bit 0: mode_en (1=write)
                               ; bit 1: cke (MEM_CLK_EN)
                               ; bit 2: ddr (DDR mode on)
                               ; bit 3: ref_en (Refresh enable)
                               ; bits 4-6: Reserved
                               ; bit 7: hi_addr (XLA[4:7] as row/col
                               ;   must be set to '1' 'cuz we need 13 RA bits
                               ;   for the Micron chip above
                               ; bit 8: reserved
                               ; bit 9: drive_rule - 0x0
                               ; bit 10-15: ref_interval, see UM 0x0f
                               ; bits 16-19: reserved
                               ; bits 20-23: dgs_oe[3:0] (not sure)
                               ;  but I think this is req'd for DDR 0xf
                               ; bits 24-28: Resv'd
                               ; bit 29: 1 = soft refresh
                               ; bit 30 1 = soft_precharge
                               ; bit 31: reserved

WM32    0x80000104  0xf10f0f02 ;SDRAM Control: precharge all
WM32    0x80000104  0xf10f0f04 ;SDRAM Control: refresh
WM32    0x80000104  0xf10f0f04 ;SDRAM Control: refresh

WM32    0x80000100  0x018d0000  ; SDRAM Mode Samsung
                    ; bits 0-1: MEM_MBA - selects std or extended MODE
reg 0x0
                    ; bits 2-13: MEM_MA (see DDR DRAM Data sheet)
                    ; bits 2-7: Operating Mode -> 0x0 = normal
                    ; bits 8-10: CAS Latency (CL) -> Set to CL=2 for
DDR (0x2)
                    ; bit 11: Burst Type: Sequential for PMC5200 ->
0x0
                    ; bits 12-14: Set to 8 for MPC5200 -> 0x3
                    ; bit 15: cmd = 1 for MODE REG WRITE

WM32    0x80000104  0x710f0f00 ;SDRAM Control: Lock Mode Register (was
0x514f0000)

; *********** Initialize the serial port ***********
; Pin Configuration
WM32    0x80000b00  0x00008004  ; UART1

; Reset PSC
WM8     0x80002008  0X10         ; Reset - Select MR1

WM16    0x80002004  0          ; Clock Select Register - 0 enables both Rx &
Tx Clocks
```

```
WM32    0x80002040    0            ; SICR - UART Mode
WM8     0x80002000    0x13         ; Write MR1 (default after reset)
                                   ; 8-bit, no parity
WM8     0x80002000    0x07         ; Write MR2 (after MR1) (one stop bit)

WM8     0x80002018    0x0          ; Counter/Timer Upper Reg (115.2KB)
WM8     0x8000201c    0x12         ; Counter/Timer Lower Reg (divider = 18)

; Reset and enable serial port Rx/Tx
WM8     0x80002008    0x20
WM8     0x80002008    0x30
WM8     0x80002008    0x05


;
; define maximal transfer size
TSZ4    0x80000000    0x80003FFF   ;internal registers
;
; define the valid memory map
MMAP    0x00000000    0x07FFFFFF   ;Memory range for SDRAM
MMAP    0xFF000000    0xFFFFFFFF   ;ROM space
MMAP    0xE00E0000    0xE00EFFFF   ; PowerPC Logic
MMAP    0x80000000    0x8fffffff   ; Default MBAR
MMAP    0xC0000000    0XCFFFFFFF   ; Linux Kernal


[TARGET]
CPUTYPE      5200          ;the CPU type
JTAGCLOCK    0             ;use 16 MHz JTAG clock
WORKSPACE    0x80008000    ;workspace for fast download
WAKEUP       1000          ;give reset time to complete
STARTUP      RESET
MEMDELAY     2000          ;additional memory access delay
BOOTADDR     0xfff00100
REGLIST      ALL
BREAKMODE    SOFT    ; or HARD
POWERUP      1000
WAKEUP       500
MMU          XLAT
PTBASE       0x000000f0


[HOST]
IP           192.168.1.9
FORMAT       ELF
LOAD         MANUAL        ;load code MANUAL or AUTO after reset
PROMPT       uei>


[FLASH]
CHIPTYPE     AM29BX16          ;Flash type (AM29F | AM29BX8 | AM29BX16 | I28BX8 |
I28BX16)
CHIPSIZE     0x00400000    ;The size of one flash chip in bytes
BUSWIDTH     16            ;The width of the flash memory bus in bits (8 | 16 |
32)
```

```
WORKSPACE     0x80008000     ;workspace in internal SRAM
FILE          u-boot.bin
FORMAT        BIN 0xFFF00000
ERASE         0xFFF00000     ;erase a sector of flash
ERASE         0xFFF10000     ;erase a sector of flash
ERASE         0xFFF20000     ;erase a sector of flash
ERASE         0xFFF30000     ;erase a sector of flash
ERASE         0xFFF40000     ;erase a sector of flash

[REGS]
FILE          $reg5200.def
```

Index

Page numbers followed by *n* indicate footnotes.

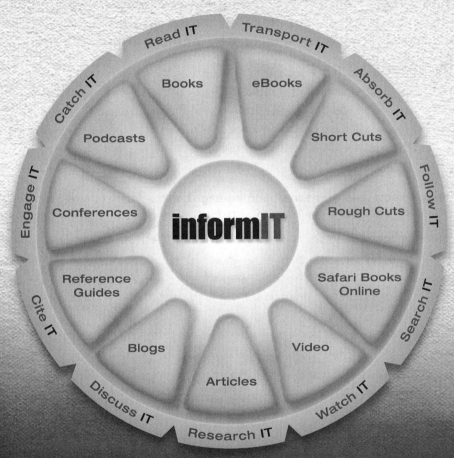

Safari®
BOOKS ONLINE
ENABLED

THIS BOOK IS SAFARI ENABLED

INCLUDES FREE 45-DAY ACCESS TO THE ONLINE EDITION

The Safari® Enabled icon on the cover of your favorite technology book means the book is available through Safari Bookshelf. When you buy this book, you get free access to the online edition for 45 days.

Safari Bookshelf is an electronic reference library that lets you easily search thousands of technical books, find code samples, download chapters, and access technical information whenever and wherever you need it.

TO GAIN 45-DAY SAFARI ENABLED ACCESS TO THIS BOOK:

- Go to **informit.com/safarienabled**
- Complete the brief registration form
- Enter the coupon code found in the front of this book on the "Copyright" page

If you have difficulty registering on Safari Bookshelf or accessing the online edition, please e-mail customer-service@safaribooksonline.com.

林

紹

義

Shawyee Lin

購

自

Amazon.com